THROBBING GRISTLE

intellect Bristol, UK / Chicago, USA

GLOBAL PUNK

Series editors: Russ Bestley and Mike Dines

Produced in collaboration with the Punk Scholars Network, the Global Punk book series focuses on the development of contemporary global punk, reflecting its origins, aesthetics, identity, legacy, membership, and circulation. Critical approaches draw upon the interdisciplinary areas of (amongst others) cultural studies, art and design, sociology, musicology, and social sciences in order to develop a broad and inclusive picture of punk and punk-inspired subcultural developments around the globe. The series adopts an essentially analytical perspective, raising questions over the dissemination of punk scenes and subcultures and their form, structure, and contemporary cultural significance in the daily lives of an increasing number of people around the world. To propose a manuscript, or for more information about the series, please contact the series co-editors Russ Bestley and Mike Dines (contact details available at www.intellectbooks.com).

The Punk Reader: Research Transmissions from the Local and the Global (2019)
Edited by Russ Bestley, Mike Dines, Alastair Gordon and Paula Guerra
Trans-Global Punk Scenes: The Punk Reader Vol. 2 (2021)
Edited by Russ Bestley, Mike Dines, Alastair Gordon and Paula Guerra
Punk Identities, Punk Utopias: Global Punk and Media (2021)
Edited by Russ Bestley, Mike Dines, Matt Grimes and Paula Guerra
PUNK! Las Américas Edition (2022)
Edited by Olga Rodríguez-Ulloa, Rodrigo Quijano and Shane Greene
Blank Canvas: Art School Creativity From Punk to New Wave (2022)
Simon Strange
Punk Pedagogies in Practice: Disruptions and Connections (2023)
Edited by Francis Stewart and Laura Way
Punk Art History: Artworks From the European No Future Generation (2023)
Marie Arleth Skov
In Search of Tito's Punks: On the Road in a Country that No Longer Exists (2023)
Barry Phillips
Throbbing Gristle: An Endless Discontent (2023)
Ian Trowell

THROBBING GRISTLE

AN ENDLESS DISCONTENT

IAN TROWELL

First published in the UK in 2023 by Intellect, The Mill, Parnall Road, Fishponds, Bristol, BS16 3JG, UK

First published in the USA in 2023 by Intellect, The University of Chicago Press, 1427 E. 60th Street, Chicago, IL 60637, USA

Produced in collaboration with the Punk Scholars Network

A catalogue record for this book is available from the British Library.

Copy editor: MPS Limited
Cover designer: Russ Bestley
Cover image: Akiko Hada
Indexing: Ian Trowell
Production manager: Sophia Munyengeterwa
Typesetting: Russ Bestley

Part of the Global Punk series
ISSN 2632-8305 | ONLINE ISSN 2632-8313

Hardback ISBN 978-1-78938-826-8
Paperback ISBN 978-1-78938-829-9
ePDF ISBN 978-1-78938-827-5
ePUB ISBN 978-1-78938-828-2

Printed and bound by CPI Group (UK) Ltd, Croydon, CR0 4YY

To find out about all our publications, please visit www.intellectbooks.com. There, you can subscribe to our e-newsletter, browse or download our current catalogue and buy any titles that are in print.

This is a peer-reviewed publication.

Opening image: Throbbing Gristle graffiti in Hackney, 1970s, from *Camouflage* by Timeless Editions, 2018. Courtesy of Laurence Dupré.

TG

CONTENTS

ACKNOWLEDGEMENTS 9

1. DISPLACEMENTS 11

2. ORIGINAL SINNERS – TOWARDS *PROSTITUTION* 43

3. IN AND AGAINST PUNK – 1977 THROUGH THE LOOKING GLASS 73

4. ANTI-GIG – ARCHITECTURAL ASSOCIATION, 3 MARCH 1978 97

5. IN THE MACHINE – WAKEFIELD COLLEGE, 1 JULY 1978 119

6. ANACHRONY IN THE UK – DERBY AJANTA THEATRE, 12 APRIL 1979 153

7. RESTLESSNESS – SHEFFIELD UNIVERSITY, 10 JUNE 1980 185

8. ENDGAMES/AFTERLIVES 229

REFERENCES 267

INDEX 281

ACKNOWLEDGEMENTS

This book took substantially longer to write than planned, not least due to the COVID-19 pandemic and a series of lockdowns interrupting my research and writing. My thanks go to my partner Clare for putting up with me vanishing down a Throbbing Gristle black hole for nights on end. My parents and my children have also offered me continual encouragement.

For all-round support, resources and knowledge I'd like to thank Simon Dell and his encyclopaediaelectronica.com archive, Amy Chiros, Ben Waddington, Matthew Worley, Mick Fish, Frank Maier and his Tape-Mag project, Wes Moynihan, Tim Jones, and Roger Quail and his *My Life in the Mosh of Ghosts* podcast.

Various people have put up with reading drafts of sections of this work including the known and unknown peer reviewers. Thanks to those, and also to David Bell, Paul Gorman, Matthew Cheeseman, Chris Low, Kevin Shepherd, and Howard Slater.

Photographic resources are credited where the material has been kindly provided, and I'd like to extend my thanks to all involved, in particular Edward Bottoms at the Architectural Association Archives.

Chapter research and testimony saw the help of numerous correspondents. A special mention to Chris Westwood, Stephen Mallinder, Ada Wilson, Mark Trout, Michael Fawcett, Paul Hayes, Peter Norton, Glyn Lenney, Aaron Williamson, Tim Etchells, Phil Taylor, Johnny Vincent, Richard Lammell, Darrell Buxton, Dave Bonsall, Hector Heathcoate, Alan Hempsall, Geoff Davis, Mark Albrow, Ron Wright, Paul Bower, Bob Baker, Klive Humberstone, Andrew Darlington, and Sam Mills.

Russ Bestley and Mike Dines, the editors of Intellect's Global Punk series, have been incredibly supportive in giving this project a safe home.

1. DISPLACEMENTS

INDUSTRIAL INTRODUCTION

> Tonight we're going to do a one hour set called 'Music from the Death Factory'. It's basically about the post-breakdown of civilization. You know, you walk down the street and there's lots of ruined factories and bits of old newspaper with stories about pornography and page three pin ups blowing down the street, and you turn a corner past the dead dog and you see old dustbins. And then over the ruined factory there's a funny noise.

And so it begins with this assiduously prepared statement, delivered back in October 1976 in the hallowed gallery space of the Institute of Contemporary Arts (ICA) on London's Mall, 'within spitting distance of Buckingham Palace'.[1] A statement that is often reprinted with much of the work that attempts to pin down and understand the confrontational, scabrous, and enigmatic band called Throbbing Gristle. The gradual coming together of four disparate but like-minded individuals drawn from art and performance, looking to explode boundaries, affront moral codes, and demolish preconceptions. The spark for a short-sharp career lasts half a decade within the shadows of punk and post-punk and garners around 30 live performances and a handful of self-produced records. The quoted statement is an overused opening gambit to succinctly characterize these four individuals drawn from underground and confrontational art, noise and mischief, sex, sedition, and seediness. Their imagery, intent, ideology, and awareness (and perhaps celebration) of the abrupt nihilism of the times are summed up through this opening delivery of their first proper foray into the murky world of popular music made unpopular. As punk breaks, then four individuals, briefly united as one band, set out to break punk; whether through twisting the format of live appearances, taking lyrical themes to places where it should never go, or producing music that fluctuates between an evil noise and a glibbed-out mix of odd genres past (lounge music) and future (synth-pop). Mythology disrupted at its point of origin – punk as anti-music, chaos, and the abject or punk just as a continuation of rock 'n' roll. Choose your side. These well-honed words that comprise the opening speech are transcribed again and again onto the page as the event, and this spoken utterance retreats into more distant history. Darkly seductive, the words amass a totalitarian and authoritarian quality as we replay them in our head, imagining the sound in the gallery space with the assembled proto-punks, press-hacks, and art-fans. The statement conjures a stentorian and strident manner of delivery, offering itself for an imaginative reconstruction of the event as we contemplate the words. In contrast, recorded footage reveals it to be slightly hesitant, disjointed, and (dare we say) weak and underwhelming. Tremulous not tremorous. But let's not allow the facts of the matter to get in the way of the powerful mythology, because mythology is a key part of this game.

What followed the short proclamation was definitely not apprehensive, opaque, or ambiguous. Throbbing Gristle proceeded to perform a truncated set to accompany the opening of the COUM Transmissions (henceforth COUM) retrospective around the walls and vitrines of the ICA gallery. Commencing immediately on the conclusion of the address with a low-throb and escalating electronic clutter that would define their sonic bombardment, COUM and Throbbing Gristle switched places in priority. Frontman Genesis P-Orridge, sporting the remnants of a hippie haircut seemingly restyled by the inmate of a psychiatric unit, delivers the script of the opening piece 'Very Friendly'. This concerns the murder of teenager Edward Evans by Ian Brady and Myra Hindley, with P-Orridge beginning the narration as if reading a children's bedtime story. He perfects an enchanting drollness that will define his style throughout the short lifespan of Throbbing Gristle. He hams up the final syllables for effect, followed by the introduction of a comedy stammer. This stammering does not refer back to the 'cool' stutter of the Who's Roger Daltrey whirring through 'My Generation' and evoking the pilled-up mod, a stammer that would surface again within the punk culture. Mythology and reality again, the Who as pre-punk heroes, but not welcome here. P-Orridge's stammer is the opposite, redolent of the boozy, besuited comedians who defined the 1970s with skits about malfunctioning equipment to end up as fringe characters in *Carry On* films. Skilled in the art of bathos, the band draw their references from the high and low. His narrative drives on in a disconcerting assault, inserting references to the everyday world of products (German wine, Ovaltine) and outlets (Marks & Spencer, Tesco), thus blurring the abhorrent events into a trivialized realm. Instantly apparent is the key tactic of exposing the seamless continuity of the everyday with the monstrous, a theme that will animate and drive the work of Throbbing Gristle and maintain a constant presence and pressure of self-doubt when thinking about this music, or worse still when thinking about enjoying this music.

Switching performative tactics, he screams and implicates the audience – 'alright you fuckers' – accusing them of browsing the facts as simple information from the front page, forcing what Valencia (2018: 182) declares as an 'eschatological rupture'. Pushing forward, holding back, exposing, implicating, and horrifying – the game is in play. The dissensus in amoralist intent is matched by the sound; swirls of synth that would fit with the brain-fried prog-rock soundscapes of Tangerine Dream chopped into the mix with slabs of discordant sound and viciously mangled guitars. Instead, we are subjected to what post-punk historian Simon Reynolds (2005: 224) labels as an 'inverted psychedelia', in which, according to Encarnacao (2019: 71), the freethinking of the 1960s is taken to 'eccentric corners of cultural expression'. After extended sections of intensifying noise, a lyrical theme is resumed with 'Slug Bait', in which P-Orridge takes a first-person voice to narrate a gruesome murder of a heavily pregnant woman. And on it went, not up to the full promised hour, but ending after around 40 minutes with a screeching feedback blast that emulated an alarm to clear the building. Not provoking an immediate response but having the desired effect of creating a long-term ripple of controversy by virtue of the strategically invited guests to the event, Throbbing Gristle enters the cultural canon.

Following this ICA intervention, a spluttering machine rhythm commenced defining the insidious creep of the band into the subcultural psyche, with sporadic appearances confounding expectation and confronting the audiences in and around the creative (and destructive) era of punk. Summarized by Reynolds (2005: 235) as 'sadistic assaults on the audience', Throbbing Gristle quickly outstripped punk's live confrontational emphasis by turning it back onto the punk audience as a 'complete clash of ideologies' (Savage 1991: 516).[2] Aside from the barrage of pre-existing sounds of distressing aurality (loud and non-harmonic) and disturbing content, the band slowly introduced an arsenal of sensory devices beyond the domain of hearing. Whereas psychedelic-era bands invested in a multisensory approach to create a synchronized whole, Throbbing Gristle sought out a desynchronized hole. Walker (1987: 132) details a 'violent assault on the senses and preconceptions of the audience, who had to contend with dazzling lights and mirrors directed towards them', described by Reynolds (2005: 235) as a 'retinal barrage'. On occasion, a giant Tesco bag is employed, distorting the scale of the stage elements and pre-empting the totalizing of our lives by brands and logos. The lights and mirrors forced upon the audience witnessing the performance itself make them agog and dazzled in place of seeing the desired performers. This visual strategy is aligned with the replaying of recorded death threats issued to the band, serving up a reconstituted contempt where the audience consumes its own rage (and is further enraged).

Live events were buttressed by an elusive trickle of fiercely independent record releases, selective interviews, and propaganda blasts. The band, particularly

P-Orridge, made time to engage fanzines and reply to letters from intrigued fans, explaining the wider rationale behind their endeavours. For example, in issue 4 of *VOX*, we learn that Throbbing Gristle releases are not to be seen as 'exciting or important' but as 'demonstrations and research items' (1980: 23). The role of open and direct communication (through letters and telephone calls) and the willingness to support small fanzines informed the path of the band's live performances. Without the presence of a promoter or record label, gigs were often negotiated and arranged by fans through direct contact with the band. Examples of this are documented in Chapters 5 and 6 which detail the band's appearances at Wakefield and Derby. A new genre emerged – the unwanted child of an illicit liaison between punk and extreme art – industrial music. Encarnacao (2019: 75) marks this territory as the 'electronic confrontation and the rejection of rock music as being redundant'. An in-house fanzine, *Industrial News*, showcased an autodidactic philosophical, cultural, and intellectual armour that drew together disparate elements from the outer limits of taste, the dark crevices of the counterculture, the banality of the everyday, and the hypocrisy of sublimated control. The mode of engagement between the band and (potential) audience shifts and slides between the dialogical, the didactic, the encouragement of autodidactic practices, and practices of self-directed 'un-learning'. This shift in engagement with followers is subtle but evident, blossoming in the final throes of the band and their fallout projects. Ultimately, it accelerates to the indoctrinating and dictatorial as industrial music gave way to a cult-like yearning. Alongside this, the fragile unity between the band members, a counterintuitive source of the power and originality of the music, was reflected in their individual aims and intentions for the Throbbing Gristle project. Nothing exposes itself to rational explanation or harmonized resolution; everything is always at the point of breaking down or revelling in its beyondness. If a concept of a neatly defined project within industrial music is proposed by Shryane (2011: 57), as situating 'music as research and a shared desire to create disruptive, improvised sound', then Throbbing Gristle operated at the outer limits of sound, action, and ideology to blow apart such a conceptual cohesion. Walker (1987: 131) pulls no punches on this, arguing that the band took a specific aim at art and everyday life to 'destroy the barrier altogether'. In this mission, they were always at the almost-point of destroying themselves.

ABJECT MISSIVES

Shock is nurtured, captured at the point of explosion, and folded back into the flow of product, as album tracks also recycle the death threats made to the band and howls of derision from audiences. Even towards the end of their career, as the band started to gain critical acclaim and an expectant audience, there was a disjuncture that was forced back onto the audience as a concrete sound source for critical engagement. The track 'Trade Deficit', assembled after the band had fallen apart, consists of an overlaying of all the applause given to the band at their three German performances – the suggestion is that the applause is an unwanted reaction (the band demanding something else) and so it is returned as a deficit.

Pausing to think as to why we might enjoy, or find interesting, this music can lead to a self-critical breakdown. Throbbing Gristle fan, academic, and musician Drew Daniel captures the compulsive and convulsive essence of encountering and becoming enraptured by the band, describing the experience as akin to 'inhaling anti-matter', provoked by the 'harsh form and ghoulish content' (Daniel 2008: 12, 59). Stubbs (2018: 321) extends this allegory of toxicity, recalling his own encounter with the music such that it exuded:

> the feeling of seepage, of effluent, of unlocked emissions. There was a sense that their music was intended to drift into the world like a toxic cloud, and that the outside world was in turn drifting into their music, mutually accenting, mutually resistant.

As novelist Iain Sinclair (2012: 333) observes, there is a hidden history of underground cultures fixing 'homeopathic doses of horror to prepare ourselves for the dark day', and Throbbing Gristle excelled in this capacity. Hegarty (2007: 119) offers the most brutally introspective attempt to articulate this, suggesting that the band provided 'a set of subtle questionings disguised as violent and offensive valorising of unacceptable imagery, movements and individuals. The strength was precisely in the uncertainty and excitement it generated'. Reynolds (2005: 226) presents another angle, arguing that the band undertook their own 'quest for some kind of authentic "pure self" via a gruelling regime of deconditioning', and anyone subscribing to the process is dragged along. It is not easy either framing this mode of working or indeed framing one's own attraction to it. Daniel (2008: 19) attempts to do so, resorting to calling up an adolescent vs. grown-up liminal border, a last fling before accountability beckons. Somehow making it not quite real is a justification, or perhaps an apology:

> And yet the knowledge that those sympathies are only being temporarily suspended is crucial to such art's effect of moral holiday, and the open secret to the perverse pleasure that such fare provides to the spectator: to do such things in reality would be utterly wrong, and so *therefore* their simulation is exciting, even pleasurable. These visions of remorseless criminality function as a kind of funhouse mirror reflection of the adolescent 'innocence' of their typical spectators and fans.

Bill Lee, in his contemporaneous review of the Throbbing Gristle album *Heathen Earth* for the music newspaper *New Music News* (7 June 1980: n.pag.), also sees this juvenile dimension. Instead of using it as a safety mechanism for enjoying the ride, he simply sees it as a failing of the band:

> I found it hard to come to terms with some of the ambiguities of their mode of expression – their idle image-mongering, their *dubious* symbolism – and their interest in all things prurient, diseased, or decayed came over less as a Sadeian exploration of morality and its limits, than as blockhead iconoclasm straight out of *everyone's* mid-teens.

As already glimpsed, much writing about the band's aesthetic and discursive dimension calls up a race-for-the-bottom of descriptive allegory, creating a paratactic convoy of anomic and degraded descriptive terms. The exercise of describing Throbbing Gristle becomes a potential product of the band's narrativized descent. This is evidently easier when you de-implicate yourself from the scene of involvement. For example, Demers (2010: 106) suggests that the band achieved a 'signal jamming that thwarts traditional aesthetics and notions of beauty', whilst Bland (2018: 165) signposts a 'surface nihilism'. Constantly striving for what Atton (2011: 325) calls a 'music of excess', the band drew on an endlessly darkening series of themes with little hope of respite or salvation: a twinning of negative eschatology and eschatological negativity. Daniel (2008) frames this juxtaposition of the banal and horrific as an affront to the generalized voluntary submission to the status quo, 'indulging in and reinforcing its ambient brutality' (128), with an intent to 'short-circuit its socio-political wiring' (129). The didactic content of live performances worked with and towards a multitude of interlocking intents: a disturbing message and sensory experience at the hermeneutic level, the direct pursue of altered states and physical bodily reactions (apparent intestinal discord through volume, bass frequencies and repetition, the mythical spontaneous orgasms that the band were obsessed with), and destabilizing the contract of performed entertainment. This latter intent, stated by Laing (1985: 88) as 'deconstructing the live performance as act', came to define the live experience of Throbbing Gristle, and the chapters in this book articulate the efforts of the band to achieve this. Lyrics and themes evolved over shows, at times forming what we might think of as a canon of defined songs or numbers in the parlance of rock and pop music, but P-Orridge tended to extemporize and take on board the mood of the crowd (and work against it).

It is necessary to get our hands dirty and ask ourselves how we are attracted to these abject missives. The difficult narrative themes – presented as established lyrics, improvised monologues, sampled dialogue or speeches, and accompanying materials –

produced by the band have been the subject of much debate. The obvious propensity of dark themes such as eulogies to human atrocities, poetic odes to serial killers, fantasized recollections of sex and violence, and withering and monotonic deliveries of an assumed sexual predator invite a multitude of interpretations. Arguing against a purely uncritical and glib celebration of the basest aspects of society, Conroy (2015: 97) frames the lyrics as a tension around control: 'what Throbbing Gristle are engaged in here is an exploration of a particular existential possibility regarding control or its absence. Control, for them, is a recurring theme'. Reed (2013: 10) proposes in his attempt to circumscribe this critical intent and method within the wider genre of industrial music: 'where there is transgression, there is law, and where we reveal law, we reveal external control'.

Other interpretations struggle to salvage an incisive thrust towards anywhere other than a descent, with Steirer (2012: 16) finding particular difficulty with the track 'Persuasion', suggesting that 'such songs often exhibited a schizophrenic logic, revelling in the very acts of manipulation they seemed to decry'. In a starkly self-interrogating chapter, Daniel (2008: 104–33) uses this same track as a case study to explore how we, as listeners to the music, process the brutal themes of the band, such that 'Persuasion' acts as a cypher for the general difficulty and unease of listening. This accrued self-doubt and nagging guilt pre-emptively haunts any discussion of Throbbing Gristle, though Duff (2019: 218) offers a diversion from the argument by drawing on disturbing work from other disciplines:

> People sometimes ask why anyone would actively choose to listen to music that makes them feel unsettled or even scared. Although the question is a valid one, interestingly it's a question that is rarely asked of cinema, or literature, or fine art. The paintings of Francis Bacon are unremittingly bleak and unsettling, yet there is no question over his genius or the validity of the work. Similarly the books of Stephen King, and the films of David Lynch contain huge swathes of material specifically designed to frighten and deeply disturb. Again we accept that they are masters of their craft. But it would seem that music, the most abstract of the arts, should expect to be judged by different criteria.

This raises more questions. What is the role of popular music as compared to art? Do we, as consumers or participants in popular music and subcultures, automatically associate the purveyor of these themes as being an advocate for the same themes, this unspoken bond of belief from the songsmith such that they endorse the subject of their works? It works well in the realm of pop, with regard to songs of love, happiness, positivity, and material consumption. It even works well for the politicized or critically engaged strand of punk, with stirrings of a better world, the righting of perceived injustices, and the angry and ideological critique. We feel that the artist holds these views or is personally animated by the subject matter; that there is a *linkage*. Do we then extend this beyond the moment of engaging the commercial product to suggest that to enjoy a piece of music (or art) we automatically sympathize with the themes therein? We may at times apply this dictum to politicized lyrics, more so to any band that explores right-wing lyrics and imagery such that we label the artist and the listener with sharing the views of the work unless we can pass it off as overidentification (because that counts as being critical in an ironic way). P-Orridge described his themes and lyrics as instinctive journalism, reflecting the abjectness of society in general. A switch from narrator to objective eye, like a remote-control drone camera panning over the wastelands of humanity and asking the question 'Can the world be as sad as it seems?'. P-Orridge, and the band, transgress the barriers and structures of what can be said in certain assemblages of popular culture, art, entertainment, etc. But they also go beyond his claim for instinctive journalism, moving into the realm of the glib, putrid and seemingly celebratory. It is an important issue and uncertainty that I return to throughout this book.

EVERYTHING OVERTURNED

In practice, the lyrical extent of the live performances was not a single focus on creating an ultimate abjection of themes, and P-Orridge utilized screams and contorted utterances on tracks such as 'Eee Ahh Oooh', achieving a linguistic void that could be read as a counterbalancing reaction to the montage of horrors relayed elsewhere. However, Throbbing Gristle inspired many bands in the subsequent industrial scene who fixated singly on the simple delivery of lurid and graphic retelling of themes of sex, pain, abuse, power, and death.

Aside from the lyrics, the band worked against the accepted spatial arrangements of the performance arena, deliberately undermining a contract of performance. Even when performing in an established venue such as at the early gig at the Nags Head in High Wycombe, the band abandoned the stage over to the audience, an effort described by Ford (1999: 7.9) to reverse the 'ritualised role as a passive consumer of the rock spectacle'. This worked against the proximal codes of the rock concert identified by Fonarow (2006: 82), with performers and differing modes of engagement by the audience. If a spatial rearrangement wasn't possible the band deliberately played early or before the support band, disrupting the temporal codes of a concert. The competence and proficiency were also challenged, summarized by Kromhout (2011: 26) in his description of the band as follows:

> the four members all played instruments they initially were unable to play properly, they made extensive use of self-built electronic instruments producing a deafeningly loud sound, and their output relied heavily on improvisation, chaos, and an atavistic, brutal energy, often recorded live in rather poor, lo-fi quality.

Whilst punk made (often unsupported) claims against accomplished music as part of an origin myth default statement, there was still an accomplished standard of punk behaviour and an undertaking of punk tropes to be delivered to an expectant audience. Throbbing Gristle took it upon themselves to turn this inside out. Reed (2013: 73) further expands upon this:

> In spite of the foursome's collective intelligence and savvy, they purposefully selected instruments and musical constraints that would highlight their individual ineptitude. When punk and other genres flaunt performers' incompetence, the intent is usually to convey an underclass cultural authenticity. For Throbbing Gristle, however, incompetence wasn't just a way to resist the constraints of supposed correctness; it was a means of achieving an unpremeditated encounter between performer and music.

A note of caution needs to be exercised here, as we descend into the unchallenged punk mythology of the permanent stasis of incompetence that accompanies the music. First, many punk musicians were far from incompetent. Second, Throbbing Gristle were equally competent at the points that mattered. They also became skilled with their instruments and didn't elect to put them down or switch them around when a level of mastery was attained. Certainly, the electronics specialist in the band Chris Carter did not fetishize incompetence in any way whatsoever – he explored non-standard sounds and effects, but did so from an incredibly competent position. Third, P-Orridge in particular was also well versed in avant-garde noise traditions, borrowing from a range of sources such as Jean Debuffet's 'musique brut' (the use of instruments that you cannot play) through to Artaud's glossolalia. Even if the band (or some of the band) initially chose instruments based upon unfamiliarity, they did practice, and if not gain a competence as we would understand in terms of how to play a specific instrument, they gained a competence in their own incompetence. Or, more so, a competence in the artistic staging of incompetence. The chaotic and jarring nature of their sound (or noise) aspired to a sonic apex, through either sheer cacophony and brutality, or through an acute sense of the disconcerting. Furthermore, as I show in later chapters, there were key points during their live trajectory where a distinct Throbbing Gristle sound was attained that wasn't simply a negation of either comprehension or competence.

As if to acknowledge the impossibility of containing a radical genre in the reasoned language (as some noise music theorists argue), hyperbole abounds in writing about noise music. Atton (2011: 329) sums this up: 'It is as if the intensity of the listening experience cannot be contained by subtler discursive means'. Throbbing Gristle draw you in, and you think you are able to arm yourself with words, a Bataillean descent of descriptive terms for depravity and abjection, it fleshes out, and flushes out, the wrongness. I (you) replay them back here, end-to-end, a parataxis of the oblique and outcast, numbly and dumbly mimicking the band as they compile the hostile audience reactions onto their recorded output. A perfect circle of imperfections. An illusion of catharsis, a justification, a pathetic poetry to celebrate a non-poetry of Auschwitz, serial killers, humiliation, loss, pain, bodily functions misfunctioning, embarrassment, predation, and on and on.

JOURNEY THROUGH A BODY

The history and trajectory of the overlapping projects of COUM and Throbbing Gristle are complex and muddy, proliferating on websites and blogs in conflicting and contrasting versions befitting of the band's commitment to waging an information war of viruses, memes, falsifications, half-truths, and extremes. Their legacy persists with a constantly replenishing legion of loyal fans who are drawn to the source as they partake in resilient subcultures such as the industrial genre (see Reed 2013 for an industrial genealogy). The task of authoring a definitive history, or even a definitive set of historical versions, is not an enticing prospect, but it is thankfully not of primary concern here, having been diligently tackled by Simon Ford's magisterial book *Wreckers of Civilisation*, published in 1999. Ford patiently drew out a timeline of events through both archival research reflecting contemporaneous documentation and interviews with the disparate band members to present divergent accounts and the unfolding of mythologies, adding his own input and interpretation from his art historical and countercultural research backgrounds. Not only is it the go-to book on Throbbing Gristle but it is also the go-to archetype of how to write about a band like Throbbing Gristle.

Ford's history of COUM and Throbbing Gristle has recently been supplemented by two autobiographies from band members: first, Cosey Fanni Tutti's 2017 work *Art Sex Music*, and more recently P-Orridge's 2021 contribution *Nonbinary: A Memoir*.[3] Both books are fascinating, useful, and troublesome in equal measures; however, both of them also contain relatively lengthy gaps for some of the period of Throbbing Gristle's initial active duration. Tutti's work spans her varied and illustrious career blurring the boundaries in the production of art, sex, and music for public consumption. Her recollections of the time in Throbbing Gristle are (understandably) tainted by the corrosive relationship she entered with P-Orridge, and this festers on like a picked-at scab through the bulk of the book.[4] P-Orridge's book was written (or at least written towards completion) at the time of their terminal illness and so presents numerous hurdles in regarding it as an accurate source of information. The first part of the book (P-Orridge's early years) is dense and entertaining, whilst the period from around 1980 onwards seems hurried. Again, this is perfectly understandable as clearly time was running out (P-Orridge died of chronic myelomonocytic leukaemia in March 2020). P-Orridge has the propensity to elaborate and fantasize, and so parts of their story do not stand up to scrutiny, whilst other parts move around in the timeline of events as meticulously set out in Ford's book. Revelations in *Nonbinary*, such as P-Orridge's infamous claim that he enjoyed a close intellectual and emotional relationship with Joy Division singer Ian Curtis just prior to his suicide, are thus to be taken with a pinch of salt. If a reason for the pure energy and innovation of Throbbing Gristle was their constant tension and an impending breakdown of homeostasis, then this pulling in different directions has seemingly outlasted the band to a somewhat detrimental effect.

Acknowledging Ford's book and the two autobiographies, this book traces the history of the band Throbbing Gristle in the first phase of their existence, plotted through the research into, and contextualization of, a sequence of live performances. The band were effectively inaugurated through a statement of intent on 3 September 1975 as a further manifestation of the art project COUM and terminated in early 1981, giving them a small window of six core years of operation. I situate Throbbing Gristle within, against, and beyond the British punk and post-punk cultures, an approach that some may find controversial. They were coterminous with the first wave of British punk (1975–78) and the epiphenomenal emergence of post-punk (1978–81) which overlapped with commercial acceptance and overgrounding of the original punk scene and also a reiteration of punk as a 'second-wave'. As a band, and as individuals, they stridently declared themselves to have nothing to do with such scenes, though they performed their music, released their records, and engaged with the music press during the key period of British punk. Their audience initially consisted of an arty crowd that had alighted on punk and formed one-half of punk's pincer movement between a more workaday rock 'n' roll anger and an experimental exhibitionism. It is easy to overlook, but McLaren and the Sex Pistols set out with similar links to the arty world of London's 'them' culture, playing events for Andrew Logan and forging links with filmmakers such as Julien Temple. As Throbbing Gristle progressed to gigs in the northern provincial towns and cities their audience included a key demographic of punks nurtured upon the music press image of the scene. As I show in the chapters that follow, many audience members were so moved by the band's performance that they began to explore new music and modes of participation. In offering a punk narrative to Throbbing Gristle I am not trying to rewrite history. Throbbing Gristle emerged and existed during a time when punk raised many questions, reflective of a tumultuous period of political, social, and cultural unrest as the 1970s drew to a close in a seemingly hopeless search for a reckoning.

Throbbing Gristle had a contradictory relationship to punk, simultaneously denying it, ignoring it, exploiting it, and inciting it. However, punk ultimately provides an insightful method for reading and understanding the band. In tandem with this, Throbbing Gristle posed questions about the interventional scope and affective dimension of punk. I set this out in Chapters 2 and 3, taking both the origin moment of the band in 1975 and their immediate incubation in punk's heyday years of 1976 and 1977, to explore where connections occur and how these were articulated. Punk engaged the time of the late 1970s, as Britain lumbered like a punch-drunk heavyweight boxer through a mammoth and brutal bout. Aspects of punk were predominantly forged from circumstances of the time and reflected those times (if not necessarily satisfying both criteria). Instances of cultural unease erupted like jets from a leaky faucet: the liberal-hating comic book figure Judge Dredd rode into view in 1977, JG Ballard published dystopian works such as *Concrete Island* (1974) and *High Rise* (1975) which rooted a pervasive dread in the concrete infrastructure of the built environment, and new novelists entered the fray with bleak and futile stories such as Martin Amis's *Dead Babies* (1975) and Ian McEwen's *Cement Garden* (1978). The post-apocalyptic television series *Survivors* aired on the BBC in 1975, created by the writer Terry Nation, with a title caption utilizing a stencilled font later made popular by the anarcho-punk band Crass. Throbbing Gristle's inception in 1975, and subsequent aesthetic development, would prove to have more than a little in common with *Survivors*.

At the political level, the Labour Party government under Harold Wilson returned to power without a majority share of the votes in the April 1974 general election, ratifying their position a few months later with a second general election which saw a change in leadership within the opposition to Margaret Thatcher. A demise through the second half of the 1970s was unstoppable with inflation, unemployment, Irish Republican Army (IRA) bombing campaigns, and a pound falling against the dollar to a record low, signalling what the historian Andy Beckett termed 'declinism' (Beckett 2010: 177). This period of Labour government was split between Wilson and James Callaghan, who replaced Wilson as the leader in April 1976. Callaghan's leadership of the party and the country is effectively synchronous with punk's rise to visibility and notoriety. His denouement came with the toxic shock of the Winter of Discontent as 1978 unravelled into 1979.

As a result of a mix of negative, lazy, or inexperienced journalism, it is a commonly accepted idea that the Winter of Discontent somehow produced, or is at least symbolic of, punk. This is a misconception, as punk was clearly nurtured some years before when the political climate was slightly different and more heterogeneous. In effect, we could suggest that punk prefigured or foreshadowed the Winter of Discontent, willing and accelerating it into actuality. We only need to turn again to P-Orridge's introductory delivery before their inaugural ICA performance, included as the opening to this chapter, to envisage ruination, abandonment, collapse, and despair – a pitch-perfect vision of 1978–79 in 1976. Throbbing Gristle were thus at the heart of this prefiguration, promulgating an endless discontent. If punk offered a way of understanding and potentially undermining the political, social, and cultural climate of the late 1970s – both a lens and a crowbar so to speak – then Throbbing Gristle both amplified and distorted the process. They embodied, intensified, and warped that critique by digging hard into the repressing moral substructures of society, extending the Winter of Discontent prior to and after the focused period of 1978–79. Furthermore, the band drew punk into the critique, picking away at its codes, conventions, and concealed conformist underbelly that constituted an industry of contracts, products, advertisements, and manufactured dreams. In this sense, Throbbing Gristle were both in and against punk, and punk was both in and against 1970s Britain, allowing Throbbing Gristle's critique to perform a nuanced double refraction – in historian Mathew Worley's framing of punk and politics, they both propagated and problematized (Worley 2017: 172).[5]

Throughout this book, I take a similar chronological trajectory to Ford's endeavours in *Wreckers*, adding my own findings, but developing a different context rather than building upon Ford's work by either questioning his findings and interpretations or adding to his body of evidence. My methodology is to isolate and contextualize a selection of live performances by the band, undertaken in the initial short period of their existence. Each chapter pivots around a performance to draw out the significance of the event and allow a fuller enquiry into the shifting sound and tactical affront of the band, deconstructing the performance through textual and performative analysis of lyrics, phenomenological registers of noise and ambience, and shifting signifiers and metaphors from the wider cultural sphere. Chapters 2 and 3 cover the years up to and including 1977, returning first to the *Prostitution* event of October 1976 and then panning through 1977 and alighting on a March performance at Brighton that coincided with the Sex Pistols 'God Save the Queen' controversy. Chapters 4 and 5 cover 1978, a time when the band were refining a sound and mode of operation to provoke punk and subsequently picking up an initial music press interest. These chapters document a gig at London's Architectural Association and the band's first foray up north to perform at Wakefield. The focus is split, with Chapter

4 exploring the structural nature of performance and Chapter 5 exploring the sound and narratives of the band. Chapter 6 commences in the midst of the Winter of Discontent with a gig at Derby in the East Midlands. The research here highlights how punk was temporally stretched out as it moved into the provinces, a factor that contributed to the birth of a second wave of punk that flourished in towns and cities like Derby. Chapter 7 covers the remainder of 1979 and the start of 1980 as post-punk began to establish itself through various definitional boundaries of geography and style. The focus of the extensive chapter is the band's second appearance in Sheffield with experimental colleagues Cabaret Voltaire. The book concludes with the period through the end of 1980 and the start of 1981, a period when the band endured both increased activity and rapid dissolution. I use their performances as a way of understanding the time and the place (as a flux of societal pressures pertinent to the late 1970s and subcultural counterforces such as punk) through the critical intent of the band. Through this reverse angle shot, a shadow history of the band is also opened up, as they respond to the times and, more importantly, respond in turn to the responses that they previously provoke through probing and shaping subcultural and countercultural political formations. Throbbing Gristle engaged the times, shaped the times, and were further shaped by their own impacts.

As I have briefly indicated, and will further show throughout this book, the band were consistently unorthodox at all levels of activity; the style, content, and presentation of their music, the development and transmission of a broadly political and philosophical stance, their in-house management of record releases, their eventual eschewing of the usual channels of the music press, their approach to live events, and the emphasis of a multimedia and inter-medial approach to experimentation, communication, and output. Thus, their approach to live work did not follow the pattern of touring undertaken by successful rock and punk bands. Instead, most events were carefully and strategically put together, making a Throbbing Gristle gig both a rarity and a blank slate of expectation (or a dynamic wiping the slate clean of preconceptions). The band undertook a meagre total of 36 live performances commencing in 1976 and ending early in 1981, with all of these performances focused on England apart from three performances in Germany in the autumn of 1980 and two performances in the United States at the end of their existence.[6] In much the same way as the key punk band Sex Pistols, whose initial parallel existence strangely haunts Throbbing Gristle, the party was over, the 'mission terminated', by the time the band ventured onto American soil.

My aim is to go back to the selected performances to understand how each event was assembled and articulated, how it unfolded on the night, and how it implanted a series of affects and reverberations once the performance was over. As Ford (1999: 8·10) recounts, Throbbing Gristle claimed to undertake metabolic music, though the nature and meaning of this are never fully expounded. The metabolic is framed as a transformative moment, a bringing about of change in those who experience the band, and so the chapters here unpack the affective dimensions and extrapolate an understanding as to what this metabolic music might entail. The emphasis throughout was to stimulate and unsettle the audience in equal measure, to invoke, implicate, and embroil the audience on the night to react and shape the event, and to plant seeds of activism and dissatisfaction, including a dissatisfaction of culturally validated outlets of dissatisfaction such as punk. Duff (2019: 228) offers a partial shot of this unsettling imperative, focusing on the purely aural context and its sensorial reverberations:

> This is one of Throbbing Gristle's signature techniques, eschewing the mid-range and focusing on sounds that occupy the extreme ends of the spectrum of audibility. Then broadcasting these sounds at near deafening levels. This is without doubt mind-altering music. It impacts on my sense of space and balance and afterwards my head is swimming for about a quarter of an hour.

The band, as an affiliation of diverse artists sharing a wilful sense of artistic mischief and dark experimentalism, are often painted through a process of serendipitous creativity. For example, Encarnacao (2019: 77) suggests that 'the gradual accretion of members resulted in formidable creative resources and an army of complementary skills that allowed the group to work with uncommon autonomy'. However, as a unit, a band, and a rock group, there is a dialectic of doubt, of coherence and destruction, forming what Slater (2009: 160) has called a 'collective of non-subject agents from whom it is difficult to isolate who does what'. Artistic temperaments streaked with dark and destructive inclinations make for a volatile milieu, with bonds fluctuating between ultra-tight to antagonistic and hostile. Performances bristled with multiple tensions played out across different registers; within each member of the band grappling with extracting a requisite dysfunctionality of their assigned instruments, between members of the band competing and co-existing in the wider mix of interpersonal relations, between the band and the audience, and between the band and all aspects of wider society. This emphasis on the spontaneity of the event, the aleatory nature of what might happen, encroached on the performance as a deictic overload such that potentially nothing exists outside of being there, the notion that you simply cannot begin to appreciate or contextualize an event without witnessing it. However, in a typically contrary gesture to imprint a non-auratic stamp, each Throbbing Gristle performance was documented and disseminated through a series of purchasable cassettes offered as a collectable and limited-edition box set (re-released in newer formats after the dissolution of the band). These cassettes, in line with the industrial ethos of the band, were uniformly packaged in a functional style documenting time, place, and a rough outlay of tracks (though, definitive tracks or songs were elusive with the band such that much early work was instrumental, improvised, and responsive to the particular situation). As Reed (2013: 117) explains with his reference to 'the eternal network', the cassette form played a vital role, allowing music to be shared via an affordable and portable medium, and for fans to send in their own music and sound experiments in the hope that the band pay it attention and facilitate further circulation.

Shortly after the abrupt split of the band, a stream of live bootlegs appeared on vinyl, offering existing, potential, and curious fans a further chance to sample their work. There was, and remains, a great deal of mystique and trepidation around the band, and with the limited amount of records and live appearances, these live documents are now a commonplace tangible link to the band. This persistence and resilience of the live sound are further buttressed through the first official studio releases of the band, *Second Annual Report* (November 1977) and *D.o.A: The Third and Final Report* (December 1978). Each release includes live snippets from gigs, recycled samples of the audience violently reacting with a hurl of insults, and montages of their signature 'Wall of Sound' that often closed out each performance as the self-imposed and meticulously timed one-hour shutdown of power drew closer. The strategic foregrounding of these fleeting, intensified, and intimate moments of being there creates a heterotopic hinterland when the contemporary fan is faced with a barrage of releases that recycle and re-sequence past performances. A latent fan of the music is both placed at the performance but unable to partake in the drama of the time or activate any metabolic affects. This is not a claim for an overwhelming hauntological or time-out-of-joint experience, but instead an indication of a tension between being there and not being there which seeps out of each live recording. If writing about Throbbing Gristle and their propensity for extremes is difficult and unsettling enough, working through these live recordings to understand the experience and impact of being there adds a whole new burden and sense of uneasiness.[7]

Part way through the process of researching and writing this book, it occurred to me that each of my case studies also had a reverberation in the contemporary era. '*Prostitution* Revisited' took place in 2016, ostensibly as a promotional event for Tutti's book. The (anti) gig at the Architectural Association was celebrated on its 25th anniversary with an exhibition and rebroadcasting of the soundtrack on 3 March 2003. The gig at Derby Ajanta was the subject of a 2018 exhibition by We Are Kunst in the town of Belper (7 miles north of Derby) which featured photographs from the event and a new performance by Vagina Dentata Organ. Throbbing Gristle's appearance in Sheffield prompted a cassette séance by academic Matthew Cheeseman in 2013, who added to the typical confused mythology by searching for the hauntings of the 1979 gig in the space of the 1980 gig. Finally, the obscure and undocumented gig in Wakefield makes a reverberation of sorts in the harrowing writing of novelist David Peace. If anything, these recent reverberations indicate how the band have slowly crept into the critical canon, but typically claim a place here through less orthodox means than simply reforming and re-treading the same paths and songs.[8] But there is something greater attempted. As detailed above, the readily available recordings of live performances allow us to transpose time by replaying the sound of 'then' as a constant resource as we go forward. However, it is an imperfect picture, and we immediately lose a grain of context which increases as a void as the years pass by. These reverberations all attempted, in one way or another, to fill the void – a phenomenological reawakening (or implantation). This book can be seen as a further extension of this process of engaging phenomenology, undertaken with a different tack and so yielding different results or interpretations.

SPACE, PLACE, AND BEING THERE

The writing thus unfolds through the analysis of a series of performances rooted in fixed points: England in the 1970s under a distinctive political situation, the towns and cities with regional nuances in social and cultural conditions, the concomitant punk scene that proliferated, and the locus of performance in terms of the concert hall or whatever form that may take. This nested register of fixed points is positioned in the current definitional flux of space and place. The geographically bounded regions of England, and its towns and cities where Throbbing Gristle delivered their avant-garde noise and extreme poetry can be considered as a place in French thinker Henri Lefebvre's sense of the term in his 1991 book *The Production of Space*. The socially and (sub)culturally bounded milieu of punk, with its rules and rituals of operation of inclusion and exclusion criteria, exists as a field such as employed in the work of French sociologist Pierre Bourdieu.[9] Finally, the tactile understanding and appreciation of the art colleges, community spaces, and rock venues where the gigs unravelled come under the remit of Gaston Bachelard and his 1964 work *The Poetics of Space*. This place, field, and space assemblage interacted, with each part informing and shaping the others such that Throbbing Gristle intervened and applied pressure at each part and across the dynamics of a relationship.

Drawing on a critical arsenal of boredom, work, consumer culture, and everyday life, punk also contested the construction of place – the meanings, rules, structures, privileges, and inequalities of society that shape the fabric of our surroundings and our life within it. In turn, Throbbing Gristle exploited the climate around punk, in terms of a new receptivity to challenging and confrontational music (as both a sound and its mode of presentation) and a critical media climate that spanned out from specialist music newspapers through to the general media. At the same time, they seldom conformed to assorted punk archetypes and quickly move beyond punk's soon-to-be well-rehearsed shock motifs of both sonic palette and lyrical or allegorical themes. The band ploughed something of an isolated furrow amongst the new punk audiences and the various media formations that either praised or berated the scene.

In tandem with their assault on the wider structure of society and the cultural response by punk, the band applied critical thinking and practice to the space of performance in terms of where they chose to play and how they deconstructed that space. With their emergence from COUM, Throbbing Gristle were well versed in arranging performances in spaces outside of the accepted gigging circuit occupied by large commercial venues catering for successful rock bands of the mid 1970s or the pub circuit which served the buoyant pub-rock scene. Through their previous guise the band had access to, and experience of, gallery spaces and art colleges, and so often found themselves crossing paths with or aligned to the aspects of the nascent punk scene that also germinated from (and fed back into) the art colleges. This relationship with (arty) punk is complex – whether we consider it as mutually beneficial, hostile or simply proximal – and contested by the members of the band, but it is an important factor in setting a context. Even if the band did not consider themselves part of this scene, they often shared the same spaces and the same audiences and were reviewed by the same reviewers from the music press. This crossover offers an understanding of how Throbbing Gristle's live performances came to be, and how we might discover evidence of the experience of being there, beyond simply listening to the many recordings of each event.

Whilst some mainstream venues (such as London's Lyceum Theatre and Heaven nightclub) were utilized towards the end of their lifespan as they became figureheads in the post-punk industrial genre, the band also performed at one-off spaces such as schools, training colleges, and art institutions. These instances gave them an opportunity to explore and deconstruct audience expectations of proximal codes and the 'contract' of performing live music. Building upon the work of Peters (2001) around the importance of 'witnessing' in regard to live music, Danielsen and Helseth (2016: 26) propose that playing live is about: 'generating a feeling of liveness, in the sense of an immediate "living presence" that often takes the form of a special intensity in the moment'. Their writing addresses a potential breach of this contract with the switch from guitars to electronic instruments and eventually laptop music, bringing to the surface a 'logical-sensorial rupture: one can hear a sound but not see its original source' (24). In their early performances, predominantly in art or institutional spaces, Throbbing Gristle are aware of this logical-sensorial rupture well before Danielsen and Helseth problematize it. It is grasped and weaponized as an opportunity, and Chapter 4 discusses in detail Throbbing Gristle performing (if not simultaneously appearing) at the Architectural Association in London.

This breaking of the rules of cultural fulfilment was something previously practised with COUM to disputable success. Cultural professionals attending COUM performances in the early to mid 1970s would quietly sit and watch as members P-Orridge and Tutti (and latterly Peter Christopherson who briefly participated in COUM events) undressed, mutilated themselves, injected their orifices with liquid foodstuffs, extracted and shared bodily fluids, and simulated sexual encroachments. Many of the photographs in the first half of Ford's book, documenting the COUM years, show stuffy-looking men in suits with blank expressions lining the perimeter of the pristine gallery enclosure, foregrounded by a floorshow of naked bodies and debris. Viewing these photographs can make us uncomfortable, although feminist theorist Siona Wilson (2015: 107–08) problematizes the normative instinct of reading these photographs as documentation. Instead, she suggests they can be situated as a strategy that adds to the disruptive function of the event as a challenging performance by undermining practices and methods of documentation, both in a formal sense or in the 'institutional-critical' sense of 1970s conceptualist actions. However, a greater problem presented itself to COUM – art, in the age after both conceptualism and Viennese actionism, was losing its ability to shock. As much as P-Orridge spent frantic time writing to the outsider art fanzines of the time elaborating (and possibly exaggerating and embellishing) the grotesque content and hostile audience reaction to COUM performances, something new was required. By shifting to the punk circuit there was an opportunity to re-open a critical space.

The relatively underground and antagonistic status of punk at the point of its inception in the United Kingdom, twinned with the fact that a significant strand of its origin came from the art school scene, meant that many punk events would take place outside of the regular circuit of venues. As documented by James (2018), the original punk band Sex Pistols traversed the art colleges in the South of England through 1975 and into 1976. Additionally, they were also forced to play small, unorthodox venues when they ventured north of London, as recounted by Smith (2015) who witnessed the band at the North Yorkshire seaside towns of Whitby and Scarborough where punk was predominantly unknown. These venues were intimate and offered the potential for interaction, spontaneity, and experimentation, though we have little knowledge or evidence of what happened in terms of efforts by the performers or audience to react to the space and situation. These events evaded any coverage by the music newspapers, and a further problem now manifests with the post hoc myth creation of punk events that have retrospectively been attributed a seminal status (a debut performance by a minor support band who would go on to become important, the inspiration for a new city-scene). Albiez (2005) offers an indicative example through his documentation of the contradicting myths surrounding a multitude of individuals who claim attendance at the key Sex Pistols performances at Manchester in 1976, seen as a catalyst for the city's quick and unique uptake of punk. In a similar vein, Lohman and Worley (2018) unpick a complex web of mythology and contradicting versions of events that have unfolded over the years following a pivotal anarchist-punk event in London's Conway Hall in September 1979 in which fierce violence erupted between left- and right-wing factions. As this book quickly and amply shows, Throbbing Gristle packed the mythologization of many of their own performances with violence, venom, and disorder.

We know the precise occurrences of the band's performances, with the venues, times, and support acts often recorded on the many websites dedicated to Throbbing Gristle and the production of a live cassette of each event, but it is more difficult to recapture how the band explored the space and ritual of performance beyond the obvious reactions captured by enraged crowd members that seep onto the live recordings.[10] The four weekly music newspapers in the United Kingdom – *Sounds, Melody Maker, New Musical Express,* and *Record Mirror* – shared a structured format of partitioning the news, record reviews, features, and coming events that make up the industry of music consumption, and thus form a key primary resource in the documentation and subsequent historical enquiry into music and its public consumption. Each contained a significant section dedicated to gig reviews, in which a music performance from the previous week is reviewed (occasionally accompanied by a photograph of the performer or band). Aside from giving the journalist a chance to extol their proprietorial prowess, the review generally addressed the artist, in terms of their demeanour, presentational appearance, interaction with the crowd, the songs performed, and the competence of the performance on a song-by-song basis. Audiences were only invoked if they gave a particularly hostile reaction. Reviews were shared across scenes and regions, and certain journalists became associated with certain areas and styles of music (metal, punk, pop, etc.). Whereas any band would be reviewed in a staggered rotation (rather than multiple reviews appearing in a short spread coinciding with a full tour), the same venues would appear week-to-week or even in the same week. The reviewers were not reviewing the venue, seldom spoke about the space, or described how each artist made a particular utilization of the space. Thus, the primary source of the music newspaper, through advertisements for coming events and reviews, provides a simple source documentation of which spaces were utilized. Alongside this, the fanzine scene – pre-dating but energized by the punk affirmation of do-it-yourself culture – tended to mimic the structure and functionality of the inkies, if not embracing lesser artists (playing more obscure venues) and eschewing a flowery style of writing that tended to make journalists consider themselves as some sort of brand.

Outside of the near-contemporaneous music reportage, secondary and tertiary source writing on the direct experience of pop, rock, and subcultural music events, spaces, and scenes is a prolific activity, with output split between enthusiastic fan memories, recalled anecdotes from the artists, and an evolving source of academic voices. The latter fluctuates between early subcultural studies under the Centre for Contemporary Cultural Studies (CCCS) at the University of Birmingham, through the post-subcultures school of the early 2000s (which challenged the Marxist struggle-from-below framing and redressed the ethnographic lacuna of much CCCS work), to the current scene of researching the role of music via memory, nostalgia, ageing, and spatial determination of local, regional, and national scenes. In contrast, vernacular style fan-driven writing, often underpinned by nostalgia, has more likelihood to recall and describe nuances of space within a venue, and I draw on some of these examples when discussing Throbbing Gristle at Wakefield Industrial College and Derby Ajanta Theatre in Chapters 5 and 6.

ELSEWHERE

If the time and place of late 1970s England, the field of punk, and the space of performance frame this work on Throbbing Gristle, then it is important to acknowledge that their efforts to disrupt these contextual frames often pushed through to an opposite. With this in mind, the word displacement frames my heterodox and heterogeneous reading of Throbbing Gristle, being applicable to their relationship to the aforementioned structures of space, place, and field. Displacement lends itself to a rhizomatic etymology such that it extends into new contextual uses common to modern language in the grip of the post-cultural studies boom, whilst further afield, experimental artists such as Doris Salcedo claim the term due to its polyvalent heritage. For my purposes here, the meaning of the word is not deployed in a diachronic measure as a linear trail back into time but is instead appreciated as a synchronic measure by exposing a complexity at a given time that has no obvious historical lineage. First, Throbbing Gristle represented a displacement in the context of not fitting in, being shunned, and seeking something or someplace else (even if, as we see below, this someplace else borders on the elusive and inexpressible). They are displaced, voluntarily and involuntarily, from general British society, the art community, and ultimately the punk community (or at least its spokespeople in the music press). In his work on radical performance art, Johnson (2019: 94) highlights COUM's fascination with 'omissions', which he describes as 'feasible contents of a life that are omitted from polite representations', and it is this preoccupation with ontological effluent that situates COUM (and Throbbing Gristle) in the realm of the displaced. Second, they represent a displacement in the context of fluid dynamics, whereby a solid body enters a solution to displace a volume of liquid. In this regard, Throbbing Gristle entered the punk environment through their manifestoes, recorded output, and – most importantly – live appearances, to influence a new scene. Disparate small groupings, what we can term like-minded individualists and experimentalists, took away something from an encounter with the band and disconnected from the mainstream current of punk to pursue something more than punk. The volume displaced was disproportionate to the volume input. Third, in the field of linguistics, displacement refers to the ability to communicate ideas that are remote in time and/or space, and this emerged as a key strategy and effect of their work as they drew from theorists and activists from the underground press past and present offering minoritarian views and voices. Finally, its coinage in Freudian psychology as a defence mechanism to deflect dangerous or unacceptable thoughts offers Throbbing Gristle fertile ground. The extreme subjects tackled by the band in a direct and overt fashion effectively undermined Freudian displacement like a drenching in industrial strength bleach. The band offer visions and reports from everyday life that push beyond what we may ourselves consider dangerous and unacceptable but deep down crave, in turn creating psychical conflict. We are fascinated by these things but they have an unshakable aura of taboo, upsetting the equilibrium of our psyche. This unavoidable discomfort and unease in the rationalizing and justifying of Throbbing Gristle's themes strike to the core of any discussion of the band.

Struggling against the time and place of its inception and expression, punk's rallying call of no future wasn't simply a wholesale negation of place or a statement of an impossibility of place – it was a cry that the current model had outstayed its welcome and outlived its worth, and that something else was required. Some punk bands went further to propose a new place, a way of doing things, such as with the epiphenomenal anarcho-punk movement that dovetailed with the end of Throbbing Gristle's period of activity. Other artists simply accelerated to an ultimate end that could be glimpsed in doomsday scenarios running from the peripheral (outbreaks of hooliganism and the breakdown of community) to the totalitarian (nuclear Armageddon). However, punk did not always propose or imagine an alternative place in the future, and, in his engaging writing on punk and apocalyptic scenarios, Williams (2011: 112) identifies several no-future motifs that are tied into the climate of punk and its co-existence with an escalation and proliferation of nuclear armaments. This selection of end-of-the-world scenes is concomitant with the early 1980s fascination with post-apocalyptic films such as *Mad Max*, and second-wave punk bands such as the Exploited drew from this cultural trope to sing about, and depict, marauding bands of mutated punks doing battle in a devastated landscape. Whilst P-Orridge often fantasized about the violent end of the world, the no-place of this no-future punk, prophetic or eagerly anticipated, is also applied to the aura of Throbbing Gristle, albeit obliquely. Hegarty (2007: 105) offers his own overview of their approach to a societal critique such that:

> like punk, industrial music was suspicious of musicality, but its hatred of contemporary art and society went deeper, its critique harsher as a result […] like Derrida, industrial music knows there is no outside to escape to that is not already consumed by the inside.

Framing the band as anti-social and isolationist, he then prophetically adds that they were 'too late for a new society' (Hegarty 2007: 106). This forlorn search for naming and delegating a spatial realm for Throbbing Gristle is continued by Steirer (2012: 3) who calls upon situationist Ivan Chtcheglov's 'Formula for a New City' and his introduction of the Sinister Quarter such that Throbbing Gristle map this at its extremes and beyond. Just as they propose the impossibility of a place they also dwell in an unnameable place, effectively a displacement, adeptly described by Worley (2017: 36) as a 'brutalised hinterland that connected transglobal artists revelling in the abject and extreme'.

MYTH AND ART

Having set out a contextual framework for this book (Throbbing Gristle, punk and the extensible Winter of Discontent), and proposed a methodology of deconstructing a selection of live performances, there are also a couple of recurrent themes that warrant inclusion in this opening chapter before we re-tread the path of the band. I have already indicated several instances where the band crossed over into the extreme points of canonical art and where they (in particular P-Orridge) inserted stories into their history. These practices of almost-contemporaneous myth creation and manipulation, and the analytical frame of the field of art history, thus form two important contexts that enshroud any discussion of the band. These can be documented as persistent *motifs* within the operations of the band but can equally be raised to the status of *devices* necessitating a closer examination. Care needs to be taken, as employing these devices as analytical or contextual frames can quickly move between utility and hindrance.

Mythologizing first. Perpetually returning to the avant-garde thinking and writing of William Burroughs, the band's core themes of information war, systems of meaning generation, control, indoctrination, and persuasion found a generalized expression in their myth creation. Unsurprisingly, this makes any kind of standardized biographical writing on the band a challenge. The band had, and continued to have through the interviews with P-Orridge, an active tendency to mythologize and embellish the facts of their intentions, motivations, actions, and impacts, and so we have to navigate this tendency and understand it as both a strategy and (imperfect) historical axis. As Reed (2013: 127) argues, P-Orridge was an avid documenter of his artistic practices and various life philosophies, whilst at the same time being a self-confessed 'storyteller'. Though a hungry market exists for tall-tales and exotic anecdotes from the chaotic world of rock 'n' roll, jumping the divide from popular to academically informed writing necessitates caution as to treating punk autobiographical material as a means to access some kind of 'truth' of events. The rich vein of mythologizing within punk feeds consumption for the nostalgia of punk, but, for historians, it is a critical impasse that blurs the usefulness of testimony (see Medhurst 1999 and Street et al. 2018 for informative case studies). With Throbbing Gristle we can provisionally move beyond seeing this strictly as an epistemic limitation, such that whilst P-Orridge's propensity to storytelling initially challenges the use of his testimony as documentation, it can be better seen as a direct continuation of each performance. The case study in Chapter 4, the performance at the Architectural Association, develops this underlying context of myth creation. Furthermore, it can be argued that what is taken forward by consumers of the mythology of the event, and so shapes potential further interventions and actions by an inspired generation, is what people want to hear. The wider field of punk and its cottage industry of mythologizing bears witness to this. Boring events, with sparse and unmotivated crowds, do not make fertile ground for future creatives looking to be inspired.

If myth was an encouraged practice and dynamic output such that each utterance and recollection was divergent from the source and heterogeneously re-stated, then an underpinning structure was also necessary. Informational control was exerted through the formation of a clique, as they worked with a close-knit circle of journalists who initially appeared as having an understanding of their intents, if not loyalty to their cause. Additionally, a small number of fans switched across from the general punk scene to dedicate their commitment to the band, and a handful of fanzines such as *Dirt, Stabmental* and *Toxic Graffiti* gave them detailed coverage in the bridging period between the onset of the rapid commercialization of punk and the counter-movement of anarcho-punk. The band, and the core members around them, also produced a fanzine of sorts with *Industrial News,* taking a Dadaist and situationist juxtaposition strategy but overloading the content with imagery and text from the obscure and extreme corners that informed their music and expressed a 'shared distaste for the hegemonic tradition of communication' (Bland 2018: 154). This engagement with fanzines mirrored the underground coverage instigated by COUM who worked with the North American mail-art scene, providing typically sordid and inflammatory column space for independent magazines such as *Vile* and *Slash*.

From mythology we can move to art. P-Orridge and the other band members knew their art via their researched endeavours with COUM and an additional accumulation of experiencing art spaces and rubbing shoulders with other artists.[11] For example, an appearance by COUM at the Architectural Association in January 1976 as part of the *Real Space* conference saw them sharing space with prestigious names from the worlds of art, architecture, and avant-garde music: challenging architect Bernard Tschumi, conceptualist John Stezaker, musician Brian Eno, and the provocative 'Nice Style' pose band formed by Bruce McLean. Two years on from this shared platform Throbbing Gristle would return to the Architectural Association and undertake one of their most ambitious interventions in presenting live rock music, but it is intriguing to think how they may have drawn from some of their encounters. For *Real Space*, Brian Eno is listed as presenting a piece of 'music to be ignored', and this would have resonance with Throbbing Gristle's own concept of 'muzak for the traffic' which they billed as their own performance in the same space in March 1978. The shared orbit with Bruce McLean is also instructive, as his 'Nice Style' project involved a possible pop band that existed solely to undertake a series of popstar poses. An art framework also offers a possible interpretation of some of the sensory tactics used in Throbbing Gristle live performances: the aforementioned use of mirrors to implicate the audience as spectators was a common strategy explored by Robert Smithson with his enantiomorphic chambers, and the oversized Tesco carrier bag prop utilized by the band was redolent of Claes Oldenburg and his large-scale sculptures of mundane objects.[12]

As stated above, applying canonical art parallels to imagery and aesthetic assemblages that normally reside in the popular field can flip from utility to hindrance. Stallabrass (2010: 115) strikes a note of caution here, suggesting that 'more often, the identification of sources seems to be an exercise in assuring that the works receive the right kind of attention as art, imbuing them with historical depth, while demonstrating the author's perspicacity, knowledge and sensibility'. In this case, utility is lost for little more than a game of art-snob *Snap*, and we cannot ascribe anything insightful to the thing that looks like something else from art. However, what is key with Throbbing Gristle is that they knowingly applied artistic criteria and parallels, and more so were well versed in the realms of art that pushed boundaries (including art that pushed the boundaries that defined art). They recognized intent and limitations, and the ability to create a difference in regard to perception and understanding, which in turn leads to destabilization and the opening up of a critical aperture or glimpse of an enclave. Parallels between their work – performances, soundscapes, record sleeve design – and art from the canon were not just coincidence, instead they were tactical, allowing critical methodology developed in the art to be applied to their own work.[13]

A further important event coincided with the longer crossover period between COUM and Throbbing Gristle, in which P-Orridge was employed to research and assemble a substantial reference book on contemporary artists for St. James Press. Produced between February 1975 and May 1977, the large format book weighs in at 1077 pages to resemble a structural breezeblock such as employed by Carl Andre in his modular *Equivalents* series. More importantly, it gives an insight into P-Orridge's appreciative scope and awareness of the contemporary art scene, even with his self-proclaimed 'rejectionist attitude' (2021: 151). The book includes significant listings for most of the actionist art scene based around Vienna and Germany (Gunter Brus, Otto Muehl, Hermann Nitsch as well as some of the American 'happenings' artists such as Carolee Schneemann), and other COUM fellow-travellers include British artist Stuart Brisley's forays into pain and self-humiliation, Luciano Castelli's early work expressing and performing transgenderism, Bruno DeMattio's interpretations of William Burroughs, situationist painter Asger Jorn, and the countercultural activist Brion Gysin. Artists who challenged the negotiation and appreciation of space within the gallery itself – in terms of (mis)directing the audience, creating spatial dissensus, and re-orienting the proximal codes of the artist-as-present – are represented with biographies for Vito Acconci and Michael Asher. I introduce many of these as critical parallels in the chapter on the Throbbing Gristle's Architectural Association performance

P-Orridge and Christopherson also published the important text 'Annihilating Reality' for the prestigious art journal *Studio International* in the July/August 1976 edition, at the cusp of Throbbing Gristle's emergence. This text and visual collage used borrowed words and original texts from a rogue's gallery of underground and extreme sources such as De Sade, various actionist figures, Charles Manson, and Aleister Crowley.[14] Amongst the images of murderers, strippers, and body-piercers – what Ford (1999: 6·17) considers as 'a vetoable cornucopia of the good, the bad and the ugly' – are artists such as Vito Acconci. The intricate crossover between COUM/Throbbing Gristle and the art scene would potentially meet the common ground in the nascent punk scene, as both the band and the punk scene developed across a shared timeframe. However, as I explore in the following chapters, this is not as straightforward as imagined, in the main due to the very nuanced and somewhat limited relationship between art and punk even amongst

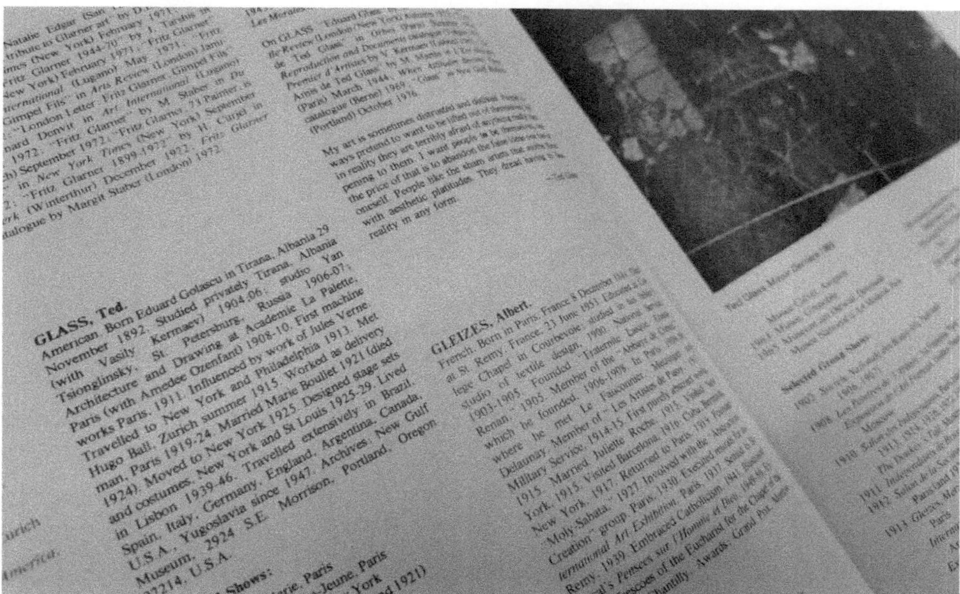
GLASS, Ted.
American. Born Eduard Golascu in Tirana, Albania 29 November 1892. Studied privately Tirana, Albania (with Vasily Kermaev) 1904-06; studio Yan Tsionglinsky, St. Petersburg, Russia 1906-07; Architecture and Drawing at Academie La Palette, Paris (with Amedee Ozenfant) 1908-10. First machine works Paris, 1911. Influenced by work of Jules Verne. Travelled to New York and Philadelphia 1913. Met Hugo Ball, Zurich summer 1915. Worked as delivery man, Paris 1919-24. Married Marie Boullet 1921 (died 1924). Moved to New York 1925. Designed stage sets and costumes, New York and St Louis 1925-29. Lived in Lisbon 1939-46. Travelled extensively in Brazil, Spain, Italy, Germany, England, Argentina, Canada, U.S.A., Yugoslavia since 1947. Archives: New Gulf Museum, 2924 S.E. Morrison, Portland, Oregon 97214, U.S.A.

Figure 1.1: Biographical entry for artist 'Ted Glass' in the volume Contemporary Artists *(1977) by Genesis P-Orridge and Colin Naylor.*

the arty strand of the first movers and shakers in the punk scene. Throbbing Gristle's embedded relationship with art scenes such as performance and conceptualist art, and a subsequently accumulated knowledge, meant that they were considerably above punk's more superficial and marketeering use of art, and above a post hoc interpretative lens of art such as may be applied to punk.

Aside from both motif and device, the St. James Press book also offers an insight into P-Orridge's self-opinion, and potentially the tense dynamics of the band, since it contains a lengthy entry for P-Orridge but no mention of his COUM and Throbbing Gristle colleagues.[15] It is also noteworthy that the tradition of graphic design and collage that fed into punk from strands such as situationism and radical montage was wholly absent such that there are no inclusions for Jamie Reid (active in creating *Suburban Press* and the graphic identity of Sex Pistols), Gee Vaucher (producer of the photo-montage magazine *International Anthem* and part of the anarchist arts performance collective Exit-Stencil), and political artist Peter Kennard. Other key absentees include US-based photomontage-activist Martha Rosler and Mary Kelly, whose provocative work would immediately precede COUM in being exhibited at the ICA.

The practice of myth also hybridizes in this writing up of art. As Ford (1999: 6.11) amusingly recounts, alongside himself and his obscure co-travellers in extreme art,

P-Orridge also insisted on including a fictitious artist in the documentation (see Figure 1.1). This occurs as Ted Glass (page 342 with an example of his art on page 343), a name previously assumed by P-Orridge for a postcard mailing action in November 1975 and for the first Throbbing Gristle gig as each band member took on a T. G. initialled name. In *Contemporary Artists*, Glass gets a write-up that paints him as a candidate for a Throbbing Gristle foot soldier declaiming the role of modern culture:

> My art is sometimes distrusted and disliked. People always pretend to want to be lifted out of themselves, but in reality they are terribly afraid of anything really happening to them. I want people to be themselves, and the price of that is to abandon the false ideas one has of oneself. People like the sham artists that soothe them with aesthetic platitudes. They dread having to face reality in any form.

The Ted Glass mythology is made plausible with a biography of exhibitions and works for the artist, suggesting inclusion in the important Harald Szeemann curated proto-conceptualist exhibition *When Attitudes Become Form* (Berne 1969). If P-Orridge's creation of an imaginary artist that persists through time via specious documentation merges his own tactical devices of myth-making and art, it also folds in another level from art by having an artist precursor. Slightly before Ted Glass is inserted into the canon the American conceptualist Gregory Battcock created his own conceptualist artist Hank Herron. As Roberts (1999: 97) recounts, Herron's 1973 work: 'entered the public discourse of post-minimalism, and therefore took on a discursive life […] his "virtual work" and "virtual biography" continue as historical events'. As a strategic seed planted in the cause of information war, P-Orridge may have well been able to foresee the automated and algorithmic information society that we live in. Every facet of web-published text and pixelated imagery is machine-harvested, stored, and represented (without quoting a source) in new manifestations and combinations of information, such that Glass and his fictitious presence at *When Attitudes Become Form* is replicated in web searches on the exhibition. Mythology outlives historical accuracy, secreting spurious facts and snippets of false information that replicate and travel automatically and algorithmically into the information sphere, a digital world that can be seen as either utopic or the latest manifestation of Throbbing Gristle's society-as-death-factory.

Finally, we can gain further insight into Throbbing Gristle employing (and often combining) myth-making and art by returning to Hegarty's discussion of noise in the context of music. If myth and art might be categorized as secondary strategies in the consideration of the band, noise is clearly a primary strategy. However, it is also possible to interpret Throbbing Gristle as layering their strategy of noise onto their strategies of myth-making and art in a feedback process. For this, we need an expanded definition of noise. We can turn again to Hegarty (2007) here, as he opens his study of noise with a wider probing of both what noise is not and what it could be after we eliminate the former. Noise is not to be confused with noises, a staple part of Throbbing Gristle's music and with many other artists as sampling became a standard means of music creation. Noise is not to be confused with noisiness, or volume, again a standard part of Throbbing Gristle's modus operandi. Noisiness can seem requisite to a situation such as a cheering crowd at a football match, even if it is discomforting it is not necessarily discomfiting, in that it never gives you the feeling that the perceptual and conceptual ground is giving way under your feet. In the noise music scene, in which Throbbing Gristle play a key part by birthing the strand known as industrial music, the tactic of noisiness is neither necessary nor sufficient to create noise music. Hegarty offers some strands of thought, a building block so to speak:

> Noise is negative: it is unwanted, other, not something ordered. It is negatively defined – i.e. by what it is not (not acceptable sound, not music, not valid, not a message or a meaning), but it is also a negativity. In other words, it does not exist independently, as it exists only in relation to what it is not. In turn, it helps structure and define its opposite (the world of meaning, law, regulation, goodness, beauty, and so on).
>
> (5)

With this more nuanced and considered definition of noise, we can now revisit the band's strategies of myth-making and avant-garde art to fold in Hegarty's explication. The deliberate creation of mythology can be understood as a *historiological noise* – a future anterior-oriented gesture to distort the possibility of fact or reportage. We see this clearly with the Ted Glass example in that references to his existence and participation in real-life events blocks access to reportage, research, and fact-checking. Similarly, an *art noise* would entail the blocking of the ease of ingestion and consumption, a surplus or supplement that disturbs the main portion of art as an agreed whole, the 'world of meaning, law, regulation' as quoted by Hegarty above. In this regard, Throbbing Gristle's reworked or extended lineage in the conceptual and actionist strands of avant-garde art continues working with art that has a troublesome aura in that it is constantly attempting to push the borders of taxonomic inclusivity. Conceptual art shifts towards utilizing the mundanity of objects, spaces, and instrumentalized processes, borrowing from earlier efforts in Pop Art where we have an attempt to shift what Groys (2014: 10) calls the 'value boundary between the cultural archive of art and the profane realm'. Whilst Pop Art took the visual culture of the everyday world of aggressive post-war consumer advertising and reproduced it as art (the tactic of Throbbing Gristle presenting the oversized Tesco carrier bag would partially belong here), conceptualist and post-conceptualist schools of art developed critical activist strands such as institutional critique and situational aesthetics that went beyond simply working against the content of the rules of inclusion. The aim instead was to destabilize the ontology of art and to rupture the habitus of privilege and function, to work against the context and structure of the rules of inclusion – a syntagmatic rather than paradigmatic shift.

It is within the turbulent period of punk and through the lenses of displacement, encompassing space, place, and subcultural fields, and noise, encompassing the discrete tactics of myth and avant-garde art, that the short but enduring history of Throbbing Gristle can now be plotted. To commence this we need to return, forewarned and forearmed, to *Prostitution*.

NOTES

1. P-Orridge used this phrase at every opportunity. For example, see Metzger (2002: 43).

2. Savage is recalling a 1978 gig at London Film-Makers' Co-op in which punk musicians in the crowd turned on the band with a violent attack.

3. In 2020 a documentary film *Other, Like Me* also added to the Throbbing Gristle history canon.

4. P-Orridge underwent a complex pandrogeny process in the late 1990s, merging with their partner to become two people with a shared identity and merged body appearance and persona, transcending both the binary of biological sex and the singularity of identity. Rae (2020: 161) interestingly contextualizes this as part of William Burroughs inspired cut-up procedure. The shared pronoun 'they' was adopted. P-Orridge's autobiography takes the title *Nonbinary*, which is a bit of a misnomer as this approximately relates to removing the ontologising structure of binary sex divides and dismantling all that has accrued through gender stereotyping. P-Orridge's quest predates the fashion for undermining gender certainty, and in some ways contrasts it by acknowledging a 'both' instead of a 'neither' or 'why'. For the time of study here coinciding with the first period of Throbbing Gristle activity, P-Orridge assumed a male identity and so the pronouns he/him are used throughout the book.

5. Worley's original source refers to post-punk band Gang of Four who favoured problematising over propagating.

6. See http://www.brainwashed.com/tg/live.php Accessed 1 December 2022.

7. For the featured gigs in each chapter I revert to the present tense, writing as listening as if I was part of the moment.

8. Of course, Throbbing Gristle did bow to pressure and reform for a second six years duration between 2004 and 2010.

9. The extension of Bourdieu's field as a way to model punk is proposed and developed by O'Connor (2016).

10. The live recording of their early gig at Brighton Polytechnic, discussed in Chapter 3, captures the breakdown of the performance and the crowd being offered the chance to vent frustrations. P-Orridge can be heard requesting to 'make sure it is all said', indicating how the band emphasised self-archiving and self-historification.

11. None of Throbbing Gristle went to art college. The extent of the band's art links and how they are often perceived as part of the art college set are explored in the conclusion of Chapter 3.

12. The use of mirrors to implicate the audience was later employed for fashion designer Alexander McQueen's S/S 2001 show *Voss*. At this point in time McQueen was utilizing the design talents of both Daniel Landin and John Gosling. The former was an early co-traveller with Throbbing Gristle (often assuming the name Stan Bingo), whilst the latter played a key part in the bands immediately following the dissolution of Throbbing Gristle. See Evans (2003: 99) for details and contextualization of this McQueen show.

13. Trowell (2020) draws links and explores critical potentialities between punk and post-punk montage work and canonical montage work.

14. Though not dwelt on here, this remains troubling. I revisit this for a more critical assessment in the conclusion of Chapter 5.

15. P-Orridge's entry runs over the pages 770–72. The book is updated with two new editions without P-Orridge as a co-editor: in these editions P-Orridge's entry is removed, as well as some of the more obscure COUM / Throbbing Gristle aligned entries that presumably were included in the original addition at his behest.

2. ORIGINAL SINNERS

TOWARDS *PROSTITUTION*

HULL AND BACK

In early 2017, the East Yorkshire city of Hull commenced its celebrations and events for its City of Culture bestowal. Geographically and in many ways culturally marooned as an abandoned annex or afterthought, the city fought against a gradual torrent of bad publicity that associated it with deprivation and desperation, depicted through the craze for 'benefits porn' programmes that functioned as fly-on-the-wall documentaries for overcrowded, run-down, and out of work households. For some strange reason, the council coincided the prestigious City of Culture opening with a chance to dig up the bulk of the city centre's pedestrian thoroughfares, as if refusing to be culturally attractive or relevant with a momentous nihilistic gesture.

The Humber Street Gallery, opened to coincide with the festival, provided a dynamic and evocative space to house ambitious and experimental art in the city alongside the well-established Ferens Gallery. Greeting the visitors on entry was the reclaimed and newly-minted-as-art 'Dead Bod', a crude graffiti of an upturned bird painted onto rusting sheets of seemingly nuclear-proof corrugated iron.[1] This readymade snatched from the world of once vernacular detritus looked a whole lot better than the ironic readymade intestinal slew of trenches, pipes, and barriers as part of the impromptu roadworks outside. The first exhibition of Humber Street Gallery celebrated the creative explosion of COUM Transmissions in the city, with the pairing of Neil Megson (later Genesis P-Orridge) and Christine Newby (later Cosey Fanni Tutti) at the heart of activities. As thoroughly documented by Ford (1999), COUM existed as a communal art and music group prior to Tutti joining in late 1969, but activities and exposure increased through the early 1970s. COUM then continued in Hackney, London following P-Orridge and Tutti's move in 1973, situated between an artist space on Martello Street christened the Death Factory due to its proximity to ancient plague pits, and a squatted house in Beck Road.

There was a heavy presence of alternative artists interweaved between these locations. P-Orridge had gained an interest in countercultural art activism such as happenings and beat-poetry writing during his time as a schoolboy in Solihull. He travelled to Hull in autumn 1968 with high hopes but ended up on a course studying social administration. He lasted barely a year, exiting the course to spend time slumming around London with David Medalla's Exploding Galaxy collective. This was not a formal art school background, more so sharing the influence of artists in the tail end of the communal hippie dream (Medalla had also worked with Pink Floyd and the UFO club). P-Orridge spent around five months with the collective before returning to Hull. By December 1969, he had procured derelict space in the docks area and set up the first of his Funhouse living spaces. It was rough. Taking liberty with the timeline we can consider Hull as the equivalent of Hackney-on-Sea. P-Orridge and his newly acquired collective moved to a new location in autumn 1970, still rough, but slightly better. COUM took shape and learnt to eke out a living by applying for arts grants and working the alternative arts festival circuit. Frustrations due to lack of opportunities and scrapes with the various underworlds of Hull forced P-Orridge and Tutti's exit to London in 1973.

Hackney was equally grim in the early 1970s, the combined sense of destitution and collective resistance summed up by Proll (2010: 11):

> Solidarity was the precept of the counterculture. The squats were the material basis and precondition for the emergence of political activism, art and alternative life. These houses, removed from the circulation of capitalist valorization, were open spaces for experimentation of all kinds towards a life lived without economic constraints.

This link between dilapidation and art activism allowed P-Orridge and Tutti to find first a studio space and then a living space (after a short period when they both lived in the studio space). The studio premises were part of the SPACE collective, a former trouser factory set up by artists Bridget Riley and Robin Klassnik, with Alberts performance artist Bruce Lacey on hand as a type of custodial caretaker role. SPACE was also connected to the Artists in Residence (AIR) galleries which would provide venues for early Throbbing Gristle performances. Meanwhile, Beck Road nurtured a concentration of artists as more properties, earmarked for clearance, were squatted, and, as Ford (1999: 3.9) recounts, a semi-legitimate status was accorded to the community of offbeat and subversive creatives.[2] An overheard conversation from the hopeful band Rinky Dink and the Crystal Set alerted P-Orridge to the immediate vacancy of a squatted house, as the band were hoping to move on to brighter pastures following the tantalization of a record contract. P-Orridge and Tutti moved into number 50, and a base for living and strategizing was established. In quick succession, the awareness of the name and notoriety of COUM intensified, and the parallel operation of Throbbing Gristle was proposed in September 1975. The following autumn, at the Institute of Contemporary Arts (ICA) Gallery,

Figure 2.1a: COUM Transmissions *installation view, Humber Street Gallery, Hull, 3 February – 22 March 2017. Courtesy of the artists, Cabinet, London and Hull 2017.*

COUM and Throbbing Gristle collided into public consciousness with the *Prostitution* exhibition, celebrating the underground canon of COUM with a generous sprinkling of Tutti's multipronged work in the pornography industry, and launching Throbbing Gristle as part of the acts to perform on the opening evening.

The 2017 exhibition in Hull reunited the wider personnel of COUM and presented a trail of artefacts commencing with the early years in Hull, to the rise of extreme actionist and performance art that characterized COUM as part of the London scene, through to the documents from the planning, executing, and immediate impact and media reaction from the ICA event. Amidst the torture devices, documents stained by bodily fluids to resemble archaic parchments, pornographic visual material, and dense manifestos was a curious document that offered another insight into *Prostitution,* and the significant shift of power and focus between COUM and Throbbing Gristle. Vitrine 14 article 153 was listed as the 'ICA Guest Invitation List' handwritten by Throbbing Gristle member Chris Carter and included all of the music newspapers and key record labels that were sniffing around the nascent punk scene. Clearly, something was afoot. With the inclusion of a punk band in support (Chelsea performing under the alias of LSD) and a curated crowd of arty punks, the recipe to make a scene was in place, and the requisite audience from the music industry were installed as key onlookers and messengers. For all intents and

Figure 2.1b: COUM Transmissions *installation view, Humber Street Gallery, Hull, 3 February – 22 March 2017. Courtesy of the artists, Cabinet, London and Hull 2017.*

purposes, this can be read as a statement of intent to admit Throbbing Gristle into the nascent punk canon.

By returning initially to the ICA performance around *Prostitution,* and then considering the handful of gigs on either side of this event, the following two chapters set out Throbbing Gristle's path within the dynamic of punk through 1975, 1976, and 1977. These three years were key for the rapid ascendance of the Sex Pistols, who rose to prominence with a series of media stunts and vitriolic engagements with wider society through searing critiques of taste, societal norms and standards of competence, and conduct. In addition, there was an element of art history awareness (and subsequent art-trashing) and performance theory nous within Pistols manager McLaren and frontman Rotten. The Sex Pistols existed as Throbbing Gristle's *bête noire,* and we can draw out parallels between the two bands. In this chapter, I examine both the shared orbit of the two bands and their clearly defined and separate realms where they each developed their music and wider aesthetic strategies. This concludes with *Prostitution,* and we see divergent and messy strands in the immediate aftermath of this curtailed event as an art scandal ensues over and above the intended din of Throbbing Gristle. In the chapter that follows, I plot the meteoric rise of the Sex Pistols in the jubilee year, and, through a series of performances, I tease out Throbbing Gristle's activity through this year as a response.

Punk informed the actions and decisions of Throbbing Gristle, though how we read this is continually up for debate. Certainly, the punk climate offered the band a backdrop to raise their own profile more so than music scenes concomitant with the activity of COUM, even if we give them the benefit of the doubt of not trying to muscle in on the scene. But, as I show, the links and coincidences are substantial.

DON'T LOOK OVER YOUR SHOULDER, BUT THE SEX PISTOLS ARE COMING[3]

Throbbing Gristle were first pronounced as a discrete working concept in September 1975. The name stems from Yorkshire slang for an erection, recounted by Ford (1999: 5·16) as being apparently derived from a passage in a pornographic magazine. Ford quotes a lengthy piece by P-Orridge from a 1979 article in which he injects a degree of idiomatic flexibility by drawing together an assemblage of post hoc connotations that can be activated, ranging from death spasms to a name for the cheap meat cuts purchased by the poor demographic of society at local market stalls. An earlier interview from 1978 references the human nature and body horror of gristle and the fact that the band throbs, and also the crude nature of the name that would potentially annoy arty types when writing about the band. Fish (2002: 17), in his autobiographical documentation of the nascent industrial scene, describes how his first live encounter with the band at the Rat Club was a brutal exposure to incessant and unrelenting noise such that his head was turning into a piece of throbbing gristle. Interestingly, in Ford (1999: 5·16), Carter suggests that the band name had been chosen before he joined to complete the quartet and that he hated the name, though one could argue that it was Carter who put the electronic throb in Throbbing Gristle. Tutti (2017: 157) presents a further version when she suggests that the name was chosen unaware of what it might become, and referenced their friend Les from early days in Hull who had spent eighteen months in prison – it was Yorkshire Les who first introduced them to the term back in the early 1970s. Tutti also dates this first use of the term to a typically challenging COUM show at Art Meeting Place in June 1974, though it is used here as integrated into the COUM performance rather than as a distinct entity or manifestation for something different.[4]

This use in 1974 puts the choice of the name in advance of the mature punk subculture, even though the name and its gutter-level denotation of the male sexual organ has a remarkable synonymity to Sex Pistols and so an obvious punk rock feel before its time, a future anterior to unfold in cultural history. For example, Hennessy's punk cash-in book *In the Gutter* had a quick-fire litany of shock-horror punk band names connoting lewdness and depravity with Throbbing Gristle nestled in there, lumping them momentarily as a punk band (Hennessy 1978: 39). This feat was repeated by Laing (1985: 46), who made a point in compiling a list of all the punk bands who constructed phallic names. In effect, the event and timelines between the two bands were incredibly coincident, though the literal link between the two names is seldom broached. The switch to making Throbbing Gristle a distinct project, a musical (sound) project, in September 1975 brought it much closer to the orbit of punk at a crucial moment, a point when the name Sex Pistols was becoming common parlance beyond an enlightened arty punk underground. What is needed is an understanding of how evolved punk was in 1975, how the punk idea had disseminated, and how close Throbbing Gristle were to this punk heartbeat.

One way of plotting the inception and rise of punk is through the deliberate and strategic management of the Sex Pistols, and the role of their manager Malcolm McLaren. The initial curation of the Sex Pistols, before a formal management role can be ascribed, is more fluid, with Bernie Rhodes also playing a part. McLaren had a history in the clothes industry, pushing boundaries with his chameleon-esque shop on King's Road and his partnership with Vivienne Westwood, a couple described by Townsend (2002: 44) as 'artfully aware cultural interventionists'. Rhodes also had an interest in the subcultural clothing business, selling second-hand clothes along with vintage records from a stall in Chelsea's Antiquarius Market up until 1973, with suggestions in historical accounts of punk such as Letts (2007: 50) that he printed his own T-shirts and overprinted buttoned shirts with slogans derived from situationist and countercultural themes. The accuracy of this claim is disputed, but what is agreed is that Rhodes purchased a high-end screen-printer in 1974 and undertook printing for McLaren (and Westwood) to produce the landmark clothing emerging from McLaren's Kings Road shop as the prototype punk identity took root. This coincided with McLaren rebranding the shop as 'Sex' in spring 1974. Cultural historian Paul Gorman has devoted endless hours unpicking this pre-punk countercultural fashion miasma, with much of it surfacing in his meticulous biography of McLaren, which is where the Rhodes screen–printer connection is stated (Gorman 2020: 218). In addition, Gorman records that Rhodes is credited with joint responsibility for the classic 1974 T-shirt bearing the design *You're Gonna Wake Up One Morning and Know What Side of the Bed You've Been Lying On* (2020: 228).

The King's Road shop under its Sex guise attracted an assortment of new customers. In its previous guises as *Let It Rock* and *Too Fast To Live, Too Young To Die* it had drawn an audience from the regurgitated and degraded rock 'n' roll subcultures that McLaren toyed with; however, it now catered for an additional core of participants in the illicit sex practices milieu. As Gorman (2020: 274) points out, one of the new customers of Sex was future Throbbing Gristle member Peter Christopherson. In a typical McLaren scheme, both sets of clientele clashed, and from this tense mix, aided and abetted by McLaren and Rhodes' inflammatory slogans, graphics, and montages, a punk identity grew. This *demi-monde* of proto-punks milled around to add to the frightening allure of the premises. A select few who had coagulated into a band caught the eye of McLaren and his wider scheming ways of hijacking the subversive potential of pop music. It is a question of opinion whether the band existed and persisted due to the presence of the shop, or whether the band was purposely assembled (or at least upgraded from a proper shambolic ensemble) to promote the shop and the clothing brand. What can be stated without doubt was that the Sex Pistols would not have existed without the shop and the later interests of McLaren.

The Sex Pistols grew from the core of Paul Cook and Steve Jones, and their amateurish band the Strand who were assembled in the early 1970s to perform various mod and rock 'n' roll cover versions. The precise date of this band formation and naming is disputed and persists as various guesses from 1971 onwards amongst internet sources. The name the Strand was taken from the proto-conceptual track by Roxy Music, 'Do the Strand', in which the arch-ironic band urged listeners to partake in a purely imaginary (and never defined) dance in the vein of earlier songs that were premised solely on an ephemeral dance craze ('The Twist', etc.). The song was released both as a standalone single and the opening track to the second Roxy Music album *For Your Pleasure* in 1973, making this the most feasible date for the formation and naming of Cook and Jones's band.[5] It was also performed and broadcast on the television show *The Old Grey Whistle Test*, giving it relatively substantial exposure in the art-rock strand of 1970s glam that had clawed back a degree of subcultural cachet following the overgrounding of glam in its populist manifestation. Cook and Jones were regulars on the King's Road boutiques circuit, and in 1974 McLaren – ensconced in his own shop – elected to help the band with their relatively unstructured and unambitious efforts. McLaren had a vision of managing a rock band and working them into a wider situationist strategy of cultural antagonism, but the Sex Pistols were not at that stage yet. The Strand adopted an on–off name change to the Swankers, quickly followed by the recruitment of Glen Matlock to give them a fixed point of musical stability to allow the more chaotic elements to shimmer on the surface as powerful illusions.[6] The idea of a rock band that went beyond the rules of music and the bounds of acceptability had always appealed to McLaren, and, as Gorman (2020: 230) informs us, the name 'Kutie Jones and his own Sex Pistols' is mooted as early as 1974 with its inclusion on the 'righteous' lying on the bedside of the aforementioned Rhodes and McLaren T-shirt. McLaren then went to America in late 1974 in an unsuccessful attempt to fulfil his ambitions through the management of the New York Dolls, leaving Rhodes to keep an eye on the band. McLaren's return in May 1975, following the collapse of New York Dolls, saw him reinvest his energies in this disparate and nebulous bunch of musicians and petty criminals who were part of the 430 King's Road shop scene. Now in a management role, McLaren commenced the search for a frontman who encapsulated the requisite look and attitude, such that Johnny Rotten (after the auditioning of other candidates) was spotted, auditioned, and selected and the project/product took shape. Subsequently, the Strand became the Sex Pistols, adumbrated by McLaren's situationist prophecy, with Rotten completing what Savage (1991: 80) evocatively called a 'gallimaufry of deviants and delinquents'.

WOUNDED BOYS

In late summer 1975, responding to a vacancy advertisement placed in *Melody Maker* on 13 September 1975, the Sex Pistols moved into premises at 6 Denmark Street in London's Soho, taking over a semi-derelict practice space that had been utilized as a studio by the rock band Badfinger. The studio shared an entrance with other businesses including the design company Hipgnosis. The company and their serendipitous proximity to the Sex Pistols is often noted due to the stark contrast between the overblown high art sleeves that were produced for clients such as Pink Floyd and the immediate and seemingly undesigned nature of the Sex Pistols initial incendiary products, particularly their eventual album *Never Mind the Bollocks*.[7] A link between the Sex Pistols and Throbbing Gristle is established through Peter 'Sleazy' Christopherson, a key part of Hipgnosis. Christopherson, born in Leeds, had spent time in America only to return to the United Kingdom in 1974 and take up work with Hipgnosis where his photographic skills and creative imagination were utilized.[8] As already noted, Christopherson was a customer at Sex, and Gorman (2020: 274) records that he pointed the Sex Pistols (in their brief pre-Rotten guise) towards the rehearsal space Crunchy Frog in summer 1975. Christopherson encountered P-Orridge and Tutti whilst watching a COUM performance in March 1974 at Oval House, Kennington, and was immediately drawn to their provocative actions through his own interest in fetish cultures, dark proclivities, and the outer limits of sexual activities. He commenced working with COUM, initially documenting then later adding an input of art techniques, equipment, and an experience of unorthodox sexual exploration, and finally joining in COUM performances in March 1975. Christopherson proved to be a principal part in the gestation of Throbbing Gristle in terms of setting out an agenda and scoping of tools and technologies; however as the band coalesced, he initially took a back seat and worked predominantly for Hipgnosis, becoming a full partner with the design firm in 1978. He called upon P-Orridge and Tutti to model for a typically provocative and surreal album cover for the rock band UFO, released in July 1975. The pair, sporting identical ponytail haircuts which make

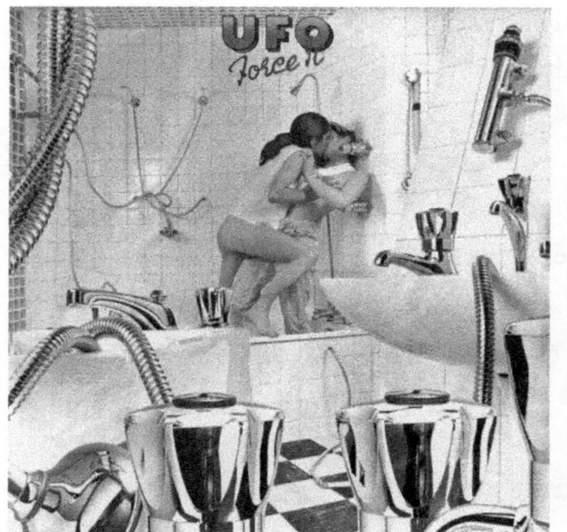

Figure 2.2: UK and US cover artwork for the album Force It *by rock band UFO.*

them discretely indiscernible and interchangeable are simulating rough sex in a bathtub under a shower (see Figure 2.2). Christopherson's warped sense of imagination is to the fore, with the pristine, white-tiled scene overwhelmed by an army of seemingly observing chrome taps and shower tubes. A *Carry On* style bathetic twist is added with the album title of *Force It,* an obvious wordplay on the plumbing phrase faucet. It would be Christopherson's presence at Hipgnosis, with the proximity of the shared entrance of 6 Denmark Street, that continued to draw Christopherson and the Sex Pistols together, putting Throbbing Gristle into a shared transient space with the Sex Pistols.

Firstly, Christopherson was extremely interested in the Sex Pistols as possible models for his ongoing photography project in which he represented prominently odd but alluring-looking boys and young males as an ambiguous and disconcerting mix of vulnerable and dangerous. His work had a visual parallel with the haunting covers from the probation workers' journal *Community Home Schools Gazette,* with lost and listless children striking thousand-yard stare poses whilst out on enforced activities such as hiking and car mechanics workshops. Like many other visual designers and artists, he was drawn to the sheer presence and raw beauty of the Sex Pistols, to their ability to draw from, mix up, and destabilize a structuring of subcultural standards. He approached McLaren to get permission to make the photographs, but the ever-sharp McLaren asked in return that any photographs could be used as potential publicity for the band. In October 1975, Christopherson created a series of images that mimicked the wounded and institutionalized boys favoured by American photographer Larry Clark, a style continued later in the iconic British film *Scum* (1979) directed by Alan Clarke.[9] Ford (1999: 5·13) goes on to state that the photographic shoot by Christopherson is located in and around a local YMCA toilet block mocked up as a tired and neglected borstal festering away from public view where *anything goes*, but the backdrops to the images also suggest one of the semi-derelict yards on and around the premises of Denmark Street.

The photographs are stunning works of fiction but proved inadequate for the purposes envisaged by McLaren. Commencing with a P-Orridge interview for *VOX* fanzine in July 1980 and continuing to his recent autobiography where they are stated as being 'too outrageous, too heavy' (P-Orridge 2021: 170), the story has passed into history such that the images were too much – too twisted – for McLaren's taste and sensibilities. However, this seems questionable bearing in mind that McLaren was already mining erotic boy magazines and the crevices of the sado-masochism scene for his own visual armoury used within the production and marketing of the clothing lines. The photographs were instead exhibited as part of *Prostitution*, and surfaced in the music newspaper *Sounds* at the end of 1979, in their 12 December edition. They were accompanied by a short paragraph that described how they never fitted into McLaren's vision for the group, which more than likely encouraged P-Orridge's version of events, indicative of an after-the-fact pissing contest between two figures wanting to appear more risqué than the other.[10] Unsurprisingly, McLaren's version of events recounted in Gorman (2020: 300) is a somewhat different feeling that the images were too bleached in final production and lacking in the both desired impact and a sense of fashion marketability.

The visual, cultural, and indeed mythical charge of the photographs persists into the current climate, with queer theorist Tavia Nyong'o (2008: 111) taking them as an integral 'archival switch point between the queer and punk seventies'. A further interesting conjecture is made by John Lydon (2013: 22), who claims that Christopherson's straitjacket photographs of himself (then using the name Rotten) were the inspiration for the legendary bondage jacket designed by Westwood and McLaren. This garment, originally produced in black sateen but later remembered for its tartan versions, marked the pivot point where Sex became Seditionaries and punk clothing, or uniform, was born proper. Bearing in mind Lydon's unreliability on historical matters, it is an intriguing theory, and the timeline certainly fits with the bondage jacket making an inaugural appearance for the Sex Pistols brief but highly publicized foray into Paris in September 1976. Published testimony around Westwood and McLaren is contradictory and increasingly fractious, though the inspiration and design lineage for this jacket (and accompanying bondage trousers) is never fully explicated. As Mendes (1999: 99) shows, the base of the garment is built upon a hybrid between a classic Belstaff outdoor jacket and military field jacket, though it is likely that the horizontal strata of restraint straps were nurtured through their experimentation with fetish clothing.

Hipgnosis co-founder Aubery Powell (2014: 92) acknowledges Christopherson's dark and disturbed genius, whilst at the same time admitting that in cases where Christopherson was given free rein to define a project from the start, the client would normally retreat in shock and horror. Troubling images of troubled boys, aestheticized violence, and visceral images of wounds (or wounds-in-the-making) were a key drive of Christopherson's vision, and much of this work would not surface until Christopherson's posthumous book on photography appeared in 2016. One set of disturbing images, recorded in Sedgwick (1982: 37), somehow got through the approval process for the soft-rock-pop band Voyager and a July 1980 album campaign. Christopherson utilized the evocatively dilapidated Denmark Street premises to mock-up a shot of two pre-teen skinhead boys enacting a blood ritual accompanied by a young girl in a bathtub with her wrists slit – the album bore the title *Act of Love*. However, there is a magic about the Sex Pistols images that is difficult to pin down, no doubt elevated by the multitude of versions of what the band, and particularly Rotten, became in the accelerated time frame of 1976–77. Christopherson rendered them something else entirely, something impossible and cognitively disruptive, a hauntological possibility of a radically different future that never came to be.

In the end, McLaren investigated other options to capture the visual prowess of his band as a patient zero of punk, assigning Mick Rock to commission a set of prints in December 1975 as the band performed at Chelsea Arts College. These were the prints used in Neil Spencer's February 1976 *NME* article announcing the band to the wider world. McLaren then called on photographer Ray Stevenson to conduct an outdoor shoot away from the rock 'n' roll standard of performing live, undertaken on a warm spring day in 1976. These photographs, an extensive set as the band careened and cavorted through London, are now also a classic set of images in their own right, but markedly more predictable than Christopherson's efforts. The band were captured goofing and gurning in stereotypical pop-cultural London tourist locations such as Carnaby Street and seen squeezing into an iconic British phone-box like schoolchildren on their awayday to the capital (these images were used by the *Daily Mirror* following the media explosion of the Bill Grundy incident in December 1976).[11]

Secondly, Throbbing Gristle and the Sex Pistols were linked simply through this Denmark Street proximity, which meant an inevitable awareness of each other. John Scanlan, in his socially contextualized history of the Sex Pistols, describes the moment when early punk fashion fan and emerging designer Ben Kelly was summoned to provide an impromptu makeover of the Sex Pistols QT Rooms studio from their decrepit and rapidly degrading state. Kelly encountered a piece of graffiti on entering the building simply declaring Throbbing Gristle (Scanlan 2016: 103).[12] The date would be early autumn 1975, the time when Throbbing Gristle as a dedicated band and plan had just been formulated, so obviously Christopherson was feeling enthused enough to spread the message (unless one of the other band members had dropped in on Christopherson whilst at work and added the tag on the corridor wall and doorbell). In his autobiography P-Orridge is predictably blasé about this proximity between the two bands, adding to the gradual accrual of ambivalence and one-upmanship he puts between himself and the Sex Pistols. He recalls: 'We'd see them quite often, going in and out. They would be doing their methedrine alcoholism with rhythm-and-blues garage rock, and we'd be upstairs, plotting the destruction of all rock and roll' (P-Orridge 2021: 170).

FACTORY SETTING

Autumn/winter 1975 was a pivotal moment beyond just a serendipitous encounter with graffiti and a contested set of photographs turned down by the arch-provocateur McLaren. Punk was about to commence in earnest with the Sex Pistols ready to perform live in what would be their first gig at St. Martins School of Art in November. Both the Sex Pistols and Throbbing Gristle had crossed paths as concepts, but we hear nothing more of it. Throughout this period, Throbbing Gristle remained in their own self-imposed background, working on their sound as the key member Chris Carter joined the operation to complete the quartet. As Ford (1999: 5·14–15) recounts, Carter had a background that dovetailed with many of the interests of P-Orridge, Tutti, and Christopherson. The key new asset that Carter brought to the party was his background in experimental electronics, having attempted to set out as a performer combining his homemade synthesizers and keyboards with his lighting rigs. The essential link between Carter and the other three was Carter's friendship and working relationship with John Lacey, the son of experimental artist and Martello Street custodian Bruce Lacey. John had joined COUM shortly after it settled in London, bringing in his electronics expertise, and Carter followed, effecting a kind of changeover of personnel with John but keeping intact the electronics specialism. By autumn 1975, with the establishment of Throbbing Gristle, the new quartet were still splitting time to work on their various projects and day jobs: P-Orridge was working full time on the St. James Press art book, Tutti was holding down many art projects and stripping and modelling assignments, Carter was working as a sound technician, and Christopherson was ploughing his energies into Hipgnosis. This ad hoc, almost hobbyist, approach continued through 1976, with the band locked into their Martello Street studio building their own instruments and sound, although Tutti (2017: 191) recalls Christopherson as being missing in action for months on end during summer 1976.

Throbbing Gristle's celebrated announcement to the world as part of their ICA *Prostitution* event was in fact the band's third performance. In July 1976, ten months into the band's formal existence, P-Orridge had been asked to curate a day of performance art at the AIR Gallery on Shaftesbury Avenue, and 'COUM with Throbbing Gristle' were included on the bill under a headline theme of 'Crime Affirms Existence', a title that drew from the article assembled by P-Orridge and Christopherson for the prestigious art journal *Studio International* (July/August 1976). For this debut live performance, Throbbing Gristle played from within an enclosed space, introducing the themes of the society as a death factory and the impending date of 1984. The specific nature of this performance in terms of challenging the spatial and proximal arrangements of serving up live music is developed in Chapter 4 when the band brought back this tactic for a larger gig at the Architectural Association two years later. The sound is dystopian and architectural, very much a soundtrack for a barely inhabited cityscape after some kind of catastrophic event. According to Tutti (2017: 190), the band (minus Christopherson who was occupied with Hipgnosis work) switched around instruments and used prepared industrial loops predominantly of performed sound rather than concrete samples and narrated segments. At this point in time, Throbbing Gristle were effectively a function of COUM that provided sound art, and this first performance was anticipated, presented, and consumed as an art event.

On 21 August 1976, Throbbing Gristle undertook their second live performance as part of the Winchester Hat Fair – a predominantly outdoor festival of performing arts established in 1974. Tutti's brief report from the event links the performance to an indoor space (the Attic Theatre in St John's Rooms), though a mixed-age audience was present in line with the family appeal of the wider festival. Myths circulate that P-Orridge attempted to book the band under the name of Punk Floyd, conjuring up an unstable dyad deliberately heretical to punk's anti-prog overtures. With Christopherson now in attendance overseeing the flow and mix, the quartet developed the first makings of a set and song titles. In contrast to the AIR event, this was a performed piece of music by musicians rather than a piece of art to be ambiently engaged. Furthermore, we see song structures that fall in with punk's celebrated non-musicality and angry disorder, though critique bubbles under the surface. 'Dead Ed/Head' gets its first airing with an instantly decomposing bass guitar solo, and a vocal utterance of 'dead ed' reduced to a barely enunciated 'de de'. This vocalization of a non-note anticipates the famous track 'Boredom' by Buzzcocks, released in January 1977 and celebrated as punk's do-it-yourself benchmark in terms of the materialization of an actual record. Sardonic Buzzcocks frontman Howard Devoto vocalizes the repeating pair of discordant notes that form the structure of the work, at the same time cleverly segueing from 'boredom' to 'b-dum'. Worley (2017: 111) declares the refrain as an 'anti-solo' and parody of virtuosity, as it is used 66 times in the song, but it stems from more astute composition skills, something Buzzcocks as a band excelled at whilst appearing to pull off an amateur and disinterested demeanour.

Throbbing Gristle would have much more to say about punk's relationship to boredom in later years, but P-Orridge's 'de de' takes the punk threat of reducing knowledge of chords to the lowest point. In contrast, a new musicality of a sort emerges with the next track 'No Two Ways', as the one-note bass pluck is thrashed and fed through feedback loops, raising to a crescendo with a wall of noise and rising and falling pulse effects. Away from the obvious glib content of their narrative tracks, this is Throbbing Gristle finding their originary signature sound and supreme embodiment of tension, an incredible sweet noise that steps confidently outside of both punk and experimental electronic music. In one fell swoop the band pour carcinogenic weed killer on what music historian Rob Young (2011: 349) calls the 'phytosonic' blooming of British folk and prog traditions. The track ascends and then descends into the 'Whorle of Sound' closing out with sound grabs (a ringside commentary of a boxing match concluding) and indiscernible spoken sections from P-Orridge. These tracks fed into the performance at the ICA, particularly 'We Hate You' which was improvised on the spot as P-Orridge playfully addressed the front row of small children in the Attic Theatre whilst sporting fake wounds oozing with blood. The parts were now in place for the next stage of Throbbing Gristle, their formal appearance at the ICA. However, the three months between this gig at Winchester and the ICA event saw a significant shift in the punk scene that ran parallel to Throbbing Gristle.

PUNK YEAR ZERO

Outside of the Death Factory, on the intersecting subcultural planes of fashion and music, things were changing rapidly. The key actors in the spread of punk were the managers of the bands associated with the scene (initially McLaren, with Rhodes momentarily fading into the background), the bands themselves (starting with the Sex Pistols), the fans who followed the bands and bought the clothes from the clothing companies owned by the managers of the bands, and eventually (but significantly) the music press. In addition, the emergence of the fanzine scene, brought into punk through Mark Perry's seminal *Sniffin' Glue* in July 1976, was also a key moment in punk's assertion of an identity and autonomy. This do-it-yourself attitude amongst punk would eventually mushroom to give the subculture an excessive strength through a proliferation of new bands and independent labels – however, punk's initial moves were dictated more by key strategists.

An incident that encapsulated this strategic synergy, and also highlighted the important role of the ICA as a platform, is the inclusion of McLaren and Westwood at the ICA fashion forum event in February 1976, with the appropriately dressed Sex Pistols (and other punks) prominent in the audience. Initially, fans were from an arty crowd as the Sex Pistols played at numerous art colleges, though punk also provided an umbrella for bands (and fans) from the rougher pub-rock scene that had flourished in a relatively low-key capacity as a reaction to the overblown gestures of prog and comedic leanings of commercialized glam.[13] The Sex Pistols quickly graduated from the art college circuit to play larger rock venues such as the Marquee and the 100 Club, where they held a brief residency. By May 1976, they were gigging around the United Kingdom, playing small venues in Yorkshire, the first of two key appearances in Manchester in June, and a visit to Sheffield in July. Often members from pub-rock and more straightforward rock bands sharing the bill would jump the gap to become punk, moved by the performative energy and visual prowess of the Sex Pistols and Rotten as a talismanic frontman. Artists such as Joe Strummer (the Clash) and Adam Ant were transformed at first sight after having the Sex Pistols support their previous incarnations. The growth of the scene and the emergence of new bands allowed managers to move into key positions. McLaren had his band, but Rhodes quickly countered with his management of the Clash which he assembled around May 1976. He encouraged a requisite image using Clash bassist Paul Simonon's idea for spray-painting shirts, adding Jackson Pollock drip patterns and applying the situationist slogans that Rhodes had utilized in his earlier days; the intent to instil the band with a message-driven missionary zeal as their punk selling point. The clothes were extolled as being homemade, partly as a street-level revolutionary gesture, but possibly as making a point of NOT wearing (and thus not marketing) items of clothing from McLaren and Westwood's production line.

A key impetus to the scene was provided with two comprehensive features on punk in the music papers following the Neil Spencer *NME* article in February which was connected to a live review of the Sex Pistols. In April 1976, the first major article appeared, written by Jonh Ingham for *Sounds*, focusing on the subcultural difference of punk. Seven months later, in November, *Melody Maker* journalist Caroline Coon set out a more studious article looking at the sociological dimension of punk, with a front cover dedicated to Rotten christened as 'punk king'.[14] The temporal gap between these articles had witnessed a phenomenal growth of punk – including the arrival of the fanzine *Sniffin' Glue* – as the 18 October date for COUM/Throbbing Gristle at the ICA *Prostitution* show approached. A two-day punk festival was held at the 100 Club in September, the Sex Pistols then signed to EMI Records on 8 October, and on 15 October – just three days before the ICA event – Judy Wade's feature on punk in *The Sun* newspaper (featuring the seemingly ever-present duo of Siouxsie and Steve Severin modelling quasi S&M clothing) brought the potentially shocking subculture to the attention of the nation. Undoubtedly, there was a punk zeitgeist, in terms of grabbing headlines to make a shock, acquiring fans, and securing potentially life-changing record contracts.

In assessing the strategic relationship between *Prostitution* and punk, there is another punk character that is important and sometimes overlooked in the history of Throbbing Gristle. Promoter John Krivine was attached to the *Prostitution* event by the involvement of his band Chelsea, but there are deeper connections. Krivine was linked through a friendship and involvement with P-Orridge and Tutti going back to his time with them in Hull in the early 1970s. Ford (1999: 1·10) introduces Krivine at the point he met P-Orridge and the COUM crowd in Hull, and Tutti (2017: 51) expands on this relationship further. For whatever reason, Krivine is constantly picked out for his wealthy status in P-Orridge (2021), described variously as having 'privileged roots' (125), being 'secretly wealthy' (186) and eventually as a 'multimillionaire' (189). During his time in London, Krivine had taken on a role similar to McLaren and Rhodes by initially working around the fringes of subcultures as a jukebox dealer. He moved on to running a clothes business and making his own designs under the ACME Attractions label, a style which highlighted an important bridge between the errant and experimental aspects of the soul subculture and an alternative early punk look (plastic 'jelly' sandals, mohair sweaters, peg trousers). ACME then evolved to the London shop BOY in early 1977, through his partnership with Stephane Raynor. Krivine, McLaren, and Rhodes formed a committee of shifting forces and powers, developing and flogging punk clothes, acquiring a 'house' band to model the clothes, and securing lucrative record contracts, effectively monetizing the punk subculture whilst encouraging it. Tutti (2017: 197) recalls that Krivine asked to manage Throbbing Gristle shortly before the ICA appearance, and the links between the band and the punk entrepreneur would continue and develop beyond the event.

Scratch beneath the surface and you see the punk-business alliances at work as the driving force: the inclusion of Chelsea at *Prostitution* indicated Throbbing Gristle's friendship with Krivine and the chance to add a bit of obvious punk appeal to the evening, yet it is suggested that the change of name to LSD was to circumvent Clash fans attending who were seen as a rival band (a fault line between Krivine and Rhodes). In fact, as Savage (1991: 240) recounts, the Clash played at the ICA just five days later and concocted their own mini-controversy headline with an audience member biting part of the ear off another fan. Christopherson and his colleague John Harwood were also underway designing interior displays and clothing iconography for Krivine's proposed new premises BOY on King's Road (see next chapter). This partnership opened up a division between Throbbing Gristle and McLaren, adumbrating a future fault line between Westwood and Krivine amidst the proximity of BOY and McLaren's shop Seditionaries on King's Road, and the seemingly casual arrangement that allowed BOY to begin reproducing past Sex and Seditionaries screen prints. Finally, as Krivine sought to assemble the right band with the right look for his clothing label and shop, Chelsea were assembled and Throbbing Gristle were asked to cast their judgements, causing friction and consternation as the budding punks of Chelsea didn't consider Throbbing Gristle as being worthy judges of punk. Chelsea disbanded shortly after the ICA performance due to differences between singer Gene October and the other band members. The latter then formed what was effectively the first pop pin-up boy-band of the punk scene, Generation X, with the Elvis sneer-a-like singer Billy Idol, managed initially by ACME accountant Andrew Czezowski, another punk entrepreneur who opened the Roxy Club in December 1976 (with Generation X being the opening night act). Complex, but all connected through rivalries and forging opportunities.

PROSTITUTION AS A PUNK GIG

In the previous chapter, I used short extracts of this opening (formal) appearance of Throbbing Gristle at *Prostitution* as a way to understand how they constructed a sound and experience; however, a fuller explication is required. This is achieved by revisiting the performance aspects in light of the newly established punk scene and then examining the aftermath in the British press. The flyer for *Prostitution* listed Throbbing Gristle as opening the proceedings and billed to perform 'Music from the Death Factory – 1984 rock', to be followed by 'professional striptease' and the 'rock band' LSD. Each member had a defined set of roles, taking them more towards a rock – or punk – archetype, though these roles were multiple and relatively unorthodox. A Throbbing Gristle archetype of performance was set in motion. P-Orridge contributed vocals and a crudely struck bass guitar, interchanged with screeches from an electric violin; Tutti, nominally seated, provided lead guitar, cornet, and effects; Christopherson added tapes and trumpet; Carter, as well as playing keyboards, had an essential controlling role of the rhythm and mix.

We know that they played a truncated set of around 40 minutes and went in hard with the deliberately enunciated tracks 'Very Friendly' and 'Slug Bait' that would have tested the tolerance of all sectors of the audience due to the theme and delivery. Such a mode of delivery, effectively a spoken narrative, had previously been applied to the punk milieu with the impromptu inaugural performance of Siouxsie and the Banshees, formed by Susan Janet Ballion (Siouxsie Sioux) and Steven John Bailey (Steven Severin) – both in the audience at *Prostitution*. This important pair started to follow the Sex Pistols in early 1976, taking the lead from another key player Simon Barker, who had seen the Sex Pistols in December 1975 at Ravensbourne College and had quickly fixed onto the crossover potential of artiness, posing, provocation, and punk music. Barker, in his part as a member of a wider group of subcultural activists known as the Bromley Contingent, sets up a highly visible early incarnation of punk affiliation, unsurprisingly ascribing to the McLaren and Westwood fashion and image faction. Appearing a month earlier at the 100 Club Punk Festival, Siouxsie and Steve Severin had roped in musicians Marco Pirroni (later to join Adam and the Ants who would make their own debut at the ICA in May 1977) and Sid Vicious (later of the Sex Pistols) to produce a twenty-minute improvisation of 'The Lord's Prayer', creating an instant talking point and facet of punk mythology. Throbbing Gristle upped the stakes here in terms of how a narrative extract can form the basis of a song.

After months in their Death Factory studio, and over these three initial gigs in July, August, and October 1976, the band's sound palette was established. Carefully contrived in terms of both sourcing and effects, they utilized processed vocals speeded up or slowed down and 'everything fed through relays of multiple effects [...] multiplied through overlay treatments' (Reynolds 2005: 228). Carter, with his electronics specialism, was working towards creating the 'gristle-izer' which modulated sound in a harsh capacity, and his expertise and diligence produced gadgets offering an early sampling capability, inserting a *musique-concrete* of media sounds, banal entertainment dialogue and catchphrases, bird noise, traffic, distressing news items, and sinister samples recorded surreptitiously by Christopherson. The latter included snippets of disturbing conversation, heavy breathing, sirens, scheming and death threats left on their answerphone, continuing the recursive tactic of the band in provoking affront and then playing this back as entertainment. Kromhout (2011: 25) frames this sound as a dialogue of noise (the 'most instructive locus') via Friedrich Kittler, with tools and techniques forged in battle and taken up for a new battle and a battle against itself – their information war: 'the noisiness and violence of their music, imagery, texts, and ideology are linked to the roots of the modern concept of noise, and thereby to questions of control, transference, and distortion of information in times of war'. He adds: 'they ventured into the commodified world of popular music using utterly uncompromising music as a weapon, physically and mentally threatening their audience with sounds, lyrics, and images' (26).

This mix and mismatch of noisy and disorienting sources also drew from literary activist William Burroughs, the band employing techniques of cut-up and information war to 'reconfigure communication in ways consistent with breaking free of social control' (Hegarty 2007: 107). This was not simply a musique-concrete that grabbed a pre-existing or pre-recorded sound for the purpose of creating a new sound in the here and now. It was also a practice and tactic that went beyond sampling in a time before sampling became a common practice in subcultural and popular music. Punk or not punk, more punk or anti-punk, these were the tensions that informed the live performance on the night of the ICA in front of the assembled crowd of art patrons, punks, journalists, record executives, and important ICA guests. As a force of sound, a display of musicians, Throbbing Gristle would have confounded all sectors of the audience, the punks included. Whilst P-Orridge wielded a bass guitar and Tutti a lead, any familiarity with a sonic palette of punk was curtailed as the instruments were relayed through Carter's effects devices. As outlined in the previous chapter, there is a misconstrued conception that amateurism is a default position of punk, a level of playing that is kind of reached without trying and then never surpassed, an entry-level so to speak. Sex Pistols musicians such as Cook, Jones, and particularly Matlock were competent and worked hard, being able to then move beyond this competency to present a controlled version of incompetency and amateurism that theatrically threatens to break down (or does break down). As Scanlan (2016: 202) observes regarding the Sex Pistols, amateurism was 'still a perception that could be manipulated to sustain their notoriety', so we must tread carefully here. Throbbing Gristle emphasized and fetishized an apparent incompetence throughout their career, and I will unpack this in later chapters as the band start to develop distinct phases of sound and character; however, the performance at the ICA gave a good impression of incompetence – or at least a thorough mangling – in terms of using the tools (guitars) of punk music. As Ford (1999: 6.30) recounts, if P-Orridge hadn't disoriented the punks through the band's unorthodox approach to music, he apparently upset them even more by spreading a rumour that Billy Idol would be hung by cheese-wire as a finale.

ART SICKNESS MEDIA FRENZY

According to the common origin myth, the performance of Throbbing Gristle at *Prostitution* is often taken to be a neat schism from their COUM incarnation, with the more transitional interpretation lost within the blaze of publicity and notoriety that accompanied the exhibition and its deliberately curated ensemble cast at the opening night. The merging of controversy in terms of a singular event of misbehaving actors and audience (with Throbbing Gristle at the core) and the opening of the exhibition itself, which contained multiple references to pornographic performance and representation, dirt and bodily fluids, and extreme sexual practices, meant that a prominent and instant backlash was created in the press and media. The go-to soundbite that has carried through history is the outrage expressed by Conservative MP Nicholas Fairbairn who declared the organizers to be the 'wreckers of civilisation' – subsequently resisted by the band as a potential album title but seized upon as an instant publicity device and chosen as the perfect title for Ford's eventual book on the band. In effect, *Prostitution* functioned as a COUM retrospective, documenting the actions of a group who carried out a strategy within art described by Sladen and Yedgar (2007: 9) as an 'ironic co-option of accepted modes of cultural production', mischievously tapping into the precarious arts climate throughout 1976. And it is as an art event, and not a rock concert (punk or otherwise), that the immediate climate of controversy was generated. Over time, with *Prostitution* being the formal introduction of the band, this knot of subsequent controversy has drifted towards being about Throbbing Gristle, a band more punk than the punks of the day. This was never the case.

This spike of controversy for the year was prompted by a spontaneously combusting argument around Carl Andre's *Equivalent VIII* (1966) which had been acquired by Tate in 1972 (acquisition number T.1534 which reads remarkably like a Chris Carter composition for Throbbing Gristle). The artwork had been intermittently exhibited peacefully from 1974 but pushed into the public realm when a February 1976 press article questioned its worth in the context of the overused phrase 'taxpayers' money'. The minimalist work consists of 120 firebricks, which – in the spirit of conceptualism – were purchased as new to create an instance of the 1966 original (whose bricks had been returned to the suppliers after Andre could not find a buyer for the work). *Equivalent VIII* was the last in this series, although Andre continued to work on other projects and returned to London's Whitechapel Gallery for a slightly less controversial retrospective in spring 1978. The 1976 furore around the Tate purchase was a microcosm of the larger media panics and moral storms that would play out as the 1970s drew to a close. The work was questioned in an April 1975 article by Bernard Denvir in the *Times Educational Supplement* based upon an annual Tate report of activities and purchases, but this seemingly elicited no wider scorn or outrage. The bones of the article were then reworked by journalist Colin Simpson for a cover feature in the business news section of *The Sunday Times* on 15 February 1976, and this was picked up by numerous other newspapers. The timing of Simpson's reloaded invective was not random, as the artwork had just returned to a period of being on display and so any constructed and conceived wrongdoing by the Tate was now explicated in full sight on the floor of the gallery. Within a couple of days, Andre was featured in the newspapers explaining how the bricks weren't the originals, and the press gleefully reported on a barrage of letters to the Tate from the public offering vacuum cleaners, children's drawings, bits of string and paper clips as donations of art. On 23 February 1976, the outrage-and-headlines spiral amplified, and the artwork was attacked with blue paint by Peter Stowell-Phillips, an apparently disgruntled but publicity-seeking member of the public. Stowell-Phillips was primed to speak to the press, and the press lapped it up, bringing out a thinly disguised repressed criticism of twentieth-century modern art with quips about *Equivalent VIII* entering its 'blue period'.

Whilst this mood of art outrage was part playful and part political rhetoric, taking on a Pythonesque dialogue about modern art strands up to and including conceptualism and minimalism, a more moralistic tone accompanied the criticism of the ICA displaying the first three parts of Mary Kelly's *Post-Partum Document* (1973–77). This challenging and very personal display was exhibited as the immediately preceding exhibition of *Prostitution*, ensuring that Kelly's display of soiled nappies would be followed by COUM's display of used sanitary towels to give a continuity of the visceral exposure of taboo bodily fluids in the art gallery environment. Johnson (2019: 96) suggests this as the opening salvo of a late 1970s culture war, a 'historically and geographically localized moment in lowering national tolerance for mischief, filth or cultural insurgence'.

COUM's contribution to this destabilizing and derailing of art's funding and exhibition structure through the notion of a public purse and taste could be construed as an example of cutting off their noses to spite their faces, an aphorism that would appeal to a band who included self-mutilation as a key signature of their art. Indeed, Johnson (2019: 95) records how COUM's actions contribute towards 'delimiting the scope of the performance of extremity with grave effects'. However, the igniting of multiple controversies was on offer with the parallel moment of punk that Throbbing Gristle also willingly exploited on the opening night of *Prostitution*. As recalled at the start of this chapter, *Prostitution* was carefully staged to encourage a punk crowd (by the inclusion of punk band Chelsea) and the strategic invitation of key music journalists who were attuned to the nascent punk scene and looking to steal a march on journalists working for rival music papers. *Prostitution* was a cleverly conceived concoction of potential flashpoints, with a guilt-by-association mechanism primed to be set in play. Fairbairn's comment of the 'wreckers of civilisation' was directed at COUM and their stirrings in the art world, though it is also possible to see it as being directed at the audience of punks who played up to the occasion of being in an art gallery (and were no doubt encouraged by the inclusion of a stripper on the bill).

Ford (1999: 6.25) assesses and proposes a four-point rationale for the motivations and reasons for the success of the moral panic that *Prostitution* provokes amongst the wider British public: firstly, the issue of money being wasted on an alien concept like art; second, the identification of COUM as an easy target since there was unlikely to be a large grouping of other artists coming out in their support; third, the potentially quirky and salacious dimensions of the story; and finally, the Arts Council and arts administration in general can be set up as a metonym of the Labour left and so allow the newspapers to use the coverage of the event as an attack on the current Labour government. A further metonym emerged in the structuring of the internal subject matter of the story, with pornography seen as a measure of the sickness of the nation. Walker (1999: 89) also sees this complex layering of pornographic seepages as key to the outrage, arguing that the proximity of the Mall (home of the ICA) and Soho (the base of London's sex trade) allowed COUM to bring across infectious material and so create 'dirt' in the context of the term used by Mary Douglas as 'matter out of place'. This contradictory proximity of spaces for incompatible imagery and practices is neatly summed up by Berry (2018: 259) in her loping study of art and bare life:

> A reassertion of proper identity through the regulation of sexual propriety is the resultant demand. Of course this did not and would not imply the abolition of actual prostitution but rather its continued obscurity, far from the salubrious auspices of public culture and the Queen's driveway.

It is not my intention to challenge or expand Ford's incisive understanding of the dynamics of this panic; he is incredibly perceptive in this regard and draws directly from a selection of newspapers reporting the event, but it is useful at this point to pause and reconsider the press furore of *Prostitution*.[15] The presentation of it in history has been deliberately skewed to good effect, part of the mischievous myth-making that the band members were adept at orchestrating. This reflection will serve several purposes: to assess the aetiology of the story with a little more detail and to try and evoke a more considered picture of the possible extent of its impact, to assess a parallel strategy of the myth which serves to historically present the story as having a constant and maximal impact, and to examine some concurrent news and cultural events within their mode of presentation in the press. To achieve this, it is necessary to return to the original newspapers rather than examine the edited collection of press clippings that were assembled by Throbbing Gristle and the ICA as a kind of hybrid documentation and (counter) publicity device.

The Fairbairn article from the following day's *Daily Mail* forms the bulwark of the recorded scandal, and this is reproduced as the main item when the controversial extent of *Prostitution* is discussed, with Ford understandably taking this as the starting point of his own critical reflection of the events following that opening evening. The article is striking and terrorizing in its layout, with Fairbairn pictured hands on hips glaring down from a small box image immediately above the first column of text, separated by a solid column of text from a large portrait photograph of Severin, Siouxsie, and Debbie Juvenile

'These people are the wreckers of civilisation'

Adults only art show angers an MP

Nicholas Fairbairn ... outraged.

By THOMSON PRENTICE

TORY MP Nicholas Fairbairn fought his way through Hell's Angels and young men with multi-coloured hair, lipstick and nail varnish last night — all in the caus of art.

But what he saw turned him blue with anger.

For the show was called 'Prostitution.' Among the 'art' was a cage of chains and images of sadism and masochism.

And the MP's critical appraisal was: 'It's a sickening outrage. Sadistic. Obscene. Evil.'

His conclusion: 'The Arts Council must be scrapped after this.'

The adults-only show is being staged for a week at the Institute of Contemporary Arts, which receives a grant of £90,000 from the council.

It is the work of ex-student Neil Megson, 26, who has changed his name by deed poll to Genesis P. Orridge. He has appeared in court on an obscenity charge.

Mr Fairbairn, QC and MP for Kinross and West Perthshire said he would demand an explanation in the Commons from Arts Minister Harold Lever.

'Public money is being wasted here to destroy the morality of our society. These people are the wreckers of civilisation. They want to advance decadence.

'I came here to look, and I am horrified,' said the MP.

Mr Orridge, wearing silver nail varnish and with his shoulder-length black hair held in place by a turquoise plastic hair slide, said: 'We are presenting information. Without people, information is dead. People give it life.

'We are out for a little fun, but I accept that some people may think we are mad,' he added.

Mr Ted Little, artistic director of the ICA, explained that he did not exercise artistic judgment. 'I see my job as giving artists exposure.

'The arts in this country are still dominated by middle-class attitudes. This has got to be broken down.'

Arts Council representatives were at the opening and Mr Little, asked what they had thought of it, smiled and said: 'They left early.'

Judges' decision soon

AN important legal decision affecting the sale of pornography in Britain will follow an appeal this week by two newsagents convicted of selling hard-core porn magazines. The judges' decision will cover the question: Can an expert say in evidence that porn can do some people good?

Visitors ... what today's connoisseur is wearing.

Figure 2.3: Daily Mail *coverage of the* Prostitution *opening event, Tuesday 19 October 1976.*

(Debbie Wilson). The three punks are pictured in an approximated contrapposto manner to allow the full of extent of their provocative clothing to be shown, and their heads craned towards the left, with a caption that reads: 'Visitors ... what today's connoisseur is wearing'. The photographs are not likely to be two crops from a single image, and we do not know what either Fairbairn or the punks are staring at, but the layout suggests that they are staring at each other in a kind of stand-off of disdain and disgust that flows both ways (see Figure 2.3). Clearly, it is a powerful image of a very real event, even if we are prompted to imbibe a narrative flashpoint that may or may not have occurred. COUM's strategy was to incorporate these press images and reports into the show in an organic

THROBBING GRISTLE AT I.C.A. OCT 76 SELECTED PRESS CUTTINGS © 1976 T.G.

'These people are the wreckers of civilisation'

TORY MP Nicholas Fairbairn fought his way through Hell's Angels and young men with multi-coloured hair, lipstick and nail varnish last night — AND SAW

sex-show

A STRIPPER, accompanied by a rock group called "Throbbing Gristle," far, far worse than anything I have ever seen. I was appalled.

"They must be very sick people indeed."

A WEIRD porn-and-pop show,

Its filth is exceeded only by its banality.

their pornography can only destroy the values of our society.

Nicholas Fairbairn . . . outraged.

And the MP's critical appraisal was: 'It's a sickening outrage. Sadistic. Obscene. Evil.' money is being wasted here to destroy the morality of our society. These people are the wreckers of civilisation. They want to advance decadence.

'I came here to look, and I am horrified,' said the MP.

THROBBING GRISTLE ARE attempting "to destroy the difference between good and bad, and right and wrong

"I'm sickened

"This show is an excuse for exhibitionism by every crank, queer, squint and ass in the business."

Mr Fairbairn said he saw:

SADISM with sticks and nails.

WEIRD music from what exhibition organisers called the Death Factory, by a rock group called "Throbbing Gristle," allowing people to promote every swill-bin attitude they can to degrade language, meaning and thought"

CEASE TO EXIST

Stripper

The show includes a stripper accompanied by masochistic performances by a rock group called Throbbing Gristle; They are devoid of any sense of proportion and respect for the decencies of life.

MASOCHISTIC performances by a rock group may be a scabrous symbol of one facet of Britain today; but not yet, thank heavens, of the whole. And the underlying impulse is not one of survival but of destruction and the death-wish–

GENETIC FEAR

BLURRED IMAGE

Visitors . . . what today's connoisseur is wearing.

SECONDARY ORGASMIC DISFUNCTION

controversial pop-and-porn show

A rock group called Death Rock [T.G.] will be taking part at the opening. They will be singing songs about mass murder and about the child murderer Ian Brady. "They offer reflections on the way TV programmes and the other media work."

"spooks with soft-belt intellectual arrogance . . . anxious to promote every swill-bin attitude they can to degrade language, meaning and thought."

"The organisers must be very sick people. I wish I'd never got involved." It was an excuse for exhibitionism by every crank, queer, squint and ass in the business."

'We're only just getting a look at the maggots in the nest. By the time the current controversy dies down their scrapbook will be fat enough to ensure gigs a plenty here and abroad for them, their rock band Throbbing Gristle and any professional striptease artiste they care to take along with them

—PARANOIA CLUB—

'We are presenting information. Without people, information is dead. People give it life.

But for me, it was like a scene out of a real-life horror show last night.

As I walked in, a drunken young woman was being carried out. She had green hair.

At the bar, a girl in trousers and bright orange hair was embracing a blonde in a gold lame dress

Next to them was a 6ft. 5in. tall West Indian transvestite in a red off-the-shoulder gown

There was also a very noisy rock group called Throbbing Gristle, dressed in more black lurex

My main concern is that it has become the phenomenon of the age in music for non-creative people to make up for their inability and lack of imagination by being obscene, vulgar and depraved." Such filthy rubbish has always been available in holes and corners for those willing to pay for it; and there have always been people ready to make a living by purveying it

A red-and-white crewcut nearby wiggled its black lurex trousers and shouted "God there are so many straights around"

Scotland Yard said today "A report is being sent to the Director of Public Prosecutions"

"This all sounds rather men among but these are always the [illegible]

Figure 2.4: *Throbbing Gristle curated press cutting reworking* Daily Mail *article.*

and dynamic context, effectively self-seeding their own feedback spiral. In documenting *Prostitution*, Wilson (2015) identifies how such was 'folded back into the exhibition' (96–97) to activate a 'slowed down feedback loop' that eventually created a 'distorted, specular mise en abyme' (106). With the *Daily Mail* article, the key piece of (anti) publicity, the band went beyond an archival functionality and reused the page in a post hoc brochure for the show. However, they tweaked and remixed the page by keeping its essential flow and structure and inserting a mix of quotes and headlines culled from similar stories in other newspapers. They then overlaid capitalized words from the fledgling Throbbing Gristle lexicon such as 'genetic fear', 'cease to exist', 'blurred self-image', 'secondary orgasmic disfunction', and 'paranoia club'. The resultant extended assemblage cleverly resembles a 'real' newspaper page, whilst morphing towards the flyer form that the band would utilize for future performances (see Figure 2.4). It is this tactically doctored image that now permeates in contemporary discussion and depiction.[16]

The prominence and singular use of this page were most likely due to this article being the only newspaper story that expressed the outrage through an on-the-spot narrative with accompanying pictures. In newspaper terms, this was the exclusive or scoop, and other newspapers would feel they were re-heating yesterday's news if they tried to run the story with similar vehemence over the following days. The story did have some reverberation, and other newspapers were obliged to plot a course through the fall-out, allowing the band to gather more headlines and snippets to mix into the original article. Stepping back to the moment of the newspaper we can ask further questions; first, we are not given, in historical accounts, an indication of the prevalence of the newspaper and assume that page 17 of the *Daily Mail* for Tuesday 19 October 1976 was dropping into everybody's letterbox or being stocked at every newsagent or newsstand throughout the United Kingdom. This was not the case, as the *Prostitution* story was only run in the evening edition of the London edition, meaning that the Fairbairn story would not have travelled outside of London.[17] For other regional variations, page 17 offered a full-page feature with an accompanying photograph of the Imperial War Museum painstakingly creating a detailed and graphic diorama of the First World War Battle of the Somme. Whilst this might have been a distant seed corn for the art-horror of the Chapman Brothers and their diorama-medium works *Hell* and *Fucking Hell*, it was not the reportage of outrage from *Prostitution*.

Second, we see little of the wider context of the newspapers that carried the main story and its trail of fall-out. It comes as little surprise that the *Daily Mail* adopts a right-wing approach to the stories it covers and the way it covers them. The headline on the day of the Fairbairn/*Prostitution* story distils anti-union sentiment around the strike at car manufacturer Range Rover, a focus and line of approach that is carried over from the previous day and was part of a wider bugbear of opposition to the Labour government and a key player in the gradual machinations that brought about the Winter of Discontent two years later. Similar themes and headlines simmer across all the newspapers with reports on strikes, crime increase (with fearmongering racist overtures), and falling education standards nestling amongst a scare story of a Colorado beetle attack, adverts for Trafalgar digital watches and Ritz crackers, and entertainment pages discussing the *New Avengers*, Demis Roussos, a *Daily Mirror* serialization of a week in the life of David Essex, and the film *Future World* (a poor follow-up to successful sci-fi-horror film *West World*). Whilst a large part of the outrage of *Prostitution* was rooted in the merging of the proximal worlds of high art (ICA) and commodified eroticism and sex (Soho), and related to various manifestations of female nudity (Cosey's own hardcore pornography, the slightly less confrontational inclusion of strippers, and the relative state of exhibitionism of audience members such as Siouxsie), the unchallenged currency of topless women held strong in the newspaper industry.[18] This can possibly be read as a valorization of Throbbing Gristle's approach to working at the extremes such that the unabridged questioning of extremes allows us to think backwards to what we accept as existing without question. Thus, during the week of the *Prostitution* scandal, we have *The Sun* running a fashion spread and a weather feature using topless women in see-through plastic macs and several newspapers reporting from the Earls Court Motor Show where topless women were modelling for the launch of the new Aston Martin Lagonda luxury car. Headlines here refer to the 'classy chassy' of model Vicki Scott, a *Daily Mirror* punchline of 'clunk, click, every strip', and most disturbing of all, the *Daily Express* running the feature on the same page as the children's serialized cartoon 'Rupert and the Worried Elves'.

As well as the *Daily Mail* running the primary coverage of Fairbairn's outburst, he also gets some of his quotes into the *Daily Telegraph* (Robertson 1976), making it onto page 2 of the newspaper and thus occupying a more prominent position. The article includes a photograph of P-Orridge, Tutti, and Christopherson posing for the camera with punk sneers and stares behind dark glasses. Rather than making reference to them as being members of the band, the photograph captions them as the organizers of the exhibition and uses the 'TG' alias of Teresa Green and Terry Goldstein for Tutti and Christopherson. In the article, Fairbairn is given the green light to vent his spleen against the links between avant-garde art and extremist or extrovert members of society, as well as his hatred of prostitutes (which would see his own downfall in years to come). He asserts:

> Every social evil is celebrated – stripping, LSD and music from what they are pleased to call the Death Factory […] Like all modern exhibitions, it was an excuse

> for exhibitionism by every crank, queer, squint and ass in the business. In a vast room there were a few photographs which attempted to make prostitutes look like victims instead of the vultures which they are.

The article then focuses on driving a stake into the liberal arts agenda, using dog-whistle phrases such as referring to ICA head Ted Little as 'the bearded director'. P-Orridge is briefly interviewed and described more as an evil hippie rather than a harbinger of demonic punk, and the music element of the evening, or the provocative punk crowd are not mentioned. Aside from these two newspapers, *Prostitution* also makes a 'comment' article in the *Daily Mirror* on the inside of the front cover, though this article focuses predominantly on attacking the Arts Council by linking *Prostitution* to the previous Mary Kelly exhibition.

The following day, Wednesday 20 October, has a total absence of reporting from the show for the newspapers outside of the London region, but the London editions of the *Daily Mail* and *Daily Telegraph* continue their assault on the Arts Council's actions in giving out grants to performers such as COUM. In addition, there is a small inclusion in *The Sun* where the newspaper links the fall-out from the show to an anti-British agenda, a mode of operating common to the newspaper that falls simultaneously outside of, and in the service of, politics. Things gather pace on Thursday, as the newspapers start to push the story out into regional editions. The *Express* runs a page 3 story by Michael O'Flaherty under the headline 'State aid for Cosey's travelling sex troupe' with a photograph of Tutti and P-Orridge that works at the theme of wasting taxpayers' money; again, the subcultural context makes no reference to punk but hippie connotations, quoting 'long-haired and bearded members of his sex troupe'. *The Times* runs a short article on page 3 on the theme of wasting money, matched with similar stories in the *Daily Telegraph* and *Daily Mirror*, the former using a cartoon of P-Orridge and others mugging the goddess of arts (an amalgamation of Minerva and Apollo) – thus linking it to the ongoing scare story of mugging (see Figure 2.5) – and the latter using the headline 'Mr P Orridge in a stir' in regard to COUM's proposed European tour funding being curtailed. Perhaps not surprisingly, a more balanced and calmly investigated piece is presented in *The Guardian* that mocks the theatrical indignation and apoplectic rage and runs the coverage into its own ongoing exchange of letters provoked by the previous Mary Kelly exhibition. The surprise piece of journalism on this day is the more sympathetic article in the *Daily Mail* by Shaun Usher, which calls on ghosts of J. M. W. Turner and James Joyce to champion the spirit of artistic experimentation.

As the weekend approaches the coverage picks up with options for humour and political mischief-making. The *Express* runs a cartoon that conflates Kelly, *Prostitution*,

RAPHIC ART"
OUPE GETS
R U.S. TOUR

a pornographic "art"
Institute of Contempory
receive a grant of £496
cil to take his troupe on
in America and Canada

the Council hinted last night
several months ago, might
complaints about his latest
is always sensitive to public
opinion," he said.

It would not assist any performance calculated to offend reasonable public taste.

The controversial I C A exhibition, called Prostitution, has been organised by Genesis Pillow Orridge—"Pillow" to his friends. It is aided by a £200 Arts Council grant.

Mr Orridge, who changed his name from Neil Megson by deed poll three years ago, was fined £100 with £20 costs by Highbury magistrates in April for sending five indecent postcards through the post.

Festival grant

The British Council, which is financed by the Government,

INSTITUTE OF CONTEMPORARY ARTS

ART

Garland

TV DROPS

Muggings increasing

The Daily

Booki
£2,00
in '87

A BOOKMAK
become a r
he had fallen a
at Leeds yeste

COLIN BARLOW, a
Manchester City foo
said he paid £2,000
shares in the horse, H

He claimed he was
had cost £7,000 at Asc

Laker, said Mr Barlow
Chancery Court, he fo
Habitual had cost Mr
WHITEHEAD, the Maltan
875gns.

Yesterday, Mr W
denied an allegation o
He defended an action
Barlow of Moadlock,
Cheshire and another
member, Mrs FREDA
of Old Edlington, ne
caster, for deceit and re
the agreement.

Sired by Habit

Mr WHITEHEAD ag
bought the horse for

Figure 2.5: Cartoon by Garland in The Daily Telegraph, *21 October 1976.*

and Andre, and *The Guardian* columnist Caroline Tisdall calls out Throbbing Gristle at their game, setting them against the artistic authenticity and integrity of Mary Kelly: 'Thanks to the press, Genesis P-Orridge and Cosy Fanni Tutti have now become household names. They themselves will carefully document the outraged headlines. Publicity is what they seek and publicity in abundance is what they are getting' (1976: 10). *The Times* revels in a blow-by-blow account of the parliamentary debate, adding bracketed indications of party cheers or laughter as an imagined sound effect. The *Daily Telegraph* prompts a quote worthy of being from a *Carry On* script from a supposedly disgruntled artist Dennis Stoll, complaining he has no funding for a trip to Egypt with a serious group of dancers: 'I feel if they called themselves Dancers of Lesbos they'd be given a special plane' (cited in Morrow 1976: 17). On Saturday, the *Express* plucks out a further example of what it sees as left-wing artistic nonsense and wastefulness, picking on the Action Space collective for getting funding to 'stage imaginary cricket matches in crowded shopping centres' (Clancy 1976: 2). This is the same Action Space that would provide an essential haven for experimental punk and post-punk acts in the late 1970s, including having a scheduled (but ultimately cancelled) performance of Throbbing Gristle in April 1979. This is the final clutch of articles – the joke finally wears thin and the newspapers move on. The question that concerns us is where do Throbbing Gristle go next?

NOTES

1. See https://inspiringcity.com/2017/09/04/the-curious-tale-of-dead-bod-the-hull-graffiti-from-the-60s-which-is-now-a-symbol-of-the-city-itself/. Accessed 10 November 2022.

2. P-Orridge (2021: 163–4) paints a picture that he single-handedly established many of the new squats on the road and effectively pioneered the artist community.

3. Headline from Neil Spencer's review of Sex Pistols at London venue the Marquee, printed on page 31 of *NME*, 21 February 1976.

4. Ford (1999: 4.12) also records the use of the name and details this COUM performance.

5. This chimes with Savage (1991: 77).

6. Documentation on the Swankers is sparse, I'm using Jones (2016: 114) here, but acknowledge that this may also be unreliable.

7. As Bestley and Burgess (2018) demonstrate, the seemingly simple and urgent design for *Never Mind the Bollocks* is incredibly well thought through to maintain a harmonic visual quality, countering Scanlon's (2016: 205) assessment of 'look[ing] as if it had cost nothing to produce'. It is also a long way from the sybaritic 1970s style, typified by the complex and readerly designs for Pink Floyd albums *Ummagumma* (1969) and *Wish You Were Here* (1975).

8. There is some discrepancy as to this timeline, I am using the dates from Ford (1999: 4.10) though Powell (2014: 20) suggests Christopherson joined Hipgnosis in 1973.

9. Originally filmed as part of BBC's *Play For Today* series in 1977 but cut from broadcast at short notice. Clarke remade *Scum* as a feature film, slightly changing the plot and emphasis points.

10. The photographs are reproduced in the plates section in Savage (1991). Savage first relays the story of the photographs being too much for McLaren in *The Face* #37 (June 1983).

11. Trowell (2016) discusses these Stevenson photographs.

12. Gorman (2020: 285) relays a slightly different version of this story, suggesting that there was a sign on the wall at the entrance announcing Throbbing Gristle.

13. Toop (1995: 261) captures this overblown prog aesthetic with his phrase 'command-centre grandiosity'.

14. Worley (2017: 30–31) discusses these initial features.

15. Ford (1999: 6.22–24) quotes and analyzes the press material. Ford doesn't indicate whether he uses original source material or the scrapbook of press cuttings assembled by Throbbing Gristle.

16. See, for example, Sladen and Yedgar (2007: 8).

17. Personal research undertaken at newspaper archives in Cambridge University and the British Library.

18. This unchallenged currency also extended into the music newspapers and was rampant through the late 1970s. Advertisements regularly featured nudity and an obsession with stockings and suspenders, whilst rock band features often included a scantily dressed or naked model on the set. Female figures were normally positioned in profile or photographed from behind such that the featured band would be depicted in the wanton presence of nudity as a kind of (desirable) rock star privilege.

3. IN AND AGAINST PUNK

1977 THROUGH THE LOOKING GLASS

SUMMIT MEETING

If the planning towards *Prostitution* and the formal appearance of Throbbing Gristle had been geared towards the context of a punk event, even if that event archetype was wilfully distorted from the start, then the immediate aftermath went in the opposite direction. The controversy, and subsequent publicity, occurred solely in an art context. The music press did not reciprocate the event, loosely adhering to the format of a gig, as either something within the now relatively mature punk subculture or as an intervention into that subculture. The evening garnered a single response, with a review for the *NME* by regular Tony Parsons published on 30 October. Parsons's review also delineated clearly between an art and a music (punk) event, having had time to digest the press furore and preface a dissection of this into his report on the evening. Following this, he establishes a mock working-class (punk?) voice by asking 'Betcha dying to know what happened, ain'tcha?' and then sets out to declare his distaste for the art audience side of things. Throbbing Gristle, linked to this arty crowd, are described through their roles and appearances, with P-Orridge's 'rap about the decay of humanity' given reference. Strangely, Tutti is credited as a male. Parsons gives the music little merit, a single short paragraph referring to 'sub-psychedelic taped sounds', 'random keyboards played plonk-plonk', and 'moronic bass' (n.pag.). After warranting Shelley the Cherry Bomb stripper with a capitalized 'GREAT!', Parsons is more enthusiastic about Chelsea, comparing them to the main punk acts of the time and delivering 'a good set of 1977 dole queue rock'. He concludes the review with a short interview with Billy Idol and a recommendation for future promoters to book the band (Chelsea, that is). Elsewhere in the newspaper, there is a Rod Stewart cover feature, an Elton John main album review (*Blue Moves*) and Julie Burchill reviewing a clutch of rock and reggae singles. An advertisement for Permaprints comedy T-shirts (with an 'I survived Butlitz' slogan that would appeal to Throbbing Gristle's humour lexicography by linking Butlins and Colditz/Auschwitz) is about as punk as things get. Another advertisement for the Philips Hipster portable cassette player (in green, grey, or denim blue) signals a surreptitious world of sound recording that would soon contour a major part of Throbbing Gristle's *modus operandi*. Other music newspapers are still mired in the mid 1970s, with *Record Mirror* (for example) employing the saggy, curvaceous fonts of the hippie era (think of the classic 'Keep on Truckin'' slogan) and structuring the pages with thickly bordered boxes with rounded corners. Content in this less forward-looking newspaper included reports on Alex Harvey collapsing on stage and Woody from the Bay City Rollers in hospital recovering from a minor operation. Punk was evident in glimpses: mention of the Sex Pistols recently signing to EMI and a vox-pop article entitled 'Punks? What Punks?' which tried to convey the view that the average young person on the street didn't care about this new subculture.

By November 1976, opportunities to make inroads into the music industry were presenting themselves to Throbbing Gristle. With punk music gradually becoming a major part of the wider subcultural fashion and music scene and still having something of a shock factor articulated through the mainstream media, then Throbbing Gristle – as overt antagonists and misfits – were ripe for potential inclusion. The crucial question remained as to whether this was a mutual attraction. Unsurprisingly, this relationship of dependence between Throbbing Gristle and punk is fiercely disputed through the testimony recorded in Ford's book, as he gives all members of the band a chance to air their differing recollections of what happened and what motives were at work. It is very easy to declare yourself as being against punk and its associated trappings of the industry – another branch of the 'death factory' with labels, production schedules, advertising, and marketing – when you have tried and failed to get a contract. Ford (1999: 4.8) details how COUM, acting on many occasions purely as a music group, had previously sought and gained coverage in the *NME* (9 September 1974) and received accolades from John Peel. From this point onwards opinions are divided, with Ford offering a heteroglossia of three different accounts of the immediate period after *Prostitution* when the interests of record labels were clearly piqued. Virgin Records' Simon Draper shows interest in the band, but a contract is not immediately forthcoming. A potential sweetener is activated, with Draper bringing Virgin's possible interest in the band to the attention of the *Melody Maker* newspaper, and so instigating the first lengthy article on the band (20 November 1976). In this initial article, an interview solely with P-Orridge, the punk culture is called into question as being part of the 'glass globe, which is the record business'. If this is not a blatant tactic to terminate a record contract before one is even on offer, it is either P-Orridge calling Virgin's bluff or putting the band across as more punk than punk by channelling a nihilism against itself (which is a tactic, as shown below, later adopted to great success by the Sex Pistols). P-Orridge praises punk's destructive experimentation but accredits Throbbing Gristle with having the nous to be both a bit more and to outlast punk, which he suggests will have a two-year shelf life.

In Tutti's 2017 autobiography, long after the band have split up, reformed and split again, and even longer after the ending of her caustic and manipulative relationship with P-Orridge, the possibility of forming deliberate links with the punk scene (and its associated courting by the record industry) is revisited. Tutti (2017: 208) makes no bones about P-Orridge's determination to land a record deal with Virgin after *Prostitution*, and a later discussion within the band in regard to the punk scene. Consulting her contemporaneous diaries from February 1977, she describes how P-Orridge was further drawn to the scene through his friendship with *Sniffin' Glue* fanzine writer and musician Mark P(erry), and his relationship with punk figurehead Soo Catwoman. This led variously to Throbbing Gristle 'appearing in *Sniffing Glue*' [*sic*], P-Orridge picking up a 'punk style' of playing his guitar through joining in with Perry and Alex Fergusson (of ATV) who were rehearsing at the studio, and P-Orridge and Soo embarking on numerous trips to inveigle record companies and agents to take a committed contractual interest in Throbbing Gristle. This then necessitated a band meeting and a resolution from the three members aside from P-Orridge to 'refocus away from anything punk' (Tutti 2017: 225–27). P-Orridge has also written about this time, though his recollections are particularly unreliable. A snapshot of his version of the time is recalled for the 'Invisible Jukebox' feature of *The Wire*, featured in the September 2006 issue and archived as an unedited transcript.[1] His posthumously published autobiography expands on these notes, though the year is wrongly remembered as 1978 instead of 1977. P-Orridge (2021: 189) attempts to mark out a delimiting stance between himself and punk, but recalls seeing bands like 'the Jam, the Lurkers, the Clash, the Damned' as part of his outings with Soo.

According to Perry, he met the members of Throbbing Gristle in late 1976, at a party held by Sheila Rock and John Krivine.[2] Perry was dating journalist Caroline Coon at the time, and would then embark on a relationship with Soo who would be introduced into the Throbbing Gristle world. P-Orridge latched on to Perry and Soo, frequenting the newly established Roxy Club which briefly flourished as a punk stronghold in the first few months of 1977. In March of that year, the nascent ATV of Perry and Fergusson were joined by P-Orridge in a loose jamming format, with both Carter and Tutti present. Perry describes the atmosphere as more convivial than bristling with the tension that Tutti portrays in her autobiography. P-Orridge was offered an opportunity to join ATV as a regular member but declined out of respect for keeping a singular vision with Throbbing Gristle. Furthermore, the inclusion of Throbbing Gristle in *Sniffin' Glue* was also more nuanced than a straight-up feature or advertisement – it was an involvement rather than an appearance. By early 1977, the ever-astute Perry was aware of the commercial interest in punk, and the fanzine was keen to explore tensions and contradictions rather

Figure 3.1: Sniffin' Glue *#11, July 1977, cover and Throbbing Gristle contribution, published by Mark Perry. Courtesy of Frank Maier.*

than act as an uncritical mouthpiece for the scene. Throbbing Gristle featured in the penultimate issue (number 11, July 1977), by which time Perry was exploring new ways to gather content and opinion. For this issue, they invited various friends to put a page together, for which they could do whatever they wanted, and contributors included Mick Jones of the Clash, Jon Savage, Sandy Robertson, and Savage Pencil. Throbbing Gristle, at the point of releasing their first album, assembled a hybrid page between an advert, a flyer and (bad) press cutting, with the dominant image consisting of a prone figure in a domestic kitchen and a short text describing her prolonged suicide efforts (see Figure 3.1). Contributors Sandy Robertson and Jon Savage would both soon play a key role in the wider dissemination of Throbbing Gristle beyond the fanzine culture.

PUNK IN ASCENDENCY

Though written over half a year apart, the 1976 music newspaper articles on punk by Ingham and Coon referred to in the previous chapter were temporally transposable, in that the different approaches taken – subcultural and sociological – were evident and consistent throughout this nascent period of punk. To move slightly forward from the Marxist strictures of understanding subcultures as simply a latent power of class oppression and struggle adopted by the Birmingham academics at the CCCS, Dick Hebdige was the first of these writers to tackle punk with his landmark 1979 book *Subculture: The Meaning of Style*. Hebdige emphasized the sociological dimension of punk as reflecting boredom and an unwillingness to play the wider game of an oppressive society, alongside the purely 'for-itself' subcultural elements that are essential to the phylogenetic mapping of post-war subcultures in the United Kingdom. Momentarily stripped away of latent political meaning, subcultures need a set of understandable and demonstrable rules evident through clothing, argot, manners, and a wider habitus. Hebdige's approach to punk was to show how this energy was generated at a crossing over of the sociological and subcultural, principally through the practices of homology and bricolage. The former demonstrated how sociological discontent was aired through aspects such as repurposed bin bags as clothing, and the latter involved pre-existing subcultures mixed up in a Frankenstein experiment such that the punk visual look set itself up as an apparent contradictory affront to the subcultural system itself.

This occurred both at the expensive high-end of punk fashion presented by McLaren and Westwood, and more predominantly at the low end of punk fashion evident in photographs by Derek Ridgers (2016) as he documents the energetic atmospheres of early punk spaces (see also Czezowski and Carrington 2016). Ridgers's photographs, often blurred through being taken amidst the energetic dancing frenzies, show the home-made fashions of ripped blazers adorned by cheap artefacts such as big badges, stitched on zips, forced tears, rips and holes, paint splatter, clips and pins assembled into long chains, and autopsied household items such as the coiled wiring of a telephone. Subjects photographed up close, particularly at rest and coated with sweat after a period of energetic engagement, picked out in the dimly lit crevices of the subterranean spaces, resemble the visual ethnographies of coal miners. A single photograph of Hennessy's *In the Gutter* (1978: 66) of the Roxy dancefloor is like a stilled outtake from a zombie film, with a sparsely populated scene of figures seemingly consuming each other in a stiffened, corpse-like manner. This subcultural and sociological flux was at a mature stage by autumn 1976, making Throbbing Gristle's point of entry into the scene most opportune. Punk had not yet crossed over into being a threat to society, or in the epic words of sociologist Stanley Cohen (1987) who unpacked the media reaction to the mods and rockers altercations of the 1960s, become a folk devil and moral panic. *Prostitution* attempted to achieve this paradigm shift but only managed it in a partial capacity; it would inevitably be fully activated by the Sex Pistols who immediately usurped *Prostitution* with their own orchestration of outrage.

As Caroline Tisdall implicated in her *Guardian* article, P-Orridge and the band played off the scandal in the immediate aftermath, seeing it have repercussions in the art world but also bringing it into the music scene with the feature in *Melody Maker*. We do not hear comment from McLaren, Rhodes, or even Krivine who was close to Throbbing Gristle but possibly concerned with getting his disintegrating band Chelsea back into shape for the punk rock horse race following their promising review in *NME*. However, just over a month later, McLaren and his Sex Pistols wrested back the upper hand and punk found a new public scandal to usurp any punk frisson manufactured by the *Prostitution* scandal. At short notice, the Sex Pistols and their entourage (including the ever-present Bromley Contingent) stood in for EMI label-mates and rock band Queen as studio guests on 1 December for the live airing of Bill Grundy's *Today* programme. In a famous 100 seconds moment, the dialogue descended to a string of obscenities, with the programme quickly fading out as members of the entourage began drunkenly dancing to the theme music. The Sex Pistols were just about to release their debut single 'Anarchy in the UK' and commence a nationwide tour starting two days later at the University of East Anglia. As Scanlan (2016: 13) remarks, even without the rebroadcasting of the footage, the news of the band 'spread like rumour of some alien invasion' with a mass of newspaper headlines. Within 24 hours, dates from the tour were being pulled, and the band's label EMI were wavering and backtracking. By the end of December, the decision had been made to release them from their contract, with a suitable compensation clause activated. Notoriety, money, record contracts gained, record contracts negated, television, and newspaper headlines; all of this was achieved overnight, casting the *Prostitution* scandal very much as yesterday's news, and Throbbing Gristle as an unknown band in the nurturing punk moment.

As 1977 commenced, the sheen of the Silver Jubilee provided a balm for an ailing country beset by strikes, power cuts, IRA bombing campaigns, and the rise of the National Front. Such events that focus away from the politics of the time are few and far between, with the hosting of sporting events such as the Olympics or the World Cup existing as pre-planned affairs, the winning (or increasingly an acceptance of nearly winning) of such events an unexpected bonus, and the manufacturing of small wars or invasions of countries another less worthy tactic. Royal weddings and celebrations are convenient placeholders in appealing for unity, calm and a sense of nationhood, and 1977 was grasped accordingly. As a dark cloud, the spectre of punk loomed large, following the very small seeds planted by the touring of bands such as the Sex Pistols in the latter half of 1976, and the explosion of publicity afforded by the *Today* incident. It was a complex process of new clubs such as the Roxy opening at the end of December

1976, and the sudden offers of contracts to punk bands from major labels for substantial fees. The entertainment industry sensed a quick cash-in, gambling that the mix of dissent, unrest, and dissatisfaction that potentially defined the core of the youthful record-buying public could be converted into hard subcultural cash through the artful hooliganism of the newly emerging punk bands and their astute managers. A feeding frenzy ensued. The Damned had quickly secured a contract with Stiff and had the accolade of releasing the first punk single ('New Rose' in October 1976) and first punk album (*Damned Damned Damned* in February 1977). The Clash gained the cover spot of *Sounds* in January 1977 as the promising new band of the scene, and had somewhat predictably signed to CBS Records by the end of January for a record fee of £100,000, prompting fanzine writer and reluctant punk spokesperson Mark P to declare this as 'the day punk died'. The Adverts soon joined the Damned on Stiff, and the Jam signed a big contract with Polydor in early March. Following the *Today* publicity, the Sex Pistols had been on a short hiatus but were back in the studio by January 1977, although EMI had quickly withdrawn the 'Anarchy' single when they parted company with the band. Glen Matlock was fired the following month, with McLaren using the opportunity to get more punk kudos for his band by framing Matlock as a fan of boring music.

As UK punk gradually expanded in the aftermath of *Today*, initially through the dedicated music press, Throbbing Gristle were split between manifestations and continents. P-Orridge and Tutti had flown out to the United States to fulfil a clutch of COUM performances (and upping the shock tactics to distress numerous American fringe artists such as Chris Burden) and Christopherson was working with John Krivine and Stephane Raynor as they redeveloped their nascent punk franchise towards the newly branded BOY shop on King's Road after attracting the wrong type of clientele to Antiquarius, where they had based ACME. Christopherson and his colleague John Harwood were called in to give an overarching theme and to design interior spaces, a risqué window display, and general iconography, drawing on Christopherson's fascination with troubled boys meeting unfortunate endings and his skill of simulating horrendous wounds. As Ford (1999: 7·4) describes, the tableau graphically constructed an imaginary scenario of a young skinhead breaking into the premises, vandalizing, inflicting arson, and then perishing in the fire. A window display was produced, along the lines of a clinical vitrine containing a burnt Doc Marten boot and severed foot with copies of Christopherson's newspaper clippings of similar real-life events.[3] As with anything conceived and actualized by Christopherson, controversy soon followed. The full extent of the shop's design ethos was explained in a short article for the *London Evening News*, dated 4 March 1977, the day before the opening of the rebranded clothing

Figure 3.2: Gary Gilmore Memorial Society T-shirt designed by Genesis P-Orridge for BOY London.

outlet. The clothing was described as being coated in dried animal blood and decorated with surgical paraphernalia, extending to accessories such as hypodermic syringe jewellery and contraceptive packet earrings. The arson look was continued with shirts daubed with metallic paint to give the impression of being charred. Soon after opening the shop, the police visited and demanded the widow display be removed. This scene is captured in Don Letts' 1978 home-move/film *The Punk Rock Movie* and includes a short clip of an agitational and cavorting P-Orridge in a shot amongst the punk customers. The next we hear of this is a short piece in the *Sunday Mirror*, dated 14 August 1977, with a report on how then owner Krivine and former manager Letts are to potentially face charges based upon the breach of a Napoleonic law outlawing the thrusting out of 'stumps' by returning wounded soldiers to solicit money.

Though the designers of this surgical post-apocalyptic clothing makeover are not named in the article, it has the feel of a COUM performance aesthetic. However, P-Orridge is named as the creator of the specific Gary Gilmore T-shirt. This had its origin in P-Orridge and Tutti's American trip, where they met up with maverick performer Monte Cazazza who would become a crucial satellite to Throbbing Gristle's operation.

SICKLY P-ORRIDGE

Now he sells firing squad postcards

GARY GILMORE MEMORIAL SOCIETY

FROM the man who has sickened you before, here is a piece of bad taste to give you an even greater shock.

By TONY ROBINSON

Martyr

ALL OUT.. AGAINST RACE HATE

LET'S DO IT MY WAY!

YOUR STARS

CONSTANCE SHARPE

EMPLOYMENT PROTECTION ACT

Two further important provisions come into force on 1 February

Part-Time Workers

Guarantee Payments

EMPLOYMENT PROTECTION ACT

A better working life for everyone

Figure 3.3: 'Sickly P-Orridge' Sunday Mirror *feature on Gary Gilmore artwork, 30 January 1977.*

The drawn-out execution of convicted murderer Gary Gilmore and an associated media feeding frenzy occupied the trio in the United States, and a Gary Gilmore Memorial Society was quickly instigated with a provocative photo shoot – a triptych of each member blindfolded, tied to a chair, facing a gun and a camera. On return to the United Kingdom in January, these were made into a set of commercial postcards and developed into a T-shirt for the proposed shop BOY (see Figure 3.2). In his autobiography P-Orridge attempts to add some distance between himself and the punk commercialization of BOY, suggesting that Krivine added 'zips and all that kind of crap to make it punk' (2021: 189). At the time of 1977, Krivine is keen to brand BOY as being a progression from punk, stating in the *London Evening News* article that 'Punk is finished. We call this stuff "Survival". These clothes are about survival in London in 1977. They are about what happens every day in the streets' (4). This fluctuating disavowal of punk would animate 1977, as creative forces moved with trepidation in anticipation of punk's balance shifting from being a rebellious energy to a watered-down stereotype.

More importantly, as Ford (1999: 7.6) recounts, the Gilmore designs gained a mention in the *Sunday Mirror* on 30 January 1977, serving to garner more Grundy-style negative publicity that can be instantly translated into punk kudos. The stunt was given a half-page feature, reproducing the postcard under the headline 'Sickly P-Orridge' (see Figure 3.3). The author, Tony Robinson, contextualized P-Orridge through his art links to *Prostitution*, though P-Orridge was described as 'an artist and rock musician'. Krivine is given the final words, justifying the project and Gilmore such that: 'It's obviously a great thing if a guy is prepared to die for something – even if it's his own feeling of despair. That's courage'. Gilmore would resurface later in the year with the Adverts hit single 'Gary Gilmore's Eyes', scurrilously documenting in B-movie style the traumatizing visions of an imaginary recipient of the killer's eyes as part of his request to donate his organs. One of punk's finest moments.

SUBVERTED JUBILEE ICONOGRAPHY

Whilst P-Orridge and Tutti were in the United States, Carter and Christopherson had been building the capability and capacity for the band's sonic power and experimentation, including Carter's legendary gristle-izer units. Retooled, the band were ready to perform again. There was, however, tension amongst the four band members and the first gig after *Prostitution* proved to be a struggle. This was an appearance at their first 'non-art' venue that had a more punk crowd, the workaday rock venue Nags Head pub in High Wycombe, on 11 February 1977. As James (2018: 354–56) documents, the Sex Pistols had already made one of their early satellite town appearances here on 2 September 1976. Throbbing Gristle's gig was chaotic on all counts, with equipment failing in sequential segments and the tensions between band members that normally animate and inspire the live performance quickly boiling over to the point of destruction. An indication of P-Orridge's thinking was evident with the opening track 'Prince Philip Licked Her Cunt', a crude affront to the Jubilee celebrations which punk already had in its sights. Obviously, P-Orridge wanted to grasp this nettle of critical fusion and push things as far as possible.

Between the Nags Head gig and the next gig at Brighton Polytechnic at the end of March, there were ongoing tensions in the band, and this period coincides with P-Orridge's initial friendship with Perry and Soo. We sense that P-Orridge is preoccupied with the punk scene and that, at the same time, this scene is rapidly accelerating outside of P-Orridge's grip and comprehension. With eye-watering contracts secured by the Clash and others in January and February, the Sex Pistols sprung back into action. March was a busy month with Sid Vicious joining the band to add his ultimately fated punk nihilism meets Goofy persona, and a significant deal was signed with A&M Records. The proposed 'God Save The Queen' single was immediately announced. This was a punk coup, with the Sex Pistols setting their stall out with an anti-Jubilee strategy to set punk in opposition to the saving grace of the country and break the spell of rapt devotion. In quick succession, the signing of the band was re-staged in front of Buckingham Palace, and made the front cover of *Sounds* newspaper on 19 March, by which time the band had been sacked from the label for beating up *Old Grey Whistle Test* presenter Bob Harris and a BBC sound engineer in the Speakeasy bar during an escalated confrontation. The finer details of this piece of punk folklore have never been verified, but its impact and exposure were immediate with the instant withdrawal (once again) of a Sex Pistols single, making it one of the rarest and sought-after punk records to date.

More importantly, *Sounds* were happy to run a feature on the band's supremely brief foray with A&M in the following week's edition and included a large image of Jamie Reid's now classic design of his détourned Peter Grugeon photograph of the Queen (the artwork was also 'leaked' to the *NME* and other music newspapers).[4] The article claimed that the obviously controversial artwork was never approved by the label, something that is disputed by Reid in later years who suggests that only the swastika variation image was not approved, so we can only speculate as to how much of the graphical package for the advertising campaign had been set in motion (Reid and Savage 1987: 65). Such an advertising campaign would include billboards and bus banners, matching the initial campaign for 'Anarchy in the UK' backed by EMI which even ran to include advertisements in matchday football programmes. The suggestion that the artwork was banned outright, conveyed by the *Sounds* article, is obviously further bad-turned-good press for McLaren's wider strategy with the band, and as a bonus, he gets to have the newspaper print the artwork (it would be used unaltered for the May release of the single on Virgin, the band's next label). In addition to the *Sounds* cover feature, rival newspaper *Melody Maker* went out with a bold front cover in part resembling a terrorist communiqué, using a provocative quote from Rotten expressing his thoughts on the record industry, set inside a red-bordered box sandwiched between the red masthead and the more regular news as bullet points. Inside the newspaper, we have a proto 'punk-effect' layout of ripped Jamie Reid artwork and a crudely reproduced photograph of the abandoned A&M pressing of 'God Save The Queen' in the act of being played. Maximum publicity for something that was pulled from happening.

Taking the stage at Brighton Polytechnic Sallis Benney Theatre, a classic academic space with plush curtains and parquet flooring, it is impossible to tell how informed

P-Orridge is with the turmoil of orchestrated events that had benefitted the Sex Pistols through March. Certainly, by the date of the gig on 26th of the month, the Sex Pistols had announced their contract and single, been photographed outside the Palace, and had the *Sounds* and *Melody Maker* cover publicity.[5] Furthermore, as Savage (1991: 315) states, the initially approved manifestations of the artwork from the single had been reproduced and widely disseminated in advance of the anticipated but ultimately aborted release. The audience at Brighton was not the punk crowd as encountered at the Nags Head wanting to pogo and spit, but an artier crowd as part of the Art and Design Department students who had invited the band to play. In the first picture section of her autobiography, Tutti reproduces as facsimile a sample page from her diary, showing an almost childlike style of vernacular craft and love as the entry is completed in neat blue ink and the page flourished with a Throbbing Gristle flash logo and carefully bordered with a demarcated red and black square boundary. The page coincides with the Brighton gig, and we learn a couple more aspects: that P-Orridge drank a bottle of whiskey in the first 'factory music section', and that he did a fantastic introduction that Christopherson failed to get on tape. This missing opening segment is a good example of the gap between thinking we are there (due to the prevalence of recordings from Throbbing Gristle performances and their aural intimacy) and actually being there, to experience the crowd, the mood, the atmosphere, the space, and to gain a context for the spontaneity.

We can only guess at the content of P-Orridge's opening speech, orated before the bottle of whiskey and presumably when (more) sober. From the live recording, the band open proceedings with their punk pastiche 'Zyklon B Zombie', offering a crude riff to jump around to and a chorus line that weaves between an Auschwitz narrative and the brainlessness of sniffing adhesives which had become a ritual within the punk craze. In Tutti's (2017: 223) notes for the 4 February 1977, the song is recalled as being a strong favourite in practice, but the Brighton airing of it would be just about the last time (before it was strangely resurrected as a single a year later). Its subsequent culling is unexplained, but there is a feeling that the song overly engages the punk milieu, the boundary between criticizing and appeasing being particularly diaphanous with the genre, and furthermore punk would soon be the target of numerous novelty and comedy records as it gained foothold in the charts. With this track out of the way P-Orridge confirms his fixation with the punk-vs-Jubilee fashion, and we get the stunning 'Last Exit', a one-off track commencing with what would become a standard device with Throbbing Gristle, an overlay of ominous readymade recordings (in this case a nuclear survival strategy), an illicit segment of recorded material, and powerful surge of electricity underpinned by a gristle-ized bass. P-Orridge then adopts an over-affected cockney accent to narrate a story about being beaten up under a poster of the Queen and Prince Philip. As the kicks and blows rain down on the prostrate figure, the poster is given an invigorated and hallucinogenic iconographic clarity revealing the Queen and her husband in a crude sexual act, seemingly moving and speaking. A journey on the Central Line offers no respite to the narrator, as the act is repeated with increasing brutality, teeth flying out as if reading from the high-octane section of a Richard Allen *Skinhead* script. The poster is still there, this time kicking the narrator. P-Orridge concludes the narrative: 'poster, fuck off, fuck off'. It was both a retelling and possibly a prescient adumbration, with Rotten himself being beaten by citizens performing their patriotic duty following the peak of his anti-Jubilee actions to come in June.

Whilst this can be construed as an improvised anti-Jubilee narrative, it also functions as an anti-anti-Jubilee message in regard to the punk scene's successful publicity seeking through this gesture. Punk's anti-Jubilee stance is read as a hedonistic pose offering no critical content. At the same time, P-Orridge is fixated on the poster, to the point where it is accosting him, first goading his actual attackers and then participating in a surreal scene as the victim succumbs to violence and pain. With Sex Pistols designer Jamie Reid extending his previous work as a cultural agitator (making fanzines and posters) to now détourne images of royalty with punk symbolism in the production of record sleeves, advertisements and posters to coincide with the single's release, one could be forgiven for thinking that it was this timely tirade of anti-royalty and shock-horror that was the source of P-Orridge's distress. Posturing punk was relentlessly beating him down. This renewed defiling of the flag and corruption of stabilizing images of royalty by Reid is augmented by Westwood and McLaren's new clothing in which flag-emblazoned clothing is cut apart and restructured with pins and straps.

In fact, P-Orridge had earlier used the apparently untouchable cultural legacy of both the union jack symbol and images of the Royal Family. The former is utilized in a provocative artwork, a piece entitled *The British Government* created for the *Ninth Paris Biennale* in October 1975. This work consisted of a conjoined pairing of crude wooden box frames, one including an upended union jack flag, the other having a more 3D construction with a photograph of a terrified and gagged boy (a mock-up by Christopherson) pasted on the back. The finishing touch was a mouse running around in the interior space to evoke the horror of George Orwell's Room 101 in *1984* (see Figure 3.4). The American stars and stripes flag had crept into the art canon as an experimental concern with artists such as Jasper Johns investigating new vision, and the early pop artists reusing it before flag-burning became a visual trope of disobedience brought to the fore with protests against the Vietnam War. In the United Kingdom, it was trickier and tied

Figure 3.4: COUM Transmissions, The British Government, *1975. Courtesy of the estate of GENESIS BREYER P-ORRIDGE and New Discretions.*

in with post-war subcultures which were intertwined with British pop art. Famously, the Who manager Kit Lambert worked with pop artist Peter Blake to refashion the band in 1965 as they structured themselves as super-mods, a concerted set of imagery and design which included a blazer fashioned from a union jack flag. This had links back to Royal College of Art student Brian Haynes, reported by Seago (1995: 196) as being the first to design clothing using the repurposed emblem as part of his degree show in the early 1960s (when he was threatened with instant expulsion for 'defiling the flag'). P-Orridge also had a form for seditiously détourning images of the Royal Family. In October 1975, he produced several montaged postcards excerpting and juxtapositioning freely available images of the Royals and their various signifiers (Buckingham Palace, etc.) with hard-core pornography, posting these out as a standard practice for those artists working in the mail art milieu. As detailed by Johnson (2019: 100–01), these missives had been intercepted by the police and P-Orridge was subsequently charged with obscenity.

Meanwhile, back at the Brighton performance, regular service is resumed with the lengthy instrumental segment 'Maggot Life', a montage of disturbing snippets and monotone recollections of brutal acts giving a typically unsettling listening experience. This is presumably the first 'factory music section' during which the whiskey is imbibed. Seemingly instilled with a fresh anger, P-Orridge picks up the vocal narration once again with 'Mary Jane/Record Contract', and here the anger at the punk scene is expressed as pure abreaction. Whereas tracks like 'Zyklon B Zombie' pre-exist in their playing live in that they are named and deliberate, tracks like 'Mary Jane/Record Contract' are not named in advance. This extemporization and accompanying noise is spontaneous and only acquires a name after the event with the documentation and production of the cassette. However, they acquire a status after the event, and so the name is reinforced and can, at times, be taken to pre-date the actual performance on the night. 'Mary Jane/Record Contract' is an important moment, masquerading as a slight against the dissolving of any potential punk integrity or something greater ... we are left to decipher the intention. P-Orridge had abandoned fostering any hope for the scene, but if he had spent weeks preceding this gig travelling around in search of a punk contract then the song takes on a larger meaning of festering frustration and possible discord in the band.

Mary Jane is introduced in a cheesy American pop voice and Bay City Rollers, David Essex, Rolling Stones, and Johnny Rotten are referenced to project a confusing anti-kudos, pop as obscenity with punk implicated. P-Orridge then starts ad-libbing about seeking anal sex with young boys in a mindless rant much like children extemporizing a slew of rhyming rude words in a corner of the playground – body cavities, sexual functions, and bodily fluids strung out in a line – cum, bum, (your) mum. It is not particularly clever or entertaining, even in the dark Throbbing Gristle way, and P-Orridge lets slip the reason for this outburst as he lists the various sexual things he is going to get, slipping in the line 'going to get a record contract'. Quickly the ode to Mary Jane is forgotten and Johnny Rotten, Sid Vicious, Sex Pistols, the Damned and 'super-punk' are invoked by name, and then by action as begging for a record contract and money. In the middle of this, a further name is brought in, with a chant of 'Steven / Steven / How's your nose / How's your teeth' – this unfortunate person (possibly the victim of some kind of attack) remains unidentified. Ending, but not resting, P-Orridge promises some music finally, and a doom-laden bass note takes over the mix and a rough promise of something about Ian Brady, presumably to drag the performance back onto recognized Throbbing Gristle territory. This breaks down, as the track is named on the spot as 'One Note One Life One Purpose' and devolves into more angry word association ranting about Brighton Rock, Brighton Pier, and Brighton pox, and it's not long before Rotten is brought back into the mix, never quite pushed away in P-Orridge's stream of consciousness. As if conforming to script, the plug is pulled and the evening descends into a free-for-all. The DJ on the night tries to coerce the angered audience into formulating their discontent and dissent, and, amidst the apparent chaos picked up on the cassette, P-Orridge can be heard asking to 'make sure everything is said'. Apparently drunk, but astute and switched on enough to know that there is art to be made here. This is recorded, and recycled back onto the album that would follow later in 1977.

TESCO DISCO

However heartfelt or bitter this rant was, it is somehow cathartic, an exorcism of sorts. The rising preoccupation was temporarily curtailed there, and a further or continued punk rage (or jealously) was not generally engaged or at least publicly expounded at this domineering level with subsequent gigs. In early May 1977, the band played at the Nuffield Theatre in Southampton and performed a strong signature set of disturbing electronic noise and pulse, with the only vocal section being P-Orridge's clever narration of 'National Affront'. You even hear polite applause between the tracks, perhaps an acknowledgement of fulfilment or accomplishment ... however, film footage from this concert later used in *After Cease to Exist* suggests that most of the audience had vacated the theatre before the climax of the show.

At the end of May, the band played the first of two gigs at the transient Rat Club, an alternative performance space held in the back room of pubs and organized by the promoter Brian Davis. The sound here was an even intensity of overlapping electronic feedback and throb, interspersed with infrequent and relatively unobtrusive samples from radio and television. If a summit meeting had been held to ascertain whether a punk influence, then this sound might well have been the result. Conversely, photographs show P-Orridge in the 'classic' early Throbbing Gristle look, as outlined by Ford (1999: 7·13–14) as a black leather jacket, T-shirt, sunglasses, and either jeans or leather trousers. By this point in time, P-Orridge had nuanced it towards more of a stereotype punk look, with studded belt and gloves, combat trousers and an army cap (see Figure 3.5). His black T-shirt is emblazoned with a classic swastika enclosed in a red square (also evidenced at the previous Southampton gig). Swastikas proliferated in the punk movement as crude armbands (introduced by Seditionaries in autumn 1976) or as chopped-up emblems in a wider melange of symbols (the famous 'Destroy' shirt produced in spring 1977), but P-Orridge's T-shirt looks to be something purchased from a specialist army memorabilia shop such as Chris Farlowe's Call to Arms in Camden.

Punk look, strange music, brooding tension and hostility, an aggressive drone. It holds a certain hypnotic power through both force and a kind of primal machine noise that would quickly attract a following who became entranced by such a sound, but something else was required to take it away from the jaws of electronic-prog doodling. P-Orridge cleverly obliges, opening his dialogue for the evening after four minutes by christening the sound 'Tesco Disco'. The whiskey comes in once again as a factor disrupting the more

Figure 3.5: Genesis P-Orridge on stage at the Rat Club, 22 May 1977. Courtesy of Michael Rorberger.

ordered oratorial and quickly moving the dialogue to match the brutality and rancorous distrust of the sounds. With the whiskey we have the punk demon briefly returning – intermittent ranting against the punk industry, but not reaching the monopolizing peak of the Brighton gig. Perhaps this was because his bête noire the Sex Pistols were back in the news with their next big record contract – signing to Virgin Records on 18 May, just four days prior to the Rat Club gig.

Up until then, punk had failed to make an impact on the mainstream, with only a pair of appearances by the Damned on LWT's Saturday morning *Supersonic* programme and the Stranglers appearing on *Old Grey Whistle Test* in early April. The latter part of May saw the first of the punk bands break onto *Top of the Pops*, with the Jam performing 'In the City' and the Stranglers with 'Go Buddy Go'. At the same time, the programme was prone to featuring banal novelty records such as the Muppets 'Halfway Down the Stairs' and the Wurzels 'Farmer Bill's Cowman'. For whatever reason, P-Orridge began calling out a litany of the accused as the Rat Club gig drew towards its conclusion. Firstly, *NME*'s punk journalist Tony Parsons was called out (he had reviewed *Prostitution* and produced a series of punk features for the newspaper from October 1976 onwards), then the poster once again, then a link between 'making a scene' and 'getting a record contract', and finally Rotten himself. In danger of simply regurgitating the venting of his spleen, P-Orridge refocuses to deliver a fantastically extemporized monologue about punters paying £1.30 to get in, a fantasy ICI-controlled project of punk mass observation and consumer demographics, a graphic encounter at the ear, nose, and throat hospital, and two people travelling down from Wolverhampton. Like an obsessive-compulsive twitching between locked themes and self-administering cognitive behavioural therapy, P-Orridge fixates on Wolverhampton, adopting the word as a drunken surrealist encounter of vocabulary. As well as distracting himself away from an anti-punk ranting, repeating the phrase works towards dissolving semantic integrity. P-Orridge gets into a locked groove asking where's Wolverhampton (initially referring to the people who have made this special trip) but eventually gets an answer from a frustrated member of the audience: 'Just off the M1'. As a finale we get an extended rant about Roger Daltrey and The Who, known for sniffing around the early punk scene, giving the impression he is in the crowd at the Rat Club. All of this is stitched together with a blend of violently processed sounds and non-stop backgrounds of sports commentaries and cinema organ music. Something was taking shape.

BUNKER MENTALITY

Punk burnt brightly through the latter half of 1977. Days after Throbbing Gristle's Rat Club event we had the rekindling of the media blaze of the Sex Pistols following their signing to Virgin and encountering a record executive (Richard Branson) who would not be phased by McLaren's antics and controversial one-upmanship. Virgin picked up the abandoned A&M release of 'God Save the Queen' with troublesome packaging and all, it was released by the end of May. It was quickly followed by the Jubilee boat trip on 7 June and the subsequent arrests and heavy publicity, with Vicious and Rotten desperately trying to outdo each other in the comedy villain stakes. Repercussions rumbled on with various members and associates of the band suffering physical attacks by the public. By summer, 'God Save the Queen' had climbed the charts and, despite a broadcasting ban, is said to have been kept off the number one spot as a matter of national emergency.

Virgin quickly followed this up with 'Pretty Vacant' which also made the UK top ten and eventually claimed the single of the year accolade with the *NME*. Punk, the Sex Pistols, and the punk fashion created by McLaren and Westwood garnered media attention; the band recorded a film for the single modelling the clothes, and a clutch of late-night shows explored punk's vestimentary centre of gravity, the King's Road.

Throbbing Gristle were elsewhere, focusing on their strengths and unique qualities, going into their studio during the summer of 1977 to produce their own film, *After Cease To Exist*, an avant-garde snuff movie that was made under the authorship of COUM and premiered in July at Arnhem Film Festival followed by a low-key showing at the Rat Club. No posing about in expensive clothes, the film included a mocked-up castration scene, shots of Soo Catwoman tied to a bed, and live footage recorded at the Southampton gig where the band were focused on their sound rather than P-Orridge's chaotic deconstruction of punk culture. The film has gained something of a cult status, bringing together Christopherson's dark visions of sexual proclivities, his skills in trauma prosthetics, and P-Orridge's added touch of merging in elements of the everyday: one contemporaneous viewer of the film I spoke to was fixated with a scene from the film in which the surgical instruments used to perform the operation were wheeled in on a 1970s cocktail trolley.

Relationships were still fragile and allegiances were shifting in flux, but productivity remained. From May onwards Cazazza spent an extended period as part of the Beck Road bunker mentality, constantly upping the stakes in extremism as the band set about producing a branded identity and quasi-advertising logic. Soo remained in the picture, causing an initial rift in P-Orridge's relationship with Tutti, though P-Orridge's autobiography strangely dates this relationship to 1978 – the year which would eventually see his relationship with Tutti terminated. As Tutti recalls in her memoirs, Soo quickly swapped P-Orridge for Cazazza, after which P-Orridge embarked on numerous other relationships. More importantly, for those interested in the genealogy of Throbbing Gristle's aesthetics rather than their domestic dramas, Christopherson and Carter were working with a strong bond to jointly explore new technologies in sound capture and transmission, enhancing the sampling capabilities of the band.

Ironically, it was the eventual payment for their work on Krivine's punk shop BOY that funded the self-release of their first album and the setting up of Industrial Records. This put paid to any more rants about record contracts. Emerging from this period of creative activity in autumn 1977, the band returned to the live circuit. Their sound and sensory assault was developing an autonomy and focus well outside of punk, and they eventually picked up interest from *Sounds* journalist Sandy Robertson in late 1977 and then landed the attention of key punk and post-punk documenter Jon Savage in 1978. This is the next stage of Throbbing Gristle, which I detail in the following two chapters.

1977 AND ALL THAT

This early period of Throbbing Gristle's history, the concurrent rise with punk, is unsatisfactorily messy. The claiming of *Prostitution* as some kind of primal scene of punk, disrespectfully usurped by the Sex Pistols and the *Today* incident, is generally what is taken away, and the other Throbbing Gristle gigs from 1977 are best forgotten. But if we work a bit harder we can find lines of flight for our reading and understanding of the time. Punk was a sign of the times, a reflective mix of the political, social, and subcultural statuses. It manifested itself as the conflation of niche schematic flows of previous subcultures, further shaped – implicitly, explicitly, and increasingly antagonistically – by wider forces and circumstances of the social, political, and cultural environment. Themes such as boredom, the built environment, the drudgery of work, and the moralistic oppression of school, church, and family were in the mix, as much as an 'enough is enough' reaction to the subcultural choices on offer as the 1970s unfolded: saccharine glam, boring rock, endlessly contemplative prog. As well as preaching an apparent do-it-yourself ethos, for some fans punk disrupted the flow of subcultures and the functional limitations of those subcultures.

All these structural issues occupied Throbbing Gristle, but they went further and deeper. At the same time, they failed to fit in. As Wilkinson (2016: 48) writes in his political study of post-punk, the break between the past and the present at the time of punk was never as totalizing as is often claimed. This statement against the assumed condition of punk requires some setting out, as Wilkinson is concerned with the political nuances of punk and its musical palette. Of course, punk borrowed from the counterculture and music scenes of the 1960s and early 1970s, but it wanted to appear to be new, and so revolted against appearances. Describing punk as a 'break as well as continuity', Wilkinson backtracks a little to reference the younger generation who sensed 'stagnation, confusion and hypocrisy within the ranks of the counterculture that prevented it from fully grasping the overall structure of feeling of the late 1970s' (2016: 48). The Clash, in their first interview for *Melody Maker* printed in November 1976 following their own riotous gig at the ICA, set out the strict demarcation to the hippie past, with Strummer associating hippies with apathy and deserving of being jeered at. This distrust manifested itself through to the end of punk's first wave, with Sex Pistols' graphic designer and cultural agitator Jamie Reid coining the 'never trust a hippie' slogan as a rebuke against Richard Branson and his Virgin label. As a subcultural formation, punk demanded something distinctive and new in terms of an immediate look, and Throbbing Gristle failed the test here, particularly P-Orridge with his obviously freak-scene early 1970s appearance. In the eyes of those constructing and reflecting upon the new scene – from McLaren to the journalists at the *NME* – P-Orridge was a subcultural anachronism. His earlier haircut experiments, consisting of shaving shapes around his crown, were a homage to Marcel Duchamp, and so had a possible punk-before-punk kudos. His straggly hippie haircut with a shaved strip up the middle might be described now as an ironic reversal of the punk Mohican crop, to make it more punk so to speak, but at the time in 1976, the Mohican was not a recognized punk trope to be reversed. P-Orridge simply had a version of the haircut of Peter Gabriel, frontman for the prog band Genesis, who had adopted this look back in 1973. Peter Gabriel was very much a part of something punk wanted to leave behind.

The role of art is more complex, although it is often wrongly simplified as stating that a strand of punk is arty whilst another is more rooted in a pub-rock rough musicality. Punk had a strong mode of visual expression, informed by expressions of anger and boredom that lent themselves to methods such as collage cut-ups calling on low-culture and shock-horror borrowings, over-wrought expressions and poses, and sartorial bricolage. This visual and performative style was rooted as much in peer-group-informed autodidacticism as in formal education. Punk was related to the art college through a function of the time and place of 1970s England: the art college offered young people a different option to life on the dole or a mapped-out future in a predictable, if not boring, job. In turn, art colleges had the potential to foster an expressive and receptive crowd who developed a subcultural hunger that fed on, and fed into, early punk as a subculture. We have to be careful of punk mythology here; art college tutors and their sessions were not all informed by proto-punkish destructive figures such as Gustav Metzger and Vienna actionists. It is a stretch to say that art colleges somehow had an inherent punk 'quality' that informed the subculture, more so we can suggest that the existing punk subculture was swelled by significant people who enjoyed the creative freedom of going to art college as an alternative to dole or work. This is in the same way that art colleges contributed to a surge in the creative glam-rock scene earlier in the 1970s. There wasn't a discursive or curricular switch in art colleges between glam and punk, it was just that they provided a refuge and supported increased creativity in whatever subculture was growing in potentiality. Subcultural expressions took influence from popular cultures, drug cultures, the beliefs held by the countercultural youth, and the strength (or otherwise) of those beliefs.

A corollary of this was the art college providing a space for early punk performances, as I have shown above with both Throbbing Gristle and the Sex Pistols. Many art students formed punk bands, but we cannot assume that they did so as an expression of art or with an intent to use punk as a way of furthering strands of avant-garde art. The previous generation had seen art and popular culture more dynamically engaged, with Pete Townshend of the Who being a good example of bringing forward an art school education under the maverick tutelage of Roy Ascott. Townshend used avant-garde practices drawn from artists such as Metzger to inform the direction of the Who's music and performance strategy. In the punk era, we can look at members of the Clash as being art school thoroughbreds, but the expressive content runs about as far as Paul Simonon applying a Jackson Pollock paint-drip onto their clothing and instruments – purely in the realm of fashion and appearance. There were exceptions: Adam Ant drew on his student experiences with erotic art specialist Peter Webb to foster an interest in artist and sculptor Allen Jones, which later informed his band's musical direction. Key band the Sex Pistols did not call upon art to broaden their musical assault. Original bassist Glen Matlock was an art student at St Martins but his artistic input culminated in painting the sign for McLaren and Westwood's shopfront. As Walker (1987: 107) surmises, in this contradictory flux and under the musical impetus of the Sex Pistols 'punk was the antithesis of artiness and pretension'.

What did occur was a masterminding by McLaren that has been rooted in the practice of the situationists, a theory that persists to the present through works such as Cooper (2017). Even though this bunch of European radicals argued against art and culture, it is considered that they somehow extended an art and culture practice and reputation to achieve this destruction. Not least, they exuded an arty countenance and accrued cool as they passed into history. Thus, McLaren's curating of the Sex Pistols is seen in this situationist-continuity light, and arty punk mythology retains a vague artistic strategy as well as a demographic basis in the art college. In the immediate period after this initial energy of 1976 and 1977, a more challenging art crossover was applied in the realms of post-punk and new wave – Gang of Four's tutoring at Leeds by Marxist art historians Terry Atkinson and Griselda Pollock being one example, XTC calling on Hipgnosis to mimic conceptualist artist Joseph Kosuth for the artwork for their album *Go 2* is another.

There were brief moments, as I have illustrated in this chapter, where lines of alliance and intent get corrupted and crossed over, but ultimately the London punk scene and Throbbing Gristle keep separate lives and paths. The strand of punk that Throbbing Gristle were exposed to was the mix between art colleges and fashion entrepreneurs looking to create subcultural energy and business opportunities, the cash from chaos formula. This was a key strand into the subculture, prominent in bringing about punk and momentarily flooding the subcultural plateau with energy, anger, and antagonism. Throbbing Gristle had an art background, even though they didn't fit the stereotype art college link discussed above. P-Orridge had attached himself to the countercultural activist strands of the hippie movement, an experience passed on to Tutti, Carter had what might be described as an art-by-osmosis effect through his friendship with Bruce Lacey's son, and Christopherson trod an odd path between professional creative and explorer of dark proclivities. Having unsuccessfully toiled in trying to create music that goes somewhere within the context of their artistic practices, COUM and Throbbing Gristle were well versed in both a subset of (extreme) art practices and also within the mechanisms of how an art career might be navigated. However, Throbbing Gristle's art pedigree would not get them a free pass into punk, and in the end, they were grateful that this didn't happen. As Ford (1999: 5·18) remarks, they reversed the standard avant-garde practice of bringing popular cultural forms into high art, and brought the extremes of high art into popular culture, although this knowledge and calling upon avant-garde practices would not be of interest to punk at its immediate point of inception.

Even though P-Orridge quickly despatched with his hippie image and went for a punk crop, the band started to dress in a style that permitted, according to Ford (1999: 7·13), a 'superficial fitting in'. They were not going to be assimilated in the 1977 punk miasma. There is an argument, put forward by Cogan (2007), that their hippie roots and associated commitment to do-it-yourself independence, communal living, disciplined ethical regimes and general societal critique aligned them (alongside the band Crass) as a founding instance of anarcho-punk, but this involves juggling time. Anarcho-punk, and its tolerance of what might be bluntly described as hippie sentiments, would not appear for a few years.[6] Instead, Throbbing Gristle developed their own sound and used this superficial fitting in to experiment with and test the limits of the punk form. Their early 1978 performance at the Architectural Association was an insightful example of this intent, and it is to this event that we now turn.

NOTES

1. See: https://www.thewire.co.uk/in-writing/interviews/genesis-breyerp-orridge.1 Accessed 11 July 2022.

2. Online discussion on a private forum, 25 March 2020.

3. P-Orridge (2021: 188) omits Harwood's role, whilst proprietor Steph Raynor (2018: 31) refers to 'two young artists'.

4. The origin of the artwork detourned by Reid is commonly stated to be a Cecil Beaton photograph. This is not the case. It is a 1975 photograph by Peter Grugeon, held in the National Portrait Gallery. The image was reversed by Reid.

5. The cover date for the newspaper is 26 March, the same day as the Throbbing Gristle performance in Brighton. This date is a Saturday, and the weekly music press is printed with the Saturday date but published in the week, giving P-Orridge and the band plenty of time to digest the story and its mode of presentation.

6. The links between Throbbing Gristle, Crass, and anarcho-punk are discussed in Chapter 8.

4. ANTI-GIG

ARCHITECTURAL ASSOCIATION, 3 MARCH 1978

The next two chapters document Throbbing Gristle in the first half of 1978 through two performances that are close in date but considered here for very different reasons. The focus of this chapter is the band's relationship to the space and codes of performance, illustrated through a highly strategic event at London's Architectural Association, whilst the subsequent chapter continues the exploration of place with the band's first excursion north of the capital to the West Yorkshire town of Wakefield. I also split the detailing of the chronology that joins the previous chapter with these two, producing a listing of events and reactions here, and a more detailed development of the band's sound in the next chapter.

INDUSTRIAL PRODUCT

Throbbing Gristle returned from the studio and their other commitments to close out 1977 with three live performances: a September date at the Highbury Roundhouse, a November return to Winchester, and a Christmas return to the Rat Club in a new venue but still offering the same mix of sordid entertainments that fitted the band's desire to be experienced live as part of a larger and unpredictable warped bestiary. Having not infiltrated the commercializing punk scene in the capital, the band drew a meagre crowd for their first performance at the Roundhouse, which had seen a four-month gap between their last live performance at the Rat Club where the mood of the evening was given over to P-Orridge's ranting against the music industry. There is clearly a retooling in this performance, the sound starts out with the industrial blueprint that had been glimpsed in parts or seen in total at select performances such as the Southampton gig and would be seen in the subsequent gig at Winchester. An important attendee amongst the sparse Roundhouse audience was *Sounds* journalist Sandy Robertson, tangentially connected to the band through his boyhood links in Renfrewshire with ATV's Alex Fergusson (who had jammed at Beck Road earlier in the year). Robertson gave Throbbing Gristle their first live review since the Tony Parsons review of *Prostitution* in *NME*. The review was terse and read at times like a pitch for a record deal, veering close to pigeonholing the band in a litany of nearly-likes but taking a final stance of uncategorizable. He concludes with a plug for the next gig in the capital and the release of the debut album *Second Annual Report*.

The album arrived as a self-released product in November 1977 with distribution arranged through the independent set-up Rough Trade which had been so far instrumental in supporting the do-it-yourself and independent offshoots of the punk scene. *Second Annual Report* effectively gathered together mismatched snippets from the live appearances, grafting bits of performance with bits of audience reaction, with only a small section on the first side consisting of new studio material. In contrast, the second side consisted of the studio soundtrack to the band's film *After Cease to Exist*. The only contemporaneous review was in *Sounds* via Sandy Robertson on 26 November 1977, who also ran a feature on the band within a larger feature entitled 'New Musick'. This collection of articles, spread across two issues and announced on the cover with a stunning photograph of Kraftwerk in front of a fogged-out Rheinkniebrücke bridge in Dusseldorf, was written by Robertson, Jon Savage, and Jane Suck after they were asked, and subsequently refused, to write something on where punk and new wave currently were. The articles they produce explored uncharted domains of music that have a new potential receptivity under the gaze of punk: the first collection included breakthrough features on Kraftwerk, Devo, Eno, and the Residents, whilst a follow-up issue covered dub, disco, and Siouxsie and the Banshees. Robertson and Savage were also early fanzine writers producing important experimental cut-up works, the former producing *White Stuff* and the latter *London's Outrage*.

The review and the article were strongly positive towards the band, ironically mutating the Clash's self-bestowed moniker as 'the sound of the Westway' into 'the sound of Tesco (with run-down batteries)' as a potential masthead for Throbbing Gristle (Robertson 1977: n.pag.). More importantly, the two features allowed the band to dictate proceedings and open up a critical front on the new wave scene, which, at the time, had displaced punk in regard to marketability if not creativity. The term new wave subsequently took on divergent and different meanings, as it became synonymous with label-produced bands that churned out a more sanitized and consumer-friendly version of punk through a surplus of sleek sleeves, coloured vinyl, and picture disc releases. In advance of this, *Sounds'* initial claiming of new wave, under the new musick edifice, embraced artists such as Devo and the Residents, and there was also a more nuanced difference at work here that links back to Throbbing Gristle's fundamental ineligibility for inclusion within nascent punk rock. Bands such as Cabaret Voltaire and This Heat would be about to break through, as part of this new wave (musick), and there was a shared background of anti-structure that has its roots in Eno, Can, and Velvet Underground, as well as P-Orridge's links to the outer fringes of the hippie milieu. In this regard of creating a scene of experimental music to deterritorialize the punk landscape and soundscape, a perceived anachronistic hippie

NEW MUSICAL EXPRESS

MAN, MUSCLE & MACHINE

THROBBING GRISTLE
The Second Annual Report Of . . . (Industrial Records)

THIS RECORD will not be repressed.

A neat double edge there. Throbbing Gristle borrowed the money to have 785 pressed, of which 500 have already been sold. That's in six weeks, with no advertising at all, and as far afield as the USA, Sweden, France and Germany. The borrowed money has been paid back and there's just enough to do another record. Which is the idea.

When the record is sold out, it is not going to be repressed. Throbbing Gristle can now do another for the same cost as repressing, so they'll move on. Which is what it's all about.

This is a very harrowing record. Darkly subjective. Not for those who feel that they perhaps can't trust themselves. On some sort of musically historical level (a debased one but an easy hanger), it's approximately John Cage, Maurice Kagel, Lamonte Young, Terry Riley even. Closer to home, it could be the first Faust album, Lou Reed's "Metal Machine Music", Fripp and Eno's "No Pussyfooting", Cluster and Eno's recent collaboration or high period Amon Duul 2.

Electronics and voice loops, echoes, effects and collage. What is this music exactly? I don't know. This is a reaction and response record. I could supply sound reasons why I er, can involve myself in this music, but that would be futile. It's up to you. This is highly personal music; it's (probably) spiritual — and therefore maybe even good for you.

On the sleeve Throbbing Gristle (Chris Carter, Peter Christopherson, Genesis P-Orridge and Cosey Fanni Tutti) proclaim: "In the forthcoming year we hope to increase the number of live demonstrations and the variety of their locations.

"We also hope to continue our film work and to extend into a new area of preparing customized tapes of piped music for shops and factories, and finally to continue releasing records for public consumption."

German composer Karlhein Stockhausen once said: "People in advertising and politics know very well what sounds do to the masses. Oh yes. The Khmer people in Cambodia moved 30 and 40 ton stones with elephants pushing and people pulling on ropes.

"Trumpet blowers who periodically blew very sharp signals had an important function, helping to synchronise thousands of people pulling on ropes in order to move such stones even one inch.

"Sounds can do anything. They can kill. The whole Indian Mantric tradition knows that with sounds you can concentrate on any part of the body and calm it down, excite it, even hurt it in the extreme."

"Second Annual Report Of . . ." is available from all Virgin Records shops, from Rough Trade, Bonaparte Records, Ramone Records and Boy Boutique in London or direct from Industrial Records, 10 Martello Street, London E8. That's at £5 including p&p, 10 dollars for the USA — and you get information, stickers, posters, postcards, etc . . .

Yes, intensity can be fun.

Paul Morley

Figure 4.1: Paul Morley's review of Second Annual Report *from* NME, *11 February 1978.*

connotation was less frowned upon. Punk favoured a structure that allowed energy to flow through both predictability of 'blokes with guitars' and a highly theatrical incompetence of said blokes and guitars. Equally importantly, Robertson's closeness to the band allowed him, and the newspaper *Sounds*, to jump the gun in running the feature and review. It wouldn't be until February 1978, when the fallout of the Sex Pistols implosion filled music newspaper column inches, that both *NME* and *Melody Maker* ran their reviews of *Second Annual Report*. The former article included a photo-conceptualist montage of Robert Smithson 'disrupted landscape' or Bernd and Hilla Becher style 'anonymous sculpture' factory photographs, giving the review the most eye-catching appearance on the page (see

Figure 4.1). It also allowed Paul Morley an opportunity to flex his tick-list of hip references and writing style as he grasped escape routes from an overgrounding punk scene, and also exposed the band to the readership of *NME*, a newspaper who were keen to explore artistic avenues opened up by punk.[1]

Celebrating the release and positive review of the debut album, the band played their Christmas gig at the Rat Club. The PA system was set out on red cloth-topped tables, mimicking a High Street electronics store, and the consumer surrealism was supplemented with the oversized Tesco bag making its first appearance as the ubiquitous supermarket took on a talismanic role for the band with P-Orridge replaying his intro rant of 'Welcome to the Tesco Disco'. Again, there was an uncanny prescience here as in years to come the supermarket chain would be emblematic of the monopoly of brands, logos, and consumer-themed spaces. There was a return switch here to a focus on extreme lyrical themes set against a constant, harsh wall of electronic noise as if to blood the potential audience of newcomers who had read the positive review of the album and accompanying article, and were expectant for some 'new musick'. The set included a one-off rendition of a track christened 'Urge to Kill' which detailed the exploits of serial killer and necrophile Edmund Kemper set to the lyrical structure of the nursery rhyme 'Humpty Dumpty'. The background samples were equally disconcerting, with snatches of disturbing film narratives and bingo caller drudgery reminiscent of the droning sample used by Lindsey Anderson in his short and caustic documentary *O Dreamland* (1953). These challenging themes are critically discussed in the next chapter, but it is worth noting that the power of these themes to mix doubt and fascination drew in upcoming music writer Jon Savage who reviewed the gig for *Sounds* and effectively entered the Throbbing Gristle inner circle. Further insight into the make-up of the crowd is given by an eyewitness: he recalls the crowd being very different to the one expected at a punk gig of the time, a performance arty crowd who were dressed fairly outrageously, but certainly not the standard safety pin/bondage uniform.[2] The support bill reflected this avant-garde strand, consisting of the keyboard player of Thunderclap Newman (who didn't turn up) and Lol Coxhill (who the band may have been familiar with from his performance art connections with Adrian Henri). Standard for the Rat Club, there was also a stripper called Candy and her performing gorilla. In keeping with the artier happening vibe, the promoter attempted to hold an impromptu debate about the whole thing after it had finished. This quickly deteriorated into a shouting match with some of the crowd shouting rubbish, suggesting that they had yet to really attract much of a following. At the same time, it was evident that the band were playing with forms and expectations, and keeping any audience (actual or potential) on their toes. Their next gigs would push this much further.

NO FUN PALACE

Throbbing Gristle's performance at the Architectural Association graduate school on the art and academia cluster of Bedford Square, Bloomsbury took place on Friday 3 March 1978, the second gig of the year following a return to Brighton Polytechnic just a few days earlier, and part of just six live performances by the band through that year. Whilst the period of the last four months of 1977 and the first two months of 1978 had allowed the band to work towards a new sound, the Architectural Association performance is an important event in its own right that offers a convergence of many of the themes that frame the band's operations – space, place, art, the unwritten 'contract' of live performance, mythology, and the continuing of their establishing of a driving industrial and totalizing sound. Sitting on top of this, as a meta-critique, was their tradition of sideswiping expectations.

In his 1985 book, effectively the first critical study devoted solely to punk rock, Laing attempts to mark out the changes (and continuities) of punk as a spectacle, subculture, and mode of entertainment. He opens the study by drawing attention to the prevalence of the prog tradition that immediately prefaced punk, coining the term 'gigantism' (Laing 1985: 3) to describe the live shows where the audience expectation was to hear an exact replication of a lavish studio album. Laing goes on to argue that punk worked to reverse the priority of studio over the event as the locus of creativity (53). Whilst this attempted reversal accounted for the creative development of punk bands, seemingly admitting the audience into having a sense of responsibility and impact, it did not address the codes of performance that had been set down by rock music. Laing realizes he has to push further here but quickly runs onto rocky ground (in both senses of the word). He argues that punk required an 'impossible dream [...] to abolish the distance, and then the difference, between performer and audience, the activity of one and the passivity of the other' (82). He mournfully concludes: 'the central grid of punk performance was inherited from the rock tradition and solidly imbued with macho values' (88). I have already quoted Laing's brief mention of how Throbbing Gristle (along with Alternative TV) attempted to undermine this, however, their performance at the Architectural Association offered the possibility of something greater.

The chance to engage the place of learning for future architects was a typically bizarre opportunity for the band. Throughout their time Throbbing Gristle displayed a manifest and multifaceted architectural imperative through a critically engaged relationship with their built surroundings that informed both their reason for making music and the music itself. As a band, they marked an abrupt end to the optimism that had lingered in utopian strands prevalent in the 1960s counterculture and its relationship to lived space. They modelled society – as a past, present and future – through the allegory of the death factory and apocalyptic wasteland, totally inverting and negating the utopian and egalitarian gestures of Joan Littlewood's London wasteland projects of the Fun Palace and Stratford Fair as documented by Miro (2018). Littlewood's plans and visions fizzled out to end in 1975, the point of inception of Throbbing Gristle, a handover from optimism to pessimism. The death factory model was total, embodying the individual parts of the machine (school, work, living, shopping) and the overall function as a meaning for society. As P-Orridge's inaugural Institute of Contemporary Arts (ICA) speech hinted at, they responded to and weaponized the material and social fabric that surrounded them. Using and abusing the tools of avant-garde art activism gained through a decade of experience they grasped the brutality and futility of the built environment and modern systems of survival to endorse a nihilist accelerationism. Their sound was a product of the industrial and post-industrial environments of the late 1970s; it was simultaneously informed and created by that environment, and it threw that environment back at the audience by creating a soundtrack both from and for the industrial individual. The wider architectural system was implicated.

Jarring architectural invocations emerge on three broad fronts in the work of Throbbing Gristle: first, within their music through a principal trio of lyrical content, compositional sources, and structure; second, in the choice of imagery used to promote the band (the inaugural 'New Musick' article in *Sounds* used a graphic consisting of a photographic-negative image of a destroyed block of flats distorted to resemble a concrete midden heap with a neon Throbbing Gristle logo in the black sky conjuring the demonic finale of the 1967 Hammer horror film *Quatermass and the Pit*) (see Figure 4.2);[3] finally, the band explored a fierce commitment to deconstruct the space of performing rock music as part of a wider strategy against preconceptions of entertainment. The counterculture, and its variant expressions in musical subcultures such as punk, had sought out marginal and autonomous spaces to relay a message, operating as a didactic model with the building as a pulpit, however, Throbbing Gristle went further to find new spaces and deliberately disrupt the assigned function of the building. Retrospectively, it is possible to grasp a sense of this by going back to the very first performance of the band, in the 'pre-historical' period prior to the ICA when they debuted at the Artists in Residence Gallery in London on 6 July 1976. P-Orridge's original notes (Ford 1999: 6·16) from the performance stress that the audience was deliberately positioned in a different room, and he re-emphasized this dissensual tactic and its importance in a more recent interview (P-Orridge 2017: n.pag.):

> The first one was in the basement of an old building in Central London with very thick concrete walls. We set all our gear in one room and then closed the doors before we played, so you could only listen to it through the wall. That was the first

Figure 4.2: Throbbing Gristle artwork from 1978.

> one. It caused a lot of frustration, people were banging on the doors. *Why can't we come in and listen?* We were trying to make it be as if you were trapped in a city of the future and you were just mystified by these noises that were coming through the walls. The building itself was part of the piece.[4]

This specific and significant detail of the structuring of the performance is surprisingly overlooked by Tutti (2017: 189–90) where she documents this first 'appearance', potentially casting doubt on P-Orridge's memory. We also see that, via P-Orridge, the mythological dimension of the event has expanded to include a frantic and violent audience reaction. Importantly, P-Orridge extends an architectural and spatial analogy, stressing the impetus to incorporate the space of the building and a dystopian allegory of being trapped in a future city, further implicating the role of the architect. This debut performance and its subsequent re-telling are indicative of a pattern that informs the Architectural Association event as it unfolds through the evening, with Ford (1999: 8·8) offering his own art parallel to avant-garde performer Tomas Schmit and his *Sixth Evening of a Grand Fluxus Festival*. Schmit proposed a concert hall locked and imagined from the outside, with taped noises of voices and clapping.

SEEING AND/OR HEARING

The performance at the Architectural Association is historically recorded as a particular and dedicated gig by the band, and an advertisement in the weekly coming events column in *Sounds* newspaper had it listed solely under the band's name. Similarly, the intricate flyer for the event depicting a montage of cut-out texts, figures, and structures (in the style of avant-garde architects Alison and Peter Smithson) was produced in-house as part of the band's tight control of information and circulated independently from other flyers produced by the school (see Figures 4.3 and 4.4). However, their appearance was part of a larger carnival that ran through the night and included a small number of other punk musicians and performers. I will return to this in detail later, but first we can examine the stated intention of the band for their performance. In a letter dated two days prior to the performance, P-Orridge ([1978] n.d.: n.pag.) details the proposed mode of appearing:

> TG play this Friday at Architectural Association. Thee idea is we are in a large cube, cage of scaffolding about 8 feet above ground in a yard which is surrounded by brick buildings. Yard floor is painted white, large 7 feet high mirrors lie at angles in yard. Black polythene roof on cage. To hear us play you have to look out of all thee windows of old brick buildings, or lean off flat roofs (they HAVE got railings). We hope to get a video camera inside cage with us, so to see us you have to go back inside buildings which will have monitors all around corridors & rooms but no sound, just image. Its at night, so we'll have halogen lamps with us, so large shadows will be cast across yard onto mirrors, people looking also in mirrors all fragmented and fused. Very Industrial as its outdoors, night, right next to Tottenham Court Road & theatre section/traffic section of central London, at roof level both sound sources will blend.

As Ford (1999: 8.13) surmises:

> the plan was to play within a cage in the central courtyard, from here the audience could listen through the open widows of the AA buildings, but not see them. For the audience away from the windows it was completely the opposite: the band could be seen performing via video cameras and monitors, but they could not be heard. The basic idea was to separate the sound of the group from the visuality of its performance.

This is clearly both an upgrade and re-combination of previous tactics employed around closing down visibility and impairing a sense of spatial awareness and certainty of role as a spectator/consumer. More importantly, it disengages the phenomenological unity

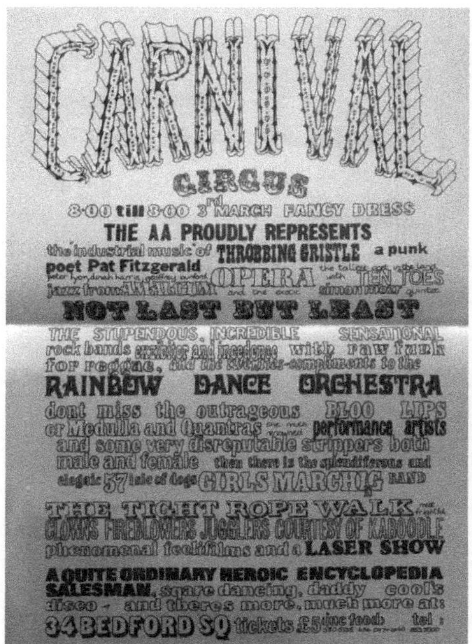

Figure 4.3: Flyer for the Architectural Association Carnival, 3 March 1978. Courtesy of AA archives.

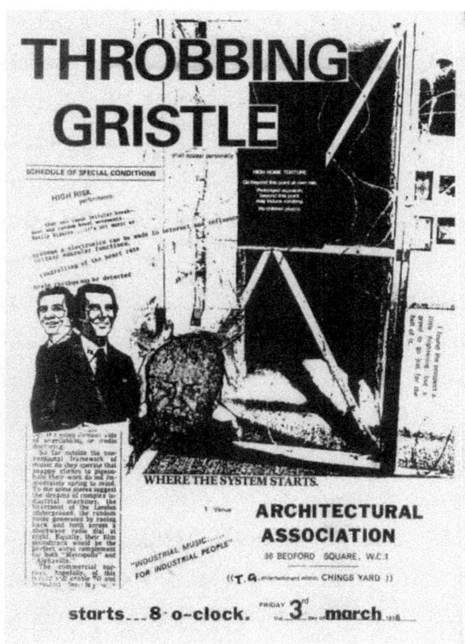

Figure 4.4: Throbbing Gristle poster for the Architectural Association Carnival, 3 March 1978. Courtesy of AA archives.

by singularizing and differentiating the elements of experience associated with how the witnessing of a live music performance is fulfilled – you need to see and hear at the same time. Stated in the parlance of phenomenology, it is an onto-epistemic (a being-of-knowing) fracturing gesture to provoke dissonance.

There are numerous parallels with radical artistic practices of the 1960s and 1970s that attempt to fracture the space of exhibition (performance) and implicate the viewer in their own act of spectating. American artist Michael Asher, as part of the crossover between conceptualism and institutional critique schools, produced numerous untitled works that disrupted the shape and space of the gallery. His work involved the subtraction of interior elements to expose the inner workings of the art business (Claire Copley Gallery, Los Angeles 1974) and the building of interior partitions to create triangles to force and funnel flows and cut off areas of the gallery (Gladys K. Montgomery Arts Center, Claremont, 1970). Rorimer (2001: 253) describes this as working with the 'contextual conditions affecting an exhibition site [...] to reveal facets of reality without creating a previously non-existent material object'. Considering the displaced role of the audience, Voorhies (2017: 38) described how Asher 'deployed the architectural language of the museum and the social behaviours expected therein to disrupt viewer expectations'. The use of video and sound, split apart and played back to the audience, informed much of the early work by Bruce Nauman; his video-feed installations *Going Around the Corner Piece* (1970) and *Live-Taped Video Corridor* (1970) presented spectators with a time-delayed moving image of themselves approaching the work, and an earlier sound-based work entitled *Get Out of My Mind, Get Out of This Room* (1968) replayed disembodied and unnerving sound in the room urging the audience to leave. In a similar vein, Dan Graham produced *Public Space/ Two Audiences* (1976) by installing a mirror system to create a self-enclosed audience feedback spectacle which has direct resonance with Throbbing Gristle's live performances. Graham also employed video and sound feeds with works such as *TV Camera/Monitor Performance* (1970) and *Present Continuous Past(s)* (1974), in which according to Rorimer (2001: 205) he aims to 'conduct images back and forth between the reality of one place and another'. Ira Schneider and Frank Gillette created *Wipe Cycle* (1969) as an early use of video and monitor to implicate the spectator of art. Another example is Paul McCarthy's *Meat Cake #5* at the Newspace Gallery in 1974, in which McCarthy undertook one of his trademark self-annihilating food rituals such that visitors first encountered a room with a monitor showing the performance and then passed through a curtain to the performance itself. Federman (2014: 3) describes the action such that it 'underscored [...] the artifice of the performance site'. An example that pre-dates all of these and ties together the relation between sound, space, and multiplied playback-as-process is Alvin Lucier's seminal performance piece *I Am Sitting in a Room* (1969).[5]

A further link is to performance artist Vito Acconci, whose projects fed directly into COUM and indirectly to Throbbing Gristle. Acconci is an awkward contraflow in the currently fashionable vector of participative art, working with the audience but with an involuntary, confrontational, and discomforting imperative, described by Ward et al. (2002: 26) as 'questioning the normative assumptions about public and private'. *Claim* (1971) consisted of a three-hour performance in a basement stairwell with Acconci posing as a psychotic derelict armed with pipes and a crowbar, warding away anyone who descended to approach, and offering the implicated-voyeuristic audience a live video feed. A year later he pushed things further with *Seedbed* (1972), lurking under a makeshift ramp structure, audible but unseen, grumbling in a threatening voice and making sounds to indicate he was constantly masturbating (using the audience walking over him to feed his thoughts). Though this work has a body-horror parallel to COUM, it also calls upon the artist as present-but-invisible. Later works such as *Air Time* (1973) and *Round Trip (A Space to Fall Back On)* (1975) felt more akin to Throbbing Gristle's sound performances as Acconci created tape recordings of challenging and disconcerting voices replayed into awkward spaces constructed within the gallery.

These artistic parallels and associated snippets of critical theory can fall foul of Stallabrass' accusation raised in the opening chapter, of serving little more purpose than partaking in a competition for spotting high-art lookalikes. What is required is a transversal in the sense of Guattari (1984), in which we transport across the critical theory associated with canonical art (Acconci, etc.) and apply it to the popular (or at least subcultural/countercultural) realm in which Throbbing Gristle operated. This, however, evinces a potential dead end. The critical theory attached to the discussion of the previously mentioned artists seldom moves away from a framing of the work in terms of a proposed artist intent, and in most instances, this intent is narrowly focused on an attack on the operational and actualization structures of high art. This tactic, common to both institutional critique and Asher's situational aesthetics (in which the site of display becomes a focus of itself), acts like a minor wrecking ball in a hall of mirrors. The impossibility of stepping outside of the 'system' to establish some kind of 'truth', whether by the activist artist or by the critical theorist who focuses on the artist. For example, we are never offered information on how Acconci's or Asher's work provokes reactions or imparts motivations or changed circumstances within those who encounter it. Perhaps the audience for this work is inured – an art world cognoscenti – referring back to Parsons' original *NME* review of *Prostitution* that went under the headline 'But mutilation is so passé', in which he delineated the art crowd and punk crowd. So how did the audience at the Architectural Association carnival react, and who was that audience?

RIOT VERSIONS

So far we have a proposal and context for this unusual performance, but how did the evening pan out? Tutti (2017: 251) does not offer much insight into the evening in her autobiography, matching P-Orridge in detailing the manner of appearing in a 'makeshift cage on a scaffolding platform covered by a large tarpaulin [...] creating a funnel of sound with surrounding buildings', followed by a short statement of the reaction as 'utter confusion, frustration and then anger'. For the actual performance on the evening, and its reaction, Ford (1999: 8.13) draws on the longer and more vivid accounts offered by P-Orridge. He quotes a letter to Throbbing Gristle correspondent Almquist:

> Thee instructions we agreed 30 minutes before we played were simply 'first 10 minutes slow ominous, then rhythm section, then 20 odd minutes, see what happens, 3 minutes of tapes, rhythm section, wall of sound'. E mentioned 3 song titles E might use if E thought of words, 'Carol Washes Brown Bread', 'Anthony'

> and 'You Smell Like A Dog'. Simple as that. We played in our cage under a hail of plates, cups, glasses, people fought, smashed windows. E leapt off cage and kicked a guy unconscious because he was about to pull our electricity. People were frustrated in not being allowed to see us except on TV monitor. We had Industrial Security Guards patrolling to provoke paranoia, which they did. There were fights afterwards.

This is an evocative, and a somewhat typical, account of events by P-Orridge, adopting standard tropes that are carried through from his embellished write-ups of COUM performances for American art fanzines, and his earlier reports of Throbbing Gristle gigs and their deliberate inflaming of punk audiences. Certain themes such as an audience member attacking the stage to disconnect electrical power and being ceremoniously knocked out by P-Orridge recall the automatic scripts utilized by subcultural pulp fiction writer Richard Allen and his *Skinhead* series, a figure I have already counterposed to P-Orridge for his Brighton punk rant during his 1976 performance. The reference to extemporizing songs with titles as prompts does not bear fruit for the Architectural Association performance, and it is likely that by denying the audience a sight line to the band also deprived P-Orridge of his impetus to create his lyrics on the hoof. Neither do the suggested track titles of 'Carol Washes Brown Bread' and 'Anthony' materialize, these songs being aired a week before the band's second visit to Brighton and meeting a more positive reaction compared to P-Orridge's tempestuous and impetuous previous appearance in the seaside town. 'Anthony' in particular is an articulate, haunting, and disconcerting work, pairing P-Orridge's flattened vocals with Tutti's rapidly improving guitar work. The track, as usual, had a troublesome subject matter, concerning young boy Anthony Nolan, born in 1971 with a serious bone marrow deficiency and in the news at the time of the performance with a heartfelt appeal for a bone marrow donor. P-Orridge tackled this delicate subject matter without recourse to trivialization or gruesome spectacularizing, giving something as intimate as possible for a Throbbing Gristle song – a palpable respite from other tracks such as 'Hamburger Lady' that were moving around in the Throbbing Gristle setlist. Whilst it does not foretoken the rash of charity singles that defined the 1980s pop scene, it destabilized the band's rigid stance between preaching self-determination and pushing out extremes of distaste.

The recording of the Architectural Association event found its way onto cassette (IRC 12) revealing the tracks as predominantly instrumental, without P-Orridge's proposed compositions.[6] Whilst the content of these instrumental marathons is by now defined structurally as Tesco Disco, or, in the words of Reynolds (2005: 231), the sound of 'rhythms based on conveyor belts', there is also an intent from P-Orridge to offer 'muzak for the traffic'. This strangely worded phrase, quoted in Ford (1999: 8·13), can be read as deliberately not music from (or of) the traffic, suggesting that the audience become (or devolve to) traffic. This reinforces and potentially transcends the aforementioned ideas of Michael Asher and his aim, according to Voorhies (2017: 39), for a 'continuity between an outside reality and its interior'.

P-Orridge is interviewed in 2017 and uses the gig as a reference point for both the innovative deconstructing of performance space and the general violence that ensued with a typical Throbbing Gristle performance. Here the consequences are embellished further to include toilets being ripped out and thrown down, and the fights are upgraded to full riot status:

> We also played at the Architectural Association where they had a courtyard between these four buildings, so we built a scaffolding cube with a platform and we put all of our PA speakers on the ground around it facing straight up. We go inside the cube, which we'd covered in tarp, and we had little cameras in there. Throughout the Architectural Association were these TV screens that we found that we could plug in to. So if you wanted to see us play, you had to be in the building, but then you couldn't hear anything. If you wanted to hear us play, you had to be on the roof and look down, and all you saw was a tarp wall and speakers. There was a riot. They threw toilets down at us. Smashed toilets and hurled them down![7]
>
> (P-Orridge 2017: n.pag.)

ANOTHER ARCHIVE

Examining the archival records from the school offers a different picture, with certain facets of the past revealed (and confirmed) through photographs and formal documentation, and further manifestations of what happened thrown into light. As stated above, the performance by Throbbing Gristle was part of a wider carnival of events, and a reinstated tradition of the Architectural Association that had been on hiatus since 1970. In the 1960s, the school hosted performances by seminal bands such as Pink Floyd, and the experimental music club UFO, launched by London underground scenester John 'Hoppy' Hopkins, functioned nearby on Tottenham Court Road in the basement of an old cinema.[8] The reinstatement of the carnival was proposed by a pair of second-year students, who threw themselves into organizing to such an extent that they failed the year. One of the students assembled a written documentation of the carnival in the hope to salvage his educational passage through the school by impressing his tutor David Greene, a member of the radical architectural collective Archigram. The project report is compiled and experienced as a partly fictional endeavour and encounter, entitled 'In Decision' and utilizing the structure of dice-throw navigation made popular with Luke Rhinehart's 1971 novel *The Dice Man*. The student added a further absurdist twist by making the accompanying dice spherical. The book itself is thus non-linear, though archival scraps can be re-arranged into a chronological sequence to establish key details of the planning for the event (letters and contracts), its happening in real time (photographs), and its aftermath (formal letters and reports).

Letters and meeting reports suggest that arrangements for re-establishing a carnival were underway from early December 1977, leaving a two-month window to put all the parts into place. This was some achievement as the included performers ran to a significant number and included a complex laser show that projected out over Bedford Square, marching bands, musicians, strippers (male and female), the Bloo Lips gay theatre company, fire-eaters, and various illusionists and magicians. A ten-foot Coca-Cola can was hoisted in with a crane, recorded as being donated by Friends of the Earth and previously used as part of a wider campaign against waste and consumerism (see Figure 4.5). According to Beckett (2010: 38), Friends of the Earth was part of a wider shift in the 1970s towards environmentalist activism and awareness, forming in 1971 as a British wing of the American group. The campaign group was allowed a free stall in the carnival to collect signatures and disseminate information about their ongoing protest against the Windscale nuclear power station in Cumbria. Friends of the Earth, in both name and deed, could be construed as anathema to P-Orridge. Their overt environmental activism contrasted with his fascination for the contemporary manifestations of the death factory and his fashion for wearing a 'Nuclear War Now' T-shirt (as depicted in Duboys 2007: 167) which deconstructed the popular 'Nuclear Power? – No thanks' symbol of the 1970s and 1980s.

There was a self-destructive edge to some of the carnival planning, with certain attractions sailing close to the wind in terms of being in proper taste or providing something that would entertain. A page of dialogue concerns the potential inclusion of an elephant, degenerating into a surreal script that rivals the 'August Bank Holiday' script sample that the band used on the night (and for other performances in 1978):

> Could we afford £350 or would a camel do for £180, alligator £70? McPherson's electronic elephant couldn't be contacted. Elephant hired, BD paid £20 for the photoshoot. Three primary schools supplied children, Capital Radio advertised. Skateboarders and equipment free, but skateboarding chimp had cold.

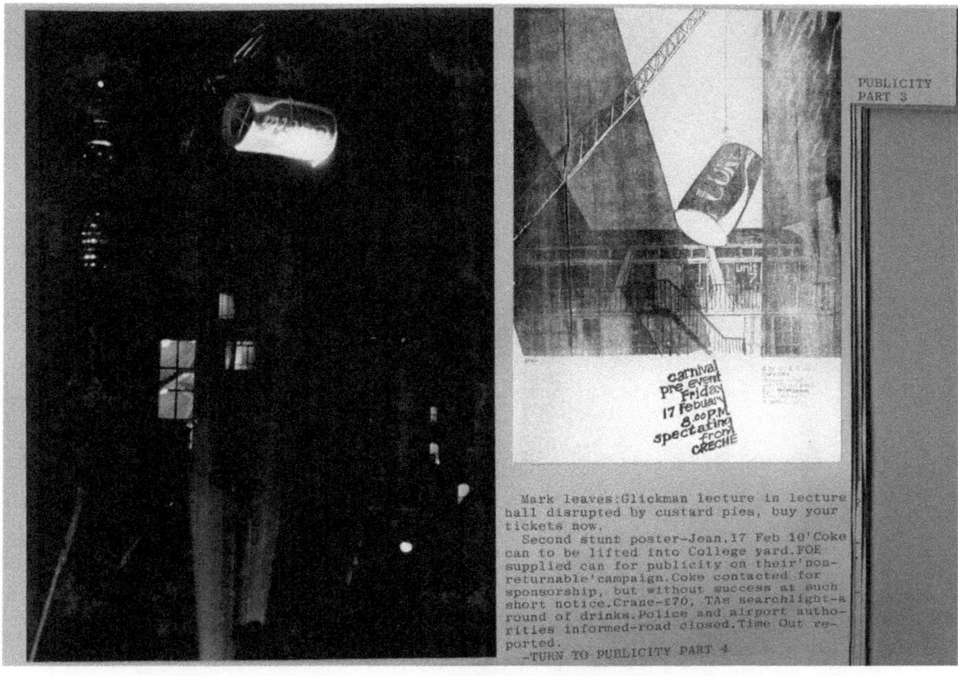

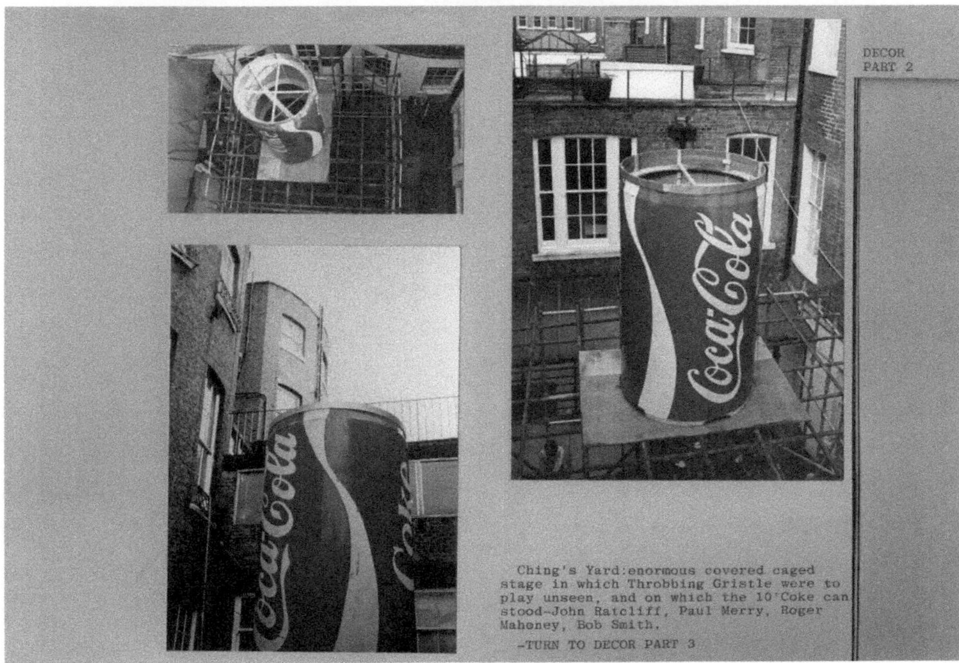

Figure 4.5: Stage setting for the Architectural Association Carnival, 3 March 1978, student workbook. Courtesy of AA archives.

Figure 4.6: Party scenes from the Architectural Association Carnival, 3 March 1978, student workbook. Courtesy of AA archives.

Throbbing Gristle potentially come into this equation of self-destruction and parody, noted as being 'discovered in answer to an enquiry for the worst band'. Worst band or otherwise, it appeared that they ask for a fee of £300 which was substantially higher than the other acts, though negotiated down to £200. We are not told anything about their demands to perform via live-feed monitors (and whether this perhaps justifies the high fee request), but the constructed cage is evident in photographs showing the Coca-Cola can move into position. Aside from this, we are shown a schedule of performers with the band slotted in to perform before midnight and a solitary photograph of two Death Factory personnel mingling in a crowd scene (see Figures 4.6 and 4.7). They certainly do not look like the intimidating figures that P-Orridge suggested as circling the premises during the performance and deliberately unsettling the crowd. A clipping from the journal *Building Design* had a brief report on the revived carnival, remarking that it was closed down at 03:30 rather than continuing to the scheduled 08:00 finish, and that security staff (real ones from Securicor) had to clear the premises of people. The main source of escalating trouble is stated as being the frantic dispersal of a vast array of theatrical custard pies. An internal report from the facilities manager of the school documents a list of damages and

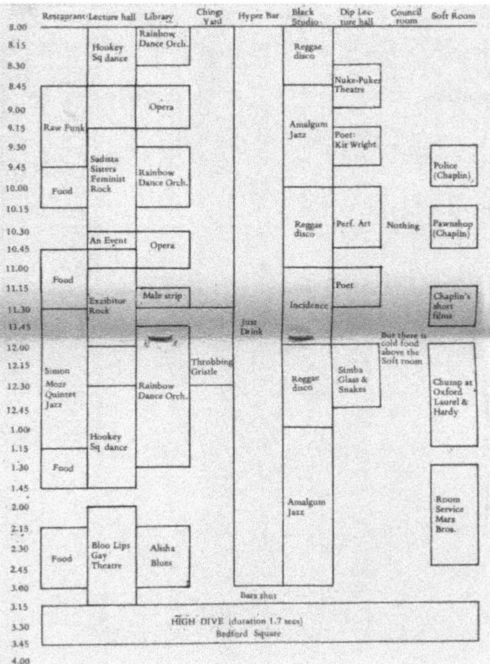

Figure 4.7: Proposed order of events for the Architectural Association Carnival, 3 March 1978, student workbook. Courtesy of AA archives.

estimated costs, though there is no evidence of the damage recalled by P-Orridge such as ripped-out toilets (and the potential damage they would have caused after being hurled off the roof). Seldomly extending beyond buoyant student pranks, damages include three fire extinguishers let off, diploma drawing destroyed by fire, a timber handrail dislodged, glass panes in Ching's Yard broken (this is the area where Throbbing Gristle performed), the Info Centre coin box was vandalized (there is an additional note that P-Orridge is to be notified in writing about this), cigarette machine broken, and finally the words 'the chandelier' followed by two exclamation marks and a note saying 'I will attend to this'. Aside from the coin box, there are no specific references to damages attributed to the band or by an audience of violent Throbbing Gristle fans or indeed general carnival attendees suddenly brought into a state of rage by the band. The photographs show the extent of foam custard pies, and a note exists to say that specialist cleaning will be required on walls and carpets (see Figure 4.8).

Whilst this list of damages might not be the only list, it suggests that the damage claimed by P-Orridge is fanciful. Furthermore, there are no clippings or reports to suggest acts of violence or bodily injury, and the physical separation between the band and the

Figure 4.8: Damage aftermath from the Architectural Association Carnival, 3 March 1978, student workbook. Courtesy of AA archives.

audience due to their covered location in a closed-off courtyard would imply that an audience member attacking the stage and being knocked unconscious was improbable. A further source of archival evidence, the live tape of the performance, reveals no audio evidence of breakdown or moments when invading crowd members are knocked unconscious, and all we detect are the usual interjections associated with many of the performances by the band: the isolated cries of 'Gerroff' at 7:24 minutes and 'Rubbish' at 48 minutes as the set nears its conclusion in the midst of somewhat noodling section of music where the band sounded as if they are bored. The suggestion of 'fights afterwards' could be attributed to little more than the custard pie fights which occurred well after Throbbing Gristle had completed their one-hour set.

OTHER PASTS AND PLACES

This performance at the Architectural Association was both a fusing of various discrete strategies employed by the band in their brief history prior to 1978 and a confluence of numerous strategies to enact and invoke a critical dialogue with architecture. The siting of the performance in an inaccessible courtyard was hindered further by adding a cloak of invisibility for those assembled to look down on the courtyard, engaging the built space of the educational institution in seeking out an unorthodox crevice for transmission. In this regard of establishing a critical metric, Throbbing Gristle immediately surpassed Pink Floyd's 1966 performance at the same venue by choosing a space out of bounds and so out of the anticipated. A performance, particularly in the tradition of rock and popular music (punk included), necessitates a contractual engagement between the audience and the performer as a kind of 'proof of the being there' of the event and so places further conditions on the arrangement of space. Throbbing Gristle immediately worked against this by severing the phenomenological elements that constitute what we now call in the neoliberalist consumer society 'fulfilment'. Sight and sound were split into separate channels, so the audience was potentially frustrated and untrusting with what it was witnessing. This splitting was achieved by working further with the spatial codes of the building, introducing television monitors that screened a live feed from elsewhere in the building. As a practice of heterotopia, this then evoked other spaces with specific functions, such as the closed-circuit environment of prisons and security facilities. There is a further iteration of heterotopia via the band opening with the lengthy track 'E-Coli', which sampled multiple dialogues from scientific and medical research sources and placed the listener in the sinister environment of a callous experimental regime. The source for dialogue that typically characterizes a performance was often the interaction between P-Orridge and the audience, however in achieving a pure separation from the audience this conduit for extemporizing a confrontational narrative was stymied, and we were given a performance predominantly consisting of the band's explorations into noise and concrete sound sources.

In retrospect, the targeted use of the Architectural Association comes across as a missed opportunity. Their appearance was by invite and part of a larger carnival, and there is no indication that the band made particular efforts to engage or critique the architectural function of the whole space in terms of it being a seat of learning connected to a custodial role of the built environment. The Architectural Association often embodies the popular opinion of such avant-garde centres of design, described by Beckett (2016: x) as a place 'where brilliant students and professors come up with multi-coloured visions of the British future, almost none of which were ever built', though Throbbing Gristle's critical engagement with architecture was demonstrably more fierce. They utilized the space within the building in an attempt to form a disruption-in-itself but seemingly failed to critique the building-for-itself. Similarly, by creating the disjuncture between the audience and performers the band forfeit the opportunity to provoke a direct dialogue with members of the audience who may be architects of death-factories-to-come, so to speak. A potential critical impetus is hinted at on the poster for the event, with collaged elements typical to their early flyers and artwork, a dissected and disconnected cybernetics. Prominent are the capitalized words 'WHERE THE SYSTEM STARTS' – though the ultimate intent of this is left ambiguous. The 'where' could be an accusation of the institution as being the birthplace of a blueprint, or it could refer to the time and space of the band performing there, heralding the start of a different 'system'. Meanwhile, the carnival as a wider assemblage of events facilitates a critical drama between the organizers of the event as students in the school, other student members who are reluctant to proceed with the planned carnival, their tutors within the school, and a wider body of custodians who author the inventories of damage. It is difficult to ascertain whether a power struggle is underway here, and it appears to end on a sour note with the threat of a failed year for the students.

Throbbing Gristle enter and leave the premises, unconcerned as to the student–tutor tensions. We do not know whether the contents of the cash box have repercussions with P-Orridge, but we do know that the band's mythology machine goes into overdrive as its own autonomous industrial process. The event was followed by the accelerating long tail of mythology that is common to other Throbbing Gristle (and indeed punk) events. A rationale for this would be to see the stories of rioting and destruction of the immediate environment provoked by the band as an act of prolepsis or apocrypha, in which P-Orridge imagines an instinctive response of destruction provoked by his words and sound. There were instances of destruction at many previous Throbbing Gristle events, some of this a factor of a generalized punk tendency and some of this aggravated further by the band – and these were gleefully recorded and added on to live recording outputs or recycled at future events. There was also more totalizing destruction played out at the Architectural Association, but this occurred long after Throbbing Gristle had performed and was influenced more by a carnivalesque (Bakhtinian inversion of order and disregard of conduct) surge brought on by the revelation of theatrical custard pies. This performance was important and insightful, but perhaps not in the way that everyone expects it to be.

NOTES

1. Morley's critical relationship to the band, which essentially defined *NME*'s relationship to the band, quickly soured. He resurrected this after the band split up (see Chapters 7 and 8 for more detailed discussion on Morley).

2. E-mail communication with Mick Fish, July 2019.

3. There is also the photo-combine of nuclear power stations used in the aforementioned *NME* album review.

4. The original notes are reproduced in Ford (1999: 6·16), the later reminisce comes from Genesis Breyer P-Orridge (2017: n.pag.) in conversation with T. Cole Rachel.

5. Lucier's work has wider reverberations for Throbbing Gristle's later practices of recording on top of recordings and questioning the certainty or necessity of presence.

6. They are listed as: E.Coli (11-29), Dead Ed (16-03), Valley of the Shadow of Death (22-03), August Bank Holiday (3-27), and Wall of Sound (7-32).

7. The riot and smashed toilets are referred to in Wolfson (2002).

8. Pink Floyd played the 'Prohibition carnival' in December 1966, a widely documented occurrence due to the cult status of the band. Ample photographs and testimony show they used the Old Lecture Hall, covering the space with plastic sheeting and creating their usual perceptual overload show with lighting. See http://collectionsblog.aaschool.ac.uk/aa-archives-pink-floyd-yardbirds-fleetwood-mac-and-allen-ginsberg/. Accessed 3 August 2020.

5. IN THE MACHINE

WAKEFIELD COLLEGE, 1 JULY 1978

Throbbing Gristle are documented as playing Wakefield Industrial Training College on Saturday 1 July 1978. The uncannily apposite name of an Industrial Training College, as if it is some kind of academy for Throbbing Gristle initiates undergoing practical sessions in extreme noise and written papers on media control techniques, is a bit of a misnomer as the college was not known by that name in the city, instead being referred to as the Technical College (or 'tech'). Recently celebrating its sesquicentennial anniversary, the foundations for the College were laid in 1868 with the establishment of The Industrial and Fine Art Institution that was set up, thanks in part to the profits from the Wakefield Industrial and Fine Art Exhibition three years earlier. This new institution aimed to benefit the young people of Wakefield by providing a practical education giving them skills necessary to survive nineteenth-century industrial life.[1] In some respects, with Throbbing Gristle performing here in this subcultural backwater in 1978, there is little change regarding exposure to industrial life, even if the tactics and understanding of industrial survival may be somewhat different across the intervening 110 years.

HAUNTED

The Wakefield performance was punctuated from the Architectural Association event by a single gig at Goldsmiths College in London, and the demarcation of these sparse performances throughout 1978 reflects the carefully considered emergence and organic growth of the band's sound towards an industrial blueprint that was everything but organic in its audible and emotive content. The band's crafty revival of the industrial name attached to this college, clever atavistic opportunism, allowed the thought of the performance to persist across time as the Wakefield gig was immortalized on cassette IRC14. However, aside from this, there survives little documentation of the event: no retained ephemera such as flyers or tickets, no announcements in either the local or national music press, no reviews in music newspapers or local newspapers, and no recollections in later studies of the band.

As a Throbbing Gristle statistic, this gig has the importance of being the band's first venture north of London, even though Tutti and P-Orridge under the COUM banner had knowledge and experience of the region due to their base being in Hull for a number of years. In this chapter, I undertake several tasks: to complete a pairing with the previous chapter in analyzing the band's dynamic through 1978, to focus more precisely on the development of the sound in terms of its construction and reception, and to open up the first of three chapters that explore Throbbing Gristle's reception outside of the fashionable base of London which had stolen a march with punk and its arty incarnations. The chapter exemplifies the role of networking and communication outside of the normal channels (record labels, managers, agents, the music press), and the efforts of dedicated individuals to engage with the band. At the same time, there are messy threads and loose ends that float in the wind, with the overlapping presence of the Yorkshire Ripper murders and an aggravated regime of general violence (hooliganism, extreme right politics) pervading the region. These threads were reopened as wounds by the author David Peace, as he directly invoked the band in his novel *Nineteen Eighty* (2001), the penultimate part of his *Red-Riding Quartet*. The novels, deeply disturbing and structured in a dizzying and angry fashion, intensified the clawing murk of his subject matter of Yorkshire Ripper Peter Sutcliffe embroiled in a quasi-fictionalized wider network of abuse, corruption, brutality, and pornography. If Throbbing Gristle, animated and electrified by mass murderers, sadistic sexual predators and their mode of coverage in the press, elected – for whatever reason – to keep this theme off their agenda when posited in the heart of Ripper Territory at the time of greatest fear, then Peace brought the things all back into the mix.

In the four-month period between the Architectural Association and the Wakefield gigs, the band enjoyed major features in the music press and the release of the single 'United'/'Zyklon B-Zombie' to universally favourable reviews, allowing them to gain wider recognition or a sense of intrigue throughout the United Kingdom. Whilst the band had developed a core of dedicated followers from their challenging and threatening London performances, many of whom would make this first trek up the M1 (beyond even Wolverhampton), the prominent and positive press attracted music fans native to towns and cities outside of London. In general, provincial towns would be picking up on punk a year or so after its explosion in London, listening to a glut of more chart-destined tracks by bands such as Buzzcocks, Generation X, and Sham 69, whilst at the same time having local punk bands forming amidst new scenes in satellite towns and cities. This complex, multiple, and overlayering of the temporal dynamic of punk is further unpicked in the next chapter, whereas the situation of Throbbing Gristle transpiring to play in Wakefield was down to precise local factors and figures slightly ahead of any punk time-lag scene that was evident in the city.

WEIGHING IN

The Wakefield gig was bookended by two major features in the British national music press. The month before the gig Jon Savage (1978) gave the band coverage in *Sounds*, and a couple of weeks after the gig Bob Edmands (1978) gave them a substantial feature in the *NME*. In contrast to the 'New Musick' umbrella feature in *Sounds* at the end of 1977, these were dedicated features. Obviously, for the Wakefield public, only the *Sounds* feature would contribute as an incentive to see the band, though Savage was at the time one of the rising stars of the new journalism whose recommendations would widely reverberate amongst the clamour to be part of an underground or cutting-edge cognoscenti. The layout for Savage's article straddled two pages, and embodied the style of the band in mixing between communiqué and corporate report, and, as with all of these early features, the band appeared to call the shots (or at least inveigle the journalist) in terms of both the content and form of the article. The article used the ambivalent photograph of the garages and brutally lit housing projects from the picture sleeve of 'United', the image sharing a dark ambivalence with much of the cover artwork for the handful of Throbbing Gristle singles (see Figure 5.1). Sargeant (2015: n.pag.) sees a parallel with the work of dystopian sci-fi author J. G. Ballard:

> These images, ambiguous close-ups of body parts, machinery, unpopulated suburban (or at least appearing suburban) locations, speak to a dislocated and de-contextualised everyday. Like the unconscious everyday that leaked into Ballard's car crashes and adverts, there is something uncanny at play [...] Meanwhile behind the closed folding doors of the barren garages a hundred guilty secrets lurk waiting to be uncovered. Like J G Ballard's crashed cars and oblique re-imagined advertising imagery, there is something more at stake. The heterogeneous comes into play – those elements that exceed closure dance through the margins of these images, and the viewer is compelled to look at and attempt to engage with these works.

These visual schemata no doubt drew upon Christopherson's immense experience at the cutting edge of photography and design. The work juxtaposed images from real death factories closely cropped to invite a less obvious and so jolting reading, with everyday images of society as it starts to resemble a contemporary death factory. The de-peopled nature of the photograph, combined with a scattering of litter and the harsh sunlight that picked out narrow slithers of unappetizing brickwork, fixes your attention and evades a comforting solution to the search for both contemplative reassurance ('I'm ok with this image') and indexical resolution ('I fully understand this image').

Figure 5.1: Throbbing Gristle 'United' sleeve, Industrial Records, 1978.

The starkness of the whole assemblage of the newspaper article was matched by Savage's chiselled prose, as he opened with a definition of background muzak, extending it from unchallenged ambient sounds to the flow of news and information. He then relayed the experience of encountering and listening to Throbbing Gristle, his language and structure of prose simultaneously acting out his experience of listening, giving the impression he is listening as he writes ... breaking down, giving up, transforming. This performative textual method also permeated into the *NME* with new writers such as Paul Morley. Savage comes out the other side affected and potentially inert: 'Things are not the same afterwards. Not easy to describe or to evaluate' (Savage 1978: 24). Pulling himself together, he then offered the idea of control, suggesting that Throbbing Gristle – through their autodidactic media learning and experiences – are 'granted insights into and through the reality control'. However, this is not a shining light for the listener with the band using these insights to help us leave something behind and find something new, instead it means they are able to push the listener deeper into the mess, in a controlled but arguably sadistic experiment. A balanced conversation ensued with Savage's perspicuity pitted against P-Orridge's highly informed but incendiary manner; a discussion of making records as independently as possible, the nature of using and upscaling society's own language of unquestioned wrongs and whether that achieves a liberatory or ensnaring effect, the talk of a film project with Fred and Judy Vermorel. Seemingly and befittingly savaged, the journalist closed off with his language once again breaking down, sentences reducing to segments, then to words, pre-empting the communiqué from the 1979 film *Apocalypse Now* as the narrator travels further into the abyss. He indicates his attendance at recent performances, their unpredictability, and sense of violence, a sense of post-punk post-traumatic stress disorder (including the Architectural Association gig covered in the previous chapter). The article is signed off: JON 'TESCO' SAVAGE, the author seemingly inculcated and subsumed into the system.

As well as the *Sounds* article prior to the Wakefield date, there was also a four-page spread in the glossy monthly magazine *ZigZag*. This was a longstanding magazine catering to emergent subcultures and countercultures from the late 1960s onwards, and it had a reach into newsagents across the United Kingdom whilst also retaining a subcultural cachet. The magazine was not afraid to undergo editorial changes when it felt a new music scene emerged, and in 1977 Kris Needs took over as the dedicated editor as the magazine embraced the punk and new wave scenes. Needs produced the article on Throbbing Gristle, opened with the striking image of the negatively inverted print of the destroyed building used the previous year in the first *Sounds* 'New Musick' feature, and went on to undertake a detailed interview with the band. The pitch was once again strong, verging on totalitarian propaganda: 'You do not forget any encounter with Throbbing Gristle. They make sure of that' (Needs 1978: 10). The interview, as with *Sounds*, took place at their Hackney headquarters with all present except Christopherson. The first two pages undertake a potted history from the early days of art activism, the *Prostitution* controversy, the recent gig at the Rat Club and the imminent gig at the Architectural Association, and an outlining of the band's approach to performing live and their understanding, so far, of the audience demographics and expectations: 'infiltrating, insinuating into the normality of rock' (10). Needs gives a visceral account of the standout 'tour-de-shit-yourself' track of the first album, 'Slug Bait': 'The backing sounds like a tube train crashing in slow motion accompanied by the Phantom of the Opera on synthesiser' (11). The live experience is re-emphasized, with a sly dig at Jon Savage who is accused of making a bolt for the door at a recent gig, and a finale suggesting that amongst the more unalluring instances of body trauma and freaking out is the breaking out of instant sex. This isn't included as a contribution to a Reichian discussion of the dialectics of the libido, but stated in the somewhat unreconstructed language of the time: 'During another gig two blokes were spotted weighing in with a bird in front of the stage' (11). As an added bonus, P-Orridge (with Alex Fergusson) also reviewed the singles for the magazine. What do we learn? Very little. P-Orridge excels in the pop sarcasm skills (extolled a year later by John Lydon on *Jukebox Jury*) with his crafted cynicism underlined by substantial knowledge.

FANTASY TERRACES

These lengthy articles were also buttressed by a quartet of strong reviews of the single in the music newspapers during May 1978, including the awarding of single of the week for *NME*. The single is typically schizophrenic on several levels, from the crossover between sinister and ubiquitous on-the-sleeve images to the twinning of two divergent tracks. 'United' offers up a superior synth-pop moment, predating the nascent (and now heavily bestowed) electronic post-punk tracks later in 1978 by the likes of the Normal and the Human League.[2] It gathers elements of the industrial force that the band had assembled, building from a muted and slightly off-centred 4/4 beat and hisses of compressed air escaping, to sequence in squalls of synth bursts (said to be equivalent to the sound of a Coke bottle having its lid flipped off) and P-Orridge's deadpan vocal. Aspects of 'United' can be heard in later tracks such as Fad Gadget's 1980 release 'Ricky's Hand', which intersperses the Throbbing Gristle air-hiss sample with drilling noises, formulating the 'cold-wave' genre, a dystopian variant of the more saccharine synth-pop ubiquity. As Savage (1978) eulogizes in his review for *Sounds*: 'near perfect synthetic mantra to dance at dawn to or to chant on the terraces'. The notion of the football terrace was a mischievous ruse for Throbbing Gristle, mocking punk's own attempts to incorporate itself into terrace culture.[3] The Clash utilized football fan vernacular in both the 1977 single 'Remote Control' with a midway interjection of a staccato guitar adoption of the dun-dun-dundundun' non-linguistic chant, and then as a fade-out vocal for their February 1978 hit 'Clash City Rockers'. Punk's attempt to merge with working-class terrace culture was a flight of fancy, with football fans tending to adopt and bastardize theme tunes, advertisement jingles, and a sparse number of pop songs.

Throbbing Gristle's 'United' predates a more famous punk united, with the Sham 69 single 'If the Kids Are United' about to be released to an instant chart success, the week after Throbbing Gristle appeared in Wakefield. Sham 69 were an exemplar punk band for 1978, personifying its commercial crossover. The band had managed a debut *Top of the Pops* appearance in May for their single 'Angels with Dirty Faces', a switching point when the programme would start to feature numerous punk and new wave acts rather than the occasional act as a kind of freak inclusion.[4] Sham 69 also typified the strand of punk that pleaded for identification with a working-class grounding, prefacing their mainstream television appearance with lead singer Jimmy Pursey looking into the camera to announce 'Look 'oose on *Top of the Pops* then'. Laing (1985: 71–72) discusses this

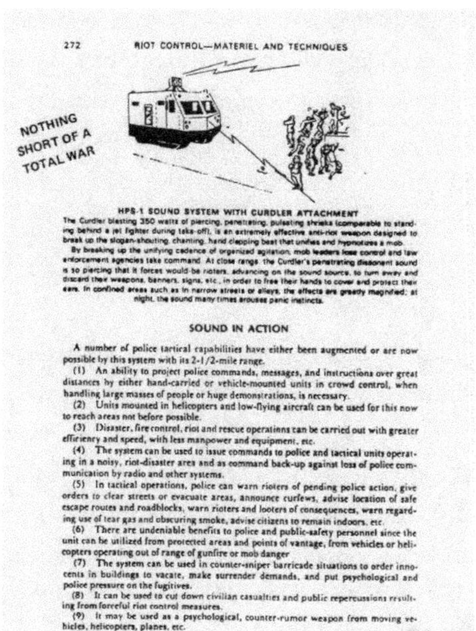

272 RIOT CONTROL—MATERIEL AND TECHNIQUES

NOTHING SHORT OF A TOTAL WAR

HPS-1 SOUND SYSTEM WITH CURDLER ATTACHMENT

The Curdler blasting 350 watts of piercing, penetrating, pulsating shrieks (comparable to standing behind a jet fighter during take-off), is an extremely effective anti-riot weapon designed to break up the slogan-shouting, chanting, hand clapping beat that unifies and hypnotizes a mob.

By breaking up the unifying cadence of organized agitation, mob leaders lose control and law enforcement agencies take command. At close range, the Curdler's penetrating dissonant sound is so piercing that it forces would-be rioters, advancing on the sound source, to turn away and discard their weapons, banners, signs, etc., in order to free their hands to cover and protect their ears. In confined areas such as in narrow streets or alleys, the effects are greatly magnified; at night, the sound many times arouses panic instincts.

SOUND IN ACTION

A number of police tactical capabilities have either been augmented or are now possible by this system with its 2-1/2-mile range.

(1) An ability to project police commands, messages, and instructions over great distances by either hand-carried or vehicle-mounted units in crowd control, when handling large masses of people or huge demonstrations, is necessary.

(2) Units mounted in helicopters and low-flying aircraft can be used for this now to reach areas not before possible.

(3) Disaster, fire control, riot and rescue operations can be carried out with greater efficiency and speed, with less manpower and equipment, etc.

(4) The system can be used to issue commands to police and tactical units operating in a noisy, riot-disaster area and as command back-up against loss of police communication by radio and other systems.

(5) In tactical operations, police can warn rioters of pending police action, give orders to clear streets or evacuate areas, announce curfews, advise location of safe escape routes and roadblocks, warn rioters and looters of consequences, warn regarding use of tear gas and obscuring smoke, advise citizens to remain indoors, etc.

(6) There are undeniable benefits to police and public-safety personnel since the unit can be utilized from protected areas and points of vantage, from vehicles or helicopters operating out of range of gunfire or mob danger

(7) The system can be used in counter-sniper barricade situations to order innocents in buildings to vacate, make surrender demands, and put psychological and police pressure on the fugitives.

(8) It can be used to cut down civilian casualties and public repercussions resulting from forceful riot control measures.

(9) It may be used as a psychological, counter-rumor weapon from moving vehicles, helicopters, planes, etc.

Figure 5.2: Pages from Industrial News *#1, 1978.*

track as an archetype of punk's desire to express and be part of an 'inner city stratum of the working class', a punk narrative that is inclusive and movement-oriented rather than negative and individualistic (as extolled by the Sex Pistols). Whereas Sham 69, with their 'If the Kids Are United' single, reach earnestly for a bit of the 'real life' of the football fan, Throbbing Gristle offer a brief chanted section of 'love is the law' in the middle of the record, imagining the football crowd as an insurgent Crowleyesque body. At other points, the song refers to the band becoming a blended whole, P-Orridge basing the lyric on the two mail artists Rhoda Mappo and Billy Haddock who took their togetherness into life and art, and according to P-Orridge in Ford (1999: 8·17) further imagined themselves in love as P-Orridge and Tutti. The flipside, 'Zyklon B-Zombie', is anything but sweet and in the orbit of love or communality, instead merging a lyric about suffering extermination by gas (a Derrida-style impossible narration from beyond the apocalyptic event) and taking the projected knuckle-headed-ness of punk to its illogical extreme.

Finally, to complement this increased activity of dissemination and exposure, the band produced the first issue of *Industrial News* in June 1978, a timely release as they made their way to Wakefield (see Figure 5.2). The newsletter took the form of the xeroxed fanzine culture of the time and included lyrics to existing tracks with fitting cut-out images (so you can sing along to 'Slug Bait' with some pictures of a developing foetus), copied articles from sonic research into crowd control and subliminal manipulation, advertisements for products, and short biographies. In addition, the band made a plea for fans to send in their everyday sounds via recorded tapes, illustrating the point made by Reed (2013: 114) in his description of how the cassette medium acts as a way to facilitate an enacting and sharing of 'curious intimacies and budding ambitions to cross boundaries [...] to transport environments'.

NETWORKS

These elements of an interest stimulated in the music press and the release of the single could well contribute to the realization of the Wakefield gig in a standard 'band makes record, gets publicity, seeks gigs' narrative. However, Throbbing Gristle did not work like this, and there was an underpinning at work in this curious event in a northern city that previously barely registered on the punk (or avant-garde) radar. As with the previous gig at the Architectural Association, and also the Derby event studied in the chapter that follows, there was an overriding narrative that brought things to fruition, with an individual (or small group) who had a dedication to the band and their project, and a desire to inflict Throbbing Gristle on their town, city, or environment (in the case of the Architectural Association). Inspiration leads to contact, and then initiative and imperative bring the event to a realization. Whereas the coming-to-be of the Architectural Association performance was driven by a parallel dynamic from the curricular (a student project) to the extracurricular (an end-of-year party), the Wakefield performance was rooted within the network of journalism and the music press. In both cases, the elements and bi-directional push-and-pull forces justify an Actor-Network Theory case study with the role of journalism at the centre of the Wakefield event: the treasured prize of a published article as the principle object with a rising power of agency, the affordances that being a successful journalist offer to a fan of music, the form, status and scope of publishing in the punk and post-punk period, the afterlife of a prominent feature in a circulated publication, and the linkages between unknown bands in remote locations and the writing of letters.[5] The key actor was Wakefield school-leaver Chris Westwood who, in 1978, was looking to gain a foothold in journalism and explore some of the more unorthodox music being developed down the road from Wakefield in Sheffield. It was a motivation powered by the love of music:

> I must have been just finishing – or had just finished – high school, though I'd been freelancing for *Record Mirror* and *ZigZag* (Kris Needs era) since around April that year. I wasn't aware of much of a scene in Wakefield at the time; maybe great things were passing me by, but Strangeways, a guitar-based pop band, were

> the only ones I knew, so I'd started looking slightly further afield to Leeds and Sheffield for new music to cover: Gang of Four in Leeds, and 2.3, the Human League, Cabaret Voltaire, Vice Versa and Clock DVA in Sheffield. You can probably imagine what a thrill it was as a young, wannabe rock writer to have all of this so close to the doorstep.[6]

A frenetic few days in Sheffield led to an urgent impetus to contact Throbbing Gristle:

> I don't have any record of the interviews I did that summer, but no doubt Throbbing Gristle came up in conversation a few times – I'm sure it did with Cabaret Voltaire. I'd been listening to *Second Annual Report* ever since reading Sandy Robertson's rave review in *Sounds*, and although I can't say I loved what TG were doing I was fascinated and knew it was somehow important. I wanted to know more, and struck up a correspondence (by phone) with Genesis P., who was lovely, engaging, always accommodating. Maybe I was the one who first suggested a Wakefield show, or maybe Genesis did when I mentioned that I lived nearby, but in any case we forged a little plan.

This series of chance encounters and previously unlinked instances instigated by a single individual and outside of a feeling of consensus amongst other Wakefield music fans formulated the possibility of a Throbbing Gristle appearance in the city. The role of the schizophrenic single, or at least one facet of it, now came into play. The release of the track 'United' is something that puzzles many Throbbing Gristle fans, as it seemed at the time unrepresentative of a perceived confrontational aim and so far removed from in terms of sound and composition from where the band were as a live experience. Outside of it actually being a great synth-pop precursor, the alternative thinking on 'United' is that it supplements a strategy of disorientation, misinformation, cognitive dissonance, and obfuscation. Westwood certainly deployed this eccentric affordance of the record:

> I contacted the student union at the college, hand-delivered a copy of 'United' Gen had sent me, and the student rep made the booking on the basis of that. After all, 'United' was so tuneful and poppy – what could possibly go wrong? If they'd bothered to listen to the B-side, 'Zyklon-B Zombie', they might have thought twice about it.

As Westwood states, the role of Sheffield band Cabaret Voltaire was crucial in instigating the Wakefield event. His article on the band surfaced in the September 1978 issue of *ZigZag*, sandwiched within a series of articles that give the first exposure of the new Sheffield scene in a national music magazine. Cabaret Voltaire were given a double-page spread marked by the author's positivity and somewhat precocious style that regularly inserts references from art and literature. The layout is futuristic and embodies the band's sense of angular and ambiguously navigated cut, paste, and mix, with the first page seemingly printed on a flattened origami cube. Westwood confesses to most of his interview tape being unintelligible (how very much generic to the scene) and has to ad-lib at times, though the references to link the band with Throbbing Gristle were prominent. I will further emphasize and document the importance of this band in Chapter 7, but it is instructive to point out that Cabaret Voltaire had secured a full feature in *Sounds* in April 1978 following an appearance at London's Lyceum the previous month, as a part of a typical punk package. The journalist is, unsurprisingly, Jon Savage, and the style is similar to his Throbbing Gristle feature that would follow a month later. Savage reflected and embodied the methods and sonic output of the band in his writing, taking a Burroughsian approach of cut-up and scene-shifting themes driven by a flickering and spluttering television set. Throbbing Gristle aren't mentioned, but the dyadic code word of 'Tesco Disco' is slotted into the article.

Cementing the triangle between Chris Westwood's Wakefield vision, Sheffield's independent electronic underground, and Throbbing Gristle, Cabaret Voltaire's Stephen Mallinder gives an insight into exploring and encountering the punk and post-punk scenes, recounting the band making the short journey from South Yorkshire to West Yorkshire:

> We did travel to gigs quite frequently in those days. Manchester, Leeds, and Doncaster – I remember Can at Doncaster Outlook – and sometimes if it was mates with cars we'd all pile in. But the TG gig we went by train and blagged a lift back so I think it was just us three plus perhaps Maggie, Chris's girlfriend (now wife), but that would have been it. We'd had some early communication with Gen and so we knew they were playing up there so we'd planned to go up and say hello as well as see the show. This was a time when people actually wrote letters, and we would have just made contact through the Industrial postal address on the record.[7]

This writing of letters also involved the swapping and sharing of domestic cassette tapes, previously flagged as a method to transport people from place to place and to tease out the sonic minutiae of places and non-places. Cabaret Voltaire made tapes of their music and sound experiments (which incorporated the sonic minutiae of their own environment) and sent these to Throbbing Gristle – we know this because the band are mentioned in the first issue of *Industrial News* (June 1978), topping the list of 'tapes received' with the mention of two C60 cassettes.

An identical overlapping triangle was mapped with fellow Sheffielders Clock DVA, the band being interviewed by Westwood on two occasions after he mislaid the first tape to offer an almost perfect symmetry to his Cabaret Voltaire deliberations. Clock DVA, as was their borderline uncooperative and antagonistic modus operandi, appear more difficult to interview than Cabaret Voltaire, and the volatility that marked the band through their career was evident from the start through talking to band founders Adi Newton and Steven 'Judd' Turner. Westwood's interview with the band was published somewhat later in November 1978, and the links to Throbbing Gristle are much more explicit, with mention of a proposed film by Adi entitled *Genitals and Genosis* which is reported to be a film both of and inspired by P-Orridge. As Mallinder notes, the Sheffield scene of experimental electronic music was close-knit with Throbbing Gristle evolving as a shared interest:

> DVA – Adi was part of all this – understandably as we saw each other all time. Judd was a good mate, and Widge, Clockdva's guitarist lived in same house as me – and made contact with Gen. But we did respect everyone doing their own work – it wasn't competitive, we were all doing our thing and those things overlapped constantly.

HUNTED

Leaving Sheffield and heading to Wakefield in the typical excitement of seeing Throbbing Gristle for the first time, Mallinder's testimony gives us a starting point for understanding the experience of encountering the band live in this place that sits on the real map between Leeds and Sheffield, but is almost absent from the punk map:

> I think we were front-loading and drinking on the train so we somehow figured our way to the venue – Wakefield is pretty small and the college was central. The venue was a very typical college hall – probably used to give prizes and speeches – with capacity of a couple of a few hundred maximum, and it seemed relatively full. There was a sense of tension and anticipation – the early punk scene had elicited a vibe of both anticipation and confrontation. That was the dynamic then – gigs weren't 'entertain me' but rather more challenging like 'ok bring it on!'. And TG through the grapevine had a reputation, through word of mouth, but no one had really seen or heard them so it was a feeling of 'what are they all about'.

Based loosely on Raymond Williams (1977) structure of feeling concept, an evolving methodology that unpicks at the totalizing nature of Gramscian hegemony, examining aspects such as social and cultural conventions and their role in implementing plausibility, it is instructive to gain an understanding of the affective dimension of both 'punk life' and general youth experience in Wakefield.[8] This generality stems from the band's appearance at the College attracting not just an informed audience of Throbbing Gristle fans (a regular following and an in-the-know inquisitive demographic), nor a more diffuse punk audience befitting the growth of the subculture in the city, but also a core of regular night-lifers as the gig formed part of the Saturday night 'tech-disco', an axis of the habitual entertainment options. This structure of feeling approach is utilized in earlier chapters, particularly with setting out a wider context of the press for their reporting of the *Prostitution* scandal to assess the dimensions of the scandal at the time, and I will call on it more systematically in this and the following chapters as we track Throbbing Gristle outside of the niche environment of London. Taking a barometer reading of the popular cultural climate allows intersecting frames of meaning-making and reference points to be brought to the surface.

The principal cinema in the centre, the ABC, was showing the David Cronenberg body horror *Rabid*, produced in 1977 but gaining popularity in the United Kingdom through 1978. Though early in his filmography, the feature was a key moment and typical of Cronenberg's futuristic and visceral style, adding in ideas of infection, transmission through sexual encounters, fleshy phallic protuberances and penetration, panic, and imminent collapse of functioning society – it is very much a 'throbbing gristle' film in the priapic sense. *Rabid* starred the actress Marilyn Chambers, known primarily as a porn star, and featured in many of the cutting-edge porn films that marked the 1970s era when this genre was considered a viable part of mainstream cinema. A consequence of this was that it became standard practice to pair up horror and pornography in the age when a trip to the cinema was often constructed as a double bill, to offer another link to throbbing gristle through its Yorkshire slang for an erection. In 1978 Wakefield, *Rabid* was paired with the 1975 film *Penelope Pulls it Off*, which was then labelled as softcore pornography in that it subscribed to a plot and included large elements of slapstick humour. Ostensibly speaking, the plot allowed a sequence of sex scenes to be played out with a binding layer of humour, though most people treated the film's (non) plot as essentially a series of sex scenes that had an approximately increasing arc of explicitness.

Whilst I return to the idea of sex and pornography as a loose end that extends beyond the reportage of the Wakefield gig, there was an uncanny Throbbing Gristle narrative to the film's premise. The plot concerned an art dealer looking to entrap people into buying faked art, using the insatiable sexual appetite of the main star Anna Bergman as a lure: art, forgery, sex, money, prostitution … it was more or less a *Carry On* makeover of the Institute of Contemporary Arts debacle. The film was 3 years old, though may just have been a cheap support film dredged up from somewhere. The other possible reason for the film's appearance may be that Bergman had just taken a key role in the second season of the ITV comedy *Mind Your Language*. This was a popular programme that played on xenophobic insecurity, with contrived stereotypes representing European countries and a clinging to regurgitated colonial outposts. Bergman portrayed a Swedish au pair, played on for her sexualized attributes but also conforming to the formula whereby each character had various insurmountable comedic lapses in their grasp of spoken English. In this case, Bergman regularly transposed words in short phrases and stubbornly used the same wrong words in place of other words. Whilst P-Orridge's splutterances and deformation of language ('E' for the nominative pronoun 'I') had roots in occult thinkers, it would also have a wider cultural resonance in the 1970s through the comedy of the time. The fashionable Nadsat language developed in *A Clockwork Orange* (novel 1962, film 1972) and adopted by many punk and post-punk bands had a precursor in comedy, with Anthony Burgess' clever structuralist hybrid of Russian and rhyming slang having a resonance with comedian Stanley Unwin's 'Unwinese'. This serendipitous double bill of throbbing gristles would only loiter for the week of the band's performance; the following week saw the somewhat milder body horror film *The Incredible Melting Man* and the Spielberg sci-fi epic *Close Encounters of the Third Kind* on show. The latter would attempt to take the mantle of the summer blockbuster, a trend set in 1975 with the feel-good-forget-Vietnam film *Jaws*.

1978 was a melting pot of genres across the music newspapers, with punk figuring less than in its energetic year of 1977. This was partly because the Sex Pistols had disintegrated and so their media-driven manager McLaren was marketing various shoddy offcuts with figures like retired criminal Ronnie Biggs joining the fray. Pastiche was also in the mix, with dreadful offerings such as Johnny Rubbish and his 'Living in NW3 4JR (Anarchy in the UK)' jibe at Rotten and the Pistols. Not that they, or anyone, cared. For the month of June, immediately preceding the Throbbing Gristle gig, the music press was giving cover space to Buzzcocks and their steady string of pop-punk missives, Siouxsie and the Banshees and their final signing to a major label, plus bands such as Penetration and the Cramps who were starting to create a buzz. The pop charts were in a strange summer lull, topped by John Travolta and Olivia Newton John performing music from *Grease*, only challenged by Father Abraham and the Smurfs with their 'Smurf Song'. For June, punk presence on *Top of the Pops* was spartan and relatively lukewarm, and the programme was cancelled at the start of the month for the opening of the World Cup in Argentina where much attention was fixed. On the screen, Plastic Bertrand is accompanied by Pan's People, Elvis Costello and the Attractions perform 'Pump it Up', and two days before Throbbing Gristle's gig the nation are treated to Boomtown Rats jerking around to 'Like Clockwork'. The Wakefield public were ripe for an onslaught of Throbbing Gristle transgression and a different type of clockwork machine rhythm.

Outside of popular culture, the West Yorkshire political climate was in flux, a prolonged season of disconcertedness in anticipation of the Winter of Discontent and a general election call by Callaghan. In anticipation of this, the Conservative tacticians were sharpening their teeth and claws, with the 'Labour Isn't Working' poster campaign by Saatchi and Saatchi unleashed in August 1978. Whilst the evolving mythology of this poster under the scrutiny of visual studies demonstrates an early case of insidious political opinion-making (the people in the photographed dole queue were stand-ins from the Hendon Young Conservatives, and sections of the queue were repeated to give it added length as it tails off into infinity due to only twenty people turning up), the poster had the desired effect.[9] In contrast, as retold by Beckett (2010: 499), Wakefield asserted itself as a Labour stronghold, with the MP Walter Harrison seen as an authentic working-class person from a poor background with the people at his heart. In further contrast to this, the British far right had a visible and vocal presence in the wider area of West Yorkshire and Leeds in particular, focusing on the football ground at Elland Road and the punk scene around the F-Club where promoter John Keenan was trying to keep a peaceful and positive-looking punk scene up and running. Leeds had nominal far right bands the Dentists and the Ventz in the mix, though more alarmingly local activist Eddy Morrison launched Punk Front as both a juncture of National Front members and fellow travellers and a dedicated fanzine in 1978 in a bid to wrestle a pre-politicized punk cohort away from the Anti-Nazi League. Worley (2017: 153) unpicks this complex arena of punk subcultures and extreme politics, whilst Rouska (2019: 40–43) provides direct testimony of encountering razor blades and ground glass under far right posters. If Wakefield was, as stated above, almost absent from the punk map, then one of its points of inclusion was Eddy Morrison's proposed opening gig for Punk Front scheduled for 17 June.

For nascent punk (or even post-punks) in Wakefield, the city offered only a smattering of points to engage the subculture. There was a small independent record outlet called The Record Bar and the large venue Unity Hall was visited by some of the punk bands who had ridden the wave of success through 1977. Past gigs included the Stranglers, the Vibrators, Boomtown Rats, and the Adverts in 1977, with the Saints, Johnny Thunders and the Heartbreakers, and the Pretenders appearing at various points in 1978. Punk clothing shops, normally secreted away on run-down back streets, were totally absent. Nearby Leeds was the biggest draw for punks in West Yorkshire, forming what Goldhammer (2018: 363) calls an 'urba-normative mecca' in the wider network of towns, in which Leeds was often felt as a version of London against the rural othering of smaller towns in West Yorkshire. Within Leeds, the work of promoter John Keenan was essential in running small clubs, booking bands, and creating a scene. As Spracklen et al. (2016: 153) recount, Keenan would extend his advertising into places such as Wakefield.

The handfuls of punks in Wakefield tended to adopt a more mundane look, with the scene of a gig described by local Paul Hayes as 'not exactly ripped jeans and safety pins, it was more proto-post-punk Oxfam, with a contingent of older, still long haired and flared-trousered kids checking out the band'.[10] Paul continues to set out the dangers of looking a bit different, with Wakefield having demarcated spaces (pubs etc.) for the remnants of the Teddy boy and soul boy scenes. The Wakefield Teds were known as the 'Tin Town Teds', after the pre-fabricated housing scheme they tended to come from. As Worley (2017: 15) documents, 'Teds liked to dance and were up for a fight: they existed in a space somewhere between the home and the workplace'. Strangely enough, the Wakefield Teds gain a mention in Gorman (2020: 159) as a named group arriving by coach trips to terrorize punks on London's King's Road. In addition, the city was the stopping-off point for many football coaches, creating an added layer of random violence that persisted through until the end of the 1980s. This constant alert status for punks in provincial towns and cities is reaffirmed by Wakefield musician Peter Norton, who played with the band Strangeways. Norton and colleague Ada Wilson saw a shared lineage of Velvet Underground and New York Dolls informing the first stirrings of punk, and quickly adopted a modest punk look and feel. However, straight-leg trousers and scruffy hair were enough for you to attract trouble.[11] On the night of the Throbbing Gristle gig, the glam rock showband Mud were performing at the Wakefield Theatre Club, so maybe this was enough to distract any stray Teds bristling for a fight.

The threat of the Yorkshire Ripper also stifled the atmosphere of West Yorkshire. Murders were gaining frequency with three occurring in early 1978 across Bradford, Manchester, and Huddersfield. Tension was ramped up in March 1978 with the letters created by 'Wearside Jack', a hoaxer claiming to be the murderer. Many of the testimonies concerning the Leeds punk and post-punk scenes address the creeping shadow of fear that these horrendous and targeted attacks instilled, overlapping with the dark shadows of racism and hooliganism. As Haslam (2005: 290) glumly remarks, there was a 'gulf of incomprehension' between anxious and desperate Reclaim the Night marches and Leeds United fans taunting the police about not being able to catch the Ripper. Inevitably, the fear pervaded into the wider region, as Cabaret Voltaire member Mallinder attests:

> It was a weird unspoken thing but particularly with our female friends there was such an awful tension, it was always odd if you were in pubs that were unfamiliar and you'd be conscious of strangers. It built up over time, by the time he was caught it was stifling. But it was also removed from our world in some respects

> and we moved in our own circles so felt slightly distant from it. It's weird to explain, you just had to live through that period to understand the vibe, you were always on your guard – pubs were hard back then, tough places, we were quite scared of some bloke smacking you for wearing strange clothes. That was the reality, not just one psycho.

INDUSTRIAL MUSIC FOR INDUSTRIAL PEOPLE

Throbbing Gristle perfected the industrial sound as a multiform concept in 1978, taking the meaning of the term to a manifold of interpretations and levels. Industrial related to the mode of production and how consumption and conformity were built into everyday life at an increasing rate. This was the fascination of Tesco, the ubiquitous supermarket chain that aggressively rose to power during the band's formative years and became akin to an ironic exemplar for the band. Much like Throbbing Gristle, Tesco had a strong logo and corporate identity, and the band saw Tesco as both emblematic and synergetic in their typically ambiguous way. The pervasive reach of the supermarket was signalled by the band with their famous photograph of them lined up under a huge hoarding announcing a new Tesco development, and further featured in *Industrial News* issue 1 with photographs of 'control agents' Glenn Wallis and Alan Phillips mocked up as Tesco security guards and the question and answer section of the newsletter suggesting that shops of interest include 'your local Tesco supermarket' alongside independent record outlets. However, the multiplying presence of Tesco had a sinister interpretation provoked by the band's use. The corporate branding encompassed a way of doing things and a way of appearing, whilst at the same time hinting at a discernible hidden depth of layers of staff working out of site keeping the function going.

This invoking of a well-oiled machine of layers of drone staff, with a subterranean undertone, is now predominantly associated with Amazon, with their 'big grey shed' architecture of fulfilment centres arranged up and down the motorways of the United Kingdom with staff working to strict quota schedules of fetching and carrying products from endless bays of storage racking. In a 2002 updating of Throbbing Gristle's critical extrapolation of the Tesco behemoth, Belgian conceptual artist Guillaume Bijl completed the latest project in his installation strategy series turning Tate Liverpool into a Tesco Express branch with the installation *Your Supermarket*. Bijl's installation work initially concerned challenging the usefulness and purpose of the gallery by transforming them into socially useful spaces, but the transformation of Tate Liverpool into Tesco also harboured a strong element of critique in that the function of the art gallery had not necessarily been disturbed due to an implied synergy between the twinned power-brands of Tate and

Tesco. Clearly, the ubiquitous supermarket giants were a perfect analogy and metaphor for Throbbing Gristle, and P-Orridge was on the lookout for signs of their consumer creep as the band began to travel around. As Chris Westwood recalls, the first thing Throbbing Gristle had seen driving into Wakefield was a great big Tesco development with P-Orridge remarking 'after "Tesco Disco", it had to be a sign'. West Yorkshire was the province of the Morrisons chain of supermarket, with a new branch announced in the local paper for the week of gig at the college. In this instance, Throbbing Gristle and Tesco were sharing a timed sense of (southern) invasion into the West Yorkshire terrain.

'Tesco Disco' stood for a sound as well as an industrial mode of creating music for consumption. We associate the supermarket queue, prior to the recent divergence into self-service, pre-scanned, and other options such as online delivery, as an endless sequence of blips and bleeps as product is skilfully rotated in search of the barcode. Goods pass along a conveyor belt which is modulated by the sensors detecting a product at the end of the belt awaiting scanning. The conveyor belt is silent, but we imagine a noise that stands for the endless process of things moving, it plays in the back of our minds: from shelf, to basket or trolley, to conveyor, to checkout operator, to bag, to home, to oven, to plate, to body, to excrement. Bleep, bleep, bleep. The acoustics of a 1978 Tesco were somewhat different to what we perceive now, due to the absence of barcodes and scanners through a computerized system, a system that wouldn't be introduced until 1982. Tesco celebrated this computerization with a widescale advertising campaign, 'Checkout 82'. This entailed an advertisement shown on television and at cinemas with a computerized till jerking out prices and pictures, animated by a synth-pop theme written by musician David Reilly with a vocal by singer Clare Torry who had previously worked with Pink Floyd and would go on to work with Culture Club and Tangerine Dream. Even if the bleep of Tesco Disco is a post hoc construction due to the pervasive reach of the modern supermarket giants, the relentless flow of products and the imagined sound of the pure process would still have been the aural evocation of the environment of the supermarket in the 1970s.

The call-to-arms of a mechanical imperative came to the fore in Throbbing Gristle's music in this period, pounding out an industrial grinding, chugging rhythm to both coincide and compete with the routine wall of noise that had been established from those early performances in the punk arena. Early instances included the performance at Southampton's Nuffield Theatre in May 1977 which momentarily transformed into a pure blend of grinding and bleeping, and then an intense industrial section of relentless and metronomic machine noise at Roundhouse in September of the same year, which Ford links to the sawmill of both futurist filmmaker Dziga Vertov (Ford 1999: 8·8) and the workaday soundscape of Hackney (7·23) as quoted by P-Orridge. This was intensified at the subsequent gig at Winchester in November, the band embodying a machine effect that no longer allowed the listener to effectively stand outside of the sound and imagine a potential source, but instead posited the listener within the machine itself. The effect is both calm in calculation and brutal in execution, neither counting down nor up, just onwards, a sonic equivalent of Hegel's bad infinity theory of the straight line ever delaying the final moment of its finitude in the endless progression of its series.

The collective dimension of being immersed in a noisy repetitive machine soundscape under the loose guise of entertainment is difficult to ascertain. The metabolic description and tactic of Throbbing Gristle's sonic assault approximated to a collective and mutual metastasis or subcultural metempsychosis but fell outside of models of music sociability that addressed the role of repetition. This ran counter to traditional models adopted from Durkheim's theory of collective effervescence, instead veering towards Reed's (2013: 12) understanding of industrial music as an approximation of intersubjective assimilation or a 'mutual absorption'. Hesmondhalgh (2013) wrestles with this briefly in his work, calling upon the Freudian observation of the fascination of repetitive certainty in the 'fort–da' game, the negative standoffishness of Adorno as he studied repetition and formulaic genres in early popular music, and jumping forward to the contemporary era of raves and repetitive club music celebrated by rave-theorist Malbon (1999). However, Throbbing Gristle came well before the rave and club diversifications into genres that prioritize jackhammer beats with minimal variation, and their collective reception posed a dilemma.

Aside from P-Orridge's Hackney sawmill, the situated industrial clustering of the north of England is commonly understood as the basis for an associated industrial sound and its proliferation as both distinctive genre (within cities such as Sheffield) and as a feeling or aesthetic supplement within distinct city scenes (the grey obtuse pop-punk of Manchester's Factory Records, Leeds' goth music scene). For example, Milestone (2018: 306) in her study of 'Madchester' and its post-punk lineage suggests that 'gritty, rainy, damp industrial landscapes had long been synonymous with northerness', an overused pop-culture trope that is only matched by a suggestion that (Manchester) punk was a response to Thatcherism. This is, of course, just a simplification, based upon a further simplification of the north of England being the sole bastion of heavy industry, either as an enduring legacy or current state with coalmines, shipyards, steel foundries, cotton mills, etc. Hegarty (2007: 6) in his study of noise sets out a noisy working class 'sound swill and sewage', and then adds the further noise of machinery as 'a layer of volume and continuity to unwanted sound'. However, primary industry (ostensibly coal mining) and its associated noise were part of the fabric of life of Wakefield. The weekend of Throbbing

Gristle playing also had a nostalgic celebration of industry and noise with the Ryhill Steam Rally on the edges of the urban area. These rallies, formed in the 1950s as the bringing together of preservationist activists, were noisy in the industrial sense. A cornucopia of restored heavy vehicles from agriculture, public transport, road haulage, and military were brought together with re-enactments of past scenes of industrial and rural life, historic battles, and massive 'steam-ups' where a line of engines would shovel coal into boilers to generate steam and potential power – there would even be an authentic sawmill or two.[12] To top matters off, the local newspaper also had a report on industrial noise regulations and recent examples of red tape, presented in something of a joking manner as if to put across the view that Wakefield people were environmentally accustomed to any noise.[13]

DEFAULT SPONTANEITY

The concept of a strapline for supermarkets did not appear until recent years, even if competing giants of grocery and general goods retail had mottoes. For Tesco it is recorded as 'pile it high, sell it cheap', which would obviously not translate well as a banner headline on stores or carrier bags, but would no doubt appeal to the humour of Throbbing Gristle.[14] The emergence of a strapline for Tesco came to the fore in recent years with the now ubiquitous phrase 'Every Little Helps', though Throbbing Gristle were clearly ahead of things here with their own strapline: 'Industrial Music For Industrial People'. So, what industrial music were the industrial population of Wakefield presented with? The Wakefield performance was structured roughly along the same lines as the Goldsmiths gig two months earlier, with certain identifiable tracks appearing that persist from gig to gig in terms of order (syntagm) and content (paradigm). Whereas this can be approximated to the workaday routines of a rock band, and indeed some Throbbing Gristle fans do mourn this point as a departure from the previous raw spontaneity that reflected both the current news and the atmosphere on the night, there is still room for spontaneity.

The band open with 'IBM', a sound piece debuted at Goldsmiths, and allegedly created from a discarded computer tape salvaged by the band outside the International Business Machines (IBM) offices (Ford 1999: 8.24). Somehow the band extracted from this tape the sound of it either performing its data duties or forced the computer tape to 'play' in an alien media, in much the same way that swathes of code can be churned out when an image file such as a JPEG is opened in a text handing program. This deliberate strategy of making an audience conscious of the playback system was used by later industrial bands and would also resurface in the hauntology scene of the early 2000s, described by Fisher (2014: 21) as 'a sensibility, an existential orientation'. This was also a Brechtian reflexive trope adopted in the avant-garde film industry, where films would often include segments showing the leader tape spooling on or off the reel. In terms of music performance, it was a strategy that extended the physical playing back of the content of a sampled source, which served to buttress the message of the band in the here and now, and also to evoke a sense of being at the place (and time) of the origin of the source in regard to its original playback. Shortly after Throbbing Gristle ceased to operate, the experimental band 23 Skidoo (initially close colleagues of Throbbing Gristle) released the track 'Porno Base' as part of the seminal album *Seven Songs*, in which the playing back of the recording of Diana Mitford's speech against the pernicious threats of pop music is made doubly disconcerting by the sound of an archaic tape spool.

At Wakefield, the cold and invasive sounds of the IBM disk are quickly augmented by P-Orridge narrating a story that barely registers in the mix. He intones twice: 'There's been a death in the family' and then adds the name 'Ian' at the end of his third recital – we are not provided with further details or clues on the nature of this incident as everything is quickly drowned out by soaring noises from the band's treated instruments. A beguiling monotone recital of an unnamed product purchase follows, given a short broadcast as the noise momentarily parts like a pair of curtains opening for a brief glimpse. This is again based upon a similar monologue extolled at Goldsmiths, with P-Orridge using the Burroughs cut-up technique which would be applied in later performances. This relaying of short sentences chopped around and idiomatic malfunctioning of partial phrases cut apart and mixed serves to muddy conceptions and create confusion, akin to the 'zone of indistinction' between poetry and prose defined by Hillyer (2013: 2) in his analysis of Maurice Blanchot. A related 'zone of indetermination' is claimed by Deleuze (1998: 11) in his pursuit of radical writing, in which we encounter a 'tour de Babil' and 'agrammaticality'. Beckman (2017: 87) captures this perfectly with her own study of Deleuze, expressing how he sought a place where you became 'a stranger within one's own literature'. It conjures up a soundscape in which, in the words of Reed (2013: 37), 'a contentlessness hovers uneasily'. The noise returns with P-Orridge clambering for traction in the mix with his 'one product' chant reverberating amidst the cacophony. After seven minutes there is a lull, the IBM tone returns, then fades to close out this first section. P-Orridge adopts his whiney punk voice to proclaim 'cheap and nasty' followed by a switch to a pastiche crooner voice obliterated by more reverb to announce 'catch me at the Cabaret Voltaire', the frontman both welcoming his new friends into the fray and extolling his avant-garde art kudos by acknowledging the Cabaret Voltaire as its original intention as a Dadaist gathering point.

Seemingly running out of interest or inspiration after ten minutes, the energetic sample of what sounds like a kids' football match with a piercing whistle and a shout of 'go on, go on' cuts into the mix as the industrial section rises from a slumber. These snatches of sampled sound are tantalizingly familiar but seldom identified. They may have come from television programmes, or be part of Sleazy's sonic rampage with the early portable cassette recorders and parabolic microphones he acquired as part of his Hipgnosis connections. P-Orridge (2021: 177) labels this activity as 'espionage field recordings' and makes a particular reference to boys playing football.[15] Again, this composition is performed previously as 'D.o.A' at Goldsmiths (and the live cut of that would form the title track of the Throbbing Gristle album at the end of 1978); however, at Wakefield it is listed simply as 'Industrial Muzak' and forms an incredible ten minutes of the band at their breath-taking best. There is a potential aural link to the football terrace culture, as the bashed rhythm sounds like being enclosed in a football stand with fans banging in unison on the corrugated sheeting that regularly formed the rear walls and low ceilings of enclosed terraces and 'popsides'. The use of the term muzak refers to the generic name of sounds used to drown out other sounds or to promote a falsified sense of place and being-in-place. Reed (2013: 21) places the origins of industrial music as sounds played into factories to break up or mask the industrial noise as an aid to bolster morale and so facilitate speedy production. The bringing out and badging up as 'industrial muzak' of the true industrial sounds that are masked by the piped muzak reverses the perspective: the cleansed everyday is invaded and reterritorialized by the hidden every day. This is the sound of cotton mills, blast furnaces, underground machinery ripping out coal; an industrial landscape. For Wakefield, in July 1978, industrial music, for industrial people, in an industrial college, within an industrial backdrop.

The sound cuts and there is a short dialogue from a medical drama; this fades but continues in the background as the new track 'Hamburger Lady' groans into life with what is now a signature introduction of droning noise and treated cornet. A Throbbing Gristle milestone moment. P-Orridge seemingly takes great pleasure in delivering the narrative of a burns victim as related by their American colleague and mail artist 'Blaster' Al Ackerman. 'Hamburger Lady' would become an enduring track that was played through 1978 and 1979, attaining the status of an ironic signature for the band. Its cloying and atmospheric nature meant that it was the antithesis of how a rock band would signal the commencement of a track with favourite status by teasing their audience with recognized intricate riffs or keyboard notes. Next, we have 'Slug Bait' revisited, albeit as a shortened version. Perplexingly, it is delivered in an atonal and staccato style with a Throbbing Gristle version of bathos – the increased original graphic horror of the track (someone being force-fed their own castrated testicles) being offset with a comedy delivery and a northern affliction ('bait' is emphasized as 'bayt').

This is followed by an overlaid and looping series of nonsense monologue samples that the band used for a number of gigs around this time. Each monologue makes little sense on its own, apart from having a brief connection to each other, and there is a link here to P-Orridge's (2021: 163) stated connections to 1970s performance artists Kipper Kids, Silvia Ziranek, and Anne Bean. Both are delivered by COUM fellow-traveller Fizzy Paet, the first concerning an unexplained patient being moved in a taxi and recalling his actions of eating various pieces of metal (sometimes listed as 'August Bank Holiday'), the second concerning a landlady advertising a bizarre range of services (listed as 'Mother Spunk' or 'Good Clean Fun').[16] The former is delivered in a deadpan northern male voice, the latter in a comedy female voice redolent of a seaside landlady in a town such as Blackpool, chiming with the classic ethnographic study by Walton (1978). Additionally, the name 'Mother Spunk' can be read as a playful parody of *Mother Courage and Her Children*, the 1939 play by Brecht (spunk is a slang word for courage). In taking this and positing it in a seedy porno-lexicographical context, the band out-Brecht Brecht. As with previous airings of this composition, background noises are cut to a minimum and the first monologue loops while the longer second monologue plays through. Samples, synths, and the foundations of a wall of noise take over as the monologues fall away, only to be cut down. Nothing holds together, and for a short while it's like a meeting of industrial machines performing improv. A microsecond of silence cuts the project down, and then Wakefield is given a sublime treat; the first live airing of 'Five Knuckle Shuffle'. This is the real Tesco Disco, punched-out and punch-drunk processing rhythms looped without deviation or acknowledgement. The click signature of 'Five Knuckle Shuffle' drives on as everything else rhythmic slips away and a new wall (whorle) of sound grows from almost nothing to almost everything. And then the hour is up.

REACTION

As stated, Throbbing Gristle's incursion into Wakefield escaped any documentation. The majority of the crowd were regulars at the 'tech disco', so it's difficult to hunt down any direct testimony over 40 years later. But, inevitably, imprints and impressions were made. Instigator Chris Westwood offers his memories of the event:

> Well, on the night the student rep was wide-eyed. So were most of the fairly thin crowd, who may have been ambivalent or bored or in shock, but there wasn't any real hostility; no projectiles, no screams of abuse, maybe a few shrugs. I might be misremembering here, or imagining, because it was so long ago, but just before the 60-minute timer shut down the show – which happened at every TG gig – I turned and saw a dozen or so of the audience at the back of the hall forming

> a human pyramid, just this great pile of clambering sweaty bodies. That's my clearest memory of the night (I wish I'd gone over to ask them why).

This bizarre reaction – a spontaneous collective metempsychosis of dithyrambic dancing – would have occurred during the grinding ten-minute close-out of 'Five Knuckle Shuffle'. It's an answer to that curious question of how Throbbing Gristle's proto-machine-dance rhythms can be responded to bodily. A boozy crowd of non-punks and non-arty-types, uninhibited by a subcultural habitus, provides an answer. Then President of the Student Union Mark Trout also recalls this: 'the thing that sticks in my mind was a long line of people prostrate and traversing the hall like a bunch of bizarre mountaineers'.[17] Michael Fawcett, also in attendance, picks up on this and gives an insight into the wider context:

> I remember that P. Orridge felt quite intimidating. His quasi neo-nazi uniform and armband seemed in direct conflict with our anti-nazi league badges. For a while we thought they were just tuning up, but it quickly became evident that this was their music. Most people drifted away from the stage (usually they'd be at the front, bouncing or headbanging) and the venue almost emptied. There were a couple of dozen people left writhing around in a bizarre human centipede/conga on the beer lubed floor.[18]

The evening had a greater impact on Paul Hayes, who recounts how they helped shape his future interests in music:

> They were something extraordinary – the Undertones they weren't. One of the bands (other being the Gang of Four) that probably saved me from going all spiky haired and leather jacketed and into that comedy punk ghetto. Plus, they were dangerous – you could tell.

MALIGNANT HUM

Whereas the other performances in this book selected as case studies and contour points have a definitive reverberation in terms of a commemorative event or an effort at reconstruction, the memory of Wakefield lies buried and forgotten. A reverberation of sorts is offered through the novelist David Peace, growing up in Wakefield but being just too young to witness Throbbing Gristle's fleeting appearance in the city. Peace crafts dark and distorted fictionalized histories of the murkier aspects of recent events, utilizing a methodology described by Laughey (2013: 95) that 'play(s) with these stark boundaries between fact and fiction, statement and rumour, truth and corruption'. Even though he shares with P-Orridge a tendency to disinter a violence that resides below the surface, it is in stark contrast to P-Orridge's hyper-mythologizing strategy. At a more granular level, Peace also employs the tactic of listening to the music of the time of his historical setting. This gives him access to the feel or the grain of a place at a certain time – something I have tried to evoke throughout this book in a more mundane way. Peace's first work to reach public acclaim was his four-part arching story of the Yorkshire Ripper woven into a vivid picture of the West Yorkshire landscape and the suffocating corruption and corruptibility of his characters. Nothing ends well, nothing looks good, and there is never ever any salvation for any character. As a reader, you cannot stake any connectivity or investment with protagonists, antagonists, narrators, or side-line players, or indeed select a character to 'root for' – everything collapses.

For the third part of this quartet, the book *Nineteen Eighty* (2001), Peace goes beyond evoking the contemporaneous music as a retrieval aid for mood and aura, and transplants Throbbing Gristle's 1980 album *Heathen Earth* into the body of the narrative. The dark mood of the album, with its preface of a Charles Manson statement rhetorically asking 'Can the world be as sad as it seems?', nourishes the forlorn soul of both antagonist and victim(s). Peace adopts P-Orridge's substitutions – 'thee' for the, and 'e' for I – as the reader is drawn into a black vortex of helpless and hapless pleading in an echo chamber:

> The italicised 'transmissions' – phantom broadcasts or 'news from nowhere' akin to electronic voice phenomena – which open each chapter of *Nineteen Eighty* cut police reports and media messages together with chilling eye witness accounts from both the Ripper and his victims. These unpunctuated transmissions pick up and leave off from one another to suggest a background noise across the narrative as a whole.
>
> (Lockwood 2011: 43)

According to cultural theorist Mark Fisher (2008: n.pag.), the arc and narrative of Peace's *Red-Riding Quartet* intensify with a foregrounded religious fervour, constituting 'not so much a negative theology as a negative theodicy', ending with a 'quasi-Gnostic treatise on evil and suffering'. Fisher knows that Throbbing Gristle, and the unabashed musing on Manson, fitted perfectly with Peace's constricted and asphyxiating reimagining of the world that allowed the Ripper to flourish, a world that (in Peace's writing) exploited and opportunized on horror and dread. If Peace retrospectively inserts Throbbing Gristle into Wakefield and the Yorkshire Ripper of 1980, a time when West Yorkshire Police were under increasing scrutiny as to why no one had been apprehended, then the Throbbing Gristle of 1978 do not bring up the spectre that haunted the region. Instead, the band produced a driving set of industrial music that was starting to find a nuanced form. Backtracking to and fro over the years, it was a soundtrack of Fisher's reading of Peace's reading of the horror of the times – accumulating, intensifying, and ending with the nihilism of 'Five Knuckle Shuffle'. Peace's reimagining of the lost underside of the Ripper decade invites reconsideration of two facets of Throbbing Gristle that have a tendency to be buried or swept under the carpet: P-Orridge's narrative foregrounding of gruesome murderers and Tutti's apparently ambiguous work in the porn industry. We left a discussion of this in Chapter 1 with a quasi-legitimization of P-Orridge's method; as deconstructing the structure of pop music narration, as offering 'instinctive journalism' in its place, as practising ironic overidentification. It feels tenuous, and P-Orridge always pushes a grounded contextualization of his methods to the point of rupture. At the same time, there is always the temptation to try and 'rescue' Throbbing Gristle from questionable connotations, which, in my opinion, needs to be strongly resisted. But where does this take us, or leave us, as we tread in the footsteps of the Ripper?

By 1978 and his arrival in Wakefield, P-Orridge's shock tactics of foregrounding serial killers and sexual deviants had waned, his source material previously gleaned from an obsessive reading of books on these subjects. If anything, the glib aesthetics and contrived mythologization of the Ripper case mimicked Throbbing Gristle, with the June 1979 hoax tape produced by 'Wearside Jack'. The tape incorporated a residual segment of the cheesy track 'Thank You for Being a Friend' by Andrew Gold, giving it the feel of something off Throbbing Gristle's album *D.o.A: The Third and Final Report of Throbbing Gristle* released at the end of 1978. But that is just my projection. In actuality, the generation of industrial and power electronics bands that followed Throbbing Gristle were quick to exploit the shock value of this serial killer, apprehended and named in January 1981. The track 'Ripper Territory' appeared on the 1981 Whitehouse album *Dedicated to Peter Kurten Sadist and Mass Slayer*, structured around harsh industrial noise on top of the ITV *News at Ten* announcement of his capture. As with the Wearside Jack tape, the track includes a banal but quirky segment introducing a subsequent news item about the Olympic swimmer Duncan Goodhew.[19] In the same year, Whitehouse founder William Bennett released an album *Bradford Red Light District*, a field recording purporting to be from Bradford, under the mischievous name of The New Order. The sleeve notes of the album are credited to P-Orridge, but this is said to be a ruse as P-Orridge had little time for the immediate generation of deliberately controversial industrial bands seemingly inspired by his own works.[20] In the following year, 1982, ex-Whitehouse member Kevin Tomkins formed a power electronics band called Sutcliffe Jugend, continuing this exercise in bad taste.[21]

But something else does not sit well and nags at you. The timelines of Throbbing Gristle's operation and Sutcliffe's killing spree are uncannily coterminous. Embarkation and disembarkation in alignment. The band date the announcement of their formation to September 1975, one month before Sutcliffe claims his first victim. Sutcliffe is thankfully apprehended in early 1981, charged and then sentenced – the verdict coming down on 22 May 1981. This coincides with the playing out of Throbbing Gristle's 'termination', the band actually performing the first of two final gigs in America on the day that Sutcliffe is sentenced.[22] This almost perfect overlapping of existence and activity proffers an inevitable interweaving of circumstances that manifests as a conspiratorial shared narrative. For example, Throbbing Gristle's peak (live) moment of questionable context and content occurs during their Christmas 1977 gig at the Rat Club, where they performed 'Urge to Kill' followed by 'Assume Power Focus' which ended with P-Orridge exhorting the audience to 'go out and kill'. As Ford (1999: 7·12) notes in his discussion of Jon Savage's thoughts on this gig (edited down for his subsequent review in *Sounds*), the ambivalence and ambiguity to extreme matters were open to misinterpretation. Sutcliffe's killing spree accelerated in early January 1978, with the murders of Yvonne Pearson and Helen Rytka. Whilst in custody in 1981, he confessed that at the time of these two murders he had 'the urge to kill any woman. The urge inside me to kill girls was now practically uncontrollable'. Peace's para-historical fictionalizing reverberates in Throbbing Gristle's dark cultural domain, and you are left to concoct your own morbid conspiracies as you assume the persona of Peace and implicate the band in a morbid multiverse.[23]

Worley (2017), in his overarching study of punk formations and practices, explores the lyrical content and projected aesthetics of punk with regard to certain bands electing to pursue themes such as class sensibility and social realism, aspects that situate punk outside of the mainstream pop process and give it a critical cutting edge. His work builds upon Laing (1985: 27) who documents punk as a progression from earlier set themes of 'love, dance, hard luck and so on'. Worley is a safe pair of hands in these matters, working through contexts with a taxonomical methodology and gradient of extremity. However, he ultimately reaches the point where 'punk gave rise to tendencies keen to recover the marginal and the suppressed, to scrape away the veneer of British propriety to reveal what lay beneath' (105). Throbbing Gristle enter the dialogue, where the intent shifts to 'shock and disrupt the fragile equilibriums of modern society', and by the time we arrive at Whitehouse the historian acknowledges in a defeatist manner that 'things got messy if the propensity to shock fell out of context' (107). Pantagruelic one-upmanship. Shits and giggles. The critical detachment initiated by Throbbing Gristle becomes a trump card to be bettered each time. If, and I use the term with caution, Throbbing Gristle had a didactic or even dialogical imperative when summoning up these heinous crimes and their perpetrators, then Whitehouse and their ilk simply drip-feed a subcultural identity that has a need to appear controversial as part of its general facets of appearance, identity, and connotation.

Let's return to entertain the possibility of a didactic or dialogical dimension in Throbbing Gristle's work in the abject domain. Steirer's (2012) academic paper on Throbbing Gristle's malefic tendencies necessarily touches upon this moment at the Rat Club in 1977, but a resolvable critical appraisal is lost within Steirer's wider and overly-ambitious arc of linking valences of situationist thought (towards urban space and art), Throbbing Gristle and the industrial subculture, information art, and the politics of neo-liberalism. Whereas previous discussions towards a potential contextualization and validation of Throbbing Gristle's grim themes have orbited around ideas of legitimizing cultural and critical practices – the suggestion that making certain aesthetic and lyrical themes taboo stifles and excludes criticality of what is NOT taboo – Steirer calls upon P-Orridge and Christopherson's text 'Annihilating Reality' from the June/July 1976 issue of art magazine *Studio International*.[24] He suggests that this text can be read in the situationist valence of Raoul Vaneigem such that anything can be art, and so Throbbing Gristle's explosive litanies of the acts of serial killers are raising the consideration of aesthetic phenomena:

> The anti-progressive aspect of Throbbing Gristle's aesthetic was achieved, in a manner that resembles Gray's representation of the Situationist City, primarily through the selection for representation of objects that cannot rationally be accounted for by any functioning utopia. Exemplary in this regard was the band's handling of murder, which (especially in its early days) was a frequent topic of its music, writing, and performances. Songs like 'Urge to Kill' and 'Slug Bait' reported the activities of serial killers like Edmund Kemper and Charles Manson not as calls for moral outrage (and subsequent corrective action), but as aesthetic phenomena.[25]
>
> (Steirer 2012: 10)

Steirer continues, shifting the context slightly onto a dubious and dangerous terrain:

> Certainly the band did not actually hope to incite murder, but wished instead to open up modes of experiencing murder and the fantasy of committing it that are not wholly determined by the familiar problem oriented discourses of sociology and psychology.
>
> (11)

He then returns to the aesthetic dimension, summoning 'Annihilating Reality' and proposing that it:

> does not actually advocate murder; rather it argues for the separation of the act's formal qualities from its social effects and moral value. Instead of immorality, murder, the band argued, can be seen as an aesthetic event, as art. Furthermore, when the concept of art was thus expanded so as to include murder as a paradigmatic example, it shed the need to reflect what ought to be and contribute to that ought's utopian realization.
>
> (11)

He directly quotes a section from the text, where P-Orridge and Christopherson call upon numerous multiple murderers from history, to refocus on their proposal of an aesthetic dimension (in this case the work of German avant-garde shamanic artist Joseph Beuys):

> Rais, Prelati, Poitou made crosses, signs, and characters in a circle. Used coal, grease, torches, candles, a stone, a pet, incense. Words were chalked on a board. Could these rituals preceding child murders, in another context and properly photographed, become Beuysian performance?
>
> (11)

Steirer avoids the more scandalous claim that Ian Brady be considered as a conceptualist artist (Brady and Hindley photographed the Moors as landscape, encoding a hidden reading of the photographs referring to where the bodies of their child victims were buried in much the same way that conceptualist art operates with latent readings). However, even the Rais-Beuys homology does not sit well. Perhaps it is not meant to … a meta-ethic or meta-aesthetic game in play? A further swipe at the dead end of avant-gardism as discussed in the previous chapter? Indeed, it would require a degree of art knowledge to link P-Orridge and Christopherson's adjectival Beuysian with the German artist, and further knowledge to know that he specialized in the ritualized use of wax and fat.

This is a brutal allegory, bringing together the ways that Throbbing Gristle approach the darkness of thought with Peace's own fiction, through the cipher of the Ripper. There is a dark synergetic return to Sutcliffe again, grim reality filtered through Peace's occult cartography as both the author and Throbbing Gristle offer their responses to the underbelly of the lost decade. A neat conclusion of thoughts is evasive. Sutcliffe, when captured, was found to be wearing (underneath his outer clothes) a knitted sweater worn upside down with his legs in the sleeves such that the void offered by the inverted v-neck allowed his genital area to be exposed. Presumably also keeping him from getting a chill in cold January air. The jumper had leather patches on the elbows, now coinciding with Sutcliffe's knees, as he crouched over his victims. In the homological pairing and semantic games of 'Annihilating Reality', we could consider this as avant-garde clothing design, Sutcliffe as a protégé dynamic for the Antwerp fashion designer Martin Margiela with his re-worked gloves made into sweaters and sweaters made into jackets? Is this the intent and endgame? If this serves as an extreme example to delegitimize the hallowed bubble of authenticated art production, circulation and critical reflection, then we can allay any concerns. But, taking shots at art through escalating abjection and extremism is a safe game – taking this into the realm of pop and rock music is something different. 'Annihilating Reality' and its pop medley of society's ultra-sadistic overspill was a parting shot to the art world, prefaced by the short section 'Scenes of Victory' in which P-Orridge and Christopherson pronounce: 'For every interesting performance artist there was a psychopath, fetishist or intense street individual who created more powerful and socially direct imagery' (1976: 44). This can be read two ways as a chiasmus: legitimate art is made meaningless and worthless by the aesthetic inventiveness of serial killers, or serial killers need to be escalated to the role of higher artists and role models of creative expression. Which is it to be?

'FIVE KNUCKLE SHUFFLE'

The second controversial aspect of Throbbing Gristle that Peace's novels invite a critical reappraisal of is Tutti's role in the pornography industry as model, actress, and striptease artist. Tutti's pornographic work was folded back into the collective Throbbing Gristle aesthetic affront at the outset, with her portfolio forming a key part (and moral bait) of the *Prostitution* exhibition. Her work then continued as a separate endeavour during the period of Throbbing Gristle without ever being foregrounded as an aesthetic dimension. It is only in recent years that this work, perhaps best understood as simple wage labour, has taken on a new valence of critical thinking within and around performance art.

Looking at Tutti's pornography contribution to the *Prostitution* exhibition, Ford (1999: 6·25) classes this work – if it is to be considered in a critical canon of art practice – to be in the genre of body art. Battista (2019: 54) expands on this term in her survey of female body artists (including Tutti and Mary Kelly) by structuring it in terms of a dilemma or a 'feminist binary'; either using or declining to use one's body. This invites an epiphenomenal dilemma between reclaiming the body and re-emphasizing an idealized image of the body. Ford (1999: 6·25) uses Lippard's label of the 'subtle abyss', admitting that such art is often: 'marginalised or misunderstood by male critics, or found to be problematical by female critics'. The question hangs as to whether Tutti finds a way out of this art-world impasse. Ford suggests:

> In the context of the initial publication of the magazines themselves Tutti could not escape being 'reduced' to the role of an interchangeable fetishized object of private male sexual fantasy. But where Tutti's roles were multiplied, as in the public exhibition, to become both subject and object, artist and model, viewer and viewed, the work became difficult to consume as pornography.

This is a bold approach by Ford, as it circumvents the reduction of the argument to being simply about the divide between art and popular or mass culture – the artistic nude vs. the tabloid consumption of topless women. He concludes with an argument of sorts that suggests Tutti's stance in the anti-censorship camp can be validated through both a repossession of identity and questioning of the 'real' of identity:

> It was Tutti's ability to draw on 'real' experiences as a 'real' model in the fantasy world of pornography that made the work so difficult to reconcile at the time. Today it is this explicit play of notions of authenticity and identity through a foregrounding of pornography as a signifying system, that marks out Tutti's work for magazines as a significant contribution to the feminist critique of an essentialised femininity.

The 'today' of Ford is now a further twenty years in the past, and a contextual resolution of this deeply embedded pornography work by Tutti remains elusive. Johnson (2019: 116), drawing on a contemporary ontology of labour, sees the magazine actions as a 'recasting of Cosey's immaterial labour – posing for pornographic images – as a surreptitious conceptual art project'. His assessment of the exploitative role of the pornographer (or, at least, the photographer) is such that Tutti 'declares herself an agent of self-representation, under whose control the photographer is unwittingly subordinated' (117). In contrast to Johnson's neat encapsulation of a motivation and means for the work, there is a transitoriness in Tutti's explanation, moving between a means of subsistence, the creating of 'self-sourced collaging material' (Roberts 2020: 257) and a 'rich visual time capsule of the blatant 1970s sexism' (Tutti 2017: 340).

Roberts (2020: 244) opens her critical reflection on these works by drawing attention to their 'foundation for re-thinking resistance to classification', particularly in regard to previous categorizations of not art and not feminist. However, she finds it hard to dispute that the work is 'produced within material conditions that are explicitly grounded in pornography' (247) such that the 'ontological "fixing" of the image reaches a dead-end' (256) and 'the images lose distinctiveness in the echo of their familiar expression' (264) – the reductive tropes of pornography. Again, agreement here cannot be found as to a liberating potential (or otherwise) of this apparently reclaimed labour of pornography, as Berry (2018: 254) situates the 'overly legible and derivative quality of the gestures' as playing on the 'replicative amoral indifference'. There is a constant push and pull between who has power and agency, with the suggestion that Tutti's projects allow her a process of self-exploration that transforms her understanding of self, sex, and femininity. This chimes with Dean and Zamora (2021: 204) and their analysis of Foucault's final transition into a politics that prefigured neo-liberalism such that 'politics had become a question of subjectivity and its transformation through limit-experiences, transgressions and ordeals, and that the core of resistance would henceforth be found in the relation of self to itself'. However, the articulation and debate feel messy, inadequate, and imbued with academic seediness.[26] Worley (2017: 183–84) is again useful, capturing something of this messy ambiguity with his analysis of Tutti's extended sleeve notes to the 1988 release *Time to Tell* and the 2010 project *Cosey Complex*. Whereas he holds back on critically assessing Throbbing Gristle as part of the race towards abjection, he is more committed with his reading of these incursions into the pornography industry. He responds to the necessity of the (neo-liberalist) self-journey of bad-archetypal becoming (acquiescing to the language and situational aesthetics of pornography's world) with a stark counter view: 'equally, of course, Cosey's "agenda" as an artist ensured her relationship to porn's subterranean world differed from most of the those she met on the way through'.

Those people whom Tutti might have met on this 'way through' form an accumulating part of Peace's *Red-Riding Quartet*. Women seldom come out of the narrative with any sense of worth or dignity. Victims of the murderer(s), sidekicks relegated to the function of extra-marital affairs for always corruptible male characters, diligent wives carrying the burden of the secrets of their partners, and photographs on the stuck-together pages of porn magazines such as *Spunk* assembled in nondescript flats above nondescript shopping precincts. Peace's fictionalization of the porn industry that runs through the heart of his four novels has no artistic underbelly, autoethnographic endeavour, or Foucauldian voyage of discovery through self-imposed ritual. It's just grot and exploitation. Desperate women hooked in and then drawn in further – brutal, seedy, relentless, degrading, insatiable, exploitative. Everything under the rule of the Five Knuckle Shuffle. Objectified forms that Tutti knew (and played) so well: the bored housewife, the up-for-it secretary, the girl next door, 'Tessa from Sunderland'. A nested set of well-rehearsed archetypes – roles, demeanour, sensibilities, stances, settings, accoutrements. Fantasy is directed into a codified and objectified cul-de-sac with an accompanying script in which you know every word by heart.

Throbbing Gristle's 'Five Knuckle Shuffle', first aired at Wakefield, represented the conveyor belt end point of boredom – the boredom of doing nothing, of penniless and purposeless punk life on the council estate, and of shitty drugs and anti-depressants. The detumescence of your own Throbbing Gristle – industrialized boredom, industrialized relief. The nuances of the pornography industry would come to the fore in the following year, with tracks such as 'Persuasion' and 'Convincing People', replacing the 'aesthetic celebration' of serial killers with an equally unsettling narrative. The Yorkshire Ripper would continue to terrorize through 1979, and Throbbing Gristle would start to explore 'the north' with a more strategic assault, starting with a remarkable gig at Derby.

NOTES

1. https://www.wakefield.ac.uk/college-life/news/2018/04/150-year-launch/?fbclid=IwAR1Q4LG7pHSRyg0-G27pzRD-ALC-Ro-gZEqhNyXbqnSlJBXpMHV2wsTB1X8. Accessed 13 July 2022.

2. 'United' was reviewed in the music newspapers through May into June. The Normal's 'TV-OD' was reviewed around the same time but then re-booted in October with the more commercially friendly 'Warm Leatherette' as the lead track. In the collected book of Mute writing, Reid (2019: 15) has the single released in November. Human League's 'Being Boiled' was released and reviewed in June, shortly after 'United'. Kraftwerk also went 'pop' in 1978 with the German-only release of 'The Model', though this would not find popular appeal in the UK until its 1981 re-release.

3. The band would also include a football hand-clap for the intro of their 1980 single 'Adrenalin'.

4. Sham 69 performed on 11 May 1978 programme as the lone punk act. The following week's programme saw three punk acts with Plastic Bertrand ('Ça plane pour moi'), the Stranglers ('Nice 'n' Sleazy'), and X-Ray Spex ('The Day the World Turned Day-Glo').

5. For the general theory of ANT, see Latour (2005); for a worked case study in art history which has a similar field to my proposal here, see Pezzini (2019). My study of the Sex Pistols producing early publicity photographs on Carnaby Street is also framed within ANT based upon the agency of the camera taking the photograph and the backdrop of Carnaby Street – see Trowell (2016).

6. E-mail conversation on July 2019; as well as for any following uncited Westwood quotes. Westwood's regional gig reviews can also be found in 1978 issues of *Record Mirror*. He mainly reviewed punk and post-punk bands but strangely did not review the Throbbing Gristle gig he put on in Wakefield. The edition of *Record Mirror* following the gig (cover date 8 July 1978) has a Westwood review of the heavy metal band UFO at Sheffield City Hall.

7. E-mail conversation in July 2019; as well as for any following uncited Mallinder quotes.

8. Gildart (2013) adopts a similar methodology and describes structure of feeling as 'a way in which the working class experienced economic and social life in cultural terms' (3).

9. See https://en.wikipedia.org/wiki/Labour_Isn%27t_Working. Accessed 19 August 2021.

10. E-mail conversation in July 2020; as well as for any following uncited Hayes quotes.

11. E-mail conversation in November 2021; as well as for any following uncited Norton quotes.

12. For an analysis of the industrial soundscape of the steam rally, see Trowell (2019).

13. *Yorkshire Evening Post*, 29 June, page 6.

14. See https://en.wikipedia.org/wiki/Tesco. Accessed 10 May 2022.

15. Identifying samples from Throbbing Gristle (and many other post-punk electronic artists) becomes something of a trivial pursuit played out over the internet. This 'go on, go on' shout sample is used as a midpoint in the 'United' single – presumably to emphasize its mock football appeal. It was rumoured to come from an episode of children's television programme *Grange Hill* which first aired in February 1978, putting it close to the recording of the single. However, archive footage of the first few episodes of *Grange Hill* have not revealed the source.

16. *Industrial News* issue 1 (June 1978) has a note of Fizzy Paet sending these tapes to the band.

17. E-mail conversation on 1 July 2020.

18. E-mail conversation in July 2020.

19. The Wearside Jack tape was incorporated into the rough punk single 'Northern Ripper' by The Blanks. The bassist, Allen Adams, was a Throbbing Gristle fan and is listed as among the attendees at the *Heathen Earth* recording in 1980.

20. P-Orridge's relationship to Whitehouse, and Bennett's relationship to Throbbing Gristle is covered in the final chapter.

21. P-Orridge eventually succumbed, with the track 'Leeds Ripper' appearing on the 1995 re-release of the 1982 Throbbing Gristle out-takes compilation *Assume Power Focus*. It is credited as a 1979, composition but is actually a 'fake' track produced by P-Orridge and Larry Thrasher.

22. The overlap between Throbbing Gristle and Sutcliffe is picked up by Ken Hollings in his review of the 2003 reissuing of TG24. Hollings (2003: 58) describes Sutcliffe (and Colonel Kurtz from *Apocalypse Now*) as 'TG contemporaries touched by similar destinies'.

23. We have to include here the Swedish noise-rock band Brainbombs and their more contemporary revivalist Ripper fascination. Most of this is concentrated on the 1999 album *Urge to Kill*, particularly the track 'Driving Through Leeds'. Though by 1999 anything with this title would more than likely summon up thoughts of the notoriously perplexing ring-road around the city centre.

24. Facsimile and transcript available at https://magazine.sangbleu.com/2014/02/22/coum-transmission-annihilating-reality/. Accessed 15 April 2021.

25. The subject of 'Slug Bait' is the murder of a wife of a farmer in the former Rhodesia, but it is often confused with the Manson Family murder of Sharon Tate. P-Orridge 'splices' the narratives together, see https://userpages.umbc.edu/~vijay/tg/texts/text6.html. Accessed 13 July 2022.

26. The paper that promises most, Conroy (2015) for the academic journal *Porn Studies*, delivers the least – a meek celebration of how Throbbing Gristle paved the way for a more expressive and divergent alt culture.

6. ANACHRONY IN THE UK

DERBY AJANTA THEATRE, 12 APRIL 1979

The Winter of Discontent grew through the final few months of 1978 and the first months of 1979, a culmination of British politics and trade unionism dovetailing and conflicting with a power play and series of bluffs to concoct a nadir of economic and social conditions. Strikes began in late September and quickly escalated, the climate of unrest fused with a period of freezing temperatures that gripped the country throughout December and again into the months following the New Year. It felt like the world (or this little bit of the world) was coming to an end. Lorry drivers joined the strike in December, intensifying the social and material extent of the battle into everyday life such that supply lines were threatened with being cut off, thus resulting in shortages and panic buying. The recruitment of gravediggers and waste collectors to the striking sectors in early January acted as a glib metonym, giving the period a defining and long-lasting visual and mythical legacy.

The term Winter of Discontent, taken from Shakespeare's *Richard III*, was not used until the day of the general election in early May 1979 – coined by the editor of *The Sun* as a post hoc description in anticipation of a new dawn of politics. The Labour and Conservative parties had taken turns through the 1970s to steer the country in a more (capitalist) manageable direction, but neither could get to grips with the complexity and rootedness of the 'problems'. Thatcher had taken leadership of the Conservatives in early 1975, following Edward Heath's failure to defeat Harold Wilson in the 1974 general election. Wilson had subsequently handed over the leadership of the Labour party to James Callaghan, a poisoned chalice if ever there was, and Thatcher was waiting to pounce with an aggressive agenda that would go on to define the next decade and beyond. By the end of March 1979, there was a vote of no confidence in the Labour government prompting a general election. Parliament was dissolved in early April to allow campaigning for the election, held on 3 May 1979.

Throbbing Gristle lurched through this period in fits and starts – ending the summer of 1978 with an orchestrated riot at one of their gigs, releasing their second album that cemented their widening recognition, undergoing a series of traumatic relationship events, and emerging to 1979 with a series of gigs at typically bleak and semi-derelict punk venues. This chapter tracks the band through these intense few months, hinging upon their performance at Derby Ajanta Theatre as the 1979 general election takes shape.

ART-PUNK RIOT

Following their first venture to perform north of London, the band saw out the remainder of 1978 in the capital with two prominent gigs at the London Film-Makers' Co-op in Camden on 6 July (five days after the Wakefield gig) and their regular pre-Christmas appearance this time taking place at a space called Cryptic One in the basement of Paddington's Trinity Church. London was lurching towards a post-punk scene that had not yet cohered, with artistic agitators looking for something new that continued the antagonistic lineage of punk with explorations of sonic possibilities. Both of these London gigs, and more specifically the time between them, were important moments in Throbbing Gristle's history and are covered in detail in Ford's history and Tutti's autobiography. It is necessary to set out the key points of this late 1978 period as this allows us to understand the direction the band took in 1979. The year commenced with a relatively compacted period of gigs in the industrial north, bringing the music, imagery, and political complexity of Throbbing Gristle to bear upon new audiences. Whilst the band played to audiences in Sheffield and Manchester that were a part of distinctive city scenes semi-autonomous from the directives of London punk and post-punk, the appearance in Derby is less amenable to an obvious sociocultural contextualization. Developing such a contextualization for what can be considered a proper provincial punk scene forms the basis of this chapter, but first we must return to London.

The July 1978 gig at London Film-Makers' Co-op saw Throbbing Gristle return to a more countercultural arts-based environment, with the co-operative and its associated space on Gloucester Avenue emerging from, and embodying, the squatting initiatives of the 1960s counterculture. The performance was a free event and included the band The Distributers as support and a selection of films, including the notorious *After Cease to Exist* that generally provoked some form of response whenever it was shown. Fish (2002: 29–30) recalls in his book on industrial culture how the audience had to climb a set of metal stairs and were handed a Throbbing Gristle badge before entry into the cramped space, adding:

> There was a very weird vibe at the Film-Makers' Co-op gig from the very beginning. Due to the venue probably, they had decided to show some films including their film (*After Cease to Exist*) with a castration scene (almost definitely Sleazy's idea). There was a very abundant cheap bar and I think it all became too much for the Slits/Raincoats crowd.

The live set progressed in much the same way as Wakefield a few days earlier – 'IBM' as an introduction, the b-movie schlock horror of 'Hamburger Lady' – only for the intensity and brutality of the sound to take on an extra edge. The band then produced a particularly gruelling and caustic industrial section entitled 'Sawmill' followed by an extended sample of the Rolling Stones current disco-based hit 'Miss You' segueing into the 'Mother Spunk' monologue. Finally, the venomous click-loop of 'Five Knuckle Shuffle' breaks through amidst a wall of noise that sounds as if the building is being ripped into a localized black hole. P-Orridge neglects vocal duties as all-out war breaks out in the crowd, with members of the Slits and Raincoats plus punk scenester and photographer Annette Weatherman turning on the band and other members of the audience. Robert Rental's son Dylan is attacked and held aloft, and the antagonists (to Throbbing Gristle's inbuilt antagonism) confront the band and attempt to unplug various leads. In turn, members of the band strike back and use their instruments as weapons in a typical punk affray. As John Gill poetically remarks in his review of the gig, 'the room resembled a furniture warehouse being attacked by poltergeists' (1978b: 34). This gig gradually replaced the Architectural Association gig as the focal point of the mythology machine for the band's provocations of violence.[1]

The period between this gig and the next one includes key incidents that have come to light in recent writings on the band. In May 1978, P-Orridge undertook a trip to Poland to gather influences and conduct a short affair, and a repercussion of this is Tutti calling time on their relationship that is slowly unravelling as a control experiment gone awry. In her autobiography (Tutti 2017: 246–47), she marks the 1st of August as the announcement of the split, and the 15th of the same month when she, under much duress, extricates herself from the domestic arrangements of Beck Road.[2] Prior to this apparently finalizing event, the band attained their first dedicated feature in *NME*, interviewed by an old colleague Bob Edmands who knew them from their Hull days. P-Orridge is returned from Poland and is evidently burning with curiosity and creative energy after experiencing the beginnings of the dark heritage culture associated with death camps such as Auschwitz. In the feature, he related how he had purchased a Polish soldier's uniform, and how the bus tickets on the tourist trip to the death camp were embellished with a fancy pattern of barbed wire (this harrowing design would subsequently grace the covers of *Industrial News*). The scandal of *Prostitution* is reanimated with P-Orridge giving a new slant to the proceedings in pointing out that The Queen is also implicated in things by taking rent from the Institute of Contemporary Arts: 'It's amusing, really, to think that Cosey's tits fed the corgis for a few weeks' (1978: 27).

DIACRITICAL OMISSION

The band also finalized their second album in this period for a release date at the start of December 1978 on their own Industrial label. The album, *D.o.A: The Third and Final Report of Throbbing Gristle*, captured a feeling of multiple crossroads, serving as both an archival document in the sense of the previous album by including several live documentations, and also indicating new material. Further, the album incorporated a dedicated track by each band member, quite possibly indicating the imminent tension and apparent dissolution that haunted the period. These individualized tracks were not added to the live repertoire, and remain as indicators of how the four members will eventually evolve as separate musicians following the actual dissolution of Throbbing Gristle two years later. The album also included numerous provocations and affronts to the concepts of product and consumption, considered as the breaking of archetypes as related to the fanzine *DIRT* #3 which devoted a whole issue to the band in early 1979. The opening track 'IBM' (which has been utilized live) is given an extended presence, designed to veer into the annoying category and also serve as a warning to those who wander into a record shop and ask to listen to the album (and so are offered the opening track as standard practice). The 'hit single' 'United' is included but accelerated and compressed to a sonically intriguing but conceptually meaningless sixteen seconds, effectively fulfilling the promise that the song is included in its entirety. The track 'E-Coli' is cleverly produced using split recordings for the left and right channels; one channel offering a commentary that relays the promotional sheen of genetic research, the other channel explicating its sinister applications, and the murky dialectics of combining them undertaken in a 'normal' listening of the track. Finally, the album includes an intermission of 'Death Threats' taken from the answerphone, including a message left by the partner of Annette Weatherman following the Film-Maker's Co-op riot.

D.o.A received critical acclaim, pushing the band into the foreground for 1979 as British post-punk began to establish and assert itself.[3] Reviews were spread over a month period reflecting the truly independent status of the operation, with *Sounds* kicking off on 16 December 1978 with a five-star review by John Gill (the recipient of P-Orridge's wrath after the previous gig). The following week saw Jon Savage review the album for *Melody Maker*, bleeding in lyrics and constructs from Cabaret Voltaire about 'entertainment' and 'fun' to act as a pivot for the review, and setting out his approach like an essay on the sociology of music to encompass theories of an inside, outside and strategies to move between the two. Savage was still unconvinced and cautious about the band's predilection for presenting, if not celebrating, pure pain and trauma, and called upon the writer Susan Sontag to try to navigate, or at least situate, this dilemma in terms of articulating a response and subsequent action. Two further reviews appeared on 13 January 1979. First, Ian Penman in *NME* who, typical for the newspaper, felt threatened by Throbbing Gristle's apparent intellectualism and avant-garde art pedigree and so turned the review over to a structurally dubious exposition of structuralism. Second, our Wakefield colleague from the previous chapter, Chris Westwood, gave the album an understandably strong review in *Record Mirror* without a need to resort to any pseudo-intellectualism.

FINALITIES

As a precursor to the album's release, the band played at Cryptic One on 11 November 1978, their final gig of the year. This was part of a larger event organized by Colin Faver under the Final Solution umbrella, who were starting to act as a focal point for the coalescing of the post-punk experimental noise, electronic and industrial scenes. Throbbing Gristle appeared with their friends Cabaret Voltaire, Robert Rental and The Normal, and Metabolist. A corresponding night of entertainment was offered a few days later involving a coach trip to a mystery location to experience American avant-gardists Pere Ubu and Red Crayola, both bands straddling the energy and innovation of the punk scene whilst having one foot in the art scene. The Cryptic One gig is where P-Orridge took an overdose prior to performing, completed the performance in an understandably distressed and downcast manner, and returned home to pass out and to be eventually recuperated from the brink of death. As much as Throbbing Gristle stage-managed publicity stunts and worked the media angle to the maximum, this incident was kept out of public knowledge. In Ford (1999: 8.19) P-Orridge relates the personal tension at the time due to the collapse of his relationship with Tutti and also the encroaching acceptance of the band with his recollection that The Clash were trying to get in on the guest list.[4] Understandably, the structure of this gig was very different to the pattern that had emerged through 1978, with P-Orridge opening the event with a sarcastically upbeat announcement (in terms of content) but delivered in a morose manner, taking on the alias of David Brooks and now employed begrudgingly as a lite-entertainer. Opening with 'Whistling Song', essentially a background noise for P-Orridge to unleash a litany of newly instated post-relationship humdrum life, the musical version of George Orwell's 1936 novel *Keep the Aspidistra Flying*. Abruptly ending with a scream, the set moved into the familiar industrial section nominated as 'Tesco Disco' with smothering samples of pop music, news snippets, television programmes (*The Professionals*), advertisements, and film extracts overlaid with processed guitar and bass. 'E-Coli' followed, as presented at the Architectural Association, and the aggressive loop that will eventually form the backbone of the track 'What a Day' was hammered out for the first time with lyrics supplanted by an increase in samples. A curious ten-minute finale of near silence with reduced shrill sound – documented as 'High Note' – completed the evening.

This performance, as a watershed marker of the recent past and the immediate future, was hugely significant. It drew a line between the industrial sound of 1978 gathered up within *D.o.A* and the direction the band will pull in through the next year. Unaware of the wider machinations, Paul Morley reviewed the event for *NME* (18 November 1978) and uses the gig, and Throbbing Gristle, as a vehicle to air his despair and apparent hatred of music and the industry. Whereas he came down on the side of the band in his review of the first album back in February, by now he feels the need to establish a critical distance as he starts to plot his own course through the burgeoning possibilities of post-punk. The year 1979 would be key, with Morley hoping to gain an authoritative voice to dictate taste through the early 1980s.

Throbbing Gristle constantly evolved, forever restless and challenging their own complacencies. Consequently, any record release was very much an archival endeavour, even if aspects of *D.o.A* indicated the potentiality of the members to make something individual of value and merit, as a quadrisected experiment. The sum total of Throbbing Gristle always exceeded these four components, oftentimes vastly so, as it inevitably included an overlaying of tensions within each member as self-doubt and commitment to self-learning, between band members in terms of differing views, tastes and not least intimate tensions, and finally between the band and the outside world of audiences and the music business. Again, we can borrow from the practical partnership of renegade philosophers Gilles Deleuze and Félix Guattari, who are described in the joint biography by Dosse (2010) as establishing a 'disjunctive synthesis' (328) and working in a 'paradoxical tandem' (368). Beckman (2017: 87) offers a clear and concise statement of this way of operating, talking of a 'productive mistrust' such that 'to get to true thinking, a philosophical friendship needs to affirm its dark regions. The friction of uneven surfaces and the ensuing sparks are what cause the creative hum'. With the terminal breakdown of the relationship between P-Orridge and Tutti, it is feasible to consider the band as entering their own personal Winter of Discontent to supplement the encroaching dread of the time as strikes escalate in public sectors. Opinions diverge as to how the band were evolving in this period, akin to an interregnum or stretch of hollowed-out time, with P-Orridge in Ford (1999: 8.30) suggesting 'structural problems' and questioning the levels of commitment within the band. In his recent autobiography, he goes further, suggesting that his suicide attempt at the end of 1978 'burned out some serious memory receptors or something […] the next year, 1979, it's a blank' (P-Orridge 2021: 228). In contrast, Tutti (2017: 254) offers a different view, suggesting that the band are 'on fire with new ideas'. Though her autobiography strangely skips over the years of 1979 and 1980, in many ways opening up her view of being alive with new ideas to a challenge, the archived documents and record releases in these years support this energy flash of creativity. The tensions within the band catalyzed a new phase of activity, which emerged instead as a counterintuitive inversion of productive recalcitrance. The band gained momentum, an incredible insatiable momentum, understood as an (e)motive force, and at the same time increased inertia, understood as a resistance to be changed.

A NEW YEAR

The year 1979 commenced with the band's third feature in *Sounds,* penned by their supporter Sandy Robertson and appearing in the first edition of the year on 6 January 1979. No mention was made of the traumas that had beset the band through November and December, and Robertson instead chose to let P-Orridge wax lyrical about the band's foregrounding of Charles Manson and death camp aesthetics, without coming to any satisfactory conclusion. Neither was there any intimation of a 'where next' nor an indication of this new creative surplus, but this would soon become evident with the band's first performance of 1979.

Whereas the band had avoided a recognizable set or repertoire, certain signatures and structural exertions formed the basis for new songs that captured a new direction. The industrial section within each set that defined the uniqueness of the Throbbing Gristle sound and united a critique of both society and the music business, exemplified at Wakefield, plotted a movement away from punk and a more coherently formed notion of the industrial as a process: repetition, factory (or supermarket) soundscape and mindset, rhythm, and noise. It was a totalizing sound outside of bite-sized and digestible morsels of entertainment akin to the rock music scene, and more geared towards a sound experiment in an art gallery. Out of this dense morass, a bunch of new signatures and compacted rhythms (developed by Carter) began to gather shape, performed as short and intense songs within an approximate set. The live debut of these songs is often misattributed to the first performance of 1979, and there is a common thread amongst many of P-Orridge's recollections that he improvised most of this material on the night. We know that 'Five Knuckle Shuffle', a key element from 1979 onwards, was given its first airing at Wakefield in the summer of 1978, sounding very much like a well-rehearsed song with a theme about punk nihilism and the purposelessness of existence as thinly veiled drudgery. Another key song, 'What a Day', was premiered at Cryptic One in an instrumental format, with P-Orridge's later vocal built up through 1979. Two other tracks debuted at the first event in 1979, a mid-afternoon performance

Figure 6.1: Throbbing Gristle arriving at Centro Iberico, 21 January 1979, photographed for The Poser *#1. Courtesy of Neil Anderson and Darren Laws.*

in the winter climate at the Centro Iberico, an anarchist space within a squatted school on Harrow Road in West London.

Taking place on 21 January 1979, amidst the biting cold that formed the apposite climatic backdrop to the Winter of Discontent, the venue embodied the apocalyptic feeling nurturing into the 1980s with films like *Mad Max* (1979) permeating the zeitgeist. With extinguished bonfires leaking smoke and steam into the crowd, the environment resembled Oscar Murillo's *Violent Amnesia* exhibition which reimagined the hanging banners of anarcho-punk legions and the 'strive to survive' aesthetic of Flux of Pink Indians. Perhaps significantly, the band members were photographed as isolated individuals in the 'straight-up' style that came to define punk and post-punk fashion documentation, for a feature in the debut issue of the fanzine *The Poser* (see Figure 6.1).

The set opens with disjointed commentary samples from the football highlights programme *The Big Match*, distorted and overdubbed with electronic noise as howling winds to appear as if it is coming from the end of the world. We hear snatches of presenter Brian Moore enthusing about Chelsea winning 3–2 away at Maine Road, the home of

Manchester City. A good win for Chelsea, but a season that ultimately saw them relegated from the First Division to commence a four-year exile from the top flight. Both City and Chelsea had notorious hooligan elements at the time as the fashion flipped from 1970s boot-boy to 1980s casual, and Throbbing Gristle's disturbing montage sounds as if it is soundtracking both the match and tense atmosphere of violence. ITV's broadcasting of *The Big Match* went out on Sunday afternoons, though a year later they would challenge BBC's exclusivity for a Saturday night highlights package with the long-running *Match of the Day* programme. The writer David Dent recalls the Iberico gig in his blog, focusing on the heterotopic moment of hearing the football commentary, placing him momentarily back in his family front room rather than the bleak confines of a punishingly loud industrial performance.[5]

This was an example of a sampling strategy at its most radical, a practice that Throbbing Gristle emphasized through 1979. It served the initial purpose to break harmony and comfort in the first instance, by bringing in an uncomfortable ambience from elsewhere such as in their performance at the Architectural Association described in Chapter 4. Sampling the sounds of other times, spaces and contexts opened up the potential to defamiliarize the current space and occasion, to create a no place, an aural hinterland. Tutti (2017: 223) emphasizes the band's intent: 'we wanted people to go out to a gig and experience a totally different sound to what they had heard before, and approach sound in a different way the next time they went out'. The rupturing of comfortable presence came to define the industrial genre, a tactic shared with colleagues Cabaret Voltaire, as Kopf (1987: 11) amply illustrates in his litany of their sources: 'Slot TV preachers and politicians, two-bit carney entertainers and vagrant conmen, lonely phone-in subscribers and their smug grinning host […] looped and looped, this flotsam and jetsam of the airwaves'. Mallinder further recounts how such sampling also served to break the passive absorption and acceptance of the media and information sphere:

> We saw ourselves as mirrors as much as anything. Building in the world around us into our work, particularly by re-appropriating the media from that world to show it back to people. We were very conscious of news and information and how that was used as a force of domination, manipulation and control […] so nothing has changed.[6]

However, Throbbing Gristle went further. As well as dragging the uncomfortable into the arena of the consumption of music (live or recorded), they also disrupted any notion of an uncritical default position of unrest in their own music. After nearly four years of building a reputation for uncompromising sounds, audiences were prone to expecting the controversial and extreme. Throbbing Gristle confronted this inuring internalization of the hostile external by bringing in mundane and banal interjections of the everyday. Hence the sudden occurrence of football commentary, or a plummy BBC voice midway through the Iberico set announcing a new programme *The Parliamentarians*.[7]

After around two minutes of disjointed and frantic football, the sound merges into a steady and unrelenting noise that resembles a mechanical lung, stretching for seven long minutes. This intro section, untitled at the time, would be radically enhanced at Derby to become 'Weapon Training'. Another first followed this, with the discomforting 'Persuasion' made up on the day, mutating from the intro under the cover of a sample of whispered dialogue. An instrumental section of sparse drones and squalls of noise punctuated with P-Orridge's violin work breaks this flow, playing with the acoustics of the space and transforming it into a sci-fi soundscape. From this gradually intensifying squall, the strains of a punch-clock rhythm overpower the complex acoustic mix. The arrangement to 'What a Day' was aired at the previous gig, but at Iberico P-Orridge adds a vocal of a sort, as garrulous grunting producing the gibberish of a transfixed simpleton, close to a Samuel Beckett dialogue that Daniel (2008: 146) associates with this track. P-Orridge (2021: 181) expands on his vocal style, the blending of his anti-charismatic charisma deadpan voice with other styles, suggesting he draws influences from the German sound poet Ernst Jandl and Gurdjieff techniques. Back at Iberico, the chaotic affront descends once again into a battering of improvised noise and feedback which, in turn, relents to allow the mechanical dominance of 'Five Knuckle Shuffle' to play out. The set concluded with the usual 'Wall of Sound' reverberating around the squatted enclosure. It must have been one hell of an experience.

This radical blueprint was the fire of new ideas to which Tutti referred. Heard at a halfway point at Centro Iberico, the band waited another three months to present this new format in a more finished state. Two cancelled gigs in the intervening period, however, prompt inclusion. The band were scheduled to take part in a 24-hour event in Dublin billed as Dark Space, running from the evening of Friday 16 February through to the following Saturday. A small selection of experimental bands were on the bill along with many local Dublin bands, films, and artworks in derelict spaces by artists such as Stuart Brisley. The three headline acts were The Mekons, Throbbing Gristle, and Public Image Ltd, though the latter two pulled out – tantalizingly depriving us of seeing P-Orridge and Lydon sharing a stage.[8] A scheduled gig for 7 April at Action Space was also cancelled, meaning that the appearance at Derby Ajanta Theatre five days later took on a heightened significance. Action Space was associated with the arty side of punk and emergent post-punk, and would be the natural place for Throbbing Gristle's dynamic to be set down for

Figure 6.2: Derby Ajanta, c.1976.

their accustomed London audience. Instead, the band headed north for the second time, to the relative backwater of Derby. The uncertainty of the time, the impending general election and demise of the Labour government, the echoey, and paranoid murmurings of post-punk would be momentarily played out in a semi-abandoned theatre in an East Midlands city that had previously hidden from the musical spotlight.

ABANDONED ENTERTAINMENTS

In many ways, Derby Ajanta Theatre was an archetypical punk venue – a once-grand landmark of expired entertainment. A building that had once been ornate to synergize the art of structure with the art of performance within, but over time had features bricked over and painted in layer after layer of weatherproof industrial paint (see Figure 6.2). In this respect, Derby's Ajanta bore a striking similarity to the Manchester Electric Circus, a building that stood isolated amongst rubble and open spaces, held intact by the exterior paint that had been applied without care or attention to the pre-existing nuances of the structure. A perfect home for punk in the provinces. Vincent (2008: 52–53) gathers some evocative testimony for his personal history of Derby's alternative music scene:

> White walls of the building darkened to grey by years of neglect and harsh weather, the windows bricked up, and loose wires hung from the side flapping about in the wind [...] With a capacity of 525 the Ajanta had an atmosphere all of its own, this was a venue that once you were inside there were no rules, you basically did what you wanted and that included smashing the place to bits, letting off fire hoses, fighting in the crowd and with the bands, throwing cans and bits of seating around [...] Like going to a cinema after it had been involved in a riot [...] the balcony was like a wooden terrace at a football ground with faded red carpet with holes in. People would sit on it pulling the thread and fraying what little was left, pulling it apart bit by bit as you would sit there waiting for the band.

Derby-born artist and performance maker Tim Etchells, attending the gig as a young teenager with a group of friends, has a vivid memory of the feeling of the place: 'The Ajanta always did feel like it was in a parallel universe – deregulated, not quite subject to the kind of organisation or law that events elsewhere might have been – a law unto itself'.[9] The intimacy of this kind of description of Derby Ajanta Theatre, its detailing of destruction reading as a dark mirror version of Gaston Bachelard's *Poetics of Space* celebrating the physical and architectural nuances of undoing and *un-dwelling,* often escapes official recording of popular music heritage. It has emerged more recently in fan-driven vernacular writing, such as Hill's (2011) documentation of the unlikely existence of the Grey Topper, a utilitarian structure that functioned as a music venue in the remote Nottinghamshire mining village of Jacksdale, and Anderson's (2009) recollection of the life and times of The Limit nightclub in Sheffield. While these are not strictly architectural readings, there is often a resonance that draws up an ontology and epistemology of the inhabited interior. For example, through Anderson's evocative references to The Limit's beer-soaked sticky carpets and sweat dripping off walls, and in the celebration of the implausible spaces that catered for the punk scene (semi-derelict cinemas and theatres, repurposed boat-houses). In an academic setting, the discursive creep of memory studies and nostalgia theory has brought this intimate study of space of pleasurable experience to new attention and audience. Forbes (2015) focuses on the single space of Glasgow Apollo to initiate a dialogue around architectural engagement, using nostalgia theory to document the corridors, rooms, and exterior gathering spots (where a free pass into the interior can be explored through an open window or unlocked backstage door). My own study (Trowell 2015), based on memories from personal experience, details Leeds Queens Hall as an interior space that enabled a northern post-punk narrative to develop in a Ballardian space of concrete and shadows. As can be gauged from the extended quote above, the Ajanta evoked strong memories and anchoring of experience for those artists who attended and for the Derby crowd of punks who felt a communal and subcultural ownership of the space.

From the stage, Derby's Ajanta Theatre looked like a 'mouth with teeth missing' (Vincent 2008: 67), as musicians stared down at the destitute theatre space with rows of plush seats long since ripped out and hurled around. It was known variously as the Ajanta Theatre and Ajanta Cinema, though ticket stubs proudly proclaimed it as a theatre, reflecting its status from 1952 as the Derby Playhouse, following a brief opening period as a school. It was burnt out and rebuilt in 1958 but went into decline soon after. It became a multi-functioning hub for the local Indian community in 1975, operating as a proper cinema for Bollywood films and then doubling with a seedy function as a porn cinema, hence instigating some confusion about its status.[10] The (porn) cinema aspect of it consisted of a back room with a large television showing adult films where a 'one hour membership' could be purchased.[11] Other concurrent uses included a laundrette and a pickling industry. It opened as a punk venue in February 1979 in a period that overlapped its use as a porn cinema, and the changing areas for the bands famously doubled as a storage space for multiple varieties of Indian pickle and chutney, a scene akin to a Tony Cragg artwork such as *Larder* (1990). Derby's punk community quickly made their mark on the fixtures and fittings by ritually smashing it up at every event, whereafter it was partially put back together, and then smashed again. The building sat off Osmaston Road on the western edge of the small shopping and business centre of Derby, the main through route to the local football ground. During its brief period as a punk venue, partly as a consequence of the audience being made to wait outside the tightly locked building right up until the start of each gig, there would be occasional fights and running skirmishes between football fans returning from the game and punks waiting for the gig. The Saturday after Throbbing Gristle played there, the local rivalry between Derby County and Nottingham Forest was rekindled as the teams met in front of 30,000 fans at Derby's Baseball Ground. Forest ran out 2–1 winners as the fortunes of the teams swapped places through the decade, reflecting the genius of the manager Brian Clough who had made the short journey between the clubs. There was no gig at the Ajanta on that Saturday evening, but the vestiges of Throbbing Gristle's mantra 'nothing short of a total war' would have been lingering as 1970s boot-boys and early 1980s casuals traded blows. Porn, pickles, decadent dereliction, and testosterone-fuelled teenagers fronting up to each other; something for everyone of a Throbbing Gristle inclination.

PUNK GHOSTS

Taking the stage on Thursday 12 April 1979, P-Orridge makes a short speech, apologizing for the inability of the film to be shown (the projector is broken) and mentioning that the local newspaper advertised the band as T.G. rather than giving them their full name. A touch of light humour is added as he apologizes for making people forgo *Top of the Pops*. Whilst we can't blame the broken projector on the Sex Pistols, subsequently sparing the Derby public a viewing of *After Cease to Exist*, the now-defunct punk band are remotely implicated in the other circumstances. The organizers of the gig, the same small group who established the Ajanta as a punk venue, had run into a brick wall with the local newspaper the *Derby Evening Telegraph*. Derby had a torrid relationship with punk and the Sex Pistols, infamously being one of the first places to ban the band's December 1976 *Anarchy in the UK* tour following the Bill Grundy incident. Desperate to keep on the right side of public opinion, with a bid for city status to be decided in 1977, the town went a step further and made minor history by demanding that the Sex Pistols perform in front of a council committee. This incident is recorded in several versions, with Scanlan's (2016: 146) account of the event suggesting it took place in the Judge's Chamber, while testimony in Vincent's (2008: 22–24) *An Alternative Derby* recalling that it was to take place during the afternoon at the venue (Derby King's Hall) but the band refused to cooperate. Apocryphal punk folklore has it that the Damned did acquiesce to the audition, and were subsequently ejected from the tour.[12] This slightly less scandal-hungry version of events is also set out by Gildart (2013: 181–83), who supports his writing with archival references to the local newspaper. The incident made good copy in the *Derby Evening Telegraph*, detailing the 'waiting game' played by five Labour and five Conservative council officials as the 2 o'clock deadline approached and passed, with one Labour official urging for the whole charade to be cancelled as he felt that acting as moral guardians of taste and culture was not something they should sign up for. Amidst photographs of queuing punks – obviously a novelty in the provincial town of Derby – the Sex Pistols attracted a headline accusing them of 'shooting off after a hard day's nowt', though the actual text of the column revealed little more than a few quotes from the hotel proprietor where the band had stayed, disappointedly reporting that the band had behaved in an exemplary fashion. The following year, Derby's near neighbours Nottingham would make more (anti) Sex Pistols history by calling upon the ancient Indecent Advertisements Act of 1899 to expedite the banning of a display of the *Never Mind the Bollocks* album in the local independent record shop (Scanlon 2016: 207).

This punk pantomime of the East Midlands ensured that the official organs, organizations, and functionaries of Derby had a distinctively wary hands-off approach

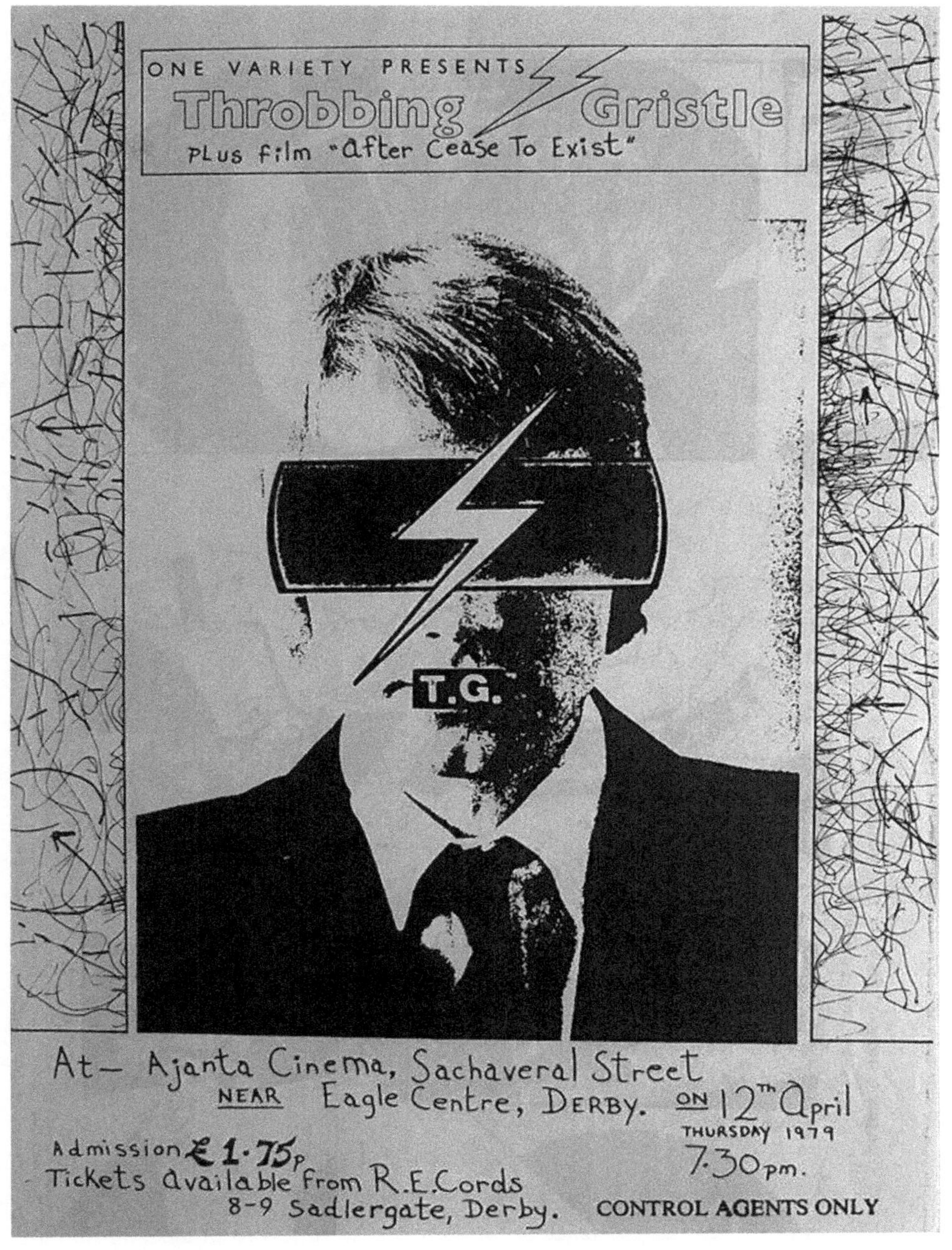

Figure 6.3: Poster for Throbbing Gristle at Derby Ajanta, 12 April 1979, designed by Val Denham.

to punk that persisted beyond 1976 and 1977, a corollary of which was that the *Derby Evening Telegraph* refused to run the advertisement for the Throbbing Gristle gig that the promoters had worked so hard to achieve. This was loosely based upon the observation that the name bore a syntactic similarity with the dreaded Sex Pistols, an echo of the discussion in Chapter 2. A compromise of sorts was reached, and the Friday before the gig the newspaper allowed a small, single advertisement for 'T.G.?' and support band Pre-De and *After Cease to Exist* (it was not made clear that the latter was a film).[13] The inclusion of a question mark did little to alleviate the lack of information, adding a sheen of mystery to the artist to appear, and possibly contributing to the eventual small attendance. The weekend edition of the newspaper, which included a music section and entertainment guide for the following week, made no reference to the gig. Instead, the Derby public were offered a double bill of horror at the Odeon cinema with *Halloween* and *Damien Omen II*, whilst the rival ABC cinema offered the obligatory porn to supplement the obligatory horror with *Kentucky Fried Movie*, *Confessions*, and *Playbirds*. The wrestling superstar Mick McManus, who plied his trade as a love-to-hate figure, was appearing at the Assembly Rooms, an attraction for all ages. No further mention was made in the run-up to the Thursday, though the paper ironically had a 24-page 'industrial survey' supplement that promoted the engineering prowess of the city. Neither were there any reviews of the gig, the only headline of a 'TG performance' appearing a few days later referring solely to a play put on by Markeaton Townswomen's Guild.

SATURATION

What about the missed edition of *Top of the Tops* that P-Orridge had offered to the audience as an apology? On Thursday 12 April 1979, the following was on show in a slightly extended 35-minute transmission hosted by an excitable Peter Powell: the Three Degrees 'The Runner', Light Of The World 'Swingin', Kate Bush 'Wow', Showaddywaddy 'Remember When', Sex Pistols 'Silly Thing' (Legs & Co.), Neil Diamond 'Forever In Blue Jeans', Racey 'Some Girls', Supertramp 'The Logical Song', Sham 69 'Questions and Answers', Kandidate 'I Don't Wanna Lose You', Sister Sledge 'He's The Greatest Dancer', and Art Garfunkel 'Bright Eyes' (number one). For a young punk audience, the standout moments were clearly Sham 69 and the Sex Pistols, the latter at the time well advanced in their disintegration, and suffering the ignominy of having 'Silly Thing' danced by the resident Legs & Co. This all-girl dance troupe gave the continuity from the long-running Pan's People and short-lived Ruby Flipper, taking over the role from 1976 to 1981, and so being saddled with having to find dance routines to the heyday of British punk and new wave which dominated the charts in 1979. Their name reflected their soft-porn approach, part of the casual sexism of the times, suggesting that a redeeming and singular feature was an attractive pair of legs.

The Sex Pistols, once the target of P-Orridge as both bands set out simultaneously on their unsteady courses from 1976, had witnessed a rapid turnover of fortunes since their breakdown concert in January 1978. Sid Vicious had been catapulted to front-of-house duties and happily obliged to record a slew of cover versions through the summer of 1978 willingly playing the fool. As Hawkins (2009: 85) surmises in his study *The British Pop Dandy*, Vicious 'negotiates a performance strategy never witnessed before'. His cover of the Frank Sinatra classic 'My Way' took this to the limit, the track starting with Sid crooning in time with the original, to a background of atmospheric orchestral strings, drawling and hiccupping his delivery with his goofy persona and upward-punching irony. In his discussion of cover versions, Mosser (2008) picks out this section of the song as deliberately lugubrious with drawn-out syllables, sounding like a 'stereotypical drunken guest at a wedding'. Heading to New York in autumn 1978, he hit a precipitous downward spiral as he lived out his cartoon character punk persona, commencing with his partner Nancy Spungen dying in a drug-related incident that was never resolved but initially saw the hapless junkie Vicious arrested and jailed. He was bailed, and then re-arrested for his part in a drunken brawl to spend 55 days in jail and undergo enforced detox. On release in February 1979, he acquired a large amount of heroin, with the help of his addict mother, and died on the same night through an overdose. If the Winter of Discontent drew from a Shakespearian history play, then Sid's demise was part tragedy part comedy.

Whereas Johnny Rotten, now returned to Lydon, disconnected himself from the crawling chaos of the punk wreckage to go into a period of productive creativity with Public Image Ltd by releasing a single and album in 1978, McLaren picked over the bones of the Sex Pistols. Throughout the latter part of 1978 and the following two years, the *Flogging a Dead Horse* strategy of music marketing went into overdrive, with hit singles twinned with raunchy or novelty b-sides, wrapped in parodic commodity sleeves by designer and artist Jamie Reid. As Bestley (2013) argues, this turn to humour within punk was embraced across the genre. The Sex Pistols shifted from being society's bête noire to a household name akin to the Bay City Rollers – quite possibly the culmination of Malcolm McLaren's intent. Their smuttiness and foul-mouthing gripped the adolescent record-buying market; playground chatter hinged around the band and the de rigueur hemp military-style school rucksacks were painted with extracts from the band's artwork.

The year 1979, particularly the first half, exemplified the commercial success of punk and new wave as an amorphous mix, a substantial distance away from the hip and happening beginnings of the scene in London and its distillation into the provinces through a cool and connected network. As can be seen above, Sham 69 and the Sex Pistols stand out on a *Top of the Pops* devoid of any other serious or forward-looking subculture. The week before had even more to offer with five punk and new wave bands: the Jam, Generation X, the Members, Siouxsie and the Banshees, and Squeeze – for all intents and purposes a majority.[14] A couple of weeks later the Dickies found success with a vaguely punk and sped-up version of the 'Banana Splits (Tra La La)' theme (pressed in banana yellow vinyl, naturally, and having the delight of two silly tracks on the b-side – 'Hideous' and 'Got it at the Store'). Juvenile punk records in novelty packaging came thick and fast – the Undertones twinned 'Jimmy Jimmy' with 'Mars Bars' (with a limited-edition clear sleeve and translucent green vinyl), whilst the Skids offered 'T.V. Stars' as the b-side to 'Into the Valley' creating a terrace and playground chant that reeled off the names of *Coronation Street* actors. All these records elicited an appearance on *Top of the Pops*. The common misconception of punk indelibly linked to the Winter of Discontent, providing a soundtrack for these days of darkness and dread, is turned upside down. As we can see, punk was both at its populist peak and silliest songwriting capacity – if it was indeed soundtracking the decline of British civil life, then it was through a Bakhtinian laugh via a medium of day-glo record sleeves and coloured vinyl.

Osborne (2015: 433) also notes that the year 1979 was the high point for punk's commercial exposure, arguing that as a subculture it would be boosted by large numbers of school kids looking for the next (or first) exciting thing. He points to 'Friggin' in the Riggin'', the infamous b-side of 'Something Else', the single that immediately preceded 'Silly Thing', as a clarion call:

> These young fans came on board after 1977 and initially had more familiarity with Sid Vicious than with Johnny Rotten. These were the consumers who fell for the 'swindle'. If my own school is anything to go by, they fell for 'Friggin' in the Riggin'' hardest of all.

The appeal of controversy and swearing, a tactic not ignored by Throbbing Gristle, was milked:

> In numerical terms 'Friggin' in the Riggin'' goes further still. Its lead vocalist, Jones, first displayed his aptitude for swearing on the Today program. The song contains an 'ass', a 'tits', a 'fuckin'', four 'bollocks', 'fuck' 15 times, and 'friggin'' 45 times. In its escalating litany of exploits 'Friggin' in the Riggin'' also highlights the sexual side of swearing.
>
> (437)

As Throbbing Gristle readied themselves for their Derby gig with the doors of the Ajanta barred shut, a crowd of provincial punks were milling excitedly outside. This was the third gig at the Ajanta since its tentative opening as a punk music venue, with a debut night a month previous featuring the upcoming punk band Stiff Little Fingers (who would go on to appear four times on *Top of the Pops* in 1980). Other young punks, including myself as a 13-year-old boy in front of a newly rented colour television three miles away from the Ajanta, were watching *Top of the Pops* and buying the records in their picture sleeves and multiple versions of coloured vinyl. Legs & Co. had already danced to the Sid Vicious-fronted Eddie Cochran cover 'Something Else' as it rose up the charts in March, adorned in coloured punk wigs and stretched out in a line executing a prototype *Riverdance* routine as they kicked their legs forwards and moved backwards. On the night of Thursday 12 April, the sextet were arranged in a diamond formation, akin to the famous Red Arrows aerobatics display team, wearing matching outfits of white stilettos, tight black trousers, boxy blazers in bright shades covering a bare chest, and black bow-ties around their slender necks. It was an attempt at early punk fashion where symbols of normalized modesty and vestimentary class and occasion were detourned. They danced a synchronized punk dance, keeping their arms taut to their sides and their hands pressed down into the side pockets of the oversized jackets. The dance included a well-rehearsed medley of punk moves; thrashing their heads from side-to-side, short bursts of dignified pogoing, alternating straight leg kicking with a swivel motion, the provocative mouthing of the simple chorus, and a vertical jump with arms unanchored from pockets and raised aloft. The camera utilized a crude stop-frame technique to capture the dancers at the pinnacle of each jump, holding the frame for a few seconds, and then returning to live action with the troupe scuttling around on another part of the small stage.

TRAINED WEAPONS

Beyond *Top of the Pops*, television for the night was a flaccid mix of pop, comedy, technology, and religious mysticism – themes that Throbbing Gristle aggressively and unremittingly mangled together and tore apart in their hour-long sets. The ITV channel featured the torpid soap operas *Crossroads* and *Emmerdale Farm*, factual programmes *Survival* and *TV Eye*, a nondescript sit-com *Leave it to Charlie* followed by *Best Sellers* which ran up to close-down at 12–15. BBC1 had the stalwart *Tomorrow's World* and the comedy quiz *Blankety Blank* bookending *Top of the Pops*, followed by nostalgic dross with *The Good Old Days*, a documentary on the Turin Shroud (which occupied the cover of *Radio Times*), and a closing out with *Crystal Gayle Sings Country*. BBC2 had little to offer, with regional drama *When the Boat Comes In* and an extended broadcasting of the opera Berg's *Lulu*. A choice of three channels, but minimal substance. Throbbing Gristle, on the day before Good Friday, were promoted under the banner of One Variety – a self-negating dyad that harked back on the pseudo concepts of choice and challenging culture. By ironic chance, the small advertisement in the local newspaper was placed under another event billed as an 'all star variety show' (complete with basket meals). Throbbing Gristle were about to explode all these standards, annihilating the increasingly tired and drab chronology of the 1970s as the decade drew to a close.

They commence with a first, the track 'Weapon Training', which would be a standard opening for the next three performances. This runs as a pure sample, where a stentorian American voice introduces a series of weapons one by one with a sample of their sound. The soundtrack is drawn from the album *The Sound of Combat Training*, a resource to familiarize new recruits with the noises of modern warfare.[15] In the hands of Throbbing Gristle, this takes on a disturbing sonic presence, the litany of missiles, guns, and other killing devices such as flamethrowers being projected into the crowd as if engaging them in battle. A high-pitched synth noise lingers, and as the flamethrower takes over the sonic foreground, the sound of Throbbing Gristle and the sound of weapons blend into one, indiscernible. A plethora of machine gun fire adds rhythmic noise and the reproduction of the helicopter-mounted missile powers into a double noise of pure force and destruction from the helicopter blades and missile propulsion system. This ushers in the three-note squashed loop from the previous gig – the mechanical lung – and the rising tones. The weapons of war are now entirely in the hands of the band, a sonic war, an information war, a total war. As Matthew Cheeseman suggests in his research into the subsequent gig at Sheffield when describing 'Weapon Training': 'there was a sense that they were training their audience, forming a cadre of disciples dedicated to unlearning, forgetting social rules, deprogramming via a confrontation with the extreme' (Kilby and Cheeseman 2013).[16]

War was at the heart of popular culture for the adolescent and teenage demographic, and as Ogg (2013) shows, the residues of war had a persistent vestigial presence that seeped into the punk subculture. Wilson (2020: 34) examines the wider sphere of cultural links to assert: 'Lives were touched in profound ways, not least with the prolonged persistence of fear'. The playgrounds were full of mock wars with children mimicking the rat-a-tat of machine guns, the fizz-and-thud of grenades, and the dramatic enacting of theatrical heroic deaths. Bloodthirsty Sven Hassel World War II fantasy books were surreptitiously passed around the classroom. Toys and games were themed on war, with break-time or between-lesson games such as Top Trumps offering fetishization of tanks, armoured vehicles, and weapons as children devoured the taxonomies of power, speed, and killing capability in a bid to outdo their opponents and win cards. Action Man figures came with a vast array of uniforms, specialist outfits (for snow or underwater scenarios), weapons, and vehicles. The comic *Battle Action,* costing ten pence, was published every Thursday, and on the day of Throbbing Gristle appearing in Derby, it bore a masthead stating 'For All Out War'. Stories included 'Charlie's War', 'The Sarge', 'Glory Rider', 'Johnny Red', and 'Crazy Keller'. The theme was past wars extended into the present, but in a parallel world Throbbing Gristle brought imaginary comic strips based upon real wars in the here and now – imagine 'H-Block', 'SPG', 'Active Cell', 'Hunger Strike', 'The Torturer', and 'Nail Bomb' as alternative weekly instalments. War, art, and entertainment were all implicated in a messy flux. The track 'IBM' doubled as a rejoinder for intercontinental ballistic missiles, and (post) punk bands such as Gang of Four were explaining away their choices for signing to record labels like EMI that had a wide portfolio of killing technologies in their aggressive capitalist practices. Sonic precursors to 'Weapon Training' include Marinetti's onomatopoeia poems and the famous Futurist work *Zang Tumb Tumb* (1912) which re-imagined machine gun fire as poetry, updated by Bill Viola's *Street Music* (1976) as he recorded himself firing bullets into the air whilst stood in the Wall Street district. Global-political tension escalated as the 1970s played out, with over 500 NATO Cruise and Pershing missiles stationed in Europe. Away from war, the potential for total destruction through nuclear capability had been brought to the fore in the previous week with the partial meltdown of a nuclear reactor at the Three Mile Island Nuclear Generating Station.

'Weapon Training' is continued for eight minutes before it gradually disassembles to a crude bass pluck and then a primitive punk bass salvo, something for the punks, which picks up further as P-Orridge commences the screamed utterance of 'Eee Ahh Oooh', sound poetry and incantation based upon ritual. The second debut for Derby follows a conjoined sample consisting of the announcement of being 'free, white and 21' (a once common phrase and made popular in Larry Buchanan's 1963 film) and an interview with pornographer John Lindsey and his *Lolita* magazine project which concerns photographing children in a sexualized manner. There is a bit of a Throbbing Gristle in-joke here as Lindsey directed Tutti in the 1976 hardcore short *Sex Angle.*[17] According to P-Orridge in Daniel (2008: 75), the track 'Convincing People' was made up on the night, though the precursor sample of apparent freedom and manipulative freedom exploiter seems to make this claim appear dubious. The blend of not quite meaning what you say and the samples meeting in a muddy zone of discomfort underpins the track that follows, a key moment of the band. 'Convincing People', and other tracks developed in this period, would form half of the album *20 Jazz Funk Greats* released later in the year.

This album has attained something of a critical cult status through the years, initially seen as a bad joke to undermine the bad jokes to be expected from the band with its swirls of lounge music and drifty noodles of sound. A casualty of the album's critical reception was that tracks such as 'Convincing People', stark, synthetic, and metronomic in their composition, would be pushed aside for fixating on the more outré aspects. Daniel's study on the album does acknowledge these tracks and he sets out the compositional power as a priority, with the metronomic snaps and underwater swilling synth sounds offered as 'spinning a hamster wheel' (72). However, the theme of 'Convincing People' is both problematic and implicative of the audience, with P-Orridge's rendition of the lyrics extrapolating this by taking both sides in the argument with consecutive switches. On the album these opposing views overlap, and this is achieved in a live context as the band employ a simple single echo which allows a phrase to initially repeat in the spaces between before the spaces are dispensed with and so opposites coincide. This is evocatively described by Daniel as 'an interplay of opposites colouring each other […] self-cancellation […] affirmation and negation become simultaneous […] anti-narrative glossolalia […] an allergic reaction to meaning' (72, 88).

The set is threaded together by a steady arpeggiator-synth rhythm but then breaks down. This midway point is the commencement of 'Hamburger Lady', heightened in horror by appearing where it does in the set bracketed by an approximate silence. An instrumental section follows, guided by a chiming clock that builds towards the industrial noise of the *D.o.A* title track overlaid with what could be one of Chris Carter's electro-pop compositions. After six minutes the hybrid noise winds down to a snatched sample from the news about the Scottish Nationalist Party (SNP) and plans for devolution, momentarily bringing in the political outside of the impending general election and the implications of the Winter of Discontent. P-Orridge utters the word pogo, addressing the predominantly punk audience of Derby, and powers into a sub-two-minute bludgeon-riffed track called 'Chat Up', the ultra-minimal lyrics chorused by a high-pitched nonsense noise. If anything was improvised on the night it was this track, which would appear only once again at the subsequent gig in Sheffield two weeks later.

The voice of the male prostitute on 'Valley of the Shadow of Death' is given prominence, extending for a lengthy period as the band members presumably regroup and reset things. The third exclusive then follows, with a first proper airing of 'What a Day' following its instrumental and garbled version in the previous two performances. Listed as 'Day Song', P-Orridge sounds sickened, shouting barely coherently, possessed by malfunctioning local accents strung together like a third-rate club-circuit entertainer. This uncontrolled splurge of exaggerated accents and guttural whistles strangely links back to the birth of recording culture, highlighted by Murphy (2014: 10) as he documents the first recordings of popular tracks such as 'The Whistling Coon' and 'The Laughing Song'. Whilst submitting to what Reed (2013: 130) classes as an 'ultra-steady metering of time', the grinding piecemeal noises of 'What a Day' are both never quite aligning and never-ending, a harmonic anti-harmony. The simultaneously hypnotic and disturbing allure of this track garners most efforts at description, from attempts at simple deconstruction of its composition to allegorical excesses. After stating its intention to 'bludgeon and chafe', Duff (2019: 222) declares that 'musically, the song is founded on a locked half rhythm, with the minimum of adornments. Just a few curlicues of synth and some brief and muted washes of guitar. It's pure sonic irritant [...] moronic architecture'. Stubbs (2018: 321) simply suggests an 'electric riff like an eel in a churn' and Daniel (2008: 142) notes the 'clipped, harsh snare defining the cyclic turnover of some vast machine'.

Another moment of silence signals a proper stop to the trapped rhythm of 'What a Day' and a montage of live insertions is grabbed from a television broadcast and thrust into the output. A banal advertisement for a sale ushers in the distressing taped wail of 'Persuasion', immediately given a bathetic sheen as two football results are mixed in, read out in the official BBC voice: 'Barnsley 1 Hartlepool 0, and from Scottish Division 2 we have East Stirling 0 Dunfermline 2'. The former game, in the old English Fourth Division, was played on the night of the gig, indicating that its inclusion was via a live radio or television grab. The game was postponed from January, part of the freezing cold weather that meteorologically framed the Winter of Discontent and caused fixture congestion. At that point in time Arthur Scargill was rising as a left-wing political force, president of the Yorkshire NUM and having made his name at the victorious Battle of Saltley Gate in 1972. This strike set the seeds for the toppling of Edward Heath's Conservative government in 1974, and a period of Labour power that was about to end. Soon after Throbbing Gristle's gig at Derby the Conservative Party, under new leader Margaret Thatcher, won the election, and Scargill and the miners were the first in the cross-hairs of her sights. He would be brutally crushed as Thatcher's ritual slaughter lamb, the government employing every technique to suppress the 1984 miners' strike. At times he claimed to be a Barnsley fan and a regular at Oakwell, and he is invoked in the future-anterior sense, as someone yet to befall their fate that they are now known for. Two crowds transposed – the punks and assorted Throbbing Gristle fans sheltered in the crumbling Ajanta, the sparse crowd of Barnsley supporters on the exposed terraces of Oakwell cheering on a team trapped in the basement of the football league system – both thin in number, seated, standing, shouting, subcultural minorities verging on non-citizens or outcasts, but also worlds apart from each other.

The finale of 'Five Knuckle Shuffle' closes the evening, the machinic shift to life as checkout process. As Worley (2017: 112) states, boredom is 'both a stimulus and explanation for punk's dissatisfaction', and boredom is bored to death in 'Five Knuckle Shuffle'. Three noises fighting for superiority until they all coalesce and pummel you, a misaligned windscreen wiper in the driving rain, light at the end of the tunnel but the train crashes before you get there – GAME OVER.

SWING CITY

Derby was personified for being in flux and uncertain, nervously acquiring city status in 1977 by creating an initial pantomime of confronting punk and the Sex Pistols. It was, however, a typical medium-sized town without a dedicated university or polytechnic in the 1970s and 1980s which would typically facilitate the influx of a transient student population that in turn inspired a creative shot in the arm. Like Wakefield, it was something of a backwater but it embraced punk as much as a small town could. By 1979, it was offering a large venue for punk and new wave bands that were touring on the cusp of punk's 1979 heyday, with the covered swimming pool of King's Hall alternating with the capacious Assembly Rooms, an egg-box brutalist building opened in the Jubilee year of 1977. Derby's original punk advance guard was well established in the city, with a host of fanzines such as *Situation Vacant, Jubilee City, Twisted Reality, Verbal Abuse,* and *Maelstrom.* Key figures such as Dave Bonsall and Hector Heathcoate were spearheading the facilitation of new fashions and styles, with Bonsall opening the clothes shop Society Styles in the early 1970s and Heathcoate undertaking various dj-ing positions and working in the local independent record shop. Bonsall's original shop was remarkably similar to McLaren and Westwood's first venture on King's Road, with the shop resembling a front room and offering meticulously sourced deadstock clothing from subcultures past, bringing it back to life as punk started to blossom. In 1977, Bonsall shifted location in Derby to open ID on Tenant Street, and this functioned as a 'proper' punk space, the shop located on a broken-down street and featuring intimidating grilles over the windows. Bonsall's connections to McLaren and Westwood allowed authenticated punk objects and ideas to flow into the city, giving Derby a punk jump-start on its provincial contemporaries. More importantly, it provided a focal point for proto-punks and adventurers in the city, with an added bonus of having a small rehearsal space for fledgling bands. This meant that bands in the city around this time were fluid, ephemeral, amorphous, and interchangeable in terms of personnel and sound. Pockets of different music fans flourished in the city, fed by the channels of the music press, John Peel and word of mouth. As Tim Etchells recounts:

> The way things moved then was much more through those forms […] rather than internet as now. So everything was by definition slower, a bit more local, a little bit more intimate and also rather random in the way it connected. We were living in the suburbs so going into Derby was a bus ride […] always a bit of an adventure. […] We never felt like a huge connected part of any scene but we were there for very many gigs […] It was a huge part of staking out who you were/what you thought you could be. I definitely gravitated to the music that was reinventing stuff in the space that had been cleared by punk, but which retained the DIY vibe. The Fall, Cabaret Voltaire, Magazine, Joy Division etc.

Derby was also a strong engineering city, with a flourishing railway centre developing futuristic trains, Rolls Royce (aerospace), and the large factory British Celanese on the eastern edge. When I was at school, everyone's dad, uncles, friends, and neighbours worked at one of these employers. The Winter of Discontent was somewhat milder in the city, and subsequently Derby was seen as a barometer seat as the general election of 3 May 1979 approached. As Beckett (2010: 516) points out, Derby, being typically contrary, gave an early misreading of the swing that suggested a continuation of the status quo. This was not to be. In many ways, the result of the election shaped Derby's punk and post-punk future, but first we have to unpack the path of Throbbing Gristle into the city.

The aforementioned Bonsall and Heathcoate were key in procuring both the space of the Ajanta and the billing of the band. In fact, Bonsall suggests that they explored the opportunity to open up the space of the Ajanta with the express aim of hosting Throbbing Gristle.[18] This was also motivated by Derby's Alan Taylor, an important figure who was an early mover-and-shaker in the local (and wider) punk scene. Taylor worked in Bonsall's shop ID and formed the band Pre-De (who were pencilled in to support on the night), adopting a more post-punk style at an early juncture. Taylor had also procured an early copy of *Second Annual Report*, and this record had been passed around the small crowd of punk and experimental music fans who frequented ID. The opening night of the Ajanta (22 February 1979) under the trio's tutelage was the Rough Trade package tour; however, the headline act – Stiff Little Fingers – ensured more of a diehard punk crowd as opposed to Robert Rental, the Normal and Essential Logic who also shared the bill. The follow-up gig a month later saw a very much post-punk trio with Pop Group, Alternative TV, and Manicured Noise. This was something of a feeler to nurture a crowd for the Throbbing Gristle gig, but the Ajanta was quickly adopted as being a punk space as much as a post-punk space. Etchells recalls that this often manifests as a feeling of tension, particularly at the opening gig and the Throbbing Gristle gig:

> It felt like there was a tension between the punk scene proper (quite conservative really) and the more art school/experimental edge was in evidence – that was definitely the case at the Rough Trade gig where Robert Rental/The Normal got short shrift from a crowd that was more focused on the three-chord approach of Stiff Little Fingers. If I'm right there was also a tension around TG cos it was perceived as a London thing […] and the Derby scene was a bit parochial, anti-London, anti-anything that was perceived as 'arty'.

On the night of the Throbbing Gristle gig, Pre-De had a change of mind, partly nerves and partly a continuation of disagreement around their constant changing of style, and pulled out of the support slot. This paved the way for the young band Corridor to step up in support. Corridor were a typically brief Derby band that seeded numerous other bands moving in post-punk directions. Bassist Aaron Williamson takes up the story:

> We were a scratchy, DIY, non-musicians, bedroom band really. Early Fall, Swell Maps, Raincoats, and the US band Chrome – and of course the Velvet Underground – were what we listened to for influences. I think someone at ID must have called the student union at Wilmorton College to round us up mid-afternoon and we went straight down to the Ajanta by bus. We didn't have time to fetch our own detuned/treated instruments so we just used Pre-De's guitars and drums, which was a bit of a setback as I could only really play on my 'treated' bass (snapped strings bits of Sellotape and so on). Nick's own guitar only had the top four strings and so this was the first occasion he'd ever played a six-string guitar. The gig had a big build up and so it was just as well we had no time to get nervous or precious about the whole thing. We just stepped up. In fact, we didn't do a soundcheck (or indeed, know what one was). We were just handed plugged in instruments and advised to start playing.
>
> Corridor played with their back to audience. They were not appreciated. The only one of TG that had anything to say to us kids in the support group was Cosey who seemed to take a shine to Nick Jackson, with his cadaverous features and inky, spidery crimped hair. Nick insisted on playing with his back to the audience so the one attractive feature of Corridor – a good looking lead singer – was negated as well as our instruments and bits of songs.
>
> Yes, it was immensely exciting. There was a really edgy, dangerous vibe and the threat of violence – as always at the Ajanta – was in the air. I just recall P-Orridge stomping around threatening to pull the gig because some kind of 'calming

Figure 6.4: Genesis P-Orridge on stage at Derby Ajanta, 12 April 1979. Courtesy of Tony Fisher.

> machine' wasn't working along with the film projector. The rest of the band aside from Cosey, were pretty anonymous, but I do recall being astounded at the banks of equipment and wiring everywhere! It was something of a momentous event as many people who were looking to avoid the growing Sid-punk scene, made future connections that night.[19]

Etchells's memories of the gig are also steeped in a mix of edgy violence and equipment awe. Recalling a small contingent of what he assumed to be fellow travellers of the band, he recounts:

> I think there was some antagonism directed at this group, and one of the guys in the group was dancing during the TG set, with a belt around his neck. (Same guy had been selling or distributing TG badges with the black, white stripe and the red flash). Seemed very into the music/out of it […] and was subjected to some pushing and shoving from other folks as he was barging into them. There was a bit of a fight eventually I think. There often was. The look of the stage has stayed with me also. It was so sparse – tables for equipment, the bass.

He adds a strong memory of what is both a touching moment and also an instance that transports us into the heart of the space, the there and then:

"....He was dazed, blinking now, holding both his hands over the hole in his stomach, trying to keep himself in himself...They never warned him that it would be like this...."

Throbbing Gristle are Genesis P.Orridge (bass/vocals), Cosey Fanni Tutti (lead guitar), Chris Carter (keyboards) and Peter Christopheson (tapes/machines).

Throbbing Gristle, provoke reaction, hostile or whatever, but some sort of reaction. They're that sort of band, they build layer, structure layer on layer of sound. Sound which is so natural it hurts, sound which is so unconventional, it would probably go down a storm with Stone Age Man. Some can't take it, they don't do that many gigs. In their history, since July '76, when they started playing live, they have performed less than twenty times.

Their first album, "2nd Annual Report" sold out very quickly, they only printed 750 copies, but it still managed to sell as far a field as Sweden and the USA. Distributed by the band themselves it is no longer available nor will it be re-printed. Listening to the album can evoke feelings you never thought existed. One side is made up of live recordings, the other their soundtrack to the film "After Cease To Exist" which was premiered in Arnhem, Holland in July '77. (There are no plansffor it to be shown this year).

The album financed the single "United"/"Zyklon B. Zombie" (which you should all have in your record collections, if only to be hip, -sorry Russell). Which has in turn gone towards financing the bands new album "D.O.A. -The Third And Final Report Of Throbbing Gristle". The band have so far lost [illegible] on the album yet still resist all efforts to be monopolised by large corporations.

COSEY: "I was just writting to someone and saying Tony Blackburn should play our records to housewives. It'd go really good with the sound of their hoovers and washing machines. They could feel a part of it then. All huming and throbbing around the house."

"....He was amazed that except for a compulsive itch, in his intestine, what remained of it, he had no sensation...

GENESIS: "I make the lyrics up...I have a title and a subject and I make them up on the spot. If you're doing improvised music, you can't have a fixed lyric, you can only have a subject.

We're trying to create a sound that is equivalent to the experience...not a sound that is normal...at the end of one hour listening to us you feel like you've been through a condensed version of it...people do come up to us and say they feel physically affected."

No/5 will contain a fuller interview, hope...

Figure 6.5: Throbbing Gristle extracts from Derby's Situation Vacant *#4. Courtesy of Glyn Lenney.*

> My brother was right up against the stage through the whole gig, on the right-hand side by the speakers. He was 16 years old at the time, looked younger. As the fight broke out and the sound was echoing at the end of the gig I remember Genesis leant down to Mark and spoke to him personally – basically told him 'that's the end, you can go home now'. This has always stayed with me – because it was such a personal piece of contact, in the context of the event and the sound which was so monstrous and so overwhelming and felt like something had arrived from another dimension. It felt like this very intimate act of taking care – this surprising small human gesture (a very everyday thing) but in the middle of this very chaotic, dark, wall-of-sound event.

The Ajanta stayed open through 1979 and 1980 as a punk and post-punk venue, allowing Derby to be a stopping-off point for many of the new bands who were looking to break out of this 'Sid-punk scene', or what Gorman (2020: 438) scathingly calls 'cookie-cutter second-wave punks'. Post-punk in the provinces, for a city like Derby which didn't have its own marketed identity (see following chapter), was a perilous business, and the general worsening decrepit state of the Ajanta saw it increasingly play host to second-wave punk bands as this scene rose to prominence through 1980. The hard-working bread-and-butter punk band UK Subs seemed to play the Ajanta every month.

Some legacy of Throbbing Gristle's fleeting visit to the city was set in (ephemeral) stone, cascading into local fanzines. Glyn Lenney's *Situation Vacant* embraced post-punk experimentalism and featured Throbbing Gristle snippets and collages for issues 4 and 5 (see Figure 6.5). The second issue of *Jubilee City* included photographs of the gig, whilst Amrik Rai's *Xpert I* issue 5 included a short interview with Christopherson. Rai would briefly run the Ajanta for a few months, before moving to Sheffield and becoming more involved with the music business. Nick Jackson, the reticent glam-punk poster boy of Corridor, took the Throbbing Gristle influence into his next band Canker Opera. Though Nick is sadly no longer with us, his Canker Opera colleague Phil Taylor recalls how both he and Nick were influenced by the gig, and also by Crass who appeared at the Ajanta in April 1980, a year later. I touch upon the various synergies between Throbbing Gristle and Crass in the final chapter, but for their gig in Derby they employed a harsh affront of noise and lyrics, a band bedecked in something approaching a uniform, and a simultaneous film show of grisly extracts. As Taylor recalls: 'Yes, it was all a bit preachy but challenging, which we liked. We were also impressed by the look and went out and bought ex-army uniforms and dyed them black in Nicks mum's bathroom'.[20]

Tim Etchells went on to found the Sheffield-based theatre and performance art group Forced Entertainment where he remains the artistic director. He considers his early post-punk experiences as formative in later life. Throbbing Gristle at the Ajanta ranks high on the register:

> It was definitely a landmark thing for me. To be in this small venue and to see something so very uncompromising, so intense. That stayed with me hugely. I ordered the cassette tape release from Industrial Records and played it a lot over the years. And I guess the DIY frame TG put around their stuff was inspirational going forwards.
>
> I've done musical bits and pieces here and there (mostly experimental stuff in the frame of performance and gallery events) but have mostly been working in performance, visual art and experimental writing. But yes.. in same way that seeing The Fall early on, or the Banshees, was important, the TG gig was a sign that you could do something on an edge, outside of the mainstream and that it could still have currency. The intensity of it was definitely something [...] and the self-organised nature of it.

If Derby was tentative about its own post-punk credentials, the city would ironically become one of the cornerstones of the second-wave 'UK82' scene (actually coming to prominence in 1981). Derby band Anti Pasti rose from the chaotic sprawl of band member musical chairs that typified Derby's scene, to take up with new bands such as the Exploited, Discharge, Anti-Nowhere League and GBH to spearhead a new (reborn) scene. Glen (2019: 200) suggests that the 1979 general election and the political situation did not elicit much of a response from the British music press, but the subsequent election of Thatcher quickly saw a critical response take shape in cultural quarters. Anti Pasti released the singalong anti-Thatcher anthem 'No Government' in 1980. Post-punk was blossoming elsewhere on a more significant scale, in cities such as Sheffield and Manchester. It is to these places where we next follow Throbbing Gristle.

NOTES

1. Tutti (2017: 252) and Ford (1999: 8.14) cover the gig and the fracas. Newspaper cuttings gathered at http://brainwashed.com/tg/live/film.htm (accessed 1 December 2022) include John Gill's review for *Sounds* 15 July 1978 and a letter in response by P-Orridge (writing as David Brooks) on 5 August 1978 suggesting that Throbbing Gristle 'withdrew the veils from his subconscious'. Sandy Robertson, himself in the thick of the action and injured by a flying chair, revisits the gig for a Throbbing Gristle feature in *Sounds* 6 January 1979, but repackages it as an advert for the band. P-Orridge's interview for the fanzine ***Vox*** (issue 3) gives another near-contemporaneous account of the fracas.

2. P-Orridge (2021: 218–23) has events wrongly dated and wrongly attributed regarding the breakdown of his relationship with Tutti. He suggests that his affair with Soo Catwoman in 1978 caused the split which occurred the same year. The affair with Soo was actually the year before, 1977, and his final split with Tutti was in 1978, following other liaisons.

3. The diacritical omission of a full-stop after the A in the title could well be a design tactic to give a logo-istic balance.

4. Again, P-Orridge's autobiography (2021: 227–32) appears unreliable, reporting two closely dated suicide attempts that are remarkably similar with details such as Valium, Mogadon and whisky, plus the intervention of artist Helen Chadwick.

5. See https://darkeyesoflondon.blogspot.com/2019/01/40-years-of-throbbing-gristle-centro.html. Accessed 11 July 2021.

6. E-mail conversation July 2019.

7. This show in which Parliamentarians talk to Robin Day was given a debut broadcast at 16:00 on the day of the Iberico performance. The 15:00 scheduled start time of the gig suggests it was a live sample from the television used by Chris Carter, its interjection at around 30 minutes into the set indicating the proceedings started slightly late. We are spared a sample from the banal theme of *Ski Sunday* which started at 16:30. See https://genome.ch.bbc.co.uk/schedules/service_bbc_two_england/1979-01-21. Accessed 12 September 2022.

8. https://abstractanalogue.tumblr.com/post/96272731534/the-strange-tale-behind-a-throbbing-gristle-bootleg (accessed 8 July 2022) suggests that the band never made the ferry crossing due to bad weather. No mention of this scheduled festival is made in Throbbing Gristle literature.

9. E-mail exchange, December 2021; as well as for any uncited quotes from Etchells.

10. See http://cinematreasures.org/theaters/50689. Accessed 1 December 2022.

11. *Derby Evening Telegraph* for Saturday 7 April 1979 advertising 'uncensored films' for members only at the Ajanta.

12. The local newspaper *Derby Evening Telegraph* for Monday 6 December 1976 reports that all bands on the tour refused to audition in front of the council.

13. Tim Etchells recalls seeing the advertisement and his prior knowledge of the reputation of the film, causing great anticipation in the group of friends he attended the gig with.

14. Bestley (2019) gives an indication of punk's integration into *Top of the Pops* through his survey of acts included on the *Top of the Pops* series of albums.

15. See https://www.discogs.com/No-Artist-The-Sound-Of-Combat-Training/release/2576862. Accessed 28 January 2022.

16. See https://www.discogs.com/release/4881486-Nick-Kilby-And-Matthew-Cheeseman-Noise-Dissonance-An-Exploration-Of-Noise-And-The-Post-Industrial. Accessed 15 May 2020.

17. Analysis draws upon Wes Moynihan's research into this gig, see https://plutoniumshores.blogspot.com/2016/05/psychick-ajanta.html.Accessed 31 January 2019.

18. Conversation with Dave Bonsall, Derby, July 2019.

19. E-mail exchange, July 2020.

20. E-mail exchange, July 2020.

7. RESTLESSNESS
SHEFFIELD UNIVERSITY, 10 JUNE 1980

The scope of this chapter is ambitious, commencing with a spring 1979 gig in Sheffield and concluding with a summer 1980 gig in the same city, and covering an intense period of activity for the band that dovetailed with substantial political and subcultural shifts. Time thickened as dramatic moments and instances of change accrued, necessitating some preliminary signposts in advance of the chapter. The latter half of 1979 and the first half of 1980 saw an incredibly restless Throbbing Gristle producing vastly divergent output that evaded compartmentalization, and one task is to track and evaluate this output. This period also saw the acceleration of a wider shift in music from punk to what we now call post-punk, with a crescendo of highly significant record releases compressed into the second half of 1979. This also requires further scrutiny. Whereas we now acknowledge post-punk as a distinct genre with clean lines of demarcation and precise timeframes, these were not necessarily defined nor obvious at the time. We tend to project backwards our neat interpretation when researching this frantic twelve months and, by studying Throbbing Gristle's contemporaneous exclusion from what became post-punk (even though we now read of them as being part of post-punk), we can gain a more finely-tuned insight. The band playfully resisted and distorted genre formation, with the contemporary music press who were both the lexicographers and gatekeepers to post-punk styles (even if the term post-punk was not uniformly applied) tending to eschew Throbbing Gristle in this period. Finally, by situating this chapter on Sheffield, I bring in a geographically determined style of music (electronic noise and proto-pop formations) that came immediately after punk (hence post-punk) that briefly saw a potential kinship with the efforts of Throbbing Gristle. However, and somewhat inevitably, this did not converge to a neat ending.

POST-PUNK CITIES

Following their early April gig in Derby, Throbbing Gristle completed two further engagements in the north of England, appearing at Sheffield University on 25 April 1979 and at Manchester Factory nearly a month later, on 19 May 1979. An epochal general election was squeezed between these two gigs, making the Sheffield appearance the band's last live event under a Labour government, a correction to Ford's (1999: 9.7) assertion that the Derby gig held this dubious honour.[1] In the keeping of a loose theme running through this book, there was a role (increasingly distant) for the Sex Pistols in both Manchester and Sheffield. Whereas in the previous chapter the Sex Pistols made Derby famous for a gig that never was, the band fulfilled key early dates in both Manchester and Sheffield through 1976. History has given a great contrast to these events. The Sex Pistols appearing in Manchester (almost a residency with quick succession gigs in June and July at the Lesser Free Trade Hall and two dates at the Electric Circus on the 'Anarchy' tour) has accrued mythical status. As Albiez (2005) patiently deconstructs, their first gig is renowned for many celebrities and musicians claiming an attendance. In contrast, the summer 1976 appearance of the band in Sheffield – which included the very first appearance by the Clash as support – is claimed (see Lilleker 2005: 8; Crossley 2015: 183) as an event that people attended but were markedly unimpressed to the point of walking out. So, for Manchester those who never went now claim attendance, whilst for Sheffield those who went claim a desire for non-attendance! The northern cities of Manchester and Sheffield were key stakeholders in the evolution of British subculture and music in the period of punk and its immediate succession, what is called post-punk, and the Sex Pistols curiously had a diametrical role to play. Whereas Manchester was enthused and energized to capture something approximating to an equivalence to original punk, Sheffield already had an autonomous and creative spirit in music and subculture that pre-existed punk but was undoubtedly mobilized by punk. Mallinder (2007: 304) captures the impetus for such ambivalence to punk through Sheffield's unique position in which subcultural and musical malcontents took to 'articulating their non-conformity through modernist forms. With a drum machine, sequencer or super-8 projector, frequently cheaper or more available than a guitar amp or drum kit, access and affordability gave modernity an ironic appeal'.

The band performing in Sheffield, particularly for their second gig in 1980, was in effect a meeting of minds that had briefly configured at Wakefield in the previous year, the nascent industrial genre instigated by Throbbing Gristle guesting within the hubbub electronic scene of Sheffield. This unique Sheffield scene is often categorized as an offshoot or displaced mirror image of the industrial scene, a connotation made through the convenience of geographic determinism and the presence of the heavy industry in the city, the synecdoche of the drop forge clanging through the night. There was, and remains, something of a collective enchantment within the city when it comes to music and sound, a phenomenon that has intrigued writers. Whitney (2019: 124) presents the arguments both for and against this geographical determinism, stating 'the external environment was integrated into the core DNA of Sheffield electronica, becoming a building block for future bands'. I do not argue against the proposal that Sheffield's post-punk imprint was primarily electronic, with a sporadic influence of industrial as either a 'backbeat' or eventual destination. The Sheffield sound emerges from both what was there and what was absent, poignantly framed by Mallinder (2007: 305) who paints the city as a 'sonic nexus of electronic technology and regional dysfunction'.

As stated in the opening paragraph, the wider arc of this chapter is an explication of post-punk determined as a late 1979 tipping-point, a time-stamp often attributed to the author Simon Reynolds with his important 2005 book *Rip it up and Start Again*. Post-punk is a popular subject of writing and discussion, set into motion by Reynolds' meticulous and wide-ranging work, but it presides as a Cartesian *res extensa* – spreading as a retrospective canonization of numerous bands and key releases but eluding a thinking core as a subcultural form. Reynolds does not set out to instantiate the contours of a genre formation, instead working to understand a range of responses or workings through (critiques or opportunities) to punk. However, he unwittingly unleashed *something*, and a post hoc genre has now formed. Forty years later we exist in a time where once obscure bands are critically lauded as essential, with a cottage industry of retrospective post-punk compilations featuring bands who often played to audiences barely breaking out of double figures back in the day. As this chapter explores the key moments and timeframe of post-punk, going to a metaphorical heart of the sun, I offer the challenge of thinking about post-punk in a different framework through subcultures as a 'being and doing' rather than as an ascribed archival checklist of 'moments' by nominated contributors. In the same way that I explore Throbbing Gristle's mutable relationship to punk, I also set out the band's relationship to post-punk and its contextualization as a subcultural palette. The hinge for this chapter is the second Throbbing Gristle performance in Sheffield, occurring one year after the 1979 gig in a slightly different location in the University, and with local band Cabaret Voltaire sharing the bill. This was a direct communication, or possible unification, between a key subset of the Sheffield scene and Throbbing Gristle, but it did not play out in this feasibly predictable fashion.[2] Typically for Throbbing Gristle, there was an adverse reaction executed as a sonic abreaction – a nihilistic deluge of anti-style.

The fourteen months elapsing between these two Sheffield appearances saw several phase changes in Throbbing Gristle marked through record releases and live performances, and these need to be unpacked before I tackle this 1980 performance in the steel city. Most notable (and forming an obvious metric) was the release of two very different albums in quick succession on their own Industrial Records label: December 1979's *20 Jazz Funk Greats*, which (in part) captured the spirit and structure of these early 1979 gigs, and summer 1980's *Heathen Earth*, a dreamy and quasi-ambient soundscape punctured with dark and gloomy interjections of sound and speech. Contemplated as negentropic and a diminuendo – the gaining of order and the quietening of chaos – these two albums marked a shift in how the band were perceived in the complexly evolving post-punk climate. With *Heathen Earth* we encounter Chris Carter's debt to Tangerine Dream coming through as the driving force, kept in check in the same way that, previously, P-Orridge's explorations of the punk form were kept in check by Carter and the other band members. A reversal of perspective, or, more so, a reversal in the power dynamics of two simultaneous and oppositional forces.

Thus, Throbbing Gristle arrived for their second date with Sheffield on the back of these two albums, a monumental distance travelled, and also reflective of the rapidly changing times in subcultural expressions. By this time, summer of 1980, the post-punk music scene (as driven by the bands and labels producing the music rather than fans of the music) was fracturing and (knowingly) on the cusp of being confronted by a music industry looking for new sources of pop-capital. Sheffield's electronic musicians were (also knowingly) in a prime position. Throbbing Gristle seemingly responded to this, tearing into a large and expectant crowd with an uncompromising wall of noise. Martin Lilleker, the much-missed supportive scene journalist for the local Sheffield newspaper, was struggling for words in his short review of the gig, stating that Throbbing Gristle offered only a 'call of inaccessible and incomprehensible sound' (1980: 10). Of greater potential interest is his suggestion of an electronic pop orbital scatter plot, with his assertion that Cabaret Voltaire (in comparison to Throbbing Gristle) were 'almost conventional', and that the evening as a whole made 'Sheffield's other premier electronic band, the Human League, sound like a pop band'. All of these factors need to be taken into account, and Lilleker's nominal scatter plot held at the forefront of our thoughts, but first it is necessary to briefly travel back to the band arriving in the city in late April 1979, on a Wednesday night, eight days before the general election.

ANTI-POLITICS

The Throbbing Gristle set that had evolved through the early 1979 gigs at Iberico and Derby was now fine-tuned, and executed in approximately the same order with the same timings. As befitting the band's experimentation and restlessness, there were slight adjustments and deviations, but only slight. Variation occurred in the gaps between 'songs', with sample collages varying from gig to gig. Their Sheffield performance in 1979 did not offer anything musically different from their previous gig in Derby, even including a second outing of 'Chat Up' that was apparently made up at Derby as an ironic pacification for the prolific punk audience. There are a couple of moments in the set where they seem to play to Sheffield's electronic sensibilities, with occasional electro effects that sound, to today's ears, somewhat naff and dated, and the inclusion of video game noises sitting alongside the usual samples drawn from the dark enclaves of underground media. As Reynolds (2005: 328) states in his synth-pop chapter within his exploration of the post-punk scenes, certain sounds had an 'ultramodern-yet-already-dated quality [...] a sonic signifier for "early eighties"'. The placement of these noises emphasizes the structuring of formulaic songs, marking beginnings, endings, and chorus sections – something apparently alien to the band. In addition, P-Orridge appears to be in a playful mood, prefacing the clunking intro of 'What a Day' with a heartfelt cry of 'stand by for action', quite possibly betraying a *Thunderbirds* affection. Current affairs are, as usual, date-stamped into the gig with numerous samples from broadcasts detailing Thatcher's election campaigns – possibly a provocation to the socialist tradition of Sheffield about to be rocked in eight days' time with a Conservative Party victory. The city was, and remained, a socialist stronghold, with Labour Party leader Jim Callaghan having been given the freedom of the city just a month earlier, and the Sheffield public not anticipating a Labour defeat. Throbbing Gristle offered typically confusing signs of appeasing the crowd with homely electronic surges and assaulting them with political heresy.

Taking place in the Raynor Lounge, the gig was billed under the Now Society banner, an organization established in autumn 1977 by various students at the University to support the nascent electronic music scene that the city had nurtured. Now having attained something of a mythical status, it was originally a low-key bring-your-own records night in the small space normally reserved for the table-tennis club. The University, considered a prestigious institution, had grown considerably since its founding and was centred on the western edge of the city centre with a cluster of buildings reflecting architectural styles from most decades of the twentieth century. The Raynor Lounge was a deeply burrowed room in the modern student union building, a typical space within a labyrinthine academic enclosure of cheap bars, drab furnishings, and plaques for the great and good. The gig was organized by Geoff Davis and a series of circumstances meant that a considerable amount of money was lost on the night, jeopardizing the continuity of the Now Society. Support came from local band They Must Be Russians, who enjoyed a cult following in the city, favoured for their relaxation of an ultra-serious and theoretical dispositif common to other Sheffield bands. On the night, this extended to a finale of 'Nellie the Elephant' which seemed to go too far for some of the crowd who had come to witness Throbbing Gristle's first performance in the city. This was further complicated by a large turnout of fancy-dress students, making a strange mix. They Must Be Russians included Martin (Russian) Lacey, an important figure in the Sheffield scene with his

stylish songs and a sound that's so...well, er....

THROBBING GRISTLE NOWSOC UNION 25 APRIL

So. Throbbing Gristle eventually play NOWSOC, to mixed feelings before and after (and during) the gig. I thought they played a good set, Genesis P. on good form. More people would've enjoyed the entertainment if it had been louder-despite the size of the PA. NOWSOC lost a lot of money on this one, but I still think it was worth putting them on-I know one kid who missed his train and had to pay £7 for a taxi. An idiot or a true fan?

Oh yes, a cordial fuck off to the pathetic slimy wanker (we think wev know who it was) who ripped off £30 of tickets. Thanks a lot.

Nowsoc is in bad shape financially, but that's never stopped us before. We've also been barred from using Univ. House facilities, so perhaps early finish from now on. So get there EARLY

What is there to say about such an intriguing and innovative bunch of wankers like Throbbing Gristle? Well, they were extremely tedious for one thing, even more so since they played after the revitalised Russians who have now developed into a pop band to enjoy rather than an 'experimental' band to [illegible] to (and not before time).

"INDUSTRIAL MUSIC...... FOR INDUSTRIAL PEOPLE"

very serious action. In fact we will do everything legally possible to bring these SICK DEGENERATES to task, after banning

Figure 7.1: Review of Throbbing Gristle's 25 April 1979 performance at Sheffield University, taken from NMX *#4. Courtesy of Frank Maier.*

fanzine *NMX*, a monthly publication that pre-dated and outlasted a bewildering number of fanzines that flickered and glowed at the heart of Sheffield's scene. Lacey was adroitly attuned to emergent music and often looked outside the specific glass globe of Sheffield for material in his fanzine – always written in a precise and informative style. He was quick to write up a short report of the Sheffield gig, indicating a mixed reaction from the audience (see Figure 7.1).[3]

ELECTRONIC CITY, 1979

A barometer reading of Sheffield's electronic music scene up to this point in April 1979 is instructive. We know that Throbbing Gristle had a close eye and ear on the Sheffield sound at least through their connections (and cassette exchanges) with Cabaret Voltaire and Clock DVA, and it is beneficial to gauge the reverse perspective. As stated in Chapter 5, Throbbing Gristle had pipped both the Normal and the Human League in producing an electronic pop single, a form of music that hybridized new electronic instruments and a desublimated disco drive. These were a curious trio of tracks, none of which managed a significant chart success but all indicated a shift towards a potential new pop phenotype. By coincidence, as Throbbing Gristle visited Sheffield in April 1979, the self-aware synthetic single 'Pop Muzik' by M (artist Robin Scott, a past colleague of Malcolm

McLaren with a shared interest in situationist-lite cultural pranking) was just about to peak at number 2 in the UK charts.

If Sheffield artists were going to turn their electronic experimentation into commercial chart material, the onus would most likely fall on the Human League. After a period of evolving line-ups and multimedia experimentation, the band secured a deal with Scottish label Fast Product and were the first Sheffield band of the electronic scene to get a record out.[4] Fast Product were already working with Sheffield band 2.3, a noisy deviation of punk that defied easy categorization, and included the important figure of Paul Bower, the producer of Sheffield's first punk-era fanzine *Gun Rubber,* described by Reynolds (2005: 163) as a 'perennial catalyst' in the evolution of Sheffield's music. Fast Product, under the stewardship of the wily and unflappable Bob Last, was a key player in the post-punk genre, with Last's familiarity with the visual prowess and ironic power of conceptual art allowing the label to create diverse output wrapped up in intellectual and art-historical sleeves – a blueprint that Manchester's Factory Records would quickly engage.[5]

'Being Boiled', backed by 'Circus of Death', was released on Fast Product in June 1978, the month after Throbbing Gristle's 'United', sharing an electronic pop sound but built around a synthesized and synthetic bombastic funk groove. The sleeve was relatively orthodox in a design sense, using a Letraset assemblage and a couple dancing alongside an undulating skyscraper-scape, borrowing from the post-pop architectural designs of the Independent Group crowd. It deservedly gained an instant critical acclaim, and their first exposure in the music press was quickly followed by Chris Westwood's August 1978 feature in *ZigZag* and John Gill's short article in *Sounds* dated 12 August 1978. Even at this early point in time, it was possible to detect some playful animosity towards Throbbing Gristle and other bands in the scene, with Martyn Ware stating in the *ZigZag* article (and presumably making reference to the important 'New Musick' feature in November 1977 *Sounds*): 'When we started, electronic music was "unknown" in the commercial sense, but since then Throbbing Gristle and Devo and those Ohio bands have surfaced and it's become something very hip' (24). Continuing in this vein, John Gill's interview recounts the jokey exchange around an earlier track entitled 'Dada Dada Duchamp Vortex' completed when the band operated as the Future, while fellow band member Ian Craig-Marsh goes on to explain an automated lyric-generating system christened CARLOS – Cyclic And Random Lyric Organisation System. This can be read as a further nudge at the Burroughs influence that informs both Throbbing Gristle and Cabaret Voltaire, being 'similar to the cut-up system, except it's more mechanical' (Gill 1978a: 17). Marsh and Ware were computer operators, so the story holds a semblance of truth, but the journalist Gill is left to fill in the blanks through his own imagination, in turn proffering:

> A computerised version of a fruit machine, where the fruit/stars/whatever are replaced with words or phrases. With a fruit machine, the permutations are considerable, but with CARLOS astronomical numbers of sentence are possible, depending on how many words/phrases the operator cares to feed in.

This comedy image of spinning reels, flashing lights, and bleeping noises was nowhere near the orbit of Burroughs's erudite work in breaking down and breaking through linguistic barriers of control.

Shortly after the *ZigZag* and *Sounds* articles, *NME* ran a scene feature on Sheffield (entitled 'This Week's Leeds') in the issue dated 9 September 1978. The article was premised on Sheffield's 'rash of experimental drummerless trios', with ex-local Andy Gill tackling Cabaret Voltaire and 2.3, and Adrian Thrills introducing the Human League. Cabaret Voltaire, about to release their first ep through Rough Trade, offer a serious and measured interview, talking about methodology and arguing against preconceptions of their situatedness, whereas the Human League toy with the interviewer and typically mix sarcasm and indifference. The double-page spread is dominated by a photograph of the band with Oakey introducing the wider world to his distinctive look and haircut, soon to become an imprimatur of the city. The band adopt a stance of a small phalanx, with three members staring into the camera and Ian Craig-Marsh staring at something out of view – the classical *hors champs* pose of post-punk intellectualism. They are dressed in a slightly futuristic fashion and adopt a rigid deportment, giving the impression of a flight crew from *Space 1999*. Oakey grabs the attention, dressed in a feminine top – long-sleeved, box-cut off the neck and shoulders, with airtex adornments – and his asymmetric fringe cropped to a stylish bob. Though he fashioned himself on the science fiction writer Michael Moorcock's polymorphous character Jerry Cornelius, he came across more as a transgendered Gerry Anderson figure. Perhaps P-Orridge's Sheffield rallying cry of 'stand by for action' had a tongue-in-cheek element?[6]

The Human League did not undertake a standard tour to promote their single, playing only sporadic dates after landing various support slots in the punk scene, notably with Siouxsie and the Banshees at the end of 1978. It was, inevitably, hard work prompting any kind of appreciation from punk audiences – even the more outré elements associated with the Banshees. In their practice of always offering a meta-critical view of their music and its performance, they developed a series of Perspex 'riot shields' to protect their equipment, and themselves, from spit, flying beer, and bottles – a proleptic gesture where they foretokened their hostile reception. In early 1979, after undertaking a brief Fast Product 'package' tour with Scars, things went up a gear for the band. However, they were typically the architects of their own downfall, constantly attempting to circumvent the obvious by being wilfully obscure and belligerent.

First, they procured a spot on Tony Wilson's *What's On* programme, a music and arts feature that had grown in the mid 1970s as part of *Granada News*, and briefly ran alongside the short-lived and controversial *So It Goes*, before returning in the late 1970s as a dedicated late Thursday evening slot. They opened the Fast Product tour at Manchester's Factory on 2 February, and they appeared on *What's On* a few days later, closing out the 15 February programme after a rousing introduction by Wilson. As a television first for post-punk ironic synth-pop it fell a bit flat. There were soon-to-be-cliché opening shots (spinning tape and film spools, plugs being pulled out and pushed in, a single finger holding down a note on a keyboard) but the band looked awkward and nervous, trying too hard to feign disinterest and pull off the requisite bored look. For these few moments, the band embodied pop-theorist Michael Bracewell's (1997: 202) description of their 'monolithic synthesizer primitivism' in which he describes the track 'Circus of Death' as being 'rather like an old favourite on *Songs of Praise*'.

Second, the band attracted attention from Virgin Records, with Last swiftly negotiating a deal where he retained a management role (Lilleker 2005: 75). The 12 inch single 'The Dignity of Labour' was released in April 1979 on Virgin, but branded as a Fast Product release to retain some independent credibility (even though Fast was at the point of closing down). The four linked tracks were awkward and at odds with the band's spoken commitment to professionalism, endeavour and success-seeking, failing to fall in with either a futurist pop sensibility or an electronic dissonance. In an arch conceptualist gesture, a flexi-disc was included with the record that relayed a conversation amongst the band discussing (and at times dismissing) the strategy and structure of the release – a nod to the 1961 minimalist/conceptualist work of Robert Morris, *Box with the Sound of Its Own Making*.

Finally, the release of the record was immediately preceded by a lengthy feature in *Melody Maker* on 24 February 1979 and, more importantly, a front cover feature in *NME* on 31 March 1979. However, this cover opportunity was not fully grasped, as for some reason Oakey and his avant-garde haircut were not present. Instead, we have the other three members lined up behind each other with deep snow in evidence – another reminder of the Winter of Discontent extending well into 1979. The article itself was dominated by typical postmodern superlatives in chunks of oblique invective from Paul Morley, and so as a historical document to the band's thinking at the time we are left with very little. However, the *Melody Maker* interview allowed the band the space to explain some of their ideas. Once again, they were being mischievous, contrary, and confrontational to the scene, first stating that the CARLOS system had been ditched because it 'had a tendency to make things over-staccato' – a potential parody of other bands' Burroughs obsession and P-Orridge's resultant strings of malapropisms and pleonasms that emerged in his live performances (22). Then, as interviewer Birch mentions Throbbing Gristle (and other bands) by name, Ware counters with a pointed response:

> Anyone can sit around and be weird. The very early stuff we did, we wouldn't even consider letting people listen to it now, but it would compare favourably with a lot of the output of those other bands that have been compared with us, because it was more overtly experimental. Are people into that? I don't believe they are. It's a matter of discipline. What we're aiming for is to be professional. People are going to be more impressed if they think a lot of work has gone into something than if you shamble on stage and do something that you self-consciously think is very valid and arty, and tell them they can either take it or leave it. We're not interested in that.
>
> (21)

The Human League were typically at war with the scene and looking to press self-destruct buttons that were now being presented to them through their contract with Virgin. 'Being Boiled' had acquired praise and accolades, and the *NME* Sheffield feature from Autumn 1978 and the Human League snowy front cover slot in March 1979 put Sheffield on the map as a main player in electronic music. However, in late April 1979, as Throbbing Gristle turned up in their city for their first gig, the band had opened up a critical distance between themselves and the industrial provocateurs from the capital.

Conversely, it would be Cabaret Voltaire who set out the blueprint of a more iconic experimental sound in the post-punk climate. Their friendship with Throbbing Gristle developed following their July 1978 meeting in Wakefield, and P-Orridge recommended Rough Trade as an outlet for an initial release as well as inviting the band as support for their Cryptic One gig in December 1978. As Mallinder recalls:

> Not long after making contact Richard and I went down to Beck Road to meet Gen and Cosey and say hello. It was a nice friendly vibe, they showed this very domesticated side, the cats, the cups of tea […] it was a counterpoint to how they were seen by outsiders. We shared an interest in 'otherness' essentially – different ways of doing things that inverted and challenged established, accepted, norms both in process – not making songs, but playing with sounds and words in a new way – and representation – how artists worked with ideas and what was not being shown, to come across as different. We dealt with taboos because we both

> felt it was important to shine a light on all aspects of life and human behaviour. There is an established music industry and media and we wanted to fuck with it.[7]

The Rough Trade partnership came to fruition in late 1978, with the 'Extended Play' ep, a moment described by Reynolds (2005: 105) when the Rough Trade label first 'tapped the emergent post-punk gestalt'. The four tracks on the ep are not in the vein of the electronic pop that defined the aforementioned trio of 1978 singles – Cabaret Voltaire served up a sludgy mix of paranoia and crackle with a dubbed and spacey atmosphere. It was not a case of trying to electronically intervene in an existing format (disco-pop), but a shot-blasting, punk-infused tearing away of pre-existing electronic standards that bloatedly sat at the heart of 1970s music genres such as prog. Having a rich and archived backlog of attic experimentation, they quickly followed this up with two tracks for the *A Factory Sample* ep released at the end of 1978, both of which explored a slightly different take to the Rough Trade release. The tracks 'Baader Meinhof' and 'Sex in Secret' immediately conjure up dangerous other-worlds with their titles, and the content matches the darkly evocative titles with treated vocals and disconcerting samples pulling the listener in and under.

Going in to 1979 Cabaret Voltaire were in a strong position with new ideas and potential releases up their sleeve, their seminal single 'Nag Nag Nag' would be released in the immediate weeks after the election. This was a driving track that summoned up Hawkwind via Fritz Lang's *Metropolis*, delivering what Reed (2013: 64) evocatively labels a 'constant 1300 Hz sizzle in its electronic timbres that sounds more like a dental suction tool than a synth'. Cabaret Voltaire and the Human League, though starting to trace out different poles in the field, seemingly held the cards to their future. In addition, they were all, to a member and as a collective, incredibly 'interesting' in looks. This practice of looking good, and salvaging an image on the cheap by repurposing everything and anything, was – according to Lilleker (2005: 30) – an important part of the Sheffield look and stemmed from the Roxy Music affection that lingered inexplicably in the city. Other Sheffield bands in an approximation of this format, utilizing the drummerless format and electronic orientation, were adding to the roster. Clock DVA, after establishing contact with Throbbing Gristle and meeting them at Wakefield, were starting out on their chaotic journey, and new band Vice Versa had managed to scoop a Doncaster support slot with Wire in May 1978. This had drawn them to the attention of Chris Westwood who was reviewing the gig for *Record Mirror*, and he subsequently included them in his series of articles for *ZigZag* in the latter half of 1978. Vice Versa took the final slot, appearing in the December 1978 issue, with Westwood trying to articulate the cynicism that seemed to surround the band and their lack of a standing amongst their Sheffield peers. Westwood admits that they were a hard band to pin down, shifting between sounding like someone else to sounding like another someone else, though he does compare their moments of structureless approach to Throbbing Gristle.

BORDER SKIRMISHES

Lacey's fanzine *NMX* was on top of this emergent sensibility within the city, but he would follow up his interest in Throbbing Gristle by making the trip across the Pennines to see the band perform in Manchester the following month – a Saturday night in May. By 1979, Manchester had developed a distinctive post-punk scene that grew in a separate direction, but with an equal pace, to Sheffield's electronic scene. At the same time, the Manchester scene mirrored the London scene in many respects, hinging around proactive entrepreneurs with pseudo-situationist credentials gained through reading journals and reciting slogans. Manchester was starting to come under the direction of Tony Wilson and his Factory cohort, the city's original take on 1976 punk having dissipated into a commercial drive with Buzzcocks delivering pop singles on a factory-farmed production line whilst the highly strategic plans of Howard Devoto's Magazine were often sailing dangerously close to a glam revivalism. Wilson established the Factory identity with the Factory club in Hulme in May 1978, taking over the vacuum left by the closure of the Electric Circus in winter 1977. The final weekend of the Electric Circus was recorded for a live album and featured the band Warsaw who changed their name to Joy Division shortly after this event. This is a story told many times over and destined to be told many times again – post-punk's fireside fable. Joy Division became a key part of the Factory mindset, appearing at the club on numerous occasions through 1978 and 1979. After the club opening, Factory Records was established as a record label with the *A Factory Sample* double 7-inch ep in December 1978 – including the aforementioned two tracks by Cabaret Voltaire who performed at the club. The Factory club in Hulme would function until the end of 1979. By the time Throbbing Gristle arrived in Manchester, the club was celebrating its first anniversary. It was well established as a post-punk venue and Throbbing Gristle's appearance was flanked the week before by a Factory Records showcase featuring Joy Division and the week after by a Rough Trade triple bill of Spizz Energi, Kleenex, and Raincoats. It was not all arty, erudite, and angst-ridden post-punks playing to meagre audiences in raincoats however; the Saturday before Throbbing Gristle's appointment had seen cartoon punksters The Dickies entertaining the punk masses.

There were a number of geographical circumstances that made this an intriguing gig for Throbbing Gristle, not least Manchester being the birthplace of P-Orridge. The band were in good spirits, hanging out with the small audience before the gig began in earnest. The set on the night ran as with the previous gigs for the year, though P-Orridge appears more animated and intimate around the sense of occasion and takes a moment to effectively welcome himself home. However, the Manchester public did not reciprocate this self-welcoming by turning up on the night in great number. Whereas the initial Sex Pistols gig in Manchester, at the Lesser Free Trade Hall in summer 1976, has accrued a mythical status whereby every Manchester musician and scenester now claims attendance, Throbbing Gristle's debut in the city was thinly attended and has little post hoc fashionable status. Punk band the Ruts, with a rough but articulate veneer, were playing across town taking some of the potential crowd, but the report in *Sounds* (dated 2 June 1979) by journalist Mick Middles asks 'When I was watching Throbbing Gristle where were you?' (37). He describes the band as 'the most interesting four people in the country' and suggests that what you are presented with, on the night, is a report or reflection of how the band feel and what they are 'seeing' at that precise moment in time: an 'honesty taken to the extreme' that becomes 'self-destructive'. His argument is that this aleatory component makes the band compelling through their unpredictability and certainty of not presenting something you are familiar with or expectant of. It is an interesting statement on behalf of the band's appeal, but it is somewhat ironic to be used to describe this particular gig which fell at the end of a quartet of well-rehearsed performances. To give the reviewer's claim some credence, the set at Manchester is slowly dismantled, distorted, interrupted, and deconstructed from its previously cohering structure – it seems to be coming apart through this explorative restlessness. The closing out with the new standard 'Five Knuckle Shuffle' is revealing, as P-Orridge introduces the sound as 'autistic disco' and dedicates it to De La Pole. This is further nostalgia, but a heterotopic transplanting of a mental hospital from Hull into the Manchester night. Many towns and cities would have a mental institution or asylum as part of their services, and the distinct names of the building would enter into folklore and teasing playground dialogue. P-Orridge invoking both autism and De La Pole brought in the spectre of mental health, something that would scar Manchester's music history through Joy Division vocalist Ian Curtis.

A sprinkling of members of the Factory Records music family were in attendance, such as A Certain Ratio and Crispy Ambulance, but Ian Curtis was not in attendance. Many of the books on Manchester's post-punk history, as well as the individual autobiographies of Joy Division members Stephen Morris, Peter Hook, and Bernard Sumner, reference the influence of Throbbing Gristle on Joy Division from *Second Annual Report* onwards – more as a benchmark of experimentalism or a liminal barrier to cross than a musical direction. However, it seems that no members of the band were moved enough to attend Throbbing Gristle's live debut in the city. This brings us onto the freighted subject of P-Orridge's complex claims for his intimate friendship with Curtis, a man suffering under attack from various demons of mental health. P-Orridge claims the origin of this friendship lies in Curtis' obsession with *Second Annual Report* and the later track 'Weeping' (P-Orridge's contribution) which supposedly speaks to Curtis of his own personal turmoil. According to P-Orridge's own autobiography (2021: 233–40) and his earlier testimony in Ford (1999: 10·17–18), the story of their dependency-at-a-distance runs to a critical juncture. P-Orridge asserts he was on the phone with Curtis on the evening that Curtis committed suicide and that a plan existed for Throbbing Gristle and Joy Division to share the billing for a French gig (to be arranged through the label Sordide Sentimental) in which both frontmen would declare that they are leaving their respective bands to embark on a joint venture. No other band members nor people on the scene in Manchester have been willing to substantiate these claims.[8]

Cross-Pennine journeying music fan Lacey, lurking in the sparsely populated Factory club, uses his *NMX* article to set out a wider context for his interest and understanding of the band. His writing and contextualization is an honest and valuable resource, offering a calm perspective from someone experiencing Throbbing Gristle away from the arty scene of London. He dates his awareness of the band back to the *Sounds* 'New Musick' feature, after which he sought out *Second Annual Report*. In a frank statement, he explains how he has heard the recorded output but seldom listened to it. He also argues that the single 'United' is so unrepresentative of the band that he questions the validity of releasing it. Lacey's first live encounter was the Cryptic One gig in November 1978, when he arrived as part of a Sheffield entourage with Cabaret Voltaire who were on the bill. To Lacey (n.d.: 16–18), the performance was not memorable for what we might consider memorable moments, and it played out as a 'collage of noise, formless and seemingly pointless'. He is also quick to notice the step change I described in the previous chapter, expanding on the band's 1979 Sheffield and Manchester gigs as something different: 'identifying individual songs [...] making more use of rhythms'. The band offer him a response that suggests that all gigs are improvised and so should share a shimmer of similarity at the unstructured-structure level. However, we know with the benefit of hindsight that this is not the case, and the improvised nature of the 1979 gigs was an improvisation within a dedicated structure – change at the paradigmatic level but not at the syntagmatic level. Lacey adds a rejoinder which is interesting in light of the added electronic effects inserted into the Sheffield set, that the band do not 'stray into Human League territory'. It is a prescient statement, with the Human League lurking in the shadows of dialogue and echoed by Lilleker a year later as Sheffield's electronic music establishes zones of demarcation. Lacey's interview with P-Orridge is revealing. He produces a lengthy article and announces that the speed of ideas presented was so great that he cannot relay it all. He is also wily enough to be distrusting of all that P-Orridge feeds him, recognizing bluff and bluster about using various psychic methods to overturn the music industry (and particularly Buzzcocks who are playing on a background tape as the interview progresses). Finally, he has the tenacity to offer rebukes and criticism on the spot, suggesting that the band have an already-converted audience of key journalists and followers. However, Lacey is impressed and would develop a relationship with the band that would give him a strong insight into their second (1980) performance in his own city.

Returning to consider the initial reticence and lack of traction of the Manchester scene with regard to Throbbing Gristle, Lacey's fanzine would later give an interesting aside regarding scene formation and localism. Two months later, in *NMX* issue 7, he reviewed the Factory Tour visiting Sheffield's Limit Club, on Thursday 5 July 1979, with Joy Division, A Certain Ratio and Orchestral Manoeuvres in the Dark all making the return trip across Snake Pass to perform. Lacey described the crowd as sparse and apathetic, whilst offering a distinctive description of the visitors from over the Pennines as embodying an appearance of 'fresh-faced young intellectuals in grey straight-leg trousers and dull coloured open neck shirts', what he characterized as 'the Manchester look'. Lacey's staging of a reluctance of the Sheffield post-punk scene public to embrace Manchester reciprocates the lack of interest shown by Manchester scenesters in accepting Throbbing Gristle and the industrial and rugged electronic emphasis. Crossley (2015) documents and illuminates – through statistical modelling – the cross-pollination of punk and post-punk scenes in northern cities, but his work cannot account for absences or non-compliance. Whereas Cabaret Voltaire (and other Sheffield bands) would freely traverse borders policed by style-conscious activists, and foster links and working relations with exogenous bands such as Joy Division and Throbbing Gristle, it seemed that for some fans a degree of localism took hold – if only momentarily – along the lines of football fandom. This was primarily an outburst of local pride rather than deliberate hostility, and the dynamic would soon change in the second half of 1979 when post-punk accelerated through a series of key releases.

Y-M-C-A

A week after their Manchester Factory gig, Throbbing Gristle performed at Northampton Guild Hall, supported by then relatively unknown local band Bauhaus. At that point in time they went under their original name of Bauhaus 1919, but this was shortened within a few weeks of the May gig as their first record was released – the seminal track 'Bela Lugosi's Dead' on the Small Wonder label. Throbbing Gristle's whistle-stop tour of

Sheffield, Manchester and now Northampton, had exposed them to the hotbed of new music bursting punk's astringency that had congealed during its 1979 commercial peak. In the way that Throbbing Gristle have been linked to starting the industrial subculture, Bauhaus, through this record, have been linked to starting the gothic subculture that would become a major shareholder in the 1980s post-punk diaspora. The origins of the 1980s goth subculture are contested and malleable, with academics such as Partridge (2015: 84–85) even suggesting that Throbbing Gristle played a key part. At Northampton Throbbing Gristle were evidently feeling restless about presenting their now standardized set, going for something radically different. According to P-Orridge in Ford (1999: 9·8), this reinforced within the band their belief in their ability to still cause upset and emotion with the audience. The set resembled their work of 1978, with the 'Wall of Sound' (albeit brief) presented first as a direct antagonism and 'Sawmill' as a finale to create a sonic palindrome.

Industrial Records productivity stepped up and diversified over the summer of 1979. A second issue of the newsletter was produced in June by Monte Cazazza and Tana Emmolo-Smith, consisting solely of (suitably disconcerting) collage and montage work.[9] This was followed by a more orthodox newsletter in September, which proudly informed readers of new releases on the label amidst mock company reports, an investigation into Burroughs and Gysin's Third Mind principle, articles on public-eye killers such as Manson and Mary Bell, and parodic pop profiles of the band members. Cazazza released his debut single in June, followed in July by Sordide Sentimental releasing Throbbing Gristle's 'We Hate You Little Girls' and 'Five Knuckle Shuffle'. Wrapping the product in consummate packaging and intellectual prose, the release cemented the relationship between the band and label owner Jean-Pierre Turmel, though it utilized previous live recordings ('We Hate You Little Girls' coming from the 1976 Winchester event, 'Five Knuckle Shuffle' lifted from its debut outing at Wakefield). Later releases through 1979 on Industrial included a debut Leather Nun single, a Thomas Leer and Robert Rental album, and – most importantly – the Throbbing Gristle *20 Jazz Funk Greats* album which would surface at the end of the year. August 1979 was also an important month for P-Orridge and Tutti in terms of art events, with a final appearance of COUM also occurring as part of a prestigious exhibition at the Hayward Gallery where both (separately) contributed a significant body of work for a printed catalogue. There was no performance aspect.

According to sleeve notes, *20 Jazz Funk Greats* was recorded 'in the week ending September 3rd, 1979', and had evidently taken shape through the live tracks developed at venues such as Derby Ajanta (notably 'Convincing People', 'Persuasion', and 'What a Day'). Additionally, some of the more subtle and moody work for the album premiered at a key gig on 3 August, two months after Northampton ('Beachy Head', 'Still Walking' and an opening track given the title 'Mask of Sarnath' which took the backbeat of 'Weapon Training' and added an uncomfortable ambient montage in place of the stentorian weapon ontology). These more spacious and dark ambient tracks would only be played live at this gig as if the sculpted mood of *20 Jazz Funk Greats* struggled to be reproduced as an appropriate live experience. The gig was part of a four-day festival organized by Colin Faver of Final Solution, drawing together the cream of experimental and arty post-punk unification in the Prince of Wales Conference Centre within Tottenham Court Road YMCA.[10] Throbbing Gristle's set on the night was a strong one, a serious pitch of sorts amongst the wider assortment of prime post-punkers covering the four days. 'Still Walking' comprised of a swirling mix of tapes and loops, and 'What A Day' narrated by a full range of inflected voices by P-Orridge as if auditioning on a distorted and demented version of the have-a-go talent show *Opportunity Knocks*. This strong pitch was muddied by typical antics to deflect from any perceived musical seriousness or movement; the band utilized white and fluorescent costumes picked out by ultra-violet lights, coming on to a controlled deceleration of Village People's 'Y.M.C.A.'. As Ford (1999: 9·9) undertakes to show, reproducing a trio of consistent negative reviews from the leading music newspapers, the band had a habit of preventing critics (and audience) from getting a firm grip on them. Ford ascribes this to the band maintaining a 'precariousness of their position – a fragility of their pose'.

AUTUMN AXIS

In many respects, the YMCA event segued into the inaugural Futurama festival, which took place in Leeds Queens Hall a month later over the weekend of 8 and 9 September. Organized by the ebullient John F. Keenan, a proud northern counterpart to Final Solution's Faver, the event included the best of the now-authenticated post-punk scene (but did not include Throbbing Gristle who were recording their album and about to embark on a group holiday to San Francisco where they would partake in an en-mass trip to watch *Apocalypse Now* at the Northpoint Theatre). Keenan had worked tirelessly to support his home city of Leeds, affirming a post-punk identity in a city beset by other problems such that the post-punk scene in the city took on a distinctive hue forged by a mix of oppositional being and doing and art school (as refuge) invective. Futurama was billed as a sci-fi festival and included many of the acts appearing at the four-day YMCA event. Keenan deduced some of these acts, such as Joy Division, as mis-encountered or under-experienced due to their propensity to play small, cramped venues, and he envisaged Queens Hall as the big stage that would aspire to a larger festival atmosphere. As it played out, Queens Hall offered a dark and cavernous enclosure – a Brobdingnagian flea-pit if such a thing can be imagined –

with attendees able to sleep on the floor between Saturday and Sunday. An altruistic gesture no doubt, but the event took on the character of a masochistic experience of icy drafts, cold concrete, echoing noises, and encroaching swill – phenomenological extremities. It didn't feel like a festival vibe, but what it felt like was decidedly post-punk and went hand in glove with the music. The YMCA event and Futurama were also united by their affordable prices and lack of overblown fanfare. At times, the mood of engagement felt serious and studious, not least the use of the conference room to stage the YMCA performances giving an aura of mundane presentations and business boredom.

The autumnal turn of 1979 that enclosed these two epic events is popularly understood as the post-punk watershed moment. Joy Division's *Unknown Pleasures* – an album that exudes a winterliness – had been released that summer, and Public Image Ltd's epic *Metal Box* – equally icy in tone – was nearing completion. We can include here also Siouxsie and the Banshees' haunting and claustrophobic second album *Join Hands* – released in September – which added to the icy and harsh aura. After the Winter of Discontent extending into early 1979, a second cold front was willed in from late summer onwards. PiL and Joy Division both played at Futurama, headlining on Saturday night.[11] *Metal Box* was PiL's second album, however, as Albiez (2003: 262) argues, the early work of the band in 1978 directly played out the issues of frontman John Lydon establishing the telling of the tale regarding the stealing of his identity and creativity. The cathartic and abreacted experiment of the first album – a literal and narrative take on post-punk – acted as a caesura and allowed their music to explore new directions with *Metal Box*. The angular funk of Gang of Four's *Entertainment!* would arrive the week after Futurama. These three albums triangulated an accelerated post-punk sonic terrain, united by confident experimentalism and a turn to spatial affectivity – whether the constricted space of Gang of Four or the capacious dub sentiments of *Metal Box*. A beguiling amount of other releases that have, over the years, become more apparent in their importance, have emerged from this period of 1979. We can consider This Heat's stunning debut album, the first output of Killing Joke with the impossibly structured 'Almost Red' remix (as if the same track is overlaid backwards), A Certain Ratio's jaw-dropping four tracks for their October 1979 John Peel Session, or the continuing work of Wire with *154* – and the Sheffield input with the release of debut albums by the Human League and Cabaret Voltaire which I return to in detail below.

CONTESTED TERMS, LOST LOOKS

It is useful at this point to pause and consider the claiming of the genre post-punk – a slippery term – and to try and understand what it actually means in an ontological sense between being a musical style and a music subculture. It was not a term in common use at the time, even though it had been coined by Jon Savage way back in 1977 in his 'New Musick' feature co-researched with Sandy Robertson. The 'post' of punk being present at the outset of punk (and Cabaret Voltaire's experimentalism that obviously pre-dated punk) invites consideration of both definitions of the term post. We can consider the meaning of post as a simple temporal delineator (as in post-war or a post-watershed television programme) or an ontogenetic shift in genre and thinking (as in postmodern). Post-punk straddles both of these interpretations. The overlapping tropes of punk that followed from the halcyon years of 1976 and 1977 were complex. They included persisting first-generation punk artists, industry-fed toned-down punk as new wave, the zenith of 1979, new artists cyclically restarting punk from 'year zero', and the genre known as 'post-punk' which offers a sound made possible by, informed by, but different to punk.

This moment in late 1979, with the YMCA and Futurama festivals and the relentless schedule of exciting new releases, certainly indicated a productivity of divergent new ideas that is seldom seen. As to be expected, it was accompanied by a matched fertility of expressive journalism, particularly within the *NME*. How might this manifest itself as a traditionally framed subculture is more of a difficult question that gets overlooked in the recent historical framing of post-punk. Reynolds's *Rip it up and Start Again* retrospectively opens up the building of a canon of releases and artists that allows him to plot a roughly geographical movement of sounds, methods, and themes embedded in record releases. The critical standing of many of the bands assembled in Reynolds's work has grown to a remarkable degree, not least because many recent and contemporary bands looking to inject life into the understanding of, and quest for, 'newness' involves turning back to revisit this period. In addition, we now have a cottage industry of artfully packaged triple and quadruple disc sets (mostly in a brutalist grey, resembling a breezeblock) that dig out releases from the depths of obscurity to canonize as post-punk vectors. What we must understand though is that this post hoc building and framing of a post-punk canon overshadows the reality of how minor and niche much of this scene was as a participatively engaged music subculture. From my own experience, gigs were sparsely attended, and there is an (in)famous example from my home town of Derby when a summer 1979 gig by The Fall was attended by an audience that barely breached single figures. As shown in the previous chapter, what predominantly occupied the subcultural youth of provincial towns and cities like Derby would be a mainstream punk and new wave that was enjoying a peak in 1979. Post-punk as a musical standard emerged within the height of this subculture, not in the aftermath of its decline. Music journalists can argue, then and now, that the rapid-fire releasing of singles by Buzzcocks,

Sham 69, etc. meant that punk had become unmoored from its critical or challenging position and something new musically was required, but this recent claiming of post-punk as a subculture is more questionable.

Reynolds's approach of framing post-punk (as a response or critique) through a metric of product(ivity) which disregards a subcultural grounding of 'being and doing' is also echoed in other works on post-punk. Wilkinson's important 2016 work *Post-Punk, Politics and Pleasure in Britain* gives a valuable insight into the political framing of post-punk, but again works from the standpoint of the product(ivity) with granularization down to lyrics, themes and statements of independence. At times the author verges on transporting himself back into an imagined scene to be a politicized consumer of these lyrics and moods, but an ethnographic lacuna haunts the writing in that we do not hear from the voices who lived this subculture. This is a partial echo of the early work of the Birmingham Centre for Contemporary Cultural Studies (CCCS) whose spirit is re-invoked by Wilkinson and the ongoing academic strand of studying subcultures. The CCCS studied youth subcultures such as skinhead, hippies, mods, and rockers defined by *their understanding* of the participative being and doing rather than setting out a history of the spokespeople (bands) or nodes (magazine culture). This was all to the good, however, their researchers attempted to jump directly from understanding to interpreting the subcultures, to attach political meaning, without undertaking the necessary ethnographical work which can prove messy and not conducive to the answers that they require. This is known as question-begging. Similarly, Wilkinson's work on post-punk seldom affords a direct view into post-punk subcultural life, aside from a quasi-epistolary approach when he studies the letters to the post-punk-era fanzine *City Fun*. This contemporary reimagining of a politicized impetus as an essentialist core to post-punk also partially resonates as a wishfulness through aspects of Gavin Butt, Kodwo Eshun and Mark Fisher's edited collection *Post-Punk Then and Now*, though this book does plough into testimony from those engaged in the scene (fanzine writers and musicians) and includes transcripts of audience questions (each chapter comes from a presentation). It's loose and messy at times, but that is how it should be. For example, the essays drill down into the unique Leeds post-punk scene which was formed in the struggle of everyday subcultural life such that consumers and bystanders, so to speak, were moved to become producers by forming do-it-yourself (DIY) bands as a taking of sides in a greater struggle. Elsewhere, chapters dwell upon the autodidactic surge that post-punk instigated, and rituals of deciphering the jargon from the music press and its new breed of journalists (see Butt 2023).

It is evident that if post-punk is to be considered as something more than a modern bestowal based upon the undisputed dazzling appeal of innovative bands and releases, then significant ethnographic work needs to be undertaken. This book is not the place for it, but it is important to bring up the issue as Throbbing Gristle move through the period which we now associate with peak post-punk (even if that is predominantly a historical back-projection). The closest we get to glimpsing a post-punk subculture of being and doing is in Sam Knee's chronology of British music subcultures from 1960 to 1990. Knee (2015: 151) describes the relatively short era of post-punk as being an active time of tape-trading and DIY culture, with a look that encompassed 'glum sobriety' and called upon 'ill-fitting, dank clobber largely sourced from army surplus stores, charity shops or old man retailers'. Certainly from my own memory, I recall it being like a constant exam of keeping up with what was in and out, and deciphering (or at least pretending to understand) the postmodern scrawl from the likes of Paul Morley with his weekly album reviews.

As well as contending with the healthy corpse of punk (both refusing to die AND being reborn), post-punk in late 1979 and early 1980 also had to contend with a reawakened mod (via the film *Quadrophenia*), a stylistically over-coded iteration of skinhead with Coventry's artful 2-Tone subculture, a flamboyant reincarnation of rockabilly, and the opening strains of the new romantic scene about to go overground as participants took to forming bands. Moving forward, tributaries of post-punk formed around bands that promoted a clan identity and sense of belonging and purpose, with bands such as Killing Joke, Bauhaus, Adam and the Ants, and Theatre of Hate all gaining prominence. These bands were very much subcultural in a being and doing sense, putting forward a tailored identikit image and various brand loyalty assemblages that afforded a discernment between bands, undergirding this with relentless touring schedules that fostered dedicated tribes who hitched up and down the country. Unsurprisingly, the mainstream music press such as *NME* had no time (or kind words) for these bands, although fanzines such as *Vague* covered these bands as a kind of autoethnographic report from the frontlines of action.

EXCLUSIONS

The uncompromising demeanour of punk had been carried through to post-punk, a signal to 'do-it-yourself', but the 'it' was not a prescribed run-through of noise, anger, and heavily gestured incompetence. However, Throbbing Gristle did not fit into this scene – or at least the music press was increasingly resistant to making them feel welcome. As we saw earlier, their efforts to present new work at the YMCA event fell upon deaf ears claiming to be deafened and disinterested ears. This even extended to Chris Bohn who was writing for *Melody Maker*, a key journalist who would take up a position with *NME* and carry the baton for reporting from the frontlines of challenging music under his alias Biba Kopf. As with many journalists, he felt his academic credentials challenged by P-Orridge's arch knowingness and knowing artfulness and used his review to adopt a position over his opponent. This became a common tactic for reviewers as they quickly realized their positions as gatekeepers to the burgeoning post-punk scene needed to be locked down.

The arrival of *20 Jazz Funk Greats* at the end of November should have sat within the small canon of key works that defined post-punk's harvest, if not in sound then at least in intent and scope of ideas. Predictably, it did not. It's a mesmerizing album that never settles into a style, moving between the aporetic clipped constructions signified by 'What a Day' and haunting uneasy listening that drifts around the suicide hot-spot of Beachy Head with fog-horns and xylophones. Over the years it has claimed a post hoc place in this flashpoint of subcultural change, indicated most brightly with Drew Daniel's (2008) deft and passionate deconstruction of the album from the sleeve, tracks, and reception, but it has had to rewrite history rather than come from a position of being relatively overlooked. Paul Morley, holding the admission keys to the post-punk club at *NME*, lumped his review with Adam and the Ants' long-awaited debut album *Dirk Wears White Sox* for the issue dated 8 December 1979. Adam and the Ants were another band regularly lambasted by the music press and issued with strict instructions of no admission into the post-punk club. If *20 Jazz Funk Greats* was an early marker of postmodernist irony, with its Martin Denny fake lounge aura, its chain-of-significations through layers of the kitsch and arty intellectual, then Morley panics at the point the exam paper is placed in front of him. The easy way out was to lump it with Adam's not-quite attempts at sado-pseudo-intellectualism. Morley confuses the kitsch elements which trick you into a surface reading, with the darker elements that necessitate some kind of intellectual analysis; the outcome is 'listless and loveless' as the imagery overwhelms the content. The album works best when you switch this around, shimmering like a Jeff Wall cinematographic photograph, with its rebus elements reaching back into literary and fine art reference points; however, Morley denies the band any insight and suggests they are simply 'licking the lolly of conscious triviality' (1979: 37). Steve Taylor's review in *Melody Maker* a week later (15 December 1979) tires at the 'expensive joke which continually threatens to turn nasty', though he at least drills down into some of the tracks (48). Writing in the same week, John Gill in *Sounds* was more impressed or at least writes without giving the impression he is in fear of his academic credentials being torn up, and he ponders how a move towards being 'acceptable' might play out. What unites all three reviews are to-and-fro references to the Human League – and one wonders whether this has repercussions as 1980 dawns?

A minor flurry of press coverage accompanies the release of the album, but the wariness of journalists to P-Orridge's games tended to produce an unedifying and uninformative contentlessness. In many cases, inquisitive readers were better directed towards the fanzine scene that P-Orridge meticulously engaged. Chris Westwood revived his earlier study of the band to bring them to the fore as part of a longer article entitled 'Syn-rock is here!!', published in *Record Mirror* on 24 November 1979, and going to press days before the album is released. The article is an approximate follow-up to the earlier *Sounds* 'New Musick' feature, but focusing entirely on the new movement of synthesizer bands which by this point warrant a spread of over three pages of portfolio pieces. Meanwhile, their old friend Sandy Robertson penned a jokey piece for the Jaws column in *Sounds* in the issue dated 15 December 1979. Befitting the column's regular features of nudity and scandal, Robertson was tasked with removing the band's image as 'frozen-zone antimusic technocrats' (12). Token outrage is injected by copious mentions of pornographic habits and the inclusion of a rejection letter from P-Orridge's job application for an Assistant Mortuary Attendant. P-Orridge also refers to Bruce Elder being commissioned to write a piece for *NME*, but rejected due to it painting the band as too rational. Throbbing Gristle managed a short mention in *NME*, part of a broad-brush two-part series of new music emerging from technological frontiers, a parallel to the *Record Mirror* piece and another echo of the original 'New Musick' article. The band featured in the first part which focused on electronics under the title 'The modern dance', issue dated 5 January 1980. The journalist Andy Gill had little time for the band or indeed for P-Orridge who was labelled as a 'headline grabber', whilst their music was described as a simple 'manipulation of old-hat ideas' that, to Gill, had a worrying link to early Futurism and its nebulous relation to fascism (24).

In between these articles going to press, the band closed the year and decade out with a Christmas gig on Sunday 23 December at Butler's Wharf, on the southern bank of the Thames in the upper part of a disused warehouse. Photographs of the event taken by Akiko Hada show a dilapidated environment, the weakening bastion of Peter York's 'Them' – avant-garde artists and figures such as Andrew Logan on the fringes of 1970s counterculture, generation-gapped by the punk whippersnappers. P-Orridge with his COUM credentials has a natural link back here, going on to work closely with people like Derek Jarman who were part of this earlier scene. Hada's photograph (see Figure 7.2) of the small group waiting to get in amidst the afternoon gloom is a crowd study of post-punk countenance and comportment – a cluster of raincoats, pointy shoes, studious introspection, and scruffy haircuts – that brings to mind Lowry's 1949 painting *The Elite Fish and Chip Shop*. Colin Faver and Final Solution again promoted the event, twinning it with a more formal appearance of This Heat three days prior at the Scala Cinema. Throbbing Gristle played in the afternoon, allowing the audience to experience the novelty of the surroundings on the deindustrialized riverside, and maintained a DIY

Figure 7.2: Fans wait outside Butler's Wharf for the Throbbing Gristle Christmas 1979 performance. Courtesy of Akiko Hada.

ambience with a low stage and employing two simple fluorescent lights for illumination. An extra effort was made with some unusual touches: sweets and a diary handed out to all punters, and the band wearing matching white sweatshirts incorporating a print of the band and an individualized word that ran to the phrase: please / touch / my / arse. The show started with the playing of a Gloria Leonard flexi-disc record that came free with her pornographic magazine *High Society*. Played in its entirety, the record is a monologue narration by Leonard enchanting the listener(s) to appreciate and visualize her erotic desires, a typical Throbbing Gristle gesture mixed in with the Christmas spirit of the other gifts.

The set performed at Butler's Wharf was highly significant in that it captured a moment of transition, like an undocumented scrap of information between two film stills. It would be natural for any band to produce a live set to promote the new album (released a few weeks before the gig), but Throbbing Gristle are moving on. We glimpse the first shoots of the suite of music for *Heathen Earth*, a live album (of sorts) recorded early in 1980. A couple of transition points were revealed. First, 'Six Six Sixties' migrated from the *20 Jazz Funk Greats* version where P-Orridge's oracular power recalled a late 1960s séance delivered with the 'clipped enunciation of an emergency broadcaster' (Daniel 2008: 153) to a more dystopian version quoting a mash-up of Burroughs and Charles Manson (eventually retitled 'The Old Man Smiled'). Second, 'Still Walking' emerged as 'Still Talking', previously busy with beats and rhythms attributable to a 'dance floor mutiny, or ischemic distress' (Daniel 2008: 56). It resurfaced almost unencumbered from musical structure, with the sinister recurring and overlapping non-dialogue between Christopherson and Tutti replacing the barely audible Austin Osman Spare influenced 'songcraft (as) spellcraft' (Daniel 2008: 62) of the album version.[12] Two new compositions were also prominent: 'The World is a War Film', a sublime example of Carter programming rhythms that consume themselves ouroboros like; and 'Don't Do as You're Told, Do as You Think', a crunching tribal rhythm that works 'in the round', with segments of programmed noise sequenced and overlapping.[13]

NEW DECADE

Cazazza was back in the fold, heading over to stay at Beck Road with P-Orridge shortly after the band's group trip to San Francisco. Ford (1999: 9·18) documents the intensification of a survivalist mentality that the pair encourage in each other, with a turn towards weapon fascination and a cultic existence with military overtones. This creeps in over the year and I analyze it more fully in the concluding chapter. At a wider level, the year 1980 saw more tectonic shifts in subcultural and post-punk formation, with the assured angst of the Joy

Division scene shattered by Curtis' suicide in May. *NME* and Paul Morley were attempting an intellectual pop coup, with early cover spreads such as the close-cropped Pink Military portrait ('The Post-Modernist Fringe') on 12 January 1980 setting a heady tone of style over substance, the championing of obscure bands and quick-fix philosophizing. A week after Curtis's death the *NME* produced another iconic cover with Anton Corbijn's photograph of Joy Division framed at the interstice of Lancaster Gate tube station about to descend into the depths with Curtis turning back to acknowledge something – the whole scene takes on the aura of a chthonic staircase descending to the bowels of the earth. The vacuum created by Curtis was quickly filled by a new pop that traded in the depressive soul searching for a new ironic stance of shallow optimism. The UK launch of *The Face* was pending, followed by *i-D* and *Blitz* creating a glossy triumvirate by the end of the year. It was a move that mirrored the American art scene of the 1960s, with the introspective angst of Abstract Expressionism ousted by Pop Art and the eventual arrival of Jeff Koons and his glib over-exuberance of product society.

Cazazza's first notable task was to film Throbbing Gristle's live recording of the album *Heathen Earth*, taking place at Martello Street on 16 February 1980, in the company of an invited audience of fans and supporters. The shift in sound evidenced at Butler's Wharf was completed, with the addition of 'Something Came Over Me', a dark driving mix of low and high energy beats with P-Orridge's screeching violin giving it the feel of a dystopian video game replicating a car chase through a midnight terrain. A spoken section, originally listed as 'free link', lays out a manifesto of sorts as P-Orridge ups the stakes from forming a subculture to something resembling a cult.[14] The album and corresponding film of the evening do not emerge for another six months, primarily due to Christopherson's fine-tuning of the sleeve design. Thus, aside from the handful of people who witnessed the recording and the small crowds present at the subsequent Leeds and London gigs (where the track 'Subhuman' joins the set), this specific time-stamped sound of Throbbing Gristle is not more widely appreciated until it is some distance into the past. By the time of the release of the album, the band were restless again and heading somewhere else.

Change was evident just five days after the live recording and subsequent Leeds gig, as the band performed at the Scala Cinema as part of an all-night event on the leap year evening of Friday 29 February. Final Solution were again at the promotional helm, and the Scala – a typical independent space – was building up a reputation for supporting this new scene of noisy experimentalism since its opening in 1978 in the basement of a new office building built on the site of the original Scala Theatre on Tottenham Street. One argument is that the tracks were finessed for the Scala gig, more confident and fuller than the two tentative performances prior to this, though this seems counterintuitive to the carefully curated release of *Heathen Earth*. Evolution or disruption, the spoken tracks 'free link' and 'Still Talking' were dispatched and the others were further constructed.[15] 'The Old Man Smiled' was now underpinned by a Kraftwerk-style motoric backbeat and 'Don't Do as You're Told' took on a powerful dubby echo quality – both tracks heading towards a nuanced musicality and away from a previous anti-structure as Carter reasserted some authority. A tribal drum track was introduced early into the set accompanied by primal screams by P-Orridge – this track to become 'Heathen Earth'. It is notable that Ian Curtis (plus other Joy Division members) paid a visit to this gig, after performing with Killing Joke, A Certain Ratio and Section 25 in a post-punk jamboree at London's Lyceum. Both the Scala and Lyceum gigs shared poster artwork depicting high-rise buildings, very much a post-punk motif.

Two weeks later the band performed at Goldsmiths College, giving the same set as the Scala, and a few days later (Mother's Day) we get the famous performance at Oundle School. This gig has attained something of a legendary status, the crowd of public schoolboys giving as good as they get to Throbbing Gristle, chanting smutty innuendo at Tutti and breaking into a spontaneous round of 'Jerusalem'. Both Tutti (2017: 257) and Ford (1999: 10.9) cover the event in detail, drawing upon the overt sexual overtones directed towards Tutti and the covert sexual tension apparently experienced by Christopherson in the massed presence of hormonal boys. In addition, the gig has been remembered and written up by several of the boarders present at the event who were suitably moved by the occasion.[16] The event was recorded and released as part of the Industrial Records film output that clicked into gear in 1980 to document the limited amount of remaining time for the band. The sound is evolving. Carter's beats and rich sounds are once again being pushed aside and challenged. It seems to be a push-and-pull affair. At Oundle there is a brief return to a semblance of order, with the disorder seemingly diverted and solely driven by P-Orridge's giddy engagement with this unique audience, the boys finishing the proceedings with a spontaneous scrum and swaying waves in the crowd.[17] Three months later, as the band perform in Sheffield for their next live engagement, any notion of stylization to foretoken a potential compartmentalization in the post-punk field is ripped apart …

SHEFFIELD CALLING

I left my description of the Sheffield scene in April 1979, as Throbbing Gristle played the first of their two gigs in the city. We can now pick up the baton as Sheffield makes its contribution to the acceleration of post-punk through late 1979 and early 1980. This will then bring us to Throbbing Gristle's return to the city, and a reckoning of forces.

As stated above, the two Sheffield bands I flagged at the start of this foray into post-punk both released debut albums in October 1979 to add to this heady musical slew. Cabaret Voltaire were in the thick of things, appearing at both the YMCA event and Futurama, having followed up the single 'Nag Nag Nag' with 'Silent Command' and finally their album *Mix-Up* on Rough Trade – described with uniform praise and context as being an act of listening that ramps up tension. In a similar manner to Throbbing Gristle, the band were using the medium of fanzines to build a fanbase of curious autodidacts, and they unusually evaded interview coverage in all mainstream music newspapers through 1979. They were, however, in control of their interpretation and destiny, and curating a critical reception that would allow them to keep to their own path. They kept this path into 1980, releasing more singles and albums such as the acclaimed *Voice of America* in July 1980. It would not be until the end of 1980 – 29 November to be precise – that they procured the front cover of *NME*, producing a classic image of a raincoat-wearing Richard Kirk amidst a fleet of black cabs and the domineering ferro-vitro roof of Sheffield Midland Station reflected perfectly in a jagged diagonal of a typical Sheffield puddle.

The Human League were in a different place, always thinking too far ahead of themselves and wrestling with handling (and ironizing) an anticipated success that never actually arrived. Whereas Cabaret Voltaire were confidently secreting their furtive box of electronic tricks into the Rough Trade imprint, the Human League had been side-swiped by Gary Numan in the race to produce a sci-fi-infused electronic pop single that would grab the charts. Their critical gripes with Throbbing Gristle had been replaced by a more pertinent beef with Numan. Under his original Tubeway Army brand he had achieved, within the space of 48 hours in late May, a swift one-two punch of dramatic television appearances on *The Old Grey Whistle Test* and then *Top of the Pops* (as the 'bubbling under' act). With their famously serendipitous embrace of synths, Numan and his band had a complete strategy, with every aspect covered, and he immediately grabbed the attention of the youth market looking for a new subcultural attachment.[18] They dressed, 'moved', and posed as gender-indeterminate automatons, fused with the instruments that created their sound, leaving the Human League bristling in an all-too-human manner. Numan and Tubeway Army instantly gave young music fans in the heat of punk and new wave's commercial high-water mark something to talk about and to aspire to as a visibly marked fan culture. The singer had already provided the estranged robotic vocals for the futuristic Lee Jeans advertising campaign 'Don't be a Dummy', and the single 'Are "Friends" Electric?' released in May 1979 topped the chart by the end of June, quickly followed by his solo release 'Cars'. The professionalism that the Human League talked about was executed with clinical precision, as Numan (2020: 64) explains by recalling that pre-planned moves and lighting were rigorously put in place before these television appearances. The accompanying album, *Replicas,* went to number one, and Numan followed this with the albums *The Pleasure Principle* and *Telekon* within a short space of just over a year. He was assiduous, responsive, and ultimately invariant and ruthlessly formulaic in his accelerated output – a product machine that offered not only processed sounds but a hermetically sealed pre-packaged music. He evolved the style into a coded cyber-mod image set, utilizing slim ties finished in PVC with red and blue split colour schemes.

Numan aside, things were on an approximately upward curve for the Human League through May and June of 1979 as the band supported Iggy Pop in Europe and arranged a brief UK tour. Their working relationship with Virgin, however, was seemingly terse and poorly planned; after releasing their 'Dignity of Labour' single by pretending it was not on Virgin, the label then released their first output proper under a different name, the Men, effectively inverting the irony and achieving the same effect; commercial and critical failure. The single that should have marked their commencement with the label, 'Empire State Human', was finally released in September 1979, followed by the album *Reproduction* in October, though the impetus had been conceded. They procured a second television appearance for the Granada programme *Mainstream,* going out on 6 November. This saw a more streamlined presentation by the band, spoilt only by a slightly geekish introduction by presenter Andy Batten-Foster, the band showcasing the new single and also the more challenging composition 'Path of Least Resistance'. A larger tour was planned for November to promote these releases, but the band inexplicably cancelled all but two dates at the last minute. The tour started on 9 November at Huddersfield, one of the two surviving dates, however, on the previous night, at the capacious venue of Sheffield City Hall, Gary Numan was completing the British leg of his sell-out 'Touring Principle' tour. An article in *Sounds,* early in December 1979, comically catches the band between moments of indecisiveness, as the tour is pulled and something else is looming but not divulged. The journalist is left thinking the band have called it a day, only for a tour, of sorts, to be announced a week later whereby the band will support rising US band Talking Heads. Their default proleptic measures immediately went into overdrive, now extended to conceptualizing an absent–presence mediated by technology – they would replace themselves with a pre-recorded version of the set and mingle in the audience to spectate upon themselves, bodies at a distance experiencing their disembodied presence. Manager Bob Last called this 'cinema you can dance to', and they set up indemnity in cases where audience members might ask for a refund. However, it proved a step too far and Talking Heads pulled the plug (literally), offering the support slots to alternating bands from Factory Records.

On 6 October 1979, the reviews of the Human League and Cabaret Voltaire debut albums were combined into a single article in *Melody Maker*, and journalist Chris Bohn hinged the review on a 'post-Numan world' that fractured between experimental and pop as ways forward. At this point in time, a greater coherence and awareness had gathered around the Sheffield scene, not least due to a feature by Martyn Ware for the pop magazine *Smash Hits* published in late August 1979. By then Vice Versa had commendably set up their own label Neutron and self-released a debut ep 'Music 4', garnering a favourable review in *NME*. The band were still not taken seriously in the Sheffield electronic milieu although the monotonic explication of the lyrical quartet 'Quatermass / tear gas / riot squad / tv ad' (from the track 'Riot Squad') is still one of Sheffield's finest moments. Finally, Clock DVA were adding and changing members, and their inclusion at the YMCA event represented their first appearance in the capital.

As 1980 commenced, Sheffield bands were embroiled in a commercial chase amidst the clamour for stylized post-punk crevices and niches, although Lilleker (2005: 7) reflected on this time by suggesting that the sense of excitement had now gone. Vice Versa had retooled with Martin Fry joining, and their Neutron Records imprint (eventually) released '1980: The First 15 Minutes' featuring Vice Versa, Clock DVA, I'm So Hollow and Stunt Kites. The ep sold well, including an impromptu stall at the Leeds Throbbing Gristle gig in February 1980, but by April 1980 Vice Versa were back to releasing self-financed cassettes and recording in their own homes.

The year would be make-or-break for the Human League, with the burden of expectation from Virgin Records now weighing down on them. Their first release for the year was a double pack 'Holiday 80' which revisited 'Being Boiled' and also segued Gary Glitter's 'Rock 'n' Roll Part 2' with Bowie's 'Nightclubbing'. This latter track – well, the first part of it – allowed them a *Top of the Pops* appearance on 8 May as part of the producer's remit to take a chance on a couple of new bands hovering outside the top 40 (the other band was Orchestral Manoeuvres in the Dark). The Human League were up first and, even though we get the trademark opening shot of wires and plugs being manipulated, the appearance is strong; Oakey offers a charismatic frontman presence and Ian Marsh oozes the subcultural melange of the time with his swept-back hair, biker jacket, and red neckerchief. Host Peter Powell offers his usual enthusiasm, grasping the sense of the burgeoning new romantic occasion by sporting what appears to be a boiler suit with biker lapels constructed from turquoise vinyl with silver and plastic vents. In contrast, Orchestral Manoeuvres in the Dark play it safe, taking the stance of a regular pop combo with a token projector reel spinning on a table. Even though this opportunity for the Human League was not reciprocated by the general public of record buyers, Orchestral

Manoeuvres would quickly change their look and manner of presentation to a more hardcore synth-pop construction. The night that the programme went out coincided with a full tour proper for the band, with the Scars as support act. Stretching across seventeen dates in large venues, the tour supported the (again poorly received) album *Travelogue* which Virgin had released just six months after *Reproduction*. This effort to fall in line and support the label exacerbated tensions between band members, and as the tour ended in May the band – as it stood – went to Europe to play what would be their final dates. As Throbbing Gristle took the stage at Sheffield for their second gig, the Human League were appearing at the Festival of Fools in Amsterdam with Magazine. A portent, maybe?

SOUTH YORKSHIRE APOCALYPSE

Martin Lacey and his *NMX* fanzine were quick off the mark, grabbing members of the band for interviews before their June gig at Sheffield.[19] At P-Orridge's suggestion interviews were undertaken separately to allow individual views to surface, though (typically) Carter evaded any communication. Christopherson had little to say, talking about his use of tapes and whether or not subliminal methods were employed. Tutti offered only a small contribution but seemed to maintain enthusiasm for live events such that these were the basis for triggering change and novelty. P-Orridge, as usual, had plenty to say. He got the last word in regarding his previous interview encounter with Lacey, by emphasizing how he was right to call out the pointlessness of Buzzcocks, such that they have now 'disappeared up their own arse'. After trying to articulate his disdain of pop music (as an industry) fostering an unthinking mentality (rather than attacking the music for music's sake), he turned to default misanthropic mode by instigating a discussion on neutron bombs. He dwells upon the apparent beauty of this latest and fashionable bomb, with its ability to leave infrastructure intact. The neutron bomb was an invention of Austrian émigré scientist Samuel Cohen as part of a general movement of economic thinking around the mass annihilation of people. The irony of people-less infrastructure was not lost on P-Orridge, and he added to the flippant mood by weighing up the pros and cons of death by gradual radiation sickness and the piecemeal melting in an atomic blast associated with earlier incarnations of nuclear weapons such as Oppenheimer's original bomb. A mood of nuclear fear gradually engulfed the counterculture and pop culture of the early 1980s, with Sheffield often at its core. The harrowing BBC drama *Threads* aired in autumn 1984, with the action set in Sheffield. P-Orridge's taxonomy of gruesome ways to expire was graphically bought to the fore in scenes that scarred many viewers for life. Whilst Vice Versa's Neutron Records was named more so for its sci-fi feel than any nuclear awareness, the band Heaven 17 (formed from the 1980 split of the Human League) specialized in apocalyptic angst with tracks like 'Let's All Make a Bomb'.

This deliberation on apocalyptic scenes and obliteration thresholds joins with other P-Orridge (and general Throbbing Gristle) motifs and visual schema such as high-rise dwelling and modernist architecture, societal entropy, renegade libido, and militaristic authoritarian trigger points – effectively building up a Ballardian head of steam, a point made apparent in Sargeant (2015). The inclusion of car crash fetishism, somewhat crudely referenced in the aforementioned synth-pop scene with tracks like the Normal's 'Warm Leatherette' and indirectly with Throbbing Gristle's 'Hamburger Lady', even enters the fray with Bauhaus member Kevin J. Haskins recalling P-Orridge's 'oddly dispassionate and curiously detached' fascination with a car crash that occurred prior to the bands shared gig at Northampton (Haskins 2014: 35). However, unlike with bands such as Joy Division and the Human League with their explicit references to the author, J. G. Ballard remains at times curiously excluded as an acknowledged touchstone for Throbbing Gristle. Tutti (2017: 185) and in a later online interview with Carter and Tutti records Carter's interest in Ballard, and reflects on something akin to a split with the camp, with P-Orridge and Christopherson being firmly rooting for Burroughs and unmoved by Ballard.[20] P-Orridge's much-dissected library listing in *RE/Search* issue 6/7 is such that Ballard is conspicuous by his absence. *RE/Search* produced a number of key publications to sustain the legacy of Throbbing Gristle and support the nascent industrial scene in the immediate period following the band's split. Interestingly, issue 8/9 was devoted to Ballard.

On this balmy June evening in Sheffield an apocalypse in the heart of the commodity was on show at the local cinema, with George Romero's film *Zombies* playing along with a porn flick on the undercard (*Sissy's Hot Summer*). Romero's film was the second in his zombie lineage and is better known under its proper title *Dawn of the Dead*. The action is filmed at the Monroeville Mall in Pennsylvania, giving the film a consumer-critical edge that has grown over the years as mall culture gradually enveloped modern life. *Dawn of the Dead* was released in 1978 in Italy but suffered at the censorship level before getting a US and then UK licence, meaning that UK cinema audiences would not see it until the middle of 1980. It has gradually attained a classic status. It was the cusp of a new era, with home videos about to take root and a subsequent shift of horror and porn consumption to this new market. Unsurprisingly, Throbbing Gristle's *After Cease to Exist* managed to remain outside of this new milieu.

On the western edge of the city, the June sunlight is pushing through the 1970s allochronic curtains of the University's Lower Refectory, their vaguely cellular pattern running the narrow gamut of colours from orange-brown to brown-orange. The floor space

Figure 7.3: Throbbing Gristle performing at Sheffield University Lower Refectory, 10 June 1980. Courtesy of Roger Quail.

is packed, with a further mass of people on the overlooking balcony to the rear of the hall. In his blog of the event, Sheffield musician Roger Quail quotes Martin Lacey in observing that 'a lot of people at the gig seemed like they'd come along because they didn't want to miss it rather than because they actually wanted to see it', post-punk's early incarnation of FOMO (fear of missing out). Quail's (2016: n.pag.) eyes are drawn to the stage:

> Throbbing Gristle have an extraordinary array of equipment for a drummerless quartet. The stage looks more like a NATO forward command-and-control post than a platform for rock music. An impression exacerbated by all personnel being dressed in camouflage and combat gear, including their personal videographer.

Klive Humberstone was a recently arrived student to the city, studying at the Psalter Lane Art College where many Sheffield bands cut their teeth. Klive was lucky enough to have attended the YMCA gig with Throbbing Gristle and Cabaret Voltaire in summer 1979, recalling the comedic entrance by P-Orridge and also the fact that Steven Severin and Robert Smith were in the audience. He had quickly integrated into the Sheffield scene and formed a band called Dachau Choir with Iain Murdoch, who accompanied Klive to the gig in Sheffield. With his new Walkman recording the sets, he recalls the air of excitement and atmosphere of studious curiosity:

> There was a lot of anticipation from the audience to see Cabaret Voltaire – the local fanzines championed CV – they hadn't played locally for over a year. It seemed like everyone was in a band at the time and if you weren't rehearsing, or sat in a pub like the Beehive or The Washington, then you were at a gig watching a 'rival' band play a gig. I spent most of the evening on the balcony. It had a good vantage point, overlooking the stage and I guess I thought the sound was probably better up there for my Walkman recording.[21]

Barnsley singer Paul Bee Hampshire, soon to form a life-long bond with P-Orridge with his connections to post-Throbbing Gristle band Psychic TV, is also encountering the band for the first time. His account of the lead up to the gig verges on the awe-struck:

> The university bar was a who's who of dignitaries from the Sheffield music scene. The volume of the rowdy banter dipped as Throbbing Gristle, decked out in camouflage and military gear, made their way through the crowd. Ditching any coolness I'd been struggling to muster, my eyes locked onto them like missiles. These were definitely the sort of people that my parents had warned me about, I was in my element.
>
> (Hampshire 2020: n.pag.)

Sheffield musician Mark Albrow, who would go on to form Hula shortly after this gig, reiterates this sense of occasion:

> Both groups being well ahead of the curve, they provided inspiration to a rash of others in and around Sheffield. I had seen the Cabs a few times prior to this and they were a massive local inspiration and touchstone for both myself and my colleagues. Throbbing Gristle I knew through their records and the music press, the experience of seeing/hearing their live performance was quite different and more interesting as it was so much more confrontational and experimental. It was quite an atmosphere generated that night.[22]

In contrast, Cabaret Voltaire frontman Mallinder understandably has less detailed memories of the event, with his mind focused on his own performance to come and his band's deployment of a new drummer. His recollections are fractured around a before and after: 'Martin Denny exotica prior to the shows seemed appropriate as it was warm summer's day and perfect contrast to what was to come!'.[23] Also in the audience are a Factory contingent; ex-Joy Division members Peter Hook and Bernard Sumner, A Certain Ratio's Simon Topping, and Crispy Ambulance frontman Alan Hempsall – the quartet having journeyed over the Snake Pass in Hooky's Jag. Joy Division were close to Cabaret Voltaire, and the latter would play a small part in progressing the former to their next incarnation as New Order who in turn would make a low-key debut as a trio the following month. As Hempsall candidly remarks: 'The atmosphere was quite strange so soon after Ian's suicide. Everyone carrying on as normal, cracking jokes. Nobody's processed anything'.[24] Hempsall had fastened on to Throbbing Gristle following his attendance at the Manchester Factory gig a year earlier, and had made two trips to London in the intervening period to see the band at the YMCA and Scala events. This prior experience positioned him as something of an expert witness to the shift in sound and affront that was about to be unleashed on the Sheffield public:

> Gen told me before he went on that this set was going to be largely made up on the spot. It's also the first gig to my knowledge where Gen and Cosey used Gizmos on their guitars. That's the string bowing effect that Godley and Creme of 10cc developed. That's why it's so totally different and many aspects never to be repeated. I have to say it was a great performance and frighteningly loud. Utterly charged. I remember feeling drained afterwards.

The set from Sheffield is listed as follows: 'Punished', 'Heathen Earth', 'Strangers in the Night', 'Tortured Smiles', 'We Said No', and 'Flesh Eaters'. Aside from 'Heathen Earth', and the brief cover version of 'Strangers in the Night', these are new titles, though of course these track names may well have been assigned without method or legacy. It is hard to ascertain what is happening, either on the soundtrack or the film of the event, shot from a single overview point behind the stage. We have a close-up of a pool of cables, like spaghetti, as P-Orridge opens proceedings with a joke – seemingly making a short speech to reassure the audience that no tape recordings are to be used, only for the short speech to be repeated and reveal itself as a taped message. Humour or irony, a suppressed laugh from the audience for a brief moment, then a pummelling noise. Carter's signatures – clipped beats and underpinning rhythms – are totally absent. After a drone and vast rush of noise for 'Punished' clocking in at ten minutes, conjuring a futile and lifeless landscape,

'Heathen Earth' ramps up its tribal structure and a traffic jam of samples (the return of Gloria Leonard) gives way to P-Orridge's mournful intonations. Patrolling the front of the stage, brief moments of clarity reveal the subject matter: a willing-on of destruction and a musing on the pointlessness of survival. Happy stuff. An interlude and 'Strangers in the Night' is crooned by P-Orridge, or, in the words of Quail: 'Bert Kampfert's smoky "Strangers in the Night" is brutally flayed, its meaning taking on a darker, sinister hue in Yorkshire Ripper country'. What comes next is a stuck tape loop, speeding up, slowing down, eating away, and being engulfed by a wall of noise. It is possibly the remnant of a previous track ('The World is a War Film'?), but it endures for six minutes before what is presumably 'Tortured Smiles'. All sense of a footing is gone, and no order or function can be discerned, as this section descends into a deep slurry. 'We Said No' momentarily offers a faint rhythm and drum machine – the tiniest glimpse of something akin to Joy Division's 'New Dawn Fades' – but soon loses its sense of composure and composition. It is possible to link this track back to an untitled work aired at the Scala and Goldsmiths gigs earlier in the year, and the handful of subsequent gigs following Sheffield, but it is smashed to pieces here. The concluding track, presumably 'Flesh Eaters' (whether this connects to the Romero film showing down the road we will never know), is almost ambient; a respite from noise but not from dread. A minor crescendo of klangs and whorls is truncated by a looped announcement: 'goodnight, goodnight, goodnight …'[25]

This switch to an aggressive, cacophonous, and amplified dismantling of everything prior invited a mix of reactions. Quail was moved, able to pick out 'occasional flashes in this relentless thunderhead of energy and noise'. Others offered an uncritical celebration, perhaps from members of the large crowd who were keen to see the band for the first time. Two of the Sheffield fanzines in attendance failed to offer any critical commentary, instead printing a page of badly reproduced photographs and a strapline: issue 2 of *Pink Flag* simply printed 'NOISE NOISE – SHEER NOISE. Dance to the beat – there is no beat. Stand + listen, grimace + smile', whilst issue 2 of *It's Different for Grils* (see Figure 7.4) went with an anti-caption of 'You can't photograph noise, so these will have to do instead' (and includes a further graphic reference to *Thunderbirds*).

Neither impressed nor docilely bemused, Sheffield-based audio–visual artist and member of The Anti-Group Bob Baker offers a more critical reflection of the night. Baker had been a fan of the band from the early days, and had a tenuous knowledge of COUM Transmissions through his friendship with Hull band Dead Fingers Talk. Furthermore, he had arranged a Sheffield coach for the Throbbing Gristle gig at Leeds earlier in the year, and would also witness their traumatic performance at Manchester Rafters later in 1980. This gives a before-and-after reference point to assess this outlier performance in

Sheffield. Sceptical from the start of the larger venue size, a fit-to-burst crowd of unfamiliar faces, the disconcerting effect of the sun still shining through the curtains, and a residual smell of school dinner cabbage, he suggests:

> The second Sheffield gig felt somewhat flat, as if forces were battling against each other rather than fusing to make a new language with noise. Throbbing Gristle at their best were ritualistic, with layers of chaotic and powerful sound weaving and colliding in one magical moment after another. The venues were often dark and small, the feel was intimate, the audience on the same eye level as the group. The sound was loud and clear, and most importantly, the audience came away feeling that they had been taken on a journey and exposed to some dark secret. At Sheffield it felt as if they were going through the motions, not an informative two-way conversation, but more like a four-way argument. After the very witty intro, the interactions seemed disjointed, aimlessly meandering, and also very tame in comparison to their first Sheffield appearance – a tour de force from the very beginning with the haunting screams and gut emptying bass sequence of 'Weapon Training'. They were never designed nor intended for such large venues and large crowds, the magic dissipated in such places, places where the experience became impersonal, less intimate, less informing.[26]

However, others were moved and motivated. Ron Wright, who would co-found Hula with Albrow and Alan Fish and still continues with experimental music and film, encapsulates this transmitted spirit of a call to arms:

> The gig had a profound effect on me. I found that set impressively brutal, and as that gig seemed to be virtually improvised it had a huge impact on me. My immediate impressions were the outfits – It was very workmanlike and I was fascinated by the way they constructed almost orchestral slabs of noise – it was as far from conventional music as I had probably experienced conceptually.[27]

TWILIGHT OF THE FUTURE

These reviews and testimonies, both contemporaneous and reflective, show a divergent range of impressions and inspirations. A discernible chunk of Sheffield music was establishing an identity – electronic experimentalism and an anticipated irruption into the pop body – and Throbbing Gristle came and offered something entirely different. The intentions and motivations are unclear and will remain so, with this Sheffield performance both unexpected in terms of a beforehand and discontinued in terms of an afterwards. It stands as a rogue piece of data in what is undoubtedly an unpredictable genealogy of

recorded it .
MXR : When you play live how much of it is improvised ?
FK : All of it . We don't rehearse very often except to make sure things are working , and although we have a piece of paper which has got titles on it they're usually titles of things we've never done before , just a title and a time for a particular kind of piece we want to do . Although we have a little bit of an idea of the sound we're producing individually quite often we get confused .
MXR : Why don't you do rehearsed things ?
FK : People have got records for that . If they want to hear a performance identical to the one on the record you might as well put on the record .

Figure 7.4: Sheffield fanzines NMX #15 *and* It's Different For Grils #2 *reporting on the Sheffield performance. Courtesy of Frank Maier.*

sonic confrontation. As Quail (2016: n.pag.) concludes in his blog: 'Throbbing Gristle's untethered, drifting super-tanker of plutonium comes violently ashore at Sheffield University'. We do not know if the intent is to chastise or to chasten, but we can plot a line of subsequent events that give us some potential clues.

Following the gig, the second half of 1980 saw Sheffield music takes steps both forwards and backwards. The electronic experimentalism of Cabaret Voltaire and Clock DVA continued in its undiluted form, with both bands continuing their links to Throbbing Gristle and finalizing cassette releases through Industrial Records. In Leeds, John Keenan organized Futurama 2 for September 1980, taking the same format of a two-day 'festival' in the cold and echoey Queen's Hall. The event included various Sheffield bands split across both days, with a notable performance from Vice Versa who used this stage as a springboard to a new incarnation. Vice Versa had returned from the Netherlands where a change away from synthesizer music and a move to vocals for Martin Fry had been explored. This would be the way forward, but at Futurama we saw a step back to the pre-existing Vice Versa with keyboards and synthesizers. The new Vice Versa, who would be known as ABC, could be seen in glimpses. The band sported causal white clothes and athletic wear, jumping around frantically – frontman Mark White (soon to hand over to Fry) constantly thrashing his hands through his hair as if he had drawn the unlucky straw on a television advertisement for anti-dandruff shampoo. The transition to ABC was neither simple nor instant, with both ABC and Vice Versa seemingly overlapping through the winter of 1980. The full flowering of ABC – as part of the post-electronic pop new funk scene – would not hijack the mainstream until the very end of 1981.

The band mooted to take the prize of electronic pop was the Human League, but this was not happening. First Gary Numan had stolen a march on them, and as 1980 came to an end, the artistic-entrepreneurs of the new romantic scene added their input as they progressed from being faces about town to forming bands. The new romantic scene, or this 'scene with no name', consisted of restless migrants from the arty strand of punk, a sprinkling of glam overtones, and figureheads from the 'them' scene that punk had served to call time on. It was primarily a club scene, dressing up and dancing to records that were several strata below the mainstream: Teutonic pop from Germany, New York avant-garde funk, and home-grown synth-pop (including 'Being Boiled'). The image culture as of 1980, set to determine the identity of the decade, was given overground status through *The Face* magazine, launched in May. Strangely, it would be Adam Ant who claimed the opening look from the dressing-up box with the chance inclusion of the single 'Dog Eat Dog' on an October 1980 broadcast of *Top of the Pops*. Meticulously styled new romantic bands such as Visage and Spandau Ballet quickly followed as the scene was rapidly monetized. Record contracts were seemingly easy to come by. Meanwhile, the Human League were under pressure and cracks were showing. A tour was planned for October and November but the band split into two. Phil Oakey and Adrian Wright took the name, added Sheffield musician Ian Burden, and famously recruited two young girls seen dancing in a local nightclub. Another post-punk fireside fable. They had two weeks to get this new set-up working before they honoured their first gig of the tour at the gloriously named Doncaster Rotters club. It was sketchy, with the band opening with a bizarre cover version of Judas Priest's 'Take on the World', and certainly not a portent of what was to come. The band, with the important addition of ex-Rezillo Jo Callis, would rocket to huge success from the middle of 1981.

The reason for extending this chapter forward is to reference a feature piece arranged and written by *Sounds* journalist John Gill, going out as a double-page spread in the 10 January 1981 issue under the title 'Forgive Us Our Synths'. Gill invited artists from both the avant-garde and populist strands of what he calls both electronic music and 'electronic rock', the format being a round table discussion with Gill providing various prompts.[28] Included in the discussion, and photographed in a huddle, are Carter,

Tutti, and P-Orridge from Throbbing Gristle, Phil Oakey and Adrian Wright from the Human League, Nash the Slash, Karl Blake and Danielle Dax from Lemon Kittens, John Fothergill from Nurse With Wound, Boyd Rice (Non), and Anthony and Paul from the band Two Daughters. Gill suggests that Fad Gadget, Daniel Miller, John Foxx, and members from Orchestral Manoeuvres in the Dark were also asked, along with a tongue-in-cheek mention of Gary Numan. It is an ambitious article and doesn't quite flow as Gill tries to solve various questions of artistic and historical lineage, weaving around the divergent strands of formal (populist) and experimentalism that he anticipates as being represented in the room. What quickly emerges, and overpowers the feature, is a simmering animosity between P-Orridge and Oakey. Chris Carter innocuously cues up P-Orridge's bile, when he suggests he is not sure where he would place the Human League in what he describes (but doesn't define) as 'two camps in the so-called electronic music field'. P-Orridge, dressed to kill in full survivalist combat mode (unlike his two Throbbing Gristle colleagues) interjects that 'It's a crossover'. Whilst this doesn't read as an overt confrontational statement, his speaking on behalf of the other band and Gill's addition of 'snipe, snipe' relays the antagonistic tone.[29]

The article then opens to a wider argument about the implied laziness in musicianship offered by synthesizers, with P-Orridge leading the charge and backed by Tutti, and the unspoken targets clearly being the Human League. The atmosphere appears tense as the focus of the discussion is changed, but the argument between P-Orridge and Oakey festers. The boil is lanced when the discussion turns again to live performance, and P-Orridge, seemingly conflating creating and performing with spontaneity, accuses the Human League of 'reproducing' rather than performing. Oakey retorts: 'We entertain. We just aim to entertain'. P-Orridge makes a churlish remark outside of a music discourse, and Gill tries to call for a truce questioning this unprovoked animosity. No luck. P-Orridge interjects: 'Because they symbolise the shit of the world'. Oakey responds: 'And you symbolise why people don't go to concerts!' We are spared the dialogue of what happens immediately after this flashpoint, as Gill just refers to some ensuing 'silly bitching', but the die is cast and the discussion drifts into inane point-scoring.

Fractured and fractious, this had been the relationship between Throbbing Gristle and the Human League throughout this chapter and its focused period of 1979 and 1980. Even though Throbbing Gristle released a pair of twinned singles in the synth-pop genre in autumn 1980, following their raucous 'disconcert' at Sheffield, they only saw this as a genre form to distort. P-Orridge in particular associated any type of popularity (even within the emergent niche genres of post-punk) with an inherent osmotic process of instilling uncriticality in its listeners. He saw the Human

League as embodying this laziness, fostering what we could ironically label as 'blind youth'. The strained dynamics evident between the two bands had, for all intents and purposes, been internalized by the Human League shortly before this January 1981 article. Disagreement consumed them, and they had split. Oakey's salvaged Human League would go on to have a further failed attempt at a hit with 'Boys and Girls' in the following month, before finding the right formula under the guidance of producer Martin Rushent. Next, it would be Throbbing Gristle's turn to be consumed by both internal dynamics and conflicted notions of loyal popularity as the industrial scene they pioneered started to congeal as its own uncritical subculture.

NOTES

1. Both Derby and Sheffield gigs fell in the interregnum period when parliament was dissolved for election purposes. Technically the country was still under a Labour government.

2. As Lilleker (2005) carefully documents, Sheffield had a vibrant punk and post-punk music scene that owed an unfeasibly disproportionate debt to Roxy Music and Brian Eno rather than the Sex Pistols. The scene included many bands other than the key electronic-labelled bands that form the focus of this chapter. Examples include: Artery, Comsat Angels, De Tian, Disease, Graph, I'm So Hollow, Naked Pygmy Voles, Surface Mutants, Tsi Tsa, and Vendino Pact.

3. *NMX* 4, 1979.

4. As an aside, it is worth mentioning that a key strand of Sheffield's experimental music in this pre-punk and punk era stemmed from a council-funded youth arts project called Meatwhistle. The phallic humour in this name has an obvious synergy with Throbbing Gristle.

5. Last famously toyed with the serious Marxist-situationist tendencies of Gang of Four when he released their debut single 'Damaged Goods' later in 1978. The band sent him strict instructions on how to assemble the sleeve and transmit the required Marxist message, instead Last disregarded some of the requests and constructed the sleeve art from the instructions themselves – effectively highlighting the awkward meeting point between conceptualism and situationism.

6. The phrase was utilized in Heaven 17's 1982 Cold War track 'Who'll Stop the Rain'.

7. E-mail conversation July 2019.

8. I am of the opinion that P-Orridge met Curtis for the first time when Joy Division played Hemel Hempstead on Bonfire Night, 1979 as support to Buzzcocks. Throbbing Gristle and Joy Division both played at the YMCA four-day series of post-punk gigs in August 1979, but on different days. Nothing suggests that they stayed around to seek each other out as bands. I do not know the closeness of their relationship through letter writing, though Stephen Morris and others confirm that letter writing and tape exchanges went on between them. The counter-argument that Ian and Debbie Curtis never had a phone has been put forward by people close to Curtis, but this does not seem to hold up. In contrast, it appears feasible that Curtis spent occasional longer periods of time with P-Orridge during Joy Division's tenure in London for the recording of the album *Closer* in March 1980, particularly as downtime was apparently plentiful due to aspects of the studio production working to different diurnal timetables. This was a period when Curtis was looking to be particularly serious about culture, partly rationalizing this as the basis for his affair with Annik Honore. A slight rift between a laddish side of Joy Division

with a world of 'japes' and a serious arty side had opened up, with this rift splitting and conflicting Curtis himself. P-Orridge talks of the pair spending time in London bookshops and Chris Farlowe's Call to Arms military (Nazi) memorabilia shop. The more recent publication of some of P-Orridge's correspondence with a French journalist confirms that Throbbing Gristle were looking to secure a joint performance in Paris with Joy Division in spring 1980, but the letter (dated 23 April 1980) indicates P-Orridge's frustration with Joy Division as 'superstars' rather than implying some unbreakable bond and plan to dissolve their respective bands.

9. Cazazza and Emmolo-Smith would go on to produce the short film *SXXX-80* (1980), a loose companion piece to *After Cease to Exist.*

10. The opening Thursday showcased Essential Logic, Joy Division, Teardrop Explodes and Echo and the Bunnymen; Friday night was Throbbing Gristle with Cabaret Voltaire and Rema Rema; Saturday included Tiller Boys (Pete Shelley's alternative band), Prag Vec, Ludus and Clock DVA; the proceedings closed on the Sunday with Red Crayola, Scritti Politti, Good Missionaries (Mark Perry's ensemble), and the Transmitters (a band with membership from Wakefield who appeared at the Film-Makers' Co-op gig).

11. Reynolds (2005: 269) suggests they headlined on consecutive days, this is incorrect and the second day had Hawkwind as headliners giving the Sunday more of post-prog sci-fi feel. Futurama is a typical post-punk event in that it was badly received in the British music press at the time but has since been raised to a seminal status.

12. Reed (2019: 35) places special emphasis on 'Still W/Talking' in the Throbbing Gristle canon by suggesting their sharing of a title stems from a similar methodology (Burroughs and Gysin Third Mind theory) rather than a matching content and structure. However, his dissection of the different versions is useful, describing *20 Jazz Funk Greats*' 'Still Walking' as 'a sputtering, reverberated sixteenth-note pulse of a low-pitched analogue synthesizer, panned cyclically between right and left channels, with drum machine snares and clinks doubling the rhythms'. Going further: 'The song enacts an obsessive arbitrariness: no pitch, no moment, no process takes center stage as the sounds careen about the stereo field in static agitation' (36).

13. Attributing song titles and unpicking their etymology of change is spurious in the world of Throbbing Gristle. The first series of *24 Hours* cassette releases immediately followed Butler's Wharf (reviewed as a concept in *Sounds* 22 March 1980), and the tracks for this gig were simply listed as 'no titles'. In later editions of the cassette these two debutant tracks were titled as 'Anal Sex' and 'Chariot and Galley'. The former could well relate to a jokingly quoted magazine of choice for Carter mentioned by Sandy Robertson in his *Sounds* article published the week before the Butler's Wharf gig. The latter could relate to the 1956 film *Ben Hur* which contained homoerotic and sado-masochistic key scenes in both of these environments, something that Christopherson was a keen fan of.

14. This track is given the title 'Heathen Earth' in later repressings of the album, but a much different track emerges in 1980 to take the moniker of 'Heathen Earth', meaning that (typically for the band) the album is missing its title track.

15. If you listen closely to the live recording of the Leeds gig, you can hear a broad local accent shout 'bit boring' during P-Orridge's spoken 'free link' section.

16. See https://www.paulgormanis.com/?p=17647 and https://www.vice.com/en/article/dygk5w/throbbing-gristle-oundle-private-school-show. Accessed 1 December 2022.

17. A parallel to the crowd reaction (from an audience of non-TG fans) at Wakefield discussed in Chapter 5.

18. Thank you to Roger Quail for pointing this out.

19. *NMX* 15.

20. See https://theartsdesk.com/node/73374. Accessed 12 July 2022.

21. E-mail conversation on 8 February 2022.

22. E-mail conversation in July 2021.

23. E-mail conversation on 5 January 2022.

24. E-mail conversation on 5 May 2020, as well as any further uncited quotes from Hempsall.

25. *Zombie Flesh Eaters* was the name give to the British release of Lucio Fulci's stylish and gratuitous film *Zombi 2*, a different film. It did not have the promotional momentum of Romero's film, though made a London debut in early February 1980, clearly putting it in Throbbing Gristle orbit.

26. E-mail conversation on 6 January 2022.

27. E-mail conversation in July 2021.

28. The date and location of the round table discussion is not stated, but a short news article in *Sounds* 27 December 1980 makes reference to the discussion having taken place 'recently' at the DinDisc offices.

29. Ford (1999: 11.5) offers a transcript of this passage of conflictual dialogue but doesn't include a verbatim script, jumping from this opening gambit to the more salacious exchanges.

8. ENDGAMES/AFTERLIVES

Though my focus on the returned intensity and discordance of the Sheffield gig in the previous chapter was to use the performance as a cipher for exploring Throbbing Gristle's simultaneous developing and distancing from the burgeoning post-punk scenes, it can also be read as a change in direction or an indication of a new dissensus or intensification of entropy. Certainly, Ford (1999: 10·29) makes this first point, and we see the commencement of a new focus for live events as they move towards having a role of 'psychic rallies' where sound becomes a carrier for psychic change, an abstract and anamorphic dimension. This change would be the final throes of Throbbing Gristle, a direction indicative more of P-Orridge's vision. The allowing of a more monomaniacal position to take hold was indicative of the simmering tensions in the band, finally overwhelming the previously precarious existence of cohesion and productivity against the odds. This chapter documents the final year of the band, starting in the immediate period after the Sheffield gig (June 1980) and running up until the official 'Mission is Terminated' statement on 23 June 1981. Within this timeframe, I also take three diversions to explore the sleeve artwork of the band, performing a thick description to draw out a number of strategic uses of graphic design. Finally, I examine a series of afterlives of Throbbing Gristle that have either fixed timeframes or continue without endpoints.

I do not follow the pattern of previous chapters by focusing on a key gig as a structure to hang discussion and analysis around; instead, I take up the method used in Chapter 3, where I document the activities of the band through an intense period of change. Whereas in Chapter 3 (which covers the year 1977) the band were more coherent as a collective and starting out to progress to releasing a record, by late 1980 the band had a wider public profile and had established a buoyant record label to release both their own work and other material from relatively unknown artists. As we see below, there was a shared feeling that the band could go no further under their original remit. There was also a nagging tension about genre formation, and that Throbbing Gristle had birthed something that they were now feeling conflicted about. This makes this final period run somewhat out of synch in itself; the public profile of the band was gauged from record releases that date to prior ideas and efforts of the band, the current status as an ongoing band was gauged from the short sequence of gigs (three compressed appearances in Germany, three 'psychic rallies' back in the United Kingdom, and two final gigs in the United States), and the actual forces that were starting to unravel the interpersonal relationships that were going on out of sight, only to be revealed (albeit subjectively) in recent autobiographies. As Hegarty (2007: 110) remarks, encounters with Throbbing Gristle are 'always process, always a work undoing itself' – in the final period of the band these encounters shifted to document undoing in itself and for itself as a complex, circumvoluted process.

As detailed in the opening of Chapter 6, P-Orridge regarded the validity and viability of Throbbing Gristle performances and output to have ended in late 1978, coinciding with his suicide attempt prompted by what he called structural problems and differing levels of commitment within the band. That this also coincided with a shift in his personal relationship with Tutti is hard to deflect, as it marked the time when Tutti left the co-habitation arrangement of Beck Road and worked towards her stronger relationship with Carter. Throbbing Gristle continued through 1979 and 1980, producing outstanding recorded and live work, as I have carefully documented in the preceding two chapters. It has not been my intention to study the complex structuring (intended or actualized) of P-Orridge and Tutti's relationship, but it is evident that this relationship also continued beyond this alleged point of no return. P-Orridge certainly doesn't shy away from implying as such in his own memoirs, and Tutti reveals instances in her autobiography to suggest that forces of attraction and expectation lingered on in an uncomfortable manner (e.g. the Sandy Robertson *Sounds* article from December 1979 implied a relationship was still functioning).

For want of a better word, this 'domestic arc' comes to define the feasibility of Throbbing Gristle as the endgame plays out. Towards the end of 1980, P-Orridge enters into a more committed relationship with a new partner, Paula Jean Brooking. His autobiography takes great pleasure in relaying the point of contact as being the local Tesco where Paula works, and he goes on to include numerous scrapes and situations encountered due to Paula already having a fiancé and a family with violent gangster connections, allowing him to strut his bravado in his typically picaresque storytelling manner. P-Orridge's rapidly accelerating relationship with Paula completes the fracturing of his relationship with Tutti, regardless of whatever bizarre conditions it previously functioned under. Inevitably, the autobiographies of both sides contradict each other in terms of mismatching timeframes and lingering forces of attractions and power games. It is neither edifying nor productive to forensically analyze the differing reports of this relationship withering, or indeed the power games and accusations of attempts to delay its withering, but it serves to underscore the tensions that saw the band cease to exist. Tutti (2017: 258–59) dates her acknowledgement of the significance of P-Orridge's new relationship with Paula to early November 1980, where a shared firework party at Beck Road sees her meeting and accepting Paula but still feeling she had an expectation (from P-Orridge) to consider herself as his partner. P-Orridge (2021: 250) dates the cementing of this relationship to February 1981 and suggests that Tutti was still expectant and desirous of maintaining a relationship (sexual, etc.) with him by turning up to Beck Road dressed in provocative clothing. He said, she said. We do not get to hear Carter's thoughts on this fraught situation, but both accounts by Tutti and P-Orridge converge in recalling that Carter, prompted by a particularly irksome pronouncement by P-Orridge on his own life being determined by destiny and Carter's by fate, finally takes a stand at a group meeting and announces he is leaving the band. This occurs some time before the band are set to fly to the United States to undertake two live dates. As with the Sex Pistols three years earlier, they are heading off to an all-American sundown with their fate already sealed, going through the motions.

DAYDREAMS AND NIGHTMARES

Though the album *Heathen Earth* took an evening to record, it took over four months to be released. It was available around the time of the Sheffield gig detailed in the previous chapter, but only Martin Lacey and his *NMX* fanzine had a copy to hand to combine with their review of the gig. Ford (1999: 10·5) suggests that Christopherson's design of the sleeve and packaging hindered an immediate release date, though as we know Throbbing Gristle never intended a release to be a purchasable foretaste of what was to come if you chose to seek them out live. The packaging and presentation, however, was somewhat celebratory with the option of blue vinyl and a gatefold sleeve. The *Heathen Earth* sleeve is our first diversion in this chapter into the uses of graphic design by the band – in this case, we can read into it a mirroring of the status of the band as individuals and a series of disintegrating and formative relationships. The outer sleeve was based upon a found drawing of a dog skull with particular regard to jaws and teeth. Christopherson hand-drew the teeth onto Kodatrace and the luminous glow was achieved by exposing and partially withholding photographic paper. It is a mesmeric cover. The band opting for the gatefold release was something of an ironic nod towards the self-indulgence and conceptual opulence associated with the no-go zones of high-prog and Hipgnosis, design concepts that were dogmatically anathema to both punk and early post-punk. In place of such opulence, punk and post-punk prioritized a reading of urgency and efficiency, with information and invectives transmitted as words or bold collage housed on inner sleeves

Figure 8.1a: Throbbing Gristle Heathen Earth *gatefold sleeve interior, Industrial Records, 1980.*

or inserts. A gatefold arrangement can be seen as a lavish visual excess, and only a handful of punk bands (such as Sham 69 with their second and third albums, plus the tongue-in-cheek *Great Rock 'n' Roll Swindle* extravaganza) employed this technique – on the whole to little artistic effect.[1] Bands that wanted to continue purveying an authentic urgency, real or otherwise, tended to keep to a simple sleeve, even in cases such as The Clash with their third album *London Calling* – a significant double album released on the cusp of the 1980s that could well be envisaged with a gatefold arrangement.

The gatefold arrangement was not wasted on Throbbing Gristle, and they used the interior unfolding *moment* to present equally sized portraits of the four band members. I am going to pause for a moment and study these photographs in detail, as they can be interpreted as representing the immediate dynamics of the band as outlined in the opening paragraphs of this chapter. The photographs are not united in terms of a 'here and now', each having come from a discrete session, and this immediately suggests the band operating in or moving towards separate domains. However, the photographs all share a common aesthetic feel, tinted in blue and framed with a gold border, suggesting that Throbbing Gristle remains, for now, a project of organizational and quasi-corporate

Figure 8.1b: Throbbing Gristle Heathen Earth *gatefold sleeve interior, Industrial Records, 1980.*

commitment, like a top-secret government department. Perhaps photographs of a work team mounted on the wall of an office or the employees of the month. As with much visual material by the band, there is a rebus element to encounter and solve. On immediate inspection, the photographs reside as a paired diptych. This visual ordering of two sets of two is initially presented structurally through the pairings of Carter and Tutti on one side sharing a cropped head and shoulders depiction, and Christopherson and P-Orridge on the other side sharing a thighs and upper torso framing. Could it be any other way? This disjointed pairing is further reinforced with regard to the mode of activity behind each portrait, with the first pair self-absorbed and seemingly in their own (shared) space, whilst the second pair projects connotations of activity and research domains in the wider world of Throbbing Gristle's discursive framework.[2] Carter's photograph, on further study, is visually beguiling, drawing on late conceptualist staging strategies. He is seen in the first instance in front of a screen looking to the right, whilst in the second instance the screen behind him projects an image looking forward. The mimicking of the fold of his sweater and his Abba badge suggests that the image on the screen is from a live feed, thus creating a third replicated presence 'behind' the grainy screen image where the bottom edge of the same screen and the close-up of his sweater fabric are evident. As well as two 'screens' (the monitor and the photograph itself), there are two cameras. These both have to be imagined – the standard camera that captures the photograph we are presented with, and a video camera that both occupies and transmits Carter. The Carter of the foreground thus appears shifted to the right of the frame and looks out of the frame, his attention elsewhere. Though we can surmise his distracted gaze engages the video camera to create the required illusion, what we are presented with in the gatefold is Carter – as photographed mediation – looking at Tutti who occupies the adjacent frame. It is only the screencast (re)mediation of Carter that engages directly the viewer of the sleeve, an uneasy disconnection with the audience. Tutti in the adjacent frame is utilizing one of her modelling shots, channelling perfection and beauty – she has no issues with staring directly into the eyes of the viewer who join Carter in staring back at her.

Switching to the right-hand pairing we have hidden meanings in each photograph rather than some coded reading that suggests members wishing to covertly and collaboratively exit the band. Christopherson and P-Orridge are acting out dissent, confrontation, discomfort, and research. Christopherson appears to be using one of his Casualties Union-style photographs, where he mocks up injuries, crouched over a prone figure with a dark substance (blood/mud) in evidence. He is in the field of operation, picked out by the flash, his eyes part-closed in a mix of contemplation and resignation. The dusk sky treated with the blue hue that is shared on all four images confuses the diurnal/nocturnal reading of the photograph, but we are clearly shown an illuminated sign for Playland atop the only structure that forms the skyline. Presumably added on for visual effect, the sign refers to the infamous amusement arcade in Piccadilly, where homeless boys were farmed out to predatory adults. According to P-Orridge (2021: 171), Christopherson frequented the arcade to pick up boys for his various photography projects (he photographed the arcade itself around 1974), but the building became notorious in the mid 1970s as it was connected with young boys going missing and a paedophile ring of high-ranking businessmen and officials. P-Orridge meanwhile fronts the camera with a thousand-yard stare, his hand manacled in a tribute to Gary Gilmore awaiting and demanding execution. It is a direct copy of Gilmore's pose/appearance on the front cover of *Newsweek* from 29 November 1976, the time when P-Orridge was championing Gilmore's defiant stance. It is a haunting pair of images, as much channelling the doomed (and manacled) youth Lewis Payne as photographed by Alexander Gardner and mediated on at length by Roland Barthes in his photographic think-piece *Camera Lucida*. In photographs, Gilmore rarely achieved such a cool and disenfranchised look, making P-Orridge's sultry portrait a somewhat hybrid affair, and partly reverberating with those early photographs by Christopherson depicting the Sex Pistols as wounded boys.

The album divided opinion in the press, typically used as cipher to project and enforce the divided opinion of the band itself. I tracked both the moment and content of *Heathen Earth* in the previous chapter, and we can be reminded that the album was released, interpreted, and reviewed as either a continuous piece of music or approximate but unnamed tracks. In a month when music newspapers are busily preoccupied carving up the post-suicide legacy of Joy Division, reviews are spread over a six-week period. The first review was written by Bill Lee in the short-lived *New Music News,* dated 7 June 1980. Lee used the review to go over some of the historic difficulties of listening to Throbbing Gristle, presumably addressing those new to the band, before summarizing the album in a dry and technical manner as 'inverse Evangelism set to two sides of non-stop music bearing the by now familiar hallmarks of the TG *oeuvre*; dense, meshing synthesizers, inexorable rhythm-machine *motorik,* and an underlying odour of obsession and pessimism' (n.pag.). Three weeks later John Gill gave the album a five-star review for *Sounds,* opening with the famous line 'If Tangerine Dream fans ever have nightmares'. Gill attempted to deconstruct what it sounds like and how the sound moves you, settling on 'S&M avant-garderie that comes at you like a bull-sized psycho intent on making you bleed internally' (36). Interestingly, Gill was mesmerized by the track we now know as 'Still Talking', suggesting the sonics of a 'highly suspect Quatermass soundtrack overlaid with a "Can I Walk You Home?" country-lane rape/seduction scenario'. This passage of sound and dialogue remains a conceptual high-point of Throbbing Gristle, always disconcerting and naggingly puzzling. Two voices create an exchange out of sync, possibly a troubled thoughtscape responding to a voiced proposal, and in many ways hauntingly a prefiguration of the out-of-sync memoirs that now document the band.

Moving on to 5 July 1980, Chris Westwood (from the Wakefield gig) was happy to champion Throbbing Gristle's cause in his review for *Record Mirror*: 'TG are significant because they remind me of the essential valuelessness of much modern pop music' (24). Continuing in this manifesto mode, he classified their music as proof of another way of doing things, 'not here to annoy or confuse or rejuvenate people. It's not here to smash barriers, to be purposely avant-garde. It's here to exist and subsist'. With *Melody Maker* not proffering a review, *NME* bring up the rear on 12 July 1980, with Chris Gill joining the regular cast from the staff pool who have little positive to say about the band. Highlights included the tongue-twisting 'the same old, same old old-hat tic-tac signifying system which thousands know and love (*because* they know it)', a round of shots fired at 'old bore William Burroughs', and a conclusion that 'the ghosts of yesterday's men still cast long shadows' (15).

THE WORLD IS A WAR FILM

Throbbing Gristle had taken towards wearing camouflage and military clothing, at times all sharing a unified, uniformed look – evident at the Sheffield gig dissected in the previous chapter. The military look served a number of purposes. It was something that transferred to the fans, though the band would deny that they were fostering some kind of subculture that had been voided of a critical capacity. Instead, they offered military-style regimental patches to sew on clothes to allow fans to semi-discreetly recognize each other. The band were also entering into a militaristic or survivalist relationship with the external world ... or at least P-Orridge (under the encouragement of Cazazza) was. There was no evidence that Throbbing Gristle wished to foster association with other bands who were using military iconography as a form a critique or protest. It is clear through the previous chapters that P-Orridge in particular enjoyed taunting those taking a dogmatic position against nuclear proliferation or state-sponsored hostilities. The military metaphor in Throbbing Gristle was both fatalistic and entrenched at a wider misanthropic level. The *Heathen Earth* track that centred on P-Orridge's deadpan lyric that 'the world is a war film' consisted of a wider mantra about the futility of going on as a race of people on a poisoned planet, and about how our eagerness for war films and documentary footage had started to outstrip reality and push it into a looped cinematized conflict. The track coincides with the release of the iconic film *Apocalypse Now* (1979) and the seemingly endless repeating of BBC's *World at War* series on Sunday afternoons.

For the subsequent video of *Heathen Earth* (released November 1980), the live footage of the audience and studio recording was intercut and overlaid with pieces of film, with the war film section suitably augmented with harrowing footage of war atrocities (such as NBC studios film of the brutal headshot execution of a Viet Cong prisoner by Brigadier General Nguyen Ngoc Loan). On top of this, we have intercut film of Throbbing Gristle playing soldiers, a cast adrift unit in the urban wastelands (Hackney), dressed approximately as soldiers but also a little like a militarized Village People in British Army fatigues. P-Orridge briefly pouts in a pair of Colonel Kilgore (*Apocalypse Now*) aviator sunglasses, Christopherson (back in the studio) wears a military sweater and channels Brigadier Lethbridge-Stewart from *Doctor Who*, whilst Carter apparently misses the memo and turns up in his leather bomber jacket and jeans like an escapee Robin Askwith from a *Confessions* film. Throbbing Gristle's war film is not a battle as such, more a sequence of survivalist manoeuvres such as cooking apparently carrion meat over a makeshift fire, P-Orridge brandishing his knife with attempted menace, various smoke flares, and the members of the band crawling on all fours across piles of debris. A long way from the disciplined and ruthless cut and thrust of the SAS storming of the Iranian Embassy in May (footage of this is inserted into the film), the vibe is more akin to the BBC series *Survivors* (1975–77) or the final *Quatermass* series (1979) set in a near-future where society has collapsed to be replaced by battling quasi-religious cults.

However, the band's military uniform predilections took a significant haute-couture turn in autumn 1980, as the Parisian designer Laurence Dupré completed a commission for the band with an incredible suite of clothing incorporating an artistic interpretation of camouflage for the industrial environment. Dupré had met the band through their Sordide Sentimental release in 1979, with sleeve designer Loulou Picasso being her brother. This instigated a brief affair with P-Orridge and the designing of a bespoke uniform, with outfits for the rest of the band to follow.[3] Military clothing and British music subcultures have a long history, with anti-military (and anti-national service) sentiments lingering in the post-war mod and beatnik scenes, whilst dandy hippies often dressed in vintage military garb as a mocking of old imperialist standards. Punk and post-punk (including second-wave punk) accelerated a critical relation to militarism, exemplified through tracks such as Gang of Four's Marxist-infused single 'I Love a Man in Uniform', UK Decay's gothic 1980 poem 'For My Country', to ex-squaddie Wattie Buchan and the Exploited's opening shot in 1980 entitled 'Army Life'. The anarcho-punk subculture, coming in to focus during the latter part of Throbbing Gristle's time, initially had a resolute pacifist and anti-war strand as part of its wider ethical carapace, culminating with the 1983 Crass album *Yes Sir, I Will* drawing its title from the discomfiting hospital exchange between HRH Prince Charles and Simon Weston, a soldier who had suffered substantial burns in the Falklands conflict.

This anti-war, anti-army, and even anti-uniform trope of the various punk and post-punk subcultures did not always translate into the various looks that punk bands, and fans, adopted. This was understandable, as the subset of punk musicians and punk fans who saw the subculture as either politicized or in some sense oppositional (against society or just against other subcultures) adopted an 'us against them' mentality and an associated need to express a tribal loyalty of struggle against oppression. The Clash's 1982 album *Combat Rock*, whilst being a statement about Vietnam and American society, encouraged a military punk look with cut-off sleeves – the band having a bespoke military-themed wardrobe designed by Alex Michon. Even the anarcho-punk figureheads Crass with their martial drum beat-driven songs adopted a look of dyed-black army clothes, making fashionable the capacious combat trousers. The military surplus look of anarcho-punk worked with a mixture of denotations and connotations: a stance of anti-designer-label consumerism and sumptuousness, a streak of survivalist mentality, and a readiness for the battle against the totalizing injustices of wider society. There were significant ideological and aesthetic parallels with P-Orridge's vision, which I explore later in this chapter. On a wider scale, an assortment of individuals from post-punk bands invested in military garb as part of the spiralling image culture of the early 1980s as every band scrambled for a unique look. A post-punk military moment occurred when Echo and the Bunnymen were kitted out from head-to-toe in advance of their special concert at Buxton Pavilion Gardens in January 1981. Perhaps they were the unseen opponents routed back to the north in Throbbing Gristle's battle of Hackney film?

INDUSTRIAL RECORDS

Almost as if they had hit upon a sense of branding, the camouflage carried across to the synchronous release of two Throbbing Gristle singles in September 1980. The visually engaging and darkly cryptic style of sleeve designed for 'United' was continued, with a large photograph and inset photograph leaving the buyer to work out the intentions and connections beyond the banal and minimal outset appearance. However, for these two releases (and re-release of 'United'), the records were housed in an additional camouflage bag designed by Carter. These two releases offer a second diversion into appreciating the band's sense of graphic design.

The compositions themselves reflected their recording in upgraded conditions, the studio of Paul McCartney according to P-Orridge (2021: 255). 'Subhuman', the track inspired by P-Orridge and Cazazza's sonic and psychic battle with the travelling community encamped in Hackney, and aired through the early gigs of 1980, formed one side of a single.[4] The artwork was relatively straightforward and obvious – a reproduction of the harrowing painting of a pile of skulls *The Apotheosis of War* (1871) by Vasili Vasilyevich Vereshchagin with an inset photograph of a modern caravan.[5] Of the four tracks across these two releases, 'Subhuman' was the runt of the litter, abrasive and confrontational. The flip side to this was 'Something Came Over Me', the most commercially sounding release with its futuristic sci-fi ident sequence ushering in the driving rhythm. It aired in an instrumental form on *Heathen Earth* and then acquired P-Orridge's onanistic manifesto as it was developed for their live sets.[6] The artwork incorporated an innocuous canal towpath image with an inset image of Christopherson's semen suspended in water (I guess you would need to know these things to recognize them – though Christopherson's father Derman was a specialist academic in lubrication).

The companion release twinned two new compositions that showcased Carter's synth and programming skills, and his preference for a lighter and more accessible music. Even though Gary Numan had stamped his authority on a successful synth-pop sound, the field was still open for interpretation and colonization. As we know, the Human League were skirting around the edges, and Carter himself was reluctant to ascribe the

Figure 8.2: Throbbing Gristle 'Adrenalin' sleeve and bag, Industrial Records, 1980.

band as inauthentic or unworthy in the heated debate at the end of the year (P-Orridge did that on his behalf). In addition, Throbbing Gristle sounding tracks such as Fad Gadget's 'Ricky's Hand' and other work from the Mute label were holding their own in the independent chart's top ten through the summer of 1980. Starting with a synthetic terrace handclap, 'Adrenalin' offered P-Orridge's autobiographical account of his childhood medical condition set to a rushing and rising pulse countered with discordant screeds of noise. Mood, music, vocal style, and lyrical content all work against each other, making this a pop single that constantly denies and defies its own purpose. The sleeve artwork took banality to the limit, with a typically people-less scene looking across a road to a wide suburban pavement, a white-topped wall on a gradual incline, and a brick residence with a heavily fortified door and tightly drawn curtains. An abandoned shoe in the foreground, positioned on its side and at a 45-degree angle (to show a clear black void where a foot once was) directs your immediate reading to imagine a road accident, taking your attention away from the building, which – according to Ford (1999: 10·14–15) – is a Ministry of Defence building.[7] The inset photograph is a close-up of the bellows from a large format camera, a method of depiction often preferred by surrealists such as Jacques-André Boiffard or Brassaï. It also had a more contemporaneous popular culture familiarity in the visual picture puzzle that was a staple of the BBC game show *Ask the Family*. Contestants were shown an extreme close-up and the camera panned back until someone 'buzzed' and correctly identified the image (normally a banal object of everyday use). Households across the United Kingdom would join in to guess first as they watched the show. The juxtaposition of the two images was clever, making the rectilinear light and dark parts of the small photograph of the equipment initially appear as part of the structure of the building in the larger photograph – a technique employed to powerful effect by the conceptual artist John Stezaker.

The flip side was the more ambient track 'Distant Dreams (Part Two)' with Carter producing music very close to the Human League and P-Orridge softly intoning (as if quietly elaborating his thoughts back to himself) on love and loss. The sleeve reversed the polarity of the close-up and scenic photographs: the main image was an abstract close view of stacked walking frames salvaged from Auschwitz, whilst the inset image was a bucolic view of a tree-lined lane (also Auschwitz). These photographs used different methods – abstraction and deflection – to deter a correct reading of the dark subject matter. The four tracks, as a joint release, were summarily rubbished in the *NME* to fall in line with their approach to the band.

Summer 1980 was a busy time for Industrial Records. In August P-Orridge and Christopherson visited William Burroughs to tie up the material that would eventually form the final Industrial Records release. There were also single releases in quick succession by Monte Cazazza, SPK (with a gross-out sleeve) and an Elizabeth Welch version of 'Stormy Weather' taken from Derek Jarman's film *The Tempest*. The final release in this burst of activity, coming after the Throbbing Gristle singles, was 'I Confess' by Dorothy, the work of musician and artist Dorothy Max Prior who was present at the inaugural ICA *Prostitution* scandal, a key member of the post-punk band Rema Rema, and would go on to work with Psychic TV in their middle period.

DON'T DO AS YOU'RE TOLD ...

Suitably attired in their designer camouflage and carrying new streamlined equipment in Carter-designed cases, the band travelled to West Germany to undertake two consecutive nights at Berlin's SO36 Club followed by a single appearance at Frankfurt's Kunsthofschule at the start of November 1980. Photo opportunities were engaged on the day off as the band posed for obligatory group shots at the Berlin Wall's Checkpoint Charlie. Even though it is commonly understood that the June 1980 gig in Sheffield marked a no-turning-back point in the sound and structure of Throbbing Gristle's live music, it can be noted that these three gigs in West Germany five months later predominantly revisited the previous *Heathen Earth* set with the insertion of noisy moments. The set list on all three nights was approximately similar, though the second Berlin gig saw P-Orridge erupt into a litany of swear words to replace the usual lyrics of 'Something Came Over Me' and the gig at Frankfurt was cut short due to an audience member pouring wine into the equipment.[8]

Originally with the wall of noise, and then 'Five Knuckle Shuffle', the band had always closed their sets with a hybrid mind-stomping foot-stomping number. Through 1980, up until Sheffield, the band had appointed the reverberating clatter of 'Don't Do as You're Told, Do as You Think' as the finale, though for West Germany a new track 'Discipline' was made up on the night.[9] The track bears a structural and narrative similarity to its predecessor, arguing for, and ultimately demanding, that the audience or the listener asserts obedience to the case in hand. Both tracks dissolve the diaphanous border between the proscriptive and prescriptive, urging and commanding the listener to do the right thing by themselves whilst at the same time being coerced into this mode of self-discipline by being told not to do something. It is a deliberately tautological and fuzzy logic, mocking philosophical aporia such as Sartre's necessitating freedom to choose freedom coming before freedom itself. 'Discipline', though only arriving as a final flourish of the band in their dying embers, has rightly been carried forward as something of a legacy moment in the history of the band. It is a stirring track and strengthened the cause for the continuing afterlives of Throbbing Gristle in the nascent industrial scene.

On returning to the United Kingdom, the band played two gigs in December 1980 – Manchester Rafters and London Heaven – with both events billed on the posters as 'psychic (youth) rallies'. The flyers employed a consistent style of a stark black page with cropped and contrasted images alongside narrow white ticker-tape strips of text. The words were printed in an even and capitalized simple font that utilized an urgent communication-under-duress aesthetic with stop–start segments of information and colon delineators. For the gig at Manchester Rafters, a grotty subterranean venue on Oxford Road, the acts and films were presented simply as 'AGENDA:'. Both of these gigs were highly charged affairs, cramped and compressed, with energy and forces saturating the atmosphere. The serious and transformational mood was set with an introduction mixing a speech by Aleister Crowley and the mystical music of Jajouka, and the sound that followed was heavy in the Sheffield mode with constant employment of the Gizmo devices on guitars. However, as opposed to Sheffield's at times indiscernible assault of noise and confusion, there were moments of structure that reached back to earlier times. At Rafters, somewhat inevitably, P-Orridge had to turn in a version of 'Very Friendly', and the *Heathen Earth*-era standard 'Something Came Over Me' marked the midpoint of the set with a semblance of order. Rafters was a tempestuous, fractious, and on-the-edge affair with P-Orridge, aided by Cazazza, fired up and adorned with survivalist knives, telescopic cosh, and other gadgets. He spontaneously sprays mustard gas on a member of the band A Certain Ratio after a misheard misunderstanding of a joke, and then aggressively barrels through a crowd of Manchester chapter Hells Angels on the way to get fish and chips. The gig itself is preceded by P-Orridge cutting the arm of a female fan a little too deeply (not that there were guidelines on how to cut a fan's arm) followed by P-Orridge then cutting marks into his own hand with the intent of infusing the stage performance with rivulets of blood.

There is an incredible moment before the close-out track 'Discipline' as P-Orridge lurches forward and delivers a short comedic broken-up statement, pushing language beyond its faculties in his tried and tested manner. A member of the audience responds shouting 'what?', a mild heckle of sarcasm that attempts to bathetically defuse P-Orridge's artistic intent. P-Orridge returns to the microphone and repeats the garbled-up segment, the heckler responds again, and a tense hostage situation is suddenly upon us as to who emerges with the upper hand. Either Christopherson or Carter has P-Orridge's back: his voice is sampled, distorted, and modulated, intensifying the words and turning them into a reverberating electronic shriek that envelops the cramped space. The punk field of performance and its audience interaction/heckling as never experienced before (and never again), via a return to Dada spontaneity and impossibility. As this sound overwhelms, at the tipping point, Carter starts the jackhammer thump of 'Discipline'. It is very much

Throbbing Gristle as a tight team, knowing each other's moves. As the local fanzine *City Fun* (1981: 9–22) reported on the gig: 'Like Tangerine Dream on speed. Like Can on acid. Cabaret Voltaire spend a night with Mark Smith and end up in a lunatic asylum'.

Three weeks later Throbbing Gristle were at Heaven, the hi-tech clubbing space in Charing Cross, which opened in December 1979 as a refuge for the gay scene and its associated music genres. The club has an important place in British music history, ushering in beatmixing and offering a test-bed to the early acid house scene that developed in the later 1980s. At the time of Throbbing Gristle's appearance, the club was also a refuge for the experimental electronic and punk-funk scenes, using umbrella concepts such as the 'Night Moves' series to showcase live music. It was an intimate space, quickly becoming claustrophobic as the tempo increased. As with Rafters, this gig was filmed, the camera utilizing a fixed point within but above the audience. The band perform in front of a small, low-lying stage with a mirrored backdrop; three of the band cast reflections, making it appear as if there are more personnel in attendance as they busily go about their multi-tasked roles. Carter stands back and to the side, casting no reflection for the angle of the camera. The set here briefly revisits *20 Jazz Funk Greats*, with 'Persuasion' and 'Still Walking' coming in quick succession. As with Rafters, it is cloying and asphyxiating. However, it is easy to miss something new briefly emerging across these two December gigs, as Carter reasserts his important role in the band. There were two new tracks – simply listed as 'first disco rhythm' and 'second disco rhythm' on the set list for Heaven – that show a potential new direction. At Rafters these were presented as (anti) instrumentals (listed as 'Playground' and 'Hastings' on the bootleg album) as P-Orridge and Tutti scrawk their Gizmo devices to Carter's pounding signatures. For their second airing at Heaven, they were given presumably spontaneous vocal chants by P-Orridge ('Tokyo Summer' and 'Spirits Flying') and acquired these names for the subsequent album of the gig. Viewed counterfactually from the vantage point of the band splitting soon after, it is intriguing as to how this sound and direction might have panned out. Throbbing Gristle at their best were a balance of counter-operational forces, each element intriguing in its own right but the coming together always so much greater than the sum of parts. With these 'disco rhythms', Carter had stepped forward, possibly his final flourish, and they were – for one brief moment – wrapped up and melded in the dissonant sonics of the rest band. It was, for two evenings, a glimpse of a radical possibility; but in the long term, it was not to be.

SOUNDTRACKS

Additional footage at Heaven was recorded by filmmaker Derek Jarman, utilizing his Super-8 format that defined his earlier work. Jarman took the film and added sound from

Second Annual Report to produce the short *Psychic Rally in Heaven*. The film was not a document of the gig, being highly abstract with close crops of P-Orridge flickering and bleached under the intensity of the lights. Throbbing Gristle's next piece of studio work was a soundtrack for Jarman's recontextualized and superimposed work *In the Shadow of the Sun*, released for the Berlin film festival in February 1981. Like Jarman's out-of-time soundtracking of the Throbbing Gristle film, *In the Shadow of the Sun* consisted of reworked Super-8 films from the early 1970s. Charlesworth (2011: 83) provides an outline of the method and effect. Jarman projected two films consecutively onto a postcard and filmed the result using a Nizo 8 mm camera. The resultant projections move slightly, giving the final film, once upgraded to 16 mm with accompanying enhanced errors and deficits of content, a quivering and pulsing quality that matches the overlaid themes of fire and ritual. The blended whole, shifting and flickering in intensity, works as a unified image rather than challenging the viewer to discern the differing inputs. Whereas Jarman had recently moved into making 'standard' medium (but challenging subject matter) films such as *Jubilee* (1978), this new project of rekindling archival Super-8 opened up a painterly style and enquiring sensibility of addressing the medium of film itself. Other filmmakers such as Richard Heslop, associated with the band 23 Skidoo, would follow in this style. Throbbing Gristle's muted and suppressed soundtrack matched this painterly and ambient feel of the film. Three years after the premiere of the film, the soundtrack was released on the suitably titled Illuminated Records label.

The debut issue of *Real Shocks* fanzine included the first part of a lengthy discussion with P-Orridge undertaken on 11 January 1981. As Throbbing Gristle picked up popularity, numerous fanzines were looking for interviews, and P-Orridge – to his credit – was normally obliging. Fanzines new to the band would often repeat potted histories and the standard shock statements that were attached to the band like barnacles on a rock. However, the interview in *Real Shocks* pushed in interesting directions. First, P-Orridge is smarting from the publication of the synth debate article in *Sounds* published only a couple of days prior. He feels strongly that the article misrepresents the discussion such that everybody present was outraged by the (unprinted) things that the Human League were saying (commercialism being a motive in particular). Second, P-Orridge clears up the misunderstanding that Throbbing Gristle have an art school background. He asserts that it was always their aim to make a mark in the art history canon as people without any formal training. This, he argues, is an outlook that they have transferred to music and would transfer to their next project of filmmaking. This is the third interesting point hinted at by P-Orridge, that music activities were potentially ceasing, that a forthcoming gig in London would be the final appearance, and that new avenues such as filmmaking and opening up an archive and research facility for 'anti-cult' studies were the future. He doesn't implicate a split in the band, nor any internal strife, but when pushed about the new activities he only mentions Christopherson as being on board.[10]

What would turn out as Throbbing Gristle's final UK gig played out at the capacious and decadent-but-derelict Lyceum Theatre, a venue popular for lengthy Sunday events where a concoction of bands roughly describing a scene would play one after the other. It was often the location in London where the post-punk and second-wave punk scenes congealed into glib spectacles, an endless array of box adverts in the back pages of *NME* and *Sounds*. I attended a few of these in the early 1980s; it could be a gruelling ordeal often starting in the afternoon where you were plucked out of the bright sun and plunged into gloom, emerging hours later to scramble for the last train home out of St. Pancras. Throbbing Gristle's evening was part of this, an industrial shebang billed as a 'Fetish night out' with Sheffield musicians Cabaret Voltaire and Clock DVA plus Americans Z'EV and Boyd Rice (Non). As with the previous gigs at Rafters and Heaven, there is a separate flyer produced by the band billing the event as a 'Psychic Youth Rally' and alerting punters that Throbbing Gristle will go on first. As Clock DVA member Roger Quail (2017: n.pag.) amusingly recalls in his blog, this ensured that 'the first few rows gathered in front of the stage appears to be a conscripted squad of serious-minded young men with buzz-cut bullet-heads clad in Millet's militia chic'.[11] It was a strange affair, with the band splitting the set between distorted invocations where P-Orridge attempted to lose and possibly obliterate himself in a shamanistic ritual, followed by a thunderous 30-minute rendition of 'Discipline'. As Stubbs (2018: 320) surmises, the gig functioned as a 'test of commitment, (to) drive out the new pop fans'. This is echoed by Ford (1999: 11·8) who concludes that the band were 'in serious danger of becoming popular', having given birth to a potentially shallow subculture of loyal disciples and uniforms.

The music press were not convinced, *NME* hauling out another name from their stable to take a few arch but generalizing pot-shots at the band. *Sounds* reviewer Chris Burkham immediately cottons on to the jaded and self-destructive inwardness of the band exhibited on the night, marking their music as 'a morass of meaningless, almost moronic electronic scratching' (1980: n.pag.). Two weeks later a pseudonymous and cryptic article (using the name Magnus Hirschfeld – an exiled German sexologist) is written in *Sounds* 'Cruelty Corner' column, under the heading 'Grimness: the great threat to our nation' (1980: 15). The article refers to the wider Lyceum event, and the subsequent reviews (or 'printed aftermath'), shifting allegorically around the newly forming world of 1980s style cultures and new pop. Throbbing Gristle and the industrial scene are chastised for becoming passé, allowing a 'new pose (to reveal) its selfish and aggressive reality'. It is a strange and unrewarding article; its intent is more to parody the high style of *NME* journalism and to snipe around the internecine family of *Sounds* journalists as they take up their positions to make claims about other bands and fan cultures championed by other journalists. It would prove to be Throbbing Gristle's final mention in the mainstream music press during their active period; a suitably pointless article to reflect the caustic attitude held by many journalists towards the band. As 1981 clicked into place, tribal image culture was at its peak with post-punk, new second-wave punk, anarcho-punk, post-*Quadrophenia* mod revivalism, 2-Tone, returning rockabilly and new romantic all in the pick and mix of styles. As with punk and post-punk, Throbbing Gristle refused to fit in and abide by the rules, though it appeared that an 'industrial look' was being taken up by others.[12]

Though billed as a 'Fetish Night Out', after the ambitious but independent record label founded to re-release the initial Throbbing Gristle album, the Lyceum showcase also paralleled the last throes of Industrial Records with a series of cassette-only releases in early 1981. These included a solo project by Chris Carter entitled *The Space Between*, a collection of early Cabaret Voltaire recordings, the solo album *Disposable Half Truths* by Cabaret Voltaire member Richard H. Kirk, and a debut release by Clock DVA *White Souls in Black Suits*. Fetish had already stepped into the void and would push on through 1981 with more vinyl releases, including a Neville Brody packaged box set of Throbbing Gristle albums and the posthumous single 'Discipline'. The label would quickly establish a niche with the industrial and new-funk crossover music that immediately followed in the wake of Throbbing Gristle, offering an escape route from the excess and vacuity of the new romantic scene as it quickly crashed and burned through 1981 as a potentially credible underground subculture.

One month after the Lyceum event the band flew to Rome at the request of Italian National Radio to develop and record a spontaneous project. It would result in the band's final studio work, and a subsequent recording albeit released as an album over a year later in an unauthorized form on an obscure German label.[13] Though we are never given a precise date as to when the band knew with absolute certainty that their time was up, it appears that most of what happened through 1981 – from the Lyceum event onwards – the band have gone beyond borrowed time. This makes the album produced in Rome – *Journey Through a Body* – a curious case, as it is no doubt a conceptual and considered work seemingly produced by a coherent unit. The recording session and album have become something of a disputed historical fact, with Ford (1999: 11.9) simply reciting that the group accepted an invitation to record the album, whilst Tutti (2017: 263) fills in a few crucial details about how this came out; namely, it was an invitation directed to herself through her ongoing communication with Robert Wyatt. There is also a bit of tit-for-tat exchange around P-Orridge inserting a dedication to Paula in one of the track titles prior to its release on the German label in 1982. P-Orridge's 2021 autobiography, written as they somewhat bitterly looked back on the breakdown of both relationships, does not include any reference to *Journey Through a Body* or the trip to Rome.

The production of the work ran to a Perecquian constraint such that the band elected to produce one improvised composition on each day and then move forward to the next. Though it is possible to frame this project in the same way as their improvised soundtrack to Jarman's film produced a few months prior, this method of working also leans towards the idea that they are now artistic strangers, or at least undergoing a trial separation. However, intellectual innovation and operational concordance won out, and the band quickly adopted the idea to build the work around the theme of the body, neatly linking back to their days as extreme performance artists. The opening work 'Medicine' recreates the unsettling discord of a hospital unit, giving the project an ouroboros aspect in that such an environment can represent the first sounds heard at the point of birth or the final sounds heard at the point of death from within intensive care. The sheer terror it invokes on close listening, through its incredible replicative power of shifting you into a hospital, suggests that there was an element of pre-planning unless the band can conjure up the obscure but precise sounds of a hospital within a few hours in a foreign studio. The radio station may well have had a library of sound effects and archived incidents, but if this is the case then they were sourced and selected with a miraculous sense of urgency and accuracy. The next two tracks link back to *Heathen Earth* and *20 Jazz Funk Greats*. 'Catholic Sex' revisits the sinister and sexual funk with P-Orridge once again trying to salvage some form of romanticism from the dark caverns of his psyche. Next, 'Exotic Functions' offers the band's truest tribute to Martin Denny, looking forward to the ethnographic funk of 23 Skidoo's 'Quiet Pillage'. The mood shifts considerably with 'Violencia', where the listener is held hostage to accompany the perpetration of an act of terrible violence. It plunges you into the inaugural Throbbing Gristle territory; perhaps 'the body' that is journeyed through is in fact the dying body of Throbbing Gristle itself? Again, the concept of being able to conjure up this dense, complex, and thoroughly unnerving composition *ex nihilo* in one studio session is beguiling. The work concludes with 'Oltre La Morte', a graceful and remorseful signing off from both the project in Rome and the recording arc of the band.

LAST EXIT

The band flew to the United States in mid May to undertake two final performances: Los Angeles Veteran's Auditorium on Friday 22 May and San Francisco's Kezar Pavilion one week later on 29 May. These were larger capacity venues befitting the growing status of the band. In between dates, they undertook interviews and also accelerated the destructive domestic tension to the point where, according to Tutti in Ford (1999: 11.10), relationships overwhelmed the viability of the band. During this short tour, Tutti announced her pregnancy which would appear to have set P-Orridge into a spin where he spontaneously married Paula at a roadside church in Mexico during a trip to pick up contraband street weapons (after dropping acid). P-Orridge claims his marriage to Paula subsequently put Tutti into a sulk. It's like bad scripted reality TV 40 years before its time.

The spectral presence of the Sex Pistols returns for one last haunting, as P-Orridge makes peace with his nemesis by acknowledging that splitting in San Francisco would give the band a sense of history by sharing such a method with the punk godfathers. As indicated in the introduction to this chapter, the dissolution and ultimate termination of Throbbing Gristle unfolded through most of early 1981, dragging itself into a three-act play where each part overlapped and is historically disputed. There was a wider agreement in kind that the band had reached an impasse of having critical importance, and this comes through in some of the more measured and circumspect interviews with Carter, as part of his newly formed music partnership with Tutti. He speaks to David Elliott for his *Neumusik* fanzine (issue 5) on 9 May 1981, revealing that the band have split but will undertake the American dates, recounting that 'Sleazy said a few weeks ago, "We've used up all our ideas now; it's coming to the end of the road. We haven't got much to say together, musically"' (40). Carter maintains a similar interpretation a year later, May 1982, as he speaks to Martin Lacey for his *NMX* fanzine (issue 23) suggesting that 'It was partly that we felt we'd said everything we had to say in that direction and as far as the music went we were getting too much like a rock 'n' roll group which is what we never wanted to become' (11). This is an interesting angle and is likely to be the most amenable way of framing the end of the project, but you felt that further possibilities were in reach such as with the new 'disco rhythms' that Carter himself had introduced in the December 1980 gigs, and the incredible suite of music conjured up in Rome.

In an interview for the *LA Times*, conducted just before the band fly out and published on 17 May 1981, P-Orridge reiterates his earlier words for his interview in *Real Shocks* fanzine. It is almost verbatim, with P-Orridge stressing the band's anti-proficient interventions into both the art and music worlds, and confirming that the two gigs in the United States will be the last undertaken by the band. He does not indicate a split, but the journalist suggests that 'the four will devote themselves to Psychic Television, an ambitious endeavour aimed at providing "non-linear" video for the hours between 1 a.m. and 6 a.m., when British television goes dark' (n.pag.). Speaking much later when interviewed by old friend Sandy Robertson for *Sounds* issue 12 December 1981, he is remarkably circumspect and echoes Carter's sentiments, indicating simultaneous private personal reasons that undermined 'a close-knit emotional unit' but preferring to state that 'on an aesthetic and conceptual level it was obvious to all of us that there were two directions developing within the group' (27). For P-Orridge, this direction concerns moving away from a rock performance archetype, as he sees this as an operation of 'diminishing returns' for audience satisfaction that condition the performer into blindly trying to surpass what went before with more of the same. The plans for a new intervention into television are still at the forefront of his mind, but by now it is just P-Orridge and Christopherson. At this point in time, before his return to chasing the rock-star archetype, P-Orridge personified what Church (2019: 35) defines as a 'post-punk polymath', namely, an individual who 'lack(s) an obvious place within the histories of any particular art form, or an easily discernible relationship to disciplinary structures'.

The second act of the play centres around the moment when the break is finalized, and the weakened animal is put out of its misery. The manner and the 'honour' of this fatal blow is a topic of contestation, but the loosely agreed feeling is that the fractious group meeting at Beck Road, where P-Orridge pushes Carter past his limit point regarding 'destiny' and 'fate' is the precise moment when it all ends. This is rooted in domestic tensions as much as any consensual agreement of a foreboding creative barrenness due to differing expectations and understandings. The final act is the announcement. It is not obvious how this is agreed and it is clear that some veneer of harmony is to be upheld for the US dates, but P-Orridge pulls a fast one and announces the end of the band on American radio just prior to the last date. This caused tension for the final gig, further amplified by the penultimate gig in Los Angeles being somewhat malfunctioning. Recollections of the two dates are typically contrary, with Tutti not enjoying the first date but feeling the second was tight and cathartic, whereas P-Orridge enjoyed the abstractly nihilistic nature of the first but feeling that the second was too much in the vein of rock 'n' roll. Tutti's opinion bears fruit; the first gig suffers from bad sound and the discernibility of songs is lost, without any exciting wall of noise taking its place. It just sounds lazy and thoughtless. The second and final gig is focused and cohesive, with melancholic tones and interjections throughout. It is also appreciated by a frantic audience bouncing (and being bounced) on a sprung floor. As Wes Moynihan (2016: n.pag.) points out in his dissection of Throbbing Gristle gigs and events, this final show references back much of *20 Jazz Funk Greats*, and includes an apposite sample from the film *Apocalypse Now*: 'Terminate with extreme prejudice. You understand Captain that this mission does not exist nor will it ever exist'.[14]

A formal announcement of termination is made via a mailing out of postcards on 23 June 1981. Of the British music newspapers, only *Sounds* makes a formal death notice on 4 July 1981.

AFTERLIVES

In his 2014 book *Ghosts of My Life*, the late Mark Fisher reflects on this period of the early 1980s and the subcultural music of the time, suggesting it represented 'the time when a whole world (social democratic, Fordist, industrial) became obsolete, and the contours of a new world (neoliberal, consumerist, informatic) began to show themselves' (50). He used the metaphor of the teetering car on the desolate quarry edge in Chris Petit's 1979 film *Radio On*, describing the scene as showing future movement into the new decade as being 'stalled on the edge of the future' (201). Throbbing Gristle had driven the car to the precipice so to speak, completing, in the words of Keenan (2016: viii), the 'disassembling of rock music' and applying 'interrogative strategies for retooling DIY to liberate music from musicians'. A swarm of afterlives was inevitable.

Throbbing Gristle thus inhabited and inspired many afterlives, informing the sonic landscape of the early 1980s as punk, post-punk, second-wave punk, and several ephemeral variations and hybrids played out their overlapping lifecycles. First, the low-key announcement of their termination wasn't helped by a stream of releases that came immediately after their end, in the form of official releases on new labels and a constant drip-feed of bootlegs emerging from various corners. This body of work formed, and remains, a significant afterlife, coinciding with the incredible series of professionally produced *RE/Search* issues by Juno and Vale that kept the flame of Throbbing Gristle aglow and coalesced the nascent industrial scene.[15] Second, the four members of the band split into two camps and retooled to start performing, recording, and – in the case of P-Orridge (with Christopherson initially by his side) – proselytizing. Third there was the widening genre of industrial and aggressive noise acts that took inspiration from the band. Also included within this grouping would be the cottage industry of tape-trading 'electronic garage' artists inspired uniquely by Chris Carter and his 'performing-in-the-shadows' manner of operating. Fourth, there were a number of co-travellers with Throbbing Gristle, increasingly assembled around Fetish Records, that carried on their sonic development, particularly picking up on the looser funk and ersatz electro strands that had been glimpsed in the final few Throbbing Gristle gigs (even though 'Discipline' was the only track from this period that made it onto vinyl). Finally, there is a tangential Throbbing Gristle afterlife in the anarcho-punk scene, coming into force and officially being named in the immediate aftermath of the band's dissolution.

Figure 8.3: Throbbing Gristle 'Discipline' sleeve, Fetish Records, 1981.

Let's look first at the posthumous releases. The corpse of Throbbing Gristle was still warm when 'Discipline' came out on Fetish Records in May 1981. In fact, the band had not formally announced its termination. This was the first 12 inch by the band, and it took the extended live recordings from the first night at the SO36 Club (where the track was apparently born out of nothing) and the claustrophobic atmosphere of Manchester Rafters a month later. As with the earlier 'Five Knuckle Shuffle', the record utilized simple live lifts of the track that concluded both gigs, the powerful sound of the band as they tentatively embraced a juddering electro beat. However, the sleeve artwork was another classic that would feed into the mythology of the band through the rest of the 1980s to settle into an 'official' but incorrect documentation much like P-Orridge's fabricated artist Ted Glass. For 'Discipline', the creepy-corporate style of the Industrial Records 7 inch singles was passed over in favour of a Stan Bingo photograph showing the band lined up on the threshold of a totalitarian-looking building as part of their Berlin visit. A vast hanging flag or banner occupies the top third of the picture plane, its emblem or message not revealed. They all face the camera but look deliberately disengaged. It is either an incredibly well-executed forced double exposure (caused by the photographer deliberately not advancing the film by a frame once the shutter has been pressed) or an act of post-photographic superimpositional wizardry, but the four figures look like ghosts in front of the building as the background features of steps and stone uprights bleed through.[16] The spectral presence of the band no more, or the spectral presence of the occupants of the building – but who were they? Throbbing Gristle mythology has perpetuated the building as the Nazi Ministry of Propaganda, but it is actually Bendlerblock, an example of authoritarian Wilhelminian-era architecture. The building has a complex history, part of the internal Wehrmacht resistance to Hitler's intensification of war crimes, and the home to Claus von Stauffenberg's attempt to assassinate der Fuhrer.[17] There was an unusually lengthy review of the single in *NME* on 27 June 1981, acting more as a space for Paul Morley to re-assess his relationship with the band now that they were newly defunct. By 1981, Morley has attained something of Svengali status within the new pop journalism field, writing with an authority that apparently makes or destroys careers. Throbbing Gristle continue to worry him. He expounds many more words than usual for the reviewing of a single, using short sentence stubs in his typical style (the first six sentences are all five words and under). This staccato style makes finding a narrative (beyond pure style) an elusive endeavour, but Morley relents. 'Discipline' has him, in its intent and its execution; the record is described as 'an open conflict between surface and depth sensibilities'. You can't help feeling that Morley is questioning his own role in the unravelling of 1980s style culture with the post-punk pop process.

In October 1981, Rough Trade compiled and released *Greatest Hits – Entertainment Though Pain*, collecting snapshots of the band's album work and sporadic singles. This can obviously be seen as derivative and counter-intuitive to the band's original intent of creating albums as a document of work at a single point in time, but was a natural part of promoting either extinct or extant bands in the usual industry format. The packaging returns to the Martin Denny exotica style with Tutti gloriously obliging for the cover and the band posing in a seaside photographic studio set-up for the back, amidst cheesy props such as a mooring rope, gigantic spider crab, and cornet. A complex essay by Claude Bessy accompanies the banal photographs. *Sounds*, with the Sandy Robertson connection, are predictably first to review the work in the first week of October but Robertson seems more intent on picking up on Morley's *volte-face*. The man himself steps forward to review the album in *NME* at the end of the month. Style and pose (from Morley) cannot be suppressed: the first paragraph is encased in square parentheses and namedrops *Nouveaux Philophes* Bernard-Henry Lévy, and the second paragraph is in standard brackets with a further encased quote from the modernist poet Rilke. Is this simply a thought, then an aside, and then the review proper? This was early 1980s *NME* in essence. In the meat of the review, Morley succumbs to Throbbing Gristle, acknowledging their canonical place within the current post-punk landscape that excites him so much. He even takes up the standard line about revealing the abject as the only way of moving beyond it, quoting absurdist playwright Eugene Ionesco in three separate chunks as a suitable ally.

The year was rounded off with the release of *Funeral in Berlin* on Zensor Records, collecting material from their consecutive appearances at the SO36 Club as documented earlier in this chapter. His confessional complete, Paul Morley is replaced by Chris Bohn (Biba Kopf) who also joins the cause of reassessing his negative opinions and validating the band's preoccupation with the intense and abject. Bohn's argument, or justification, centres around the diminishing of 'viable, valuable extremes', his scepticism of the contemporary late 1981 scene contrasting with Morley's strategic enthusiasm. He even signs off with an apology for taking so long to cotton on. Within a year of splitting up, Throbbing Gristle were now seen as both a key axis of the post-punk structure and a premonition of how this scene might quickly become derailed.

Moving on to the individual band members themselves, by early 1982, both halves of the split were strategizing, as witnessed in their consecutive week interviews in *Sounds* through the previous December. Chris & Cosey have released the album *Heartbeat* on Rough Trade and would quickly follow it up with *Trance* a year later, an indication of their productivity. Split away from the anti-structural dissensus of Throbbing Gristle, the output is more clinical and polished, at points pristine, punctilious, and verging upon geeky. Tracks such as 'Bust Stop' brought out Carter's disco rhythms that were momentarily christened in Throbbing Gristle, but they missed the rough contrast of overlaid effects, Christopherson's disorienting tapes, and P-Orridge's grunting and yelling. Whilever Chris & Cosey's output was viewed through the lens of Throbbing Gristle, it was often depicted as coming up short, offering the 'nice' part which could never be anything more. It is perhaps revealing that Chris & Cosey's substantial and continuous post-TG output does not register a mention in Simon Reynolds' authoritative survey of post-punk *Rip it up and Start Again*, and their work evades the author's detailed critical purview. However, their influence would be a slow-burning fuse. Carter in particular had a fanbase of DIY electronics specialists who related to his studious and non-attention-seeking demeanour, and this sets off a cottage industry of experimentation. Furthermore, as the 1980s wound down with post-punk running out of avenues, a new mode of electronic music swept through with the birth of the rave scene and the rise of bedroom producers. These early tracks from Chris & Cosey were suddenly heralded as seminal moments in electronic dance music.[18]

Meanwhile, P-Orridge's mind was whirring, looking to do some kind of intervention with television and establish a publishing wing partly through Vale and Juno's San Francisco-based *RE/Search* project and partly through Rough Trade. The name and logo for this potential interventionist experimental operation were set out in the advance articles: Psychic TV. We saw this in his early interviews when he suggested that this would be a project that followed on from Throbbing Gristle as a continued group concern. As Psychic TV takes shape, the original afterlife of retrospective Throbbing Gristle releases goes up a gear in March 1982 with the Fetish Records box set gathering the four studio albums plus a pressing of the final gig in San Francisco sumptuously presented in Neville Brody-designed packaging.[19] Amusingly, style magazine *The Face* announces a forthcoming Throbbing Gristle feature in their February 1982 edition, presumably mistaking the stylistic continuation of the ghost of Throbbing Gristle as a real thing and confirming their adherence to artifice above actuality. An article did appear, in the following edition (issue 23 of course), and this echoes P-Orridge's article from *Sounds* regarding television and printed material projects. A grouping of like minds – thinkers, musicians, and experimentalists – was mooted under the Final Academy banner for the not-yet-opened Hacienda in Manchester.

P-Orridge's Psychic TV also re-engaged a music direction around this time, with the addition of Paula and ex-Alternative TV member and Beck Road neighbour Alex Fergusson. In his 2021 autobiography, P-Orridge is a little disingenuous regarding Christopherson's role, downplaying him to a secondary involvement with regard to producing music.[20] P-Orridge now suggests that there were two simultaneous projects, Psychic Television (with Christopherson) as a media project and Psychic TV (with Fergusson) as a music project. Documentation also suggests a key role for Stan Bingo, but he appears to have completely dropped off P-Orridge's historical recollections. A rescheduled Final Academy took place at the end of September 1982, running for four days at Brixton's Ritzy Cinema. As well as showcasing the satellite bands around the Throbbing Gristle scene – Last Few Days, 23 Skidoo, etc. – this event also saw the debut (of sorts) of Psychic TV, appearing as a pre-recorded television transmission with added tapes and effects announcing that 'Psychic TV is not a band'. This assemblage of tapes and films also premiered at Manchester Hacienda (4 October), Liverpool Centre Hotel (5 October), and London Heaven (7 October). Whatever not being a band meant it did not extend to securing a record deal with a major label and releasing a debut album, with *Force the Hand of Chance* coming out shortly after the Final Academy shows, and P-Orridge procuring lengthy features in both *Sounds* (6 November 1982 including a highly staged cover photograph by Sheila Rock) and *NME* (13 November 1982 in a television special edition). Contrary to P-Orridge's revisionist stance, Christopherson was a key musician throughout the album, although Fergusson's diverse musical background is evident with tracks such as 'Stolen Kisses' sounding as if they are outtakes from a Postcard Records demo.

With its closing track 'Message from the Temple', the album set in place P-Orridge's wider ambitions for establishing an esoteric countercultural cult: Thee Temple of Psychick Youth (TOPY). This extra-musical aspect would continue through the second album *Dreams Less Sweet* released in November 1983, coinciding with the first 'live' gig by the band – now expanded to include Geff Rushton and John Gosling. In their typical controversial style, this was pencilled in for Prestwich Asylum in Manchester, though shifted at the last minute to the more mundane and rock-centric Ritzy Club. With Ken Thomas managing the sound, it was a fraught and quasi-religious affair, the band sporting their new TOPY haircuts and uniforms like a religious brotherhood. Through much critical reflection, TOPY has been framed variously as a set of intentions at the point of its inception and a set of warnings from the point of its dissolution and apparent corruption. Partridge (2013: 200) alights upon P-Orridge's neologisms, defining TOPY for its inroads into occulture (the expansion of the differing of religion) and esoterrorism, going on to praise its aim to 'disrupt social programming and consensus solipsism'. Keenan (2016: 119), in his journeying book that covers the bands in the immediate wake of this industrial-meets-ecclesiastical moment, describes TOPY 'at their purest' as a 'daring utopian project geared towards the total subversion of contemporary morality through disciplines designed to focus the will onto one's true desires, thus enabling the individual to live an authentic life'. Opstrup (2017: 252), in a wider study linking countercultural escape strategies, offers TOPY as a 'new ecstatic commune with a decentralized and horizontal network structure which would learn us the necessary skills to survive in an imaginary future'. P-Orridge (2021: 254) jokingly refers to an impetus to set up an organization for 'thousands of people having orgasms at the same time', but later confesses a desire for a 'paramilitary occult organisation' (261).

In her discussion of entelechy, Martin (1981: 119) encounters the dilemma of the doctrine of equality and brotherhood, such that 'equality comes to depend on authority' and complete control emerges over members in order to guard against the kind of egoism and individual privacy which erodes communal identity. Throbbing Gristle had already met such dilemmas around the group-directed individual at a more minor key such as pointed out by Bland (2018: 155) in his discussion of *Industrial News* becoming the thing it was railing against. TOPY quickly fell into this trap writ large, becoming the subject of a media scare campaign, and eventually attracting the attention of Scotland Yard.[21] The researcher Dan Siepmann currently pushes hardest in maintaining a critical affront to P-Orridge's past, with his 2019 article 'Groupthink and other painful reflections on Thee Temple ov Psychick Youth' outlining how TOPY had its origins in mimicking The People's Temple at Jonestown, The Process Church of the Final Judgement, and the Manson Family.[22]

The afterlife represented by the strands of music and discrete bands inspired by Throbbing Gristle is complex, requiring a dedicated work in its own right. A similar study is required for the distinctive industrial genre that eked out a minoritarian identity in the early 1980s to commercially bloom through the 1990s (cross-pollinating with metal and goth), though this is in part explored in Reed (2013). Most, if not all, adherents of this scene and genre acknowledge the seminal role played by Throbbing Gristle. There was also an ultra-niche genre of tape-trading electronics specialists inspired by Carter's dedicated working methods, background personality, and uninhibited spheres of influence (disco, Tangerine Dream, Abba, horror film soundtracks), and this scene came to light through *Sounds* journalist Dave Henderson and his spring 1983 series of columns under the 'Wild Planet' banner. Henderson championed key cassette releases such as *Rising from the Red Sand*, and much of this work is being retrospectively documented by Cherry Red Records under their *Noise Floor* series. Throbbing Gristle influences abound, such as on the track 'Disco Song' by O Yuki Conjugate with its mournful utilization of a Boys' Brigade bugle.

Another niche genre influenced by Throbbing Gristle was the power electronics scene instigated by William Bennett and his Whitehouse project. This legacy is also complex and contested, with both P-Orridge and Tutti expressing distaste at Bennett's amplified and contextless use of troubling subject matter and imagery. I have touched on this in the conclusion to Chapter 5, concerning the evocation of Peter Sutcliffe, and the arguments around this method continue to draw disagreement and a lack of resolution. Hegarty (2007: 109) questions P-Orridge's stance, a kind of holier-than-thou-of-the-unholy, arguing that 'the success of the particular mission of taboo-breaking and exposing the brutality of rationalized society at one and the same time is precisely in the banalisation of those images, and the absence of judgement'. Meanwhile, Keenan (2016: x) grasps this nettle of how taboo defines society and how its dismantling will unleash energy, stating that industrial music is 'often thrilling in its violence, in its erotic licentiousness, in its attraction to darkness and the taboo'. Later he gives page space to Bennett, suggesting he took inspiration from Throbbing Gristle 'by dint of the fact that they weren't enough' (96). Bennett's no-nonsense fanzine *Kata* certainly confirms this, with the writer bemoaning the loss of 'classic brighton era [*sic*]' Throbbing Gristle in issue 3, and delivering a consistent attacking review of *Heathen Earth* in issue 4 ending with a summary of 'fifth rate emerson lake and palmer'. Keenan (2016: 98) concludes that Whitehouse's 'unwillingness to provide a mediating context' serves a purpose such that it contributes towards 'a strategy to force the listener to come to terms with their own prejudices, to think about their hang-ups and desires and deal with the images without any clue as to how they're supposed to react'. It's a contextual disagreement that is set to continue.

Less contentious was the loose grouping of like-minded experimentalists or 'discontented rock rebels', many of whom had coalesced around Industrial Records and then joined forces with Fetish Records for the Lyceum showcase (Robertson 1981: 27).[23] 23 Skidoo (though not appearing on the Lyceum bill) were a case in point, briefly taken under the wing of P-Orridge, Christopherson and producer Ken Thomas to produce the shuddering ethno-funk album *Seven Songs* in winter 1981 which topped the independent album charts for the first half of 1982. There is a much wider story arc to 23 Skidoo, often buried under their brief hey-day period associated with P-Orridge, but it is possible to derive an approximation of ex-TG influences. The band spent a period rehearsing at the Death Factory and 23 Skidoo member Fritz Catlin moved into Beck Road, forming connections with Dan Landin (Stan Bingo) who initially designed the sleeve for their debut single 'Ethics'.[24] Landin introduced 23 Skidoo to the potential of tape loops which, combined with P-Orridge enthused Burroughs cut-up theory and incursions into control theory, allowed the band to land on their own brand of conjoining noise and funk. 23 Skidoo were accomplished musicians, ever pressing forward to the point where roles in the band became fluid, fulfilling the promise that Throbbing Gristle had shown with their own initial experiments into funk with their 'first disco rhythm' that had been extended to incorporate blowing whistles and striking wooden percussion.

With in-house designer Neville Brody, Fetish Records flared brightly through the first two years of the 1980s, attempting to straddle the experimental edge of nascent industrial music and the New York 'no wave' funk scene. Experimental funk was a fashionable thing briefly in 1982, though it soon gave way to other trends with a myriad of accompanying clothing styles. The label ceased around 1983, though by that time the group of artists developing a more brutalist-meets-commercial electronic approach had started to cluster elsewhere. From mid 1982 Psychic TV had aligned themselves with Stephen 'Stevo' Pearce who ran the Some Bizzare label and licensed music to some of the major labels who were sniffing around the experimental and (ex)industrial scene. Some Bizzare, originally a synth-pop label that cleverly recognized the potential of Soft Cell, quickly became the new home for early industrial music with pop leanings. Reynolds's chapter 'Conform to Deform' (one of many Stevo catchphrases) in *Rip it up and Start Again* captures and contextualizes this concentration of bands perfectly, with an aim of appearing as if 'fitting in'. Psychic TV were Stevo's first catch, followed by Cabaret Voltaire, German noisemakers Einstürzende Neubauten, Christopherson's new band Coil following his break away from Psychic TV, metal-banging percussionists Test Dept, frenetic polymath Foetus (Jim Thirwell) and New York sonic brutalists Swans. Somewhat unsurprisingly, none of this rostrum troubled the mainstream charts in the way that Soft

Cell had, though the bands, through the various deals that Stevo had arranged, enjoyed a short period of lavish design, packaging and confrontational promotion. With mainstream success proving ever elusive, the bands soon settled down to graft in their particular sonic arts. The 1987 book *Tape Delay*, consisting of short sections of interviews and artist-curated collages and missives, is the contemporaneous document of this time; it revels in esoteric endeavours and an earnestness in the power of art to engender change, demolish structures, and clarify vision, the bands sharing a common bond of transmediality with nominated art movements like dada and fiction writers such as J. G. Ballard. Of course, *Tape Delay*'s publication date of 1987 was the tipping point into a new era of music with the rave, acid house, and techno scenes about to take hold. This paradigm shift split the post-TG set in half, with a handful of bands and artists clumsily attempting to claim a place at the new table of youth-oriented dance culture.

A final tangential afterlife can also be tracked in the anarcho-punk genre, coming to force as a named thing around 1982. Whilst this might appear to return critical reflection of Throbbing Gristle to a punk grounding, there were some clear dividing lines between anarcho-punk and P-Orridge's countercultural movements. In addition, whereas I am reluctant to class a scene such as punk or post-punk as a movement, implying collective and strategized aims, beliefs and methodologies, we can tentatively apply this term to anarcho-punk. It may appear evident that this genre is far away 'musically' from the sounds that Throbbing Gristle explored, but the shared timeframe and resultant shift to something more than music invite strong comparisons. The anarcho-punk movement grew from the determined efforts of the bands Crass and Poison Girls, who spent an initial period working within punk to create something extra-musical with regard to inclusivity and ethical rigour, arriving at an approximate political anti-politics. This was followed, for Crass in particular, by a period of the band negotiating (and calling to question) their perceived role as 'scene leaders'. As Ostrup (2017), O'Sullivan (2017), and Cogan (2007) all point out, Crass had a remarkable number of synchronous similarities to Throbbing Gristle. Particular parallels are activism in the art milieu prior to forming as a band and the fostering of a unicursal cult-ish aspect in later years as the Crass brand of punk, christened anarcho-punk, ran parallel to P-Orridge's post-TG experiments with Psychic TV and TOPY.[25] O'Sullivan described this shared arc as 'performance fictions' with a 'mythopoetic character' such that both bands 'involved a focus on self-determination, and, with that, presented a challenge to more dominant fictions and consensual reality more generally' (94). Worley (2016: 288), reflecting on the anarcho-punk scene, extends this to challenging punk itself, suggesting that Crass held an 'open commitment to countercultural influences that pre-dated punk' such that it 'challenged the sense of purge that came with the Pistols' – a facet clearly shared with Throbbing Gristle. But there were key differences: Crass, and a sizable portion of the anarcho-punks, were ethical, communitarian, and responsible with regard to their challenging of 'the system'; P-Orridge in his work with Psychic TV and beyond as an artist-provocateur explored thematic elements around the mind and body (hallucinogenics, occult magick, body manipulation).

Founder member of Crass Penny Rimbaud and two other art school lecturers established the anarchist commune at the then derelict Dial House in Epping Forest in 1967, creating the base for both a performance art group and a later punk band.[26] Whereas P-Orridge opted for the decaying industrial docks of Hull, Rimbaud preferred a more bucolic location to integrate aspects such as permaculture. Artist and designer Gee Vaucher soon joined the commune and collaborated with Rimbaud in the Fluxus-inspired performance art group EXIT during the same period as COUM (the two art collectives never actually coincided at an event). Vaucher was also involved with Crass from the start, taking responsibility for their strong visual identity that buttressed their various strands of protest (anarchism, pacificism, individualism, and feminism) and critical targets (the media, the state, the church, and the monarchy). Crass were prompted to form after members of the collective, including working-class eastender Steve Ignorant, witnessed the Clash perform on their 1977 tour.[27] Whereas Throbbing Gristle's ventures into music were coincident with punk starting out, Crass were more so inspired by it at its peak point of authenticity and possibility, taking on its approximate form and mantra of 'anyone can do it', but taking it further with a politicized and politicizing impetus.[28]

Crass were initially shambolic, boozy, and disorganized, but quickly realized that a sense of collectively agreed but individually applied self-discipline would be needed if they were to achieve their intent of realizing the critical power that punk briefly suggested to them. The band moved to produce a debut album *The Feeding of the Five Thousand* (retailing as a 12 inch single) at the end of 1978 and recorded a powerful session for John Peel's BBC radio show in early 1979. Musically Crass are remembered as a playing more standardized punk style, utilizing a crude martial drum sound, frantically and angrily delivered vocals, and downplaying the necessity for musical competence or an aspired punk 'tightness'. Their intent to use the body of punk as a carrier meant that they differed from Throbbing Gristle's experiments in exploring the receptivity around the breaking points of musical definitions opened up by punk, however, the sound of both bands came together at certain moments. The harrowing track 'Mother Earth' produced for the aforementioned Peel session certainly had a feel of Throbbing Gristle, with the starting 'nails down the blackboard' guitars distorted and stretched out to limit points approximating Throbbing Gristle's wall of noise. The subject matter, Myra Hindley, also chimed. Whereas Throbbing

Gristle offered a banal narrative of Brady and Hindley in their 1976 track 'Very Friendly', designed to provoke a thought in the listener with the aim of then self-questioning that thought's basis, Crass' later effort is both more prescriptive and confusing (if not slightly over-ambitious). 'Mother Earth' attempts a critique of mainstream media pretending to be outraged but selling newspapers whilst reasserting female stereotypes, and further hinting at members of the public being jealous of the celebrity culture attached to Hindley. The pseudo-juridical clamour to kill, kill, kill (as ultimate vengeance) whipped up in the readership blurs as a perpetuation of Hindley's evil deeds. The flow of influence was seemingly reversed as Throbbing Gristle's re-recorded version of 'Zyklon B-Zombie' included an extended section of rain and train noises that echoed the 1979 Crass single 'Shaved Women'.[29]

The highly politicized and anyone-can-do-it ethos of Crass quickly inspired a new rhizome of punk, nurturing (as with Throbbing Gristle's nascent industrial scene) an important fanzine culture with a distinctive style of presentation and an angry and inquisitive subject matter. Momentum built up over 1979, with fanzines such as *Toxic Graffitti/Grafity* cutting a swathe with its frantic clustering of symbols and slogans, and by 1980, there was a fairly discernible contingent of bands and fanzines informed by Crass and their in-house label. As Worley (2017: 164) remarks: 'by the early 1980s, the number of groups citing Crass as an influence or coming to prominence through playing or recording with the band was legion'. An important release on Crass Records was the first *Bullshit Detector* compilation in late 1980, acting as a precursor to anarcho-punk as a name for this style of music and subculture.[30] This was initially understood as a shared statement of politically informed DIY music creation and networking, the 'anarcho' tag did not bed in until 1982. Concordance between Crass and Throbbing Gristle (and their 'scenes') was nurtured in the less formal milieu of fanzines, with the aforementioned *Toxic Graffitti* fanzine, whose bumper issue 5 (early 1981) included a free Crass flexi and a short think piece on Throbbing Gristle in editor Mike Diboll's typically restless and explorative style. The fanzine circulated at the point in time that Throbbing Gristle had ceased to exist, though P-Orridge in particular was setting in place the parts for his next project – Psychic TV and TOPY. Another fanzine, *Kill Your Pet Puppy,* had an interest in both scenes, and the much-missed Alistair Livingston reflected on his own time within this crossover in his 2005 essay on the fanzine's website, recalling that both Crass and Psychic TV had a 'total myth and ritual approach [...] what you got was not just a bit of noise on a record, you got a whole lifestyle and ideology' (n.pag.).[31] P-Orridge is seen sporting a classic Crass 'anarchy and peace' badge on his combat jacket, and there are undocumented reports of a one-off meeting of minds at Dial House between P-Orridge and Rimbaud – but a concrete acknowledgement of shared commitment and circumstance is never set out. As I stated at the start of this section, Crass were ethical and responsible and offered a way forward as well as a way out, whereas P-Orridge was more nihilistic in just offering a way out.

TERMINUS

The afterlives of Throbbing Gristle extend onwards, each seeded scene such as anarcho-punk persisting, diversifying, and cross-pollinating. An endpoint to this documentation has to be agreed and the onset of the new scenes infusing more dance music elements from the mid 1980s seems a sensible terminus. The band members are going their separate ways (for now). At this point, we can look back and summarize our journey. In this writing, I have plotted a straight line of history for the band, aligning with Simon Ford's *Wreckers of Civilisation*, rather than contextualizing them into modes of intent and strategy that necessitate a jumping back and forwards in time. The practical arc of the band's lifetime – dictated by a messy flux of domestic tensions, confrontations with society and its institutions, engagements with the canon of art, and moments of mischievous but supreme vision and intensity – requires this linear explication. The genealogy of ideas drew from a deep well of countercultural and high-art resources, breaking interdisciplinary delimitations to segue together cultural chimaera and then always switching paths when something starts to take shape in the category of 'acceptable practice'. This is the always-adventurous vector of Throbbing Gristle.

The proximity of the band to the emergent British punk scene is a parallel way of reading the history of Throbbing Gristle. Such a navigational device might have evoked scepticism, scorn, or even heresy at the outset of this project, but my intent here is to show a value in this approach – a value that flows both ways. Punk in the current era – approaching a fiftieth-year anniversary – attracts a mythologized status dominated by heroic narratives. Instead, there is value in exploring and exposing misrememberings, fabrications, forgotten instances, and buried moments. Throbbing Gristle's coexistence with, and ultimate frustration of, punk facilitates such a reading. A world of commercial inclinations and compromises, reactions and counter-reactions, and manipulations and opportunism. In contrast to the linear history of the band through a sequence of performances, record releases and shifts of sound, punk unfolded at different speeds and from different starting times depending upon where in the country you were. In this regard, punk's chronometer was *polytemporal* – in 1979 it was both 1977 in Derby and some time in the future in Sheffield. Throbbing Gristle passed through these instances with their own trajectory, effectively moving backwards and forwards in subcultural time when measured against the assembled audiences. Regardless, the band were always working to their own clock setting. What that clock setting indicated remained open to interpretation. Chris Carter offered programming rhythms from the future, Peter Christopherson sampled from the infra-ordinary present to expose corrupt leakages, Cosey Fanni Tutti played seated in her leather trousers portraying a malfunctioning rock archetype vision, whilst Genesis P-Orridge channelled a punk-hippie-from-hell dressed in survivalist combat mode.

In his May 1981 interview for the *LA Times*, P-Orridge is caught at a typically garrulous moment just before the band flies out to play their last gigs. Fabulating and embellishing stories on the band's history, achievements, moments of controversy, and future intents in his typical style of *auto-ekphrasis*, he makes a claim as to the influential reach of their music and style. It is an unfortunate habit he carried with him throughout his music career. He suggests that Industrial Records is the 'third-largest independent label in Britain' (n.pag.), and when asked to name the groups that have 'diluted and popularized Throbbing Gristle concepts' he reels off:

> Gary Numan, Orchestral Manoeuvres, Echo & the Bunnymen, A Certain Ratio, Public Image, Robert Fripp, Brian Eno, David Bowie, Peter Gabriel. They're all people we happen to know definitely have got all our records and have listened to them and then changed styles.

Intriguingly, the list consists of pre-punk prog and glam figureheads alongside the (then) starring names in the fractalizing post-punk and electronic music scenes. His old adversary John Lydon is slipped in, immediately following the frankly strange claims of Echo and the Bunnymen and A Certain Ratio. The latter had supported Throbbing Gristle towards the end of their tenure, and Throbbing Gristle had undoubtedly been influenced by ACR's bleak and disembodied take on funk rather than the other way around. Representatives from the punk genre, aside from the mischievous inclusion of Public Image, are absent. This is not surprising. There is no great reveal, now we are at the end of this book, affirming Throbbing Gristle as an axiomatic and archetypal punk band. Throbbing Gristle had a difficult and reluctant relationship with punk, exemplified in the first three chapters of this book which describe the band navigating the initial explosion of the genre and subculture. P-Orridge seemed partly hypnotized by the rapid acceleration of the scene, the opportunities offered, and the opportunities taken by other bands. Christopherson, fired up by his intrigue for sexual proclivities and a sense of punk-appropriate daring in his design, skirted the dark fringes of punk at its onset, proffering design ideas for the clothing shop BOY. Tutti and Carter kept things very much at arm's length. In a hastily called meeting, the band, as a grouping of artists, sat down to discuss and ultimately dismiss punk as a way forward: no truck. As this book has shown, this may have been a simple decision but it was not a straightforward yes–no binary direction that was followed. In the words again of *Kill Your Pet Puppy* writer Alistair Livingston ([2005] 2019: n.pag.): 'Throbbing Gristle never fitted into punk, they were too subversive, too knowing, too clever by half. Yet their trajectory ran parallel with that of punk'.[32]

Punk hovered around Throbbing Gristle, just as the band hovered around punk. Definitions are fluid, but punk emerged variously as a musical formation (degraded rock structures, apparent incompetence), as a musical 'approach' (DIY sensibilities, anti-rockist countenance), as a subculture of looks and poses, and as a set of engagements, oppositions, and provocations. Worley (2017: 11) prioritizes the doing and critiquing over the looking and appearing, suggesting punk as a 'cultural process of critical engagement rather than a specific musical or sartorial style'. In effect, it was all of the things without the necessary and sufficient of any one thing, evolving at different speeds depending upon the communicative distance from the key nodes. It was forever staging a negotiation between authentic intent and marketable appearance as record companies began to reel in the profit. Accordingly, clashing manifestations of punk coexisted and cohabited towns and cities. Throbbing Gristle moved through this shifting scenographic, poking and prodding, constantly changing the scenery, changing the stage, challenging the audience in both the act of looking and the act of seeing. The provocations that punk affected were further pushed by the band. They were shown up to be sometimes inadequate, sometimes illusory, but always potentially extensible. Punk offered a glimpse of critical avenues and thresholds of structure, and these possibilities interested Throbbing Gristle.

As each chapter of this book hinges around a selected performance, we are able to see how both society and punk's response to it are manifested in multiple ways. I also open up a reverse view by exploring the impetus and dynamic of each gig – understanding the motivations of the organizers and detailing what enthused witnesses took away. These people shared with the band a desire to open up subcultural extensibility and to push back against transformational invariance. The performance, in its coming-to-be and ultimate execution, was an experiment in space, place, and field. We reach down to feel the grain and scuzz of the pavement and look up to gulp the noxious air of anticipation – our own war film, our own horror story. We see punk rapidly commercialized, reinventing itself as something else, and reinventing itself as the same. Throbbing Gristle continued to work through these epiphenomenal occurrences, from original punk, to post-punk, to second-wave punk to anarcho-punk. Subcultures centred upon music genres exist in a wider network of coeval subcultures and an encompassing field of popular culture –

television, the cinema, the newspapers, supermarkets, housing estates, schoolyard games, humour, everyday sexism and prurience combined, taboos, and bogeymen. This backdrop nurtured punk, both as formative input and as something to rail against. As Throbbing Gristle showed, what you draw from and what you reject can be difficult to disarticulate. In this regard, Throbbing Gristle provided a way of thinking about punk, of reassessing its project boundaries and internalized regulations. Throbbing Gristle always wanted more; to move beyond punk and to expose blind spots and self-imposed strictures. For this, we can be eternally thankful.

NOTES

1. An exception here is Siouxsie and the Banshees' second album *Join Hands* (September 1979) which utilizes the interior space artfully, and interestingly offers an almost-synergy of singularization, cropping, stances, and stares to *Heathen Earth*. Furthermore, Siouxsie and the Banshees had (as with Throbbing Gristle) split into two at the point of the record's release. Other post-punk gatefolds prior to *Heathen Earth* include Magazine's *Secondhand Daylight* (March 1979) and PiL's *Second Edition* (February 1980).

2. Thanks to Ben Waddington for prompts and ideas in the discussion of these photographs.

3. The band and their uniforms were featured in *The Face* issue 18 (October 1981), though this was four months after the band had split. P-Orridge (2021: 255) describes the grey 'military-style non-uniform uniforms' he later developed for his band Psychic TV.

4. See Ford (1999: 9.21) for details of this conflict.

5. However, the reproduction to black and white with a calculated level of degradation gives the impression of a photographic source. Ford (1999: 10.14) falls for this, incorrectly attributing the image as a scene from a Nazi concentration camp.

6. The lyrics were deliberately puerile, bonding it to the autumn 1978 comedy single 'The Winker's Song (misprint)' by Ivor Biggun and the Red Nose Burglars. This song was not overtly punk, but received a punk endorsement of sorts from Johnny Rotten as he guest-edited the singles reviews for *NME* 22 July 1978. In the same column, he dismissed the Human League's 'Being Boiled' as created by 'trendy hippies'. Masturbation would form part of the Sex Pistols afterlives popularity with 'Friggin' in the Riggin'' released the following year (see discussion in Chapter 6).

7. Ford states the details of these sleeves but does not reveal his source of information.

8. As usual, these gigs were quickly bootlegged as vinyl releases and seemingly serendipitous track names were added. What would appear to be the same compositions from separate nights are attributed different titles.

9. Both Ford (1999: 10.25) and Tutti (2017: 260) emphasize the spontaneous nature of 'Discipline'. As with previous tracks which claim spontaneity, we have no method of proving otherwise.

10. Christopherson had recently set up Greenback Films as he put the brake on record sleeve design with Hipgnosis.

11. See https://www.mylifeinthemoshofghosts.com/2017/07/22/throbbing-gristle-cabaret-voltaire-zev-the-lyceum-ballroom-london-sunday-8th-february-1981/. Accessed 14 June 2021.

12. The Sheffield fanzine *Pink Flag* #7 includes a detailed report of the Lyceum event and begins by remarking how new romantic style tribes were cautiously present in the audience alongside 'clones' who were fans of Cabaret Voltaire.

13. The album remained on the fringe of the Throbbing Gristle canon for many years, residing in a twilight of bootlegs. It was given an official release by Mute Records in 1993.

14. See https://plutoniumshores.blogspot.com/2016/05/throbbing-gristle-at-kezar-pavilion.html. Accessed 8 October 2021.

15. *RE/Search* 4/5 (1982) was dedicated to William Burroughs, Brion Gysin and Throbbing Gristle, *RE/Search* 6/7 (1983) covered various activist and artists in the industrial scene (including a lengthy retrospective feature on Throbbing Gristle), and *RE/Search* 8/9 (1984) was devoted to J. G. Ballard.

16. To create this ghosted effect the camera would have to be perfectly still for both of the overlaid shots, achievable with a tripod and remote shutter release.

17. Thanks to Sander Janzweert for invaluable help in identifying and contextualizing this building.

18. An ironic contrast to P-Orridge's various proclamations that he (and Psychic TV) invented acid house.

19. Quickly followed by Rough Trade releasing a cassette of the Heaven gig under the title *Beyond Jazz Funk* and the unauthorized edition of *Journey Through a Body* leaking out in early summer 1982.

20. In a manner similar to neuro-linguistic programming (NLP), P-Orridge employs a methodological writing style that seldom resorts to critical words about another person but carefully removes them from a rightful history of contribution whilst seemingly speaking well of them. Christopherson and P-Orridge went separate ways in early 1984. Similarly, Paula's contribution to Psychic TV has been aggressively erased by P-Orridge.

21. For a more thorough and balanced account of this incident, see Keenan (2016: 315–25).

22. See https://www.popmatters.com/genesis-p-orridge-groupthink-2640631583.html. Accessed 23 December 2021.

23. This quote is from P-Orridge's post-split interview in *Sounds* 12 December 1981.

24. Landin and Catlin were also core members of the illusive band Last Few Days.

25. Cogan (2007: 84) repeats the easy mistake of assuming Throbbing Gristle had an art school background, rather than making explicit P-Orridge's auto-didactical art groundings.

26. As with P-Orridge, 'Penny Rimbaud' is a name changed by deed poll (from Jeremy Ratter).

27. Ignorant saw the band on 27 May 1977 at Bristol Colston Hall on the 'White Riot' tour, and three days later he attended their gig at Chelmsford Chancellor Hall with other members of the Dial House collective.

28. Dunn (2012) and Grimes (2015) offer focused critical histories of Crass and their role in encouraging a DIY punk scene and going on to build an anarcho-punk movement.

29. A further connection between Crass and Psychic TV is the brief involvement of Crass vocalist Steve Ignorant with the band Current 93, founded by David Tibet who was a close colleague of P-Orridge in the immediate period of Psychic TV forming and contributed to their first album.

30. Famously reviewed in *NME* with a scathing review against 'enshrining incompetence' (14 February 1981, the same week that Throbbing Gristle played their final UK gig at London's Lyceum).

31. See https://killyourpetpuppy.co.uk/news/throbbing-gristle-and-psychic-tv/. Accessed 8 October 2021.

32. See https://killyourpetpuppy.co.uk/news/crass-in-context-al-puppy/. Accessed 8 October 2021.

REFERENCES

Albiez, Sean (2003), 'Know history!: John Lydon, cultural capital and the prog/punk dialectic', *Popular Music,* 22:3, pp. 357–74.

Albiez, Sean (2005), 'Print the truth, not the legend: Sex Pistols, Lesser Free Trade Hall, Manchester, 4 June 1976', in I. Inglis (ed.), *Performance and Popular Music: History, Place and Time,* Aldershot: Ashgate, pp. 92–106.

Albrow Mark (2021), e-mail conversation with author, July.

Anderson, Neil (2009), *Take It to the Limit: The Story of a Sheffield Rock 'n' Roll Legend,* Sheffield: ACM Retro.

Anon. (1976a), 'Knowing what we like ...' *Daily Mirror,* 19 October, p. 2.

Anon. (1976b), 'Mr P Orridge in a stir', *Daily Mirror,* October, p. 3.

Anon. (1976c), 'Protests at use of public money for Contemporary Arts exhibition', *The Times,* 22 October, p. 8.

Anon. (1980), 'Throbbing Gristle part 2: A continuation in a similar vane', *Vox,* 4, pp. 22–24.

Atton, Chris (2011), 'Fan discourse and the construction of noise music as a genre', *Journal of Popular Music Studies,* 23:3, pp. 324–42.

Bachelard, Gaston (1964), *The Poetics of Space,* Boston: Beacon Press.

Baker, Bob (2022), e-mail conversation with author, 6 January.

Battista, Kathy (2019), *Renegotiating the Body: Feminist Art in 1970s London,* London: I.B. Tauris.

Beckett, Andy (2010), *When the Lights Went Out: What Really Happened to Britain in the Seventies,* London: Faber & Faber.

Beckett, Andy (2016), *Promised You a Miracle: UK80-82,* London: Penguin.

Beckman, Frida (2017), *Gilles Deleuze,* London: Reaktion Books.

Berry, Josephine (2018), *Art and (Bare) Life: A Biopolitical Inquiry,* Berlin: Sternberg Press.

Bestley, Russ (2013), 'Art attacks and killing jokes: The graphic language of punk humour', *Punk & Post-Punk,* 2:3, pp. 231–67.

Bestley, Russ (2019), 'The Top of the Poppers sing and play punk', *Punk & Post-Punk,* 8:3, pp. 399–421.

Bestley, Russ and Burgess, Paul (2018), 'Fan artefacts and doing it for themselves: The homemade graphics of punk devotees', *Punk & Post-Punk*, 7:3, pp. 317–40.

Birch, Ian (1979), 'The cyclic and random lyric organisation system or CARLOS', *Melody Maker*, 24 February, pp. 21–22.

Bland, Benjamin (2018), '"Don't do as you're told, do as you think": The transgressive zine culture of industrial music in the 1970s and 1980s', in The Subcultures Network (ed.), *Ripped, Torn and Cut: Pop, Politics and Punk Fanzines from 1976*, Manchester: Manchester University Press, pp. 150–68.

Bonsall, Dave (2019), conversation with author, July.

Bracewell, Michael (1997), *England Is Mine: Pop Life in Albion from Wilde to Goldie*, London: Harper Collins.

Burkham, Chris (1980), review, *Sounds*, February, n.pag.

Butt, Gavin (2023), *No Machos or Pop Stars: When the Leeds Art Experiment Went Punk*, Durham: Duke University Press.

Butt, Gavin, Eshun, Kodwo, and Fisher, Mark (eds) (2016), *Post-Punk Then and Now*, London: Repeater Books.

Charlesworth, Michael (2011), *Derek Jarman (Critical Lives)*, London: Reaktion Books.

Christopherson, Peter (2016), *Photography*, Cugnaux: Timeless Editions.

Church, Lewis (2019), 'Everyone was doing everything: The post-punk polymath on the Lower East Side', *Punk & Post-Punk*, 8:1, pp. 23–37.

City Fun (1981), review of Throbbing Gristle gig, January, 2:7, pp. 9–22.

Clancy, Patrick (1976), 'Orridge sex show move', *The Express*, 23 October, p. 2.

Cogan, Brian (2007), '"Do they owe us a living? Of course they do!" Crass, Throbbing Gristle, and anarchy and radicalism in early English punk rock', *Journal for the Study of Radicalism*, 1:2, pp. 77–90.

Cohen, Stanley ([1972] 1987), *Folk Devils and Moral Panics: The Creation of the Mods and Rockers*, Oxford: Basil Blackwell.

Conroy, Thomas M. (2015), 'In the marketplace of transgression: Throbbing Gristle and the pornographic imaginary', *Porn Studies*, 2:1, pp. 96–99.

Cooper, Sam (2017), *The Situationist International in Britain: Modernism, Surrealism, and the Avant-Gardes*, London: Routledge.

Crossley, Nick (2015), *Networks of Sound, Style and Subversion: The Punk and Post-Punk Worlds of Manchester, London, Liverpool and Sheffield, 1975–80*, Manchester: Manchester University Press.

Czezowski, Andrew and Carrington, Susan (2016), *100 Nights at the Roxy Club: 14th December 1976–23rd April 1977: A Photographic Explosion*, Streatham: Carrczez Publishing Ltd.

Daniel, Drew (2008), *20 Jazz Funk Greats*, New York: Continuum.

Danielsen, Anne and Helseth, Inger (2016), 'Mediated immediacy: The relationship between auditory and visual dimensions of live performance in contemporary technology-based popular music', *Rock Music Studies*, 3:1, pp. 24–40.

De Jongh, Nicholas (1976), 'British Council attacked for "porn subsidy"', *The Guardian*, 21 October, p. 6.

Dean, Mitchell and Zamora, Daniel (2021), *The Last Man Takes LSD: Foucault and the End of Revolution*, London: Verso.

Deleuze, Gilles (1998), *Essays Critical and Clinical*, London: Verso.

Demers, Joanna (2010), *Listening Through the Noise: The Aesthetics of Experimental Electronic Music*, Oxford: Oxford University Press.

Dosse, François (2010), *Gilles Deleuze and Félix Guattari: Intersecting Lives*, New York: Columbia University Press.

Duboys, Eric (2007), *Industrial Music for Industrial People*, Rosieres-en-Haye: Camion Blanc.

Duff, Graham (2019), *Foreground Music: A Life in Fifteen Gigs*, London: Strange Attractor Press.

Dunn, Kevin (2012), 'Anarcho-punk and resistance in everyday life', *Punk & Post-Punk*, 1:2, pp. 201–18.

Edmands, Bob (1978), 'Music from the Death Factory', *NME*, 22 July.

Elliott, David (1981), 'Chris Carter', *Neumusik*, 9 Many, pp. 38–41.

Encarnacao, John (2019), 'Throbbing Gristle's early records: Post-hippie/pre-punk/post-punk', in Z. Beaven, M. O'Dair, and R. Osborne (eds), *Mute Records: Artists, Business, History*, London: Bloomsbury Academic, pp. 71–86.

Etchells, Tim (2021), e-mail exchange with author, December.

Evans, Caroline (2003), *Fashion at the Edge: Spectacle, Modernity and Deathliness*, London: Yale University Press.

Evening News reporter (1977), 'A BIZARRE BOUTIQUE THAT SELLS VIOLENCE', *London Evening News*, 4 March, p. 4.

The Express (1976), newspaper clipping, p. 2.

Fawcett, Michael (2020), e-mail conversation, July.

Federman, Rachel (2014), '"An idealistic utopian thought": Paul McCarthy and the spaces of transmission', *Oxford Art Journal*, 37:1, pp. 1–26.

Fish, Mick (2002), *Industrial Evolution: Through the Eighties with Cabaret Voltaire*, London: Poptomes.

Fish, Mick (2019), e-mail communication with author, July.

Fisher, Mark (2008), '"Can the world be as sad as it seems?": David Peace and negative theodicy', 3 December, http://k-punk.abstractdynamics.org/archives/010867.html. Accessed 13 April 2021.

Fisher, Mark (2014), *Ghosts of My Life: Writings on Depression, Hauntology and Lost Futures*, Winchester: Zero Books.

Fonarow, Wendy (2006), *Empire of Dirt: The Aesthetics and Rituals of British Indie Music*, Middletown: Weslayan University Press.

Forbes, Kenny (2015), '"You had to be there": Memories of the Glasgow Apollo audience', in S. Cohen, R. Knifton, M. Leonard, and L. Roberts (eds), *Sites of Popular Music Heritage: Memories, Histories, Places*, New York: Routledge, pp. 143–59.

Ford, Simon (1999), *Wreckers of Civilisation: The Story of COUM Transmissions and Throbbing Gristle*, London: Black Dog Publications.

Gildart, Keith (2013), *Images of England Through Popular Music: Class, Youth and Rock 'n' Roll 1955–1976*, Basingstoke: Palgrave Macmillan.

Gill, Andy (1980), 'The modern dance', *NME*, 5 January, p. 24.

Gill, Chris (1980), 'Empty vessels', *NME*, 12 July, p. 36.

Gill, John (1978a), 'The Human League', *Sounds*, 12 August, p. 17.

Gill, John (1978b), 'Sensory overload', *Sounds*, 15 July, p. 34.

Gill, John (1980), 'Armageddon time', *Sounds*, 28 June, p. 24.

Glen, Patrick (2019), *Youth and Permissive Social Change in British Music Papers, 1967–1983*, Basingstoke: Palgrave Macmillan.

Goldhammer, Rio (2018), 'Provincial towns and Yorkshire cities: Post-punk sounds, suburban escape, and metro-hegemony', in B. Lashua, S. Wagg, K. Spracklen, and M. Selim Yavuz (eds), *Sounds and the City Volume 2*, Basingstoke: Palgrave Macmillan, pp. 347–67.

Gorman, Paul (2020), *Malcolm McLaren: The Authorised Biography*, London: Constable.

Grimes, Matt (2015), 'Call it Crass but there is no authority but yourself: De-canonizing punk's underbelly', *Punk & Post-Punk*, 4:2–3, pp. 189–204.

Groys, Boris (2014), *On the New*, London: Verso.

Guattari, Félix (1984), 'Transversality', in *Molecular Revolution: Psychiatry and Politics*, Middlesex: Penguin, pp. 11–24.

Hampshire, Paul Bee (2020), 'A tribute to Genesis P-Orridge', The Brooklyn Rail, https://brooklynrail.org/2020/04/in-memoriam/Paul-Bee-Hampshire. Accessed 1 December 2022.

Haskins, Kevin J. (2014), *Who Killed Mister Moonlight? Bauhaus, Black Magick and Benediction*, London: Jawbone Press.

Haslam, Dave (2005), *Not Abba: The Real Story of the 1970s*, London: Fourth estate.

Hawkins, Stan (2009), *The British Pop Dandy: Masculinity, Popular Music and Culture*, Farnham: Ashgate.

Hayes, Paul (2020), e-mail conversation, July.

Hegarty, Paul (2007), *Noise/Music: A History*, London: Continuum.

Hempsall, Alan (2020), e-mail conversation with author, 5 May.

Hennessy, Val (1978), *In the Gutter*, London: Quartet.

Hesmondhalgh, David (2013), *Why Music Matters*, Chichester: Wiley-Blackwell.

Hill, Tony (2011), *The Palace and the Punks*, Jacksdale: Northern Lights Lit.

Hillyer, Aaron (2013), *The Disappearance of Literature: Blanchot, Agamben, and the Writers of the No*, London: Bloomsbury.

Hirschfeld, Magnus (1981), 'Grimness: the great threat to our nation', *Sounds*, 5, 28 February, p. 15.

Hollings, Ken (2003), 'Throbbing Gristle TG24: 24 Hours of Throbbing Gristle , *The Wire*, 227 (January), pp. 58–59.

Humberstone, Klive (2022), e-mail conversation, 8 February.

James, Martin (2018), '"No I don't like where you come from, it's just a satellite of London": High Wycombe, the Sex Pistols and the punk transformation', *Punk & Post Punk*, 7:3, pp. 341–62.

Johnson, Dominic (2019), *Unlimited Action: The Performance of Extremities in the 1970s*, Manchester: Manchester University Press.

Jones, Steve (2016), *Lonely Boy: Tales from a Sex Pistol*, London: Heinemann.

Keenan, David (2016), *England's Hidden Reverse*, expanded edition, Devizes: Strange Attractor Press.

Kilby, Nick and Cheeseman, Matthew ([2012] 2013), *Noise & Dissonance (An Exploration Of Noise And The Post-Industrial)*, 3 September, https://www.discogs.com/release/4881486-Nick-Kilby-And-Matthew-Cheeseman-Noise-Dissonance-An-Exploration-Of-Noise-And-The-Post-Industrial. Accessed 15 May 2020.

Knee, Sam (2015), *The Bag I'm In*, London: Cicada.

Kopf, Biba (1987), 'Bacillus culture', in C. Neal (ed.), *Tape Delay*, London: SAF Publishing, pp. 10–15.

Kromhout, Melle Jan (2011), '"Over the ruined factory there's a funny noise": Throbbing Gristle and the mediatized roots of noise in/as music', *Popular Music and Society*, 34:1, pp. 23–34.

Lacey, Martin (n.d.), no title, *NMX*, 5, pp. 16–18.

Lacey, Martin (1981), 'Chris & Cosey', *NMX*, 5, pp. 10–12.

Laing, Dave (1985), *One Chord Wonders: Power and Meaning in Punk Rock*, Milton Keynes: Open University Press.

Latour, Bruno (2005), *Reassembling the Social: An Introduction to Actor-Network-Theory*, Oxford: Oxford University Press.

Laughey, Dan (2013), 'Ripper', in P. Bennett and J. McDougall (eds), *Barthes' Mythologies Today: Readings of Contemporary Culture*, London: Routledge, pp. 94–95.

Lee, Bill (1980), review, newspaper clipping, *New Music News*, 7 June, n.pag.

Lefebvre, Henri (1991), *The Production of Space*, Oxford: Blackwell.

Letts, Don (2007), *Culture Clash: Dread Meets Punk Rockers*, London: SAF Publishing.

Lilleker, Martin (1980), review of Throbbing Gristle gig, *Sheffield Star*, 11 June, p. 10.

Lilleker, Martin (2005), *Beats Working for a Living: The Story of Popular Music in Sheffield 1973–1984*, Sheffield: Juma.

Livingston, Alistair ([2005] 2018), 'Crass In Context: An essay by Al Puppy', 26 January, https://killyourpetpuppy.co.uk/news/throbbing-gristle-and-psychic-tv/. Accessed 8 October 2021.

Livingston, Alistair ([2005] 2019), 'Throbbing Gristle and psychic TV: An essay by Al Puppy', 31 December, https://killyourpetpuppy.co.uk/news/crass-in-context-al-puppy/. Accessed 8 October 2021.

Lockwood, Dean (2011), 'The great Yorkshire fugue: Bare life in the Red Riding Quartet', in K. Shaw (ed.), *Analysing David Peace*, Newcastle-upon-Tyne: Cambridge Scholars, pp. 41–59.

Lohman, Kirsty and Worley, Matthew (2018), 'Bloody revolutions, fascist dreams, anarchy and peace: Crass, Rondos and the politics of punk, 1977–84', *Britain and the World*, 11:1, pp. 51–74.

Lydon, John (2013), 'A beautiful ugliness inside', in A. Bolton (ed.), *PUNK: Chaos to Couture*, New York: Museum of Modern Art, pp. 20–23.

Malbon, Ben (1999), *Clubbing: Dancing, Ecstasy and Vitality*, London: Routledge.

Mallinder, Stephen (2007), 'Sheffield is not sexy', *Nebula*, 4:3, pp. 292–321.

Mallinder, Stephen (2019), e-mail conversation with author, July.

Mallinder, Stephen (2022), e-mail conversation with author, January.

Martin, Bernice (1981), *A Sociology of Contemporary Cultural Change*, Oxford: Blackwell.

Mayers, Doreen (1976), 'British Council will give "sex artist" £496', *The Times*, October, p. 3.

Medhurst, Andy (1999), 'What did I get? Punk, memory and autobiography', in R. Sabin (ed.), *Punk Rock: So What? The Cultural Legacy of Punk*, London: Routledge, pp. 219–31.

Mendes, Valerie (1999), *Black in Fashion*, London: V&A Publications.

Metzger, Richard (2002), 'Nothing short of a total war', in N. Mamatras, M. Balistreri, E. Moynihad, and D. Goede (eds), *Painful but Fabulous: The Lives & Art of Genesis P-Orridge*, Brooklyn: Soft Skull Press, pp. 43–49.

Middles, Mick (1979), 'Throbbing Gristle Manchester', *Sounds*, 2 June, p. 37.

Milestone, Katie (2018), 'Madchester', in B. Lashua, S. Wagg, K. Spracklen, and M. Selim Yavuz (eds), *Sounds and the City Volume 2*, Basingstoke: Palgrave Macmillan, pp. 303–19.

Miro, Ana Bonet (2018), 'On playgrounds and the archive: Joan Littlewood's Stratford Fair, 1967–1975', *Architecture and Culture*, 6:3, pp. 387–98.

Morley, Paul (1979), 'Berks that lurk in the corners of your psyche', *NME*, 8 December, p. 37.

Morrow, Ann (1976), 'NO FUNDS LEFT DANCERS', *The Daily Telegraph*, p. 17.

Mosser, Kurt (2008), '"Cover songs": Ambiguity, multivalence, polysemy', *Popular Musicology Online*, http://www.popular-musicology-online.com/issues/02/mosser.html. Accessed 1 December 2022.

Moynihan, Wes (2016), 'Throbbing Gristle at Kezar Pavilion', 29 May, https://plutoniumshores.blogspot.com/2016/05/throbbing-gristle-at-kezar-pavilion.html. Accessed 8 October 2021.

Murphy, Gareth (2014), *Cowboys and Indies: The Epic History of the Record Industry*, New York: Thomas Dunne Books.

Needs, Kris (1978), 'Throbbing Gristle', *ZigZag*, 82, pp. 10–13.

Norton, Peter (2021), e-mail conversation, November.

Numan, Gary (2020), *(R)evolution: The Autobiography*, London: Constable.

Nyong'o, Tavia (2008), 'Do you want queer theory (or do you want the truth)? Intersections of punk and queer in the 1970s', *Radical History Review*, 100, pp. 102–19.

O'Connor, Alan (2016), 'Towards a field theory of punk', *Punk & Post-Punk*, 5:1, pp. 67–81.

O'Flaherty, Michael (1976), 'State aid for Cosey's travelling sex troupe', *The Express*, 21 October, p. 3.

Ogg, Alex (2013,) 'For you, Tommy, the war is never over', *Punk & Post-Punk*, 2:3, pp. 231–67.

Opstrup, Kasper (2017), *The Way Out*, Wivenhoe: Minor Compositions.

Osborne, Richard (2015), 'A great friggin' swindle? Sex Pistols, school kids, and 1979', *Popular Music and Society*, 38:4, pp. 432–49.

O'Sullivan, Simon (2017), 'Mythopoesis, scenes and performance fictions: Two case studies (Crass and Thee Temple ov Psychick Youth)', *Parasol: The Journal of the Centre for Experimental Ontology*, 2, pp. 94–106.

Parsons, Tony (1976), 'But darling, mutilation is so passe ...' *NME*, 30 October, n.pag.

Perry, Mark (2020), online discussion with author, 25 March.

P-Orridge, Genesis Breyer (1978), 'MUSIC FROM THE DEATH FACTORY', *NME*, 22 July, p. 27.

P-Orridge, Genesis Breyer ([1978] n.d.), private correspondence, 1 March, https://www.brainwashed.com/tg/live/architect.htm. Accessed 27 July 2022.

P-Orridge, Genesis (1981), 'Gristle to stop its throbbing', *LA Times*, 17 May, n.pag.

P-Orridge, Genesis Breyer (2017), 'Genesis P-Orridge on destroying preconceptions', in conversation with T. Cole Rachel 18 December, *The Creative Independent*, https://thecreativeindependent.com/people/genesis-p-orridge-on-destroying-preconceptions/. Accessed 13 July 2022.

P-Orridge, Genesis (2021), *Nonbinary: A Memoir*, New York: Abrams Press.

P-Orridge, Genesis Breyer and Christopherson, Peter (1976), 'Annihilating reality', *Studio International*, 192:982 (June/July), pp. 44–48.

P-Orridge, Genesis and Naylor, Colin (1977), *Contemporary Artists*, London: St. James Press.

Partridge, Christopher (2013), 'Esoterrorism and the wrecking of civilization: Genesis P-Orridge and the rise of industrial Paganism', in D. Weston and A. Bennett (eds), *Pop Pagans: Paganism and Popular Music*, Durham: Acumen, pp. 189–212.

Partridge, Christopher (2015), *Mortality and Music: Popular Music and the Awareness of Death*, London: Bloomsbury.

Peters, John Durham (2001), 'Witnessing', *Media, Culture & Society*, 23:6, pp. 707–23.

Pezzini, Barbara (2019), 'William Gladstone, collector and collectable: Objects, networks and symbols of liberalism', *Visual Culture in Britain*, 20:1, pp. 64–89.

Powell, Aubrey (2014), *Hipgnosis: Portraits*, London: Thames & Hudson.

Proll, Astrid (2010), 'Hello London', in A. Proll (ed.), *Goodbye to London: Radical Art and Politics in the 70s*, Ostfildern: Hatje Cantz.

Quail, Roger (2016), 'Cabaret Voltaire and Throbbing Gristle, Sheffield University: Tuesday 10th June 1980', 22 October, https://www.mylifeinthemoshofghosts.com/2016/10/22/cabaret-voltaire-and-throbbing-gristle-sheffield-university-tuesday-10th-june-1980/. Acccessed 12 May 2023.

Quail, Roger (2017), 'Throbbing Gristle, Cabaret Voltair, Z'ED – The Lyceum Ballroom, London: Sunday 8th February 1981', 22 July, https://www.mylifeinthemoshofghosts.com/2017/07/22/throbbing-gristle-cabaret-voltaire-zevthe-lyceum-ballroom-london-sunday-8th-february-1981/. Accessed 14 June 2021.

Rae, Casey (2020), *William S. Burroughs and the Cult of Rock and Roll*, London: White Rabbit.

Rais, Guy (1976), '"PORNOGRAPHIC ART" SHOW TROUPE GETS GRANT FOR U.S. TOUR', *Daily Telegraph*, October, p. 19.

Raynor, Stephane (2018), *All About the Boy*, Darlington: Carpet Bombing Culture.

Reed, S. Alexander (2013), *Assimilate: A Critical History of Industrial Music*, Oxford: Oxford University Press.

Reed, S. Alexander (2019), '"Let's make love before you die": "Warm Leatherette", boredom and the invention of the 1980s', in Z. Beaven, M. O'Dair, and R. Osborne (eds), *Mute Records: Artists, Business, History*, London: Bloomsbury Academic, pp. 15–30.

Reid, Jamie and Savage, Jon (1987), *Up They Rise*, London: Faber & Faber.

Reynolds, Simon (2005), *Rip It Up and Start Again: Post-Punk 1978–84*, London: Faber & Faber.

Ridgers, Derek (2016), *Punk London, 1977: The Roxy, the Vortex, Kings Road and Beyond*, Darlington: Carpet Bombing Culture.

Roberts, Eleanor (2020), 'Performance and *Prostitution*: The *Magazine Actions* of Cosey Fanni Tutti', in M. Chatzichristodoulou (ed.), *Live Art in the UK: Contemporary Performances of Precarity*, London: Methuen Drama, pp. 242–71.

Roberts, John (1999), 'Trickster', *Oxford Art Journal*, 22:1, pp. 81–101.

Robertson, Frank (1976), 'Shut Arts Council demands MP after pornography show', *Daily Telegraph*, 19 October, p. 2.

Robertson, Sandy (1977), 'Or will it be the Tescosound?', *Sounds*, 26 November, n.pag.

Robertson, Sandy (1979), 'Mouthfuls of Gristle', *Sounds*, 15 December, n.pag.

Robertson, Sandy (1981), 'GENESIS P-ORRIDGE on Breakfast TV? It could happen', *Sounds*, 12 December, n.pag.

Rorimer, Anne (2001), *New Art in the 60s and 70s: Redefining Reality*, London: Thames & Hudson.

Rouska, Richard (2019), *It Ain't Peters and Lee: The Leeds Rock, Pop, Punk, New Wave and Indie Scene 1977–87*, Leeds: 1977cc Publishing.

Sargeant, Jack (2015), 'Operating at culture's margins: Notes towards an aesthetics of the impact zone: Beyond *Crash* and *The Atrocity Exhibition*', *Deletion*, 4 May, https://www.deletionscifi.org/episodes/episode-9/operating-at-cultures-margins-notes-towards-an-aesthetics-of-the-impact-zone-beyond-crash-and-the-atrocity-exhibition/. Accessed 1 July 2021.

Savage, Jon (1978), 'Non-Muzak for Zyklon B Zombies: Industrial paranoia: The very dangerous visions of Throbbing Gristle', *Sounds*, 3, June, pp. 24–25.

Savage, Jon (1991), *England's Dreaming: Sex Pistols and Punk Rock*, London: Faber & Faber.

Scanlan, John (2016), *Sex Pistols: Poison in the Machine*, London: Reaktion Books.

Seago, Alex (1995), *Burning the Box of Beautiful Things: The Development of a Postmodern Sensibility*, Oxford: Oxford University Press.

Sedgwick, Nick (1982), *The Photo Designs of Hipgnosis: The Goodbye Look* (selected by P. Christopherson, A. Pavell, and S. Thorgerson; designed by N. Brody and Hipgnosis; text by S. Thorgerson; edited by N. Sedgwick), London: Vermilion.

Shyrane, Jennifer (2011), *Blixa Bargeld and Einstürzende Neubauten: German Experimental Music: 'Evading do-re-mi'*, Farnham: Ashgate.

Sinclair, Iain (2012), *Ghost Milk: Calling Time on the Grand Project*, London: Penguin.

Sladen, Mark and Yedgar, Ariella (2007), *Panic Attack!: Art in the Punk Years*, London: Merrell.

Slater, Howard (2009), 'Prisoners of the earth come out! Noises towards "War at the Membrane"', in A. Iles and Mattin (eds), *Noise and Capitalism*, San Sebastian: Kritika, pp. 151–65.

Smith, Peter (2015,) 'Holidays in the sun: The Sex Pistols at the seaside', *Popular Music and Society*, 38:4, pp. 487–99.

Spracklen, Karl, Henderson, Stephen, and Procter, David (2016), 'Imagining the scene and the memory of the F-Club: Talking about lost punk and post-punk spaces in Leeds', *Punk & Post-Punk*, 5:2, pp. 147–62.

Stallabrass, Julian (2010), 'Museum photography and museum prose', *New Left Review*, 65, pp. 93–125.

Steirer, Gregory (2012), 'The art of everyday life and death: Throbbing Gristle and the aesthetics of neoliberalism', *Postmodern Culture*, 22:2, https://www.pomoculture.

org/2013/04/07/the-art-of-everyday-life-and-death-throbbing-gristle-and-the-aesthetics-of-neoliberalism/. Accessed 20 February 2023.

Street, John, Worley, Matthew, and Wilkinson, David (2018), 'Does it threaten the status quo? Elite responses to British punk, 1976–1978', *Popular Music*, 37:2, pp. 271–89

Stubbs, David (2018), *Mars by 1980: The Story of Electronic Music*, London: Faber & Faber.

Taylor, Phil (2020), e-mail exchange with author, July.

Taylor, Steve (1979), no title, *Melody Maker*, 15 December, p. 48.

Throbbing Gristle (1979), *20 Jazz Funk Greats*, sleeve notes, United Kingdom: Industrial.

Tisdall, Caroline (1976), newspaper clipping, *The Guardian*, 22 October, p. 10.

Toop, David (1995), *Ocean of Sound: Ambient Sound and Radical Listening in the Age of Communication*, London: Serpent's Tail.

Townsend, Chris (2002), *Rapture: Art's Seduction by Fashion*, London: Thames & Hudson.

Trowell, Ian (2015), 'Hard floors, harsh sounds and the northern anti-festival: Futurama 1979–1983', *Popular Music History*, 10:1, pp. 62–81.

Trowell, Ian (2016), 'Punk's dead knot: Constructing the temporal and spatial in commercial punk imagery', *Punk & Post-Punk*, 5:2, pp. 181–99.

Trowell, Ian (2019), 'Heavy metal, rolling fields and the infinite harvest: The British steam rally', *International Journal of Heritage Studies*, 26:7, pp. 635–51.

Trowell, Ian (2020), 'Counter-realities and conflicted place: Gee Vaucher's *The Feeding of the Five Thousand* in the punk art tradition', *Punk & Post-Punk*, 9:3, pp. 397–424.

Tutti, Cosey Fanni (2017), *Art Sex Music*, London: Faber & Faber.

Usher, Shaun (1976), 'Is he just P. Ractical Joker?', *The Daily Mail*, October, p. 6.

Valencia, Sayak (2018), *Gore Capitalism*, London: MIT Press.

Vincent, Johnny (2008), *An Alternative Derby*, Derby: Lulu Publishing.

Voorhies, James (2017), *Beyond Objecthood: The Exhibition as a Critical Form Since 1968*, London: MIT Press.

Walker, John A. (1987), *Cross-overs: Art into Pop/Pop into Art*, London: Comedia.

Walker, John A. (1999), *Art and Outrage: Provocation, Controversy and the Visual Arts*, London: Pluto.

Walton, John (1978), *The Blackpool Landlady: A Social History*, Manchester: Manchester University Press.

Ward, Frazer, Taylor, Mark C., and Bloomer, Jennifer (2002), *Vito Acconci*, London: Phaidon.

Westwood, Chris (1978), 'The Human League', *ZigZag*, 86, August, pp. 24–25.

Westwood, Chris (1980), review, *Record Mirror*, 5 July, p. 24.

Westwood, Chris (2019), e-mail conversation with author, July 2019.

Whitney, Karl (2019), *Hit Factories: A Journey Through the Industrial Cities of British Pop*, London: Weidenfeld & Nicolson.

Wilkinson, David (2016), *Post-Punk, Politics and Pleasure in Britain*, London: Palgrave Macmillan.

Williams, Evan Calder (2011), *Combined and Uneven Apocalypse: Luciferian Marxism*, Winchester: Zero Books.

Williams, Raymond (1977), *Marxism and Literature*, Oxford: Oxford University Press.

Williamson, Aaron (2020), e-mail exchange with author, July.

Wilson, Louise K. (2020), 'Sounds from the bunker: Aural culture and the remainder of the Cold War', *Journal of War & Culture Studies*, 13:1, pp. 33–53.

Wilson, Siona (2015), *Art Labor, Sex Politics: Feminist Effects in 1970s British Art and Performance*, Minneapolis: University of Minnesota Press.

Wolfson, Richard (2002), 'Naughty but nice', *The Telegraph*, 19 December, https://www.telegraph.co.uk/culture/music/rockandjazzmusic/3587289/Naughty-but-nice.html. Accessed 9 August 2020.

Worley, Matthew (2016), 'The end result: An interview with Steve Ignorant', in M. Dines and M. Worley (eds), *The Aesthetic of Our Anger: Anarcho-Punk, Politics and Music*, Colchester: Minor Compositions, pp. 287–98.

Worley, Matthew (2017), *No Future: Punk, Politics and British Youth Culture*, Cambridge: Cambridge University Press.

Wright, Ron (2021), e-mail conversation with author, July.

Young, Rob (2011), *Electric Eden: Unearthing Britain's Visionary Music*, London: Faber & Faber.

THROBBING GRISTLE

MUSIC AS WE KNOW IT (SAFE). THEIR NAME IS SPREADING SO WE TRIED TO SHOW WHAT THEY'RE ABOUT.

e Second Annual Report

robbing Gristle

corded during the year ending September 3rd 1977

Chris Carter, Genesis P-Orridge, Cosey Fanni Tutti and Peter Christopherson don't play around. It isn't punk rock, it isn't anything you could name.

the past and present

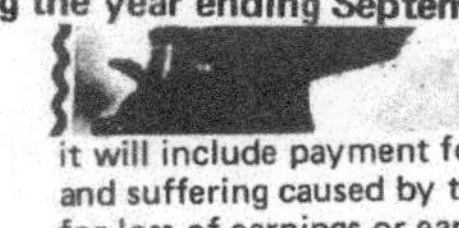

it will include payment for the pain and suffering caused by the injury, and for loss of earnings or earning capacity and out-of-pocket expenses. There are special rules for the assessment of compensation in case of death.

and arms. The Ty... slipped over leather like oiled

dreamed before that we had any sexual desires for other women, but a single, silent look told us we were in complete agreement, and the unbelievably exciting adventure continued.

I took my hands from around Carla's waist and started to unbutton her blouse, all the while kissing her face and neck. She was sucking my swollen nipples, flicking her tongue over one while pinching the other with her fingers. By the time I had her bra unfastened and off, revealing two gently swelling, soft, round boobs, her right hand had moved down between my thighs to rub my drenched pussy. It was the first time anyone had done to me the things that seemed natural to Carla. She tickled my

PARANOIA CLUB

Extended foreplay

IT HAS been a long time since my boyfriend and I made love whilst listening to a record (we use albums not singles — of course). I think the last time was the Beaver And Krause record called 'Gandharva' — and maybe some T. Dream. But he came round to my apartment here on the Left Bank a few days ago and what happened makes me wonder just where our relationship is going. He said 'I've got this album we must make it with — it's just right.' The cover was white and seemed nice. Well he had the lights off and the curtains drawn and the record on. He was good, and the record was right. But when I asked who it was he said 'Throbbing Gristle.'' My English is good and I knew what it meant. The titles of the album tracks frighten me and they look evil and now I feel somehow sick at what we did together listening to those evil English people. I don't know

There must be many rich men there. I expect they would be nice to me for the sex things I have learned to do. Girls like *PROSTITUTION*

A semi-elasticated strip is machined into the rear

MUSIC FROM THE DEATH FACTORY

This report has been assembled from recordings made during the year ending September 3rd 1977, the anniversary of, amongst other things, the approximate formation of the group Throbbing Gristle two years previously. This second year of production has shown a definite move towards establishment of a sound business foundation on which further work involving greater capital expenditure can be based. Considerable progress has been made in the fields of research and development which have enabled us to give live demonstrations in five locations. These being at the I.C.A., The Mall, London on 18th October 1976; at The Nag's Head, High Wycombe on 11th February 1977; at the Polytechnic, Brighton on 26th March 1977; at Southampton University on 7th May 1977 and at the Rat Club, Pindar of Wakefield, Kings Cross, London on 22nd May 1977. These appearances were seen by audiences varying between approximately 130 (at the Rat Club) and 800 (at the I.C.A.) and their reaction to our work has been similarly variable. We have included the reactions of the audience in Brighton and particularly of the DJ of the disco at that venue as the last track of Side One. It is worth mentioning that overall a very positive interest in our work prevails and a considerable

number have expressed a desire to see us perform on subsequent occasions. Simultaneously with our live demonstrations a weekly programme of research and composition has been maintained at the studio of Industrial Records to whom our thanks are due for their support and investment.

One side of this record has been assembled from tapes made at four out of the five live occasions and at the studio of Industrial Records in London. Side Two consists of the entire original movie soundtrack of a film produced by Coum Transmissions called "After Cease To Exist" premiered in Arnhem, Holland in July 1977 which Throbbing Gristle were

invited to score and perform. It was recorded at the Industrial Records studio. The field of film soundtrack production is one which is most suitable to our methods of work and we look forward to offers of more work in this field.

All recordings were made in one take without any overdubs or any recording treatment other than standard playing procedures that we employ. Within the limitations of the recording techniques used the sound on this record is exactly as it was heard at the moment of its production.

In the forthcoming year we hope to increase the number of live demonstrations and the variety of their locations. We also hope to continue our film work and to extend into a new area of preparing customized tapes of piped music for shops and factories, and finally to continue releasing records for public consumption.

for Throbbing Gristle
Chris Carter
Peter Christopherson
Genesis P-Orridge
Cosey Fanni Tutti

a band of the Seventies

We're sorry about that, Mr Palmer. But don't worry, outbursts aren't too unusual.

if Bill will let me buy ...oyfriend says I can' ...ard are such remark... ...hat, I'll get a spank... boyfriend got mad... ...d really spanked me ...o the file work today ...nd up—I bet I can' ...eek'. And once in a... ...verhears such advice ...o move around; the... won't leave many ...r a while, one isn' learn that bondage ...e clubs are growing

To those of us who map out the development of British Art through the pages of the SUN and MIRROR, the name of GENESIS P. ORRIDGE will, no doubt, be familiar.

Mental disorder means mental illness, arrested or incomplete development of mind, psychopathic disorder or any other disorder or disability of mind.

Your fetish is not at all unusual. As a ma... ...f fact, there is a theatre in New York ...alled The Project, in which actors pe... ...the fantasies of various people. This p... ...ular tickling fetish is one that they've ...ived many requests for.

the frustration remains the same.

Here's a fetish I want to know if you've ever heard of. I'm

Industrial Records, 10 Martello Street, London E.8, England. Tel: 01-254 9178

INDEX

Page numbers in roman represent figures.

23 Skidoo *138, 244, 247, 254, 257*

A

A Certain Ratio *202, 211, 242, 262*
ABC *see* Vice Versa
Acconci, Vito *106*
Actor-Network Theory *126*
Adam and the Ants *206, 223*
anarcho-punk *237, 246, 258–61*
  Bullshit Detector *260*
Andre, Carl
  Equivalent VIII *62–63, 70*
Asher, Michael *105, 109*

B

Bachelard, Gaston *27*
Baker, Bob *220–21*
Bakhtin, Mikhail *116, 170*
Ballard, J. G. *216, 258, 265n15*
Barthes, Roland *234*
bathos *12, 139*
Bauhaus *199–200, 205*
Bennett, William *see* Whitehouse
Bingo, Stan *see* Landin, Dan
Bracewell, Michael *193*
Brecht, Bertolt *137, 140*
Burroughs, William *33, 40n4, 60, 138, 191–92, 200, 209, 216, 226n12, 235, 240, 254n15, 257*
Buzzcocks *55–56, 131, 196, 199, 203, 215*

C

Cabaret Voltaire *127–29, 133–34, 138, 157, 186–88, 194–96, 212, 214, 219, 222, 245–46*
  'Nag Nag Nag' *195*
Carter, Chris *54, 188, 211, 231, 233–34, 243, 246, 248, 253*
cassette culture *26*
Cazazza, Monte *91, 200, 209–10, 236, 241, 242*
Chelsea (band) *59*
Chris & Cosey *253*
Christopherson, Peter *50–51, 234, 238*
  BOY retail designs *79–80, 262*
  photography *51–53, 234, 264n10*
  sampling 139
Clash, The *57–58, 79, 92, 94, 124, 157, 186, 232, 237, 259, 265n27*
Clock DVA *128–29, 195, 222, 245–46*
COUM Transmissions *29, 43–45, 62–70, 200, 259*
Crass *181, 237, 258–261*
Cronenberg, David *130*
Crowley, Aleister *242*
Curtis, Ian *21, 196–98, 219, 225–26n8*

D

declinism in British society *22, 68, 78, 132*
Deleuze, Gilles *138, 158*
Derby *163–65, 168, 176–82, 203*
Dupre, Laurence *237*
displacement *31–32*

F

far right *132*
Faver, Colin *see* Final Solution
Fergusson, Alex *75*
Fetish Records *245–46, 250, 254, 257*
Final Academy *254*
Final Solution *157, 201, 207, 210*
Fisher, Mark *137, 142–43, 250*
football *124–25, 131, 138–39, 160–61, 165, 175*
Ford, Simon *20, 23, 63–64, 103, 135, 147–48*

G

Gang of Four *173, 202, 237*
Glass, Ted *37, 38–39*
Graham, Dan *106*

H

Hackney *44*
Hegarty, Paul *38–39, 136, 256*
Hempsall, Alan *219*
heterotopia *115*
Hipgnosis *50–51, 53, 139, 231*
Hula *218, 221*
Hull *43–45, 47, 58, 155, 197, 220, 259*
Human League, The *188, 190–94, 198, 212–15, 224–25*
  'Being Boiled' *191, 264n6*
  split *223*

I

institutional critique *40, 107*

J

Jarman, Derek *207, 241, 243–44*
Joy Division *196–99, 201–02, 211, 219, 235*

K

Keenan, John *132, 201, 222*
Kelly, Mary
 Post-Partum Document 63, 69–70
Kill Your Pet Puppy 260, 263
Krivine, John *58, 75, 80–82*

L

Lacey, Martin *189–90, 198–99, 215, 217, 231*
Landin, Dan *41n12, 251, 254, 257, 265n24*
Last Few Days *254, 265n24*
Leeds *132–33, 164, 204*
 Futurama One *201–02, 226n11*
 Futurama Two *222–23*

M

Mallinder, Stephen *see* Cabaret Voltaire
Manchester *136, 187, 196, 255*
McLaren, Malcolm *48–53, 57, 94, 131, 169*
Melody Maker 83–84, 92
 1976 Throbbing Gristle feature *74*
Morley, Paul *100, 158, 193, 205–06, 252–53*
music press *30*

N

new romantic *214, 223, 245–46, 265n12*
NME 73, 99–100
 1978 Throbbing Gristle feature *155*
noise *38–39*
Numan, Gary *212–13, 223, 238*

P

Paet, Fizzy *140*
Peace, David *120, 141–44, 149*
Perry, Mark *75*
Pink Floyd *44, 50, 71n7, 109, 115, 117n8, 135*
pornography *68, 71n18, 130, 165, 168, 173, 216*
P-Orridge
 biography *43–44*
 The British Government 85
 fashion *80, 88, 89, 141, 236–37, 264n3*
 gender *40n4*
 Gary Gilmore Memorial Society *81–82, 234*
 and Paula *230–31, 247–48*
 suicide attempt *157*
 vocal style *12, 18–19, 90, 131, 138–39, 162, 174, 201, 242*
post-punk *see also* synth–pop *92, 154, 157–58, 180, 185–88, 200–05, 245–46*
 break from punk *92*
 meaning *202–03*
Prior, Dorothy Max *241*
Psychic TV *248, 254–55, 257*
Public Image Limited *162, 202, 262*
punk
 amateurism *19, 56, 61*
 art scene and methods *93–94*
 epistemology vs mythology *34, 77, 186*
 eschatology *32*
 live spectacle *101*
 popularity (1977) *79, 90–91*
 popularity (1979) *170*
 scene formation *49, 56–59, 76–77, 261*
 second wave *180–82*
 situationism *94*
 social critique *92, 263*
 versus new wave *98, 169*

R

Rabid 130
Reynolds, Simon *13, 15, 108, 187, 189, 195, 203–04, 253, 257*
Rhodes, Bernie *48–49, 57*
Robertson, Sandy *97–99, 159, 182n1, 203, 207, 230, 249, 252*
Romero, George *216*
Rough Trade *98, 177, 195, 252–53*

S

sampling *161*
Savage, Jon *98, 100, 121–24, 128, 144, 156, 203*
Sex Pistols *24, 29, 46, 57, 74, 166, 186, 197, 248*
 demise and after–life *131, 169–71, 264n6*
 formation *48–53*
 'God Save the Queen' *83, 90*
 Grundy *Today* incident *78*
Sham 69 *124–25, 232*
Sheffield *164, 186–88, 190–96, 211–12*
Siouxsie and the Banshees *59–60, 131, 170, 192, 202, 264n1*
situational aesthetics *40, 107, 149*
situationism *33, 34, 36, 48–50, 57, 94, 145, 191, 196*
Sniffin' Glue 75–76
Some Bizzare *257*
Sounds
 1978 Throbbing Gristle feature *121–23*
 1979 Throbbing Gristle first feature *159*
 1979 Throbbing Gristle second feature *207*

'Forgive Us Our Synths' feature *223–25, 244*
'New Musick' feature *98–99, 198, 203*
subcultural theories *31, 77, 204, 263–64*
Sutcliffe, Peter *120, 133, 143–47, 220*
synth-pop *124, 150n2, 190, 193, 214–16, 238, 257*

T

Tape Delay 258
Teddy Boys *133*
Thee Temple of Psychick Youth *255, 258*
They Must Be Russians *189*
This Heat *202, 207*
Throbbing Gristle
20 Jazz Funk Greats 173–74, 187, 249, 200–01, 206–07
abjectness *15–18, 32, 143–46*
'Adrenalin' *240*
After Cease to Exist 91, 154, 166, 226n9
amateurism *19, 61*
anarcho-punk (relationship to) *95*
'Annihilating Reality' *35, 145–46*
'Anthony' *108*
architecture and built space *101–03, 114–15*
art scene and methods *35–37, 39–40, 95, 105–7, 146–47, 244, 265n25*
artwork *121, 231–35, 238–40, 251–52*
Brighton Polytechnic first performance *83–88*
'Convincing People' *173–74*
crowd violence *103, 107–9, 112–14, 155*
Derby Ajanta Theatre performance *163, 171–76*
'Discipline' *241–42, 245, 251–52*
disharmony and tensions *21, 37, 75, 82, 155–59, 188, 229–31, 248–49*
'Distant Dreams (Part Two)' *240*
D.o.A: The Third and Final Report of Throbbing Gristle 156–57
'E-Coli' *115, 156*
eschatology *32–33, 102, 110, 215, 236*
fanzine scene *34–35*
'Five Knuckle Shuffle' *140, 149–50, 159, 162, 176, 197*
formation *11, 47, 54–56*
Funeral in Berlin 253
Germany performances *241*
Greatest Hits – Entertainment Through Pain 252–53
'Hamburger Lady' *139, 174*
Heathen Earth 209–11, 231–35, 238, 256
High Wycombe Nags Head performance *82*
'IBM' *137, 156, 173*
incompetence *see* amateurism
independent status *14, 91*
industrial music genre formation *14, 134–37, 139, 159, 256*
Industrial News 125–26, 128, 200
Journey Through a Body 246–47
Leeds Fan Club performance *210*
London AIR Gallery performance *55, 102–3*
London Architectural Association performance *104–17*
London Butler's Wharf performance *207–09*
London Centro Iberico performance *160–62*
London Cryptic One performance *157–58*
London Film-Makers' Co-op performance *154–55*
London Heaven performance *243, 265n19*
London ICA gig and *Prostitution 11–13, 52, 59–70, 73, 155*
London Lyceum performance *245–46*
London Rat Club first performance *88–90*
London Rat Club second performance *100, 144–45*
London Roundhouse performance *97, 135*
London Scala Cinema performance *210*
London YMCA performance *201*
Manchester Factory performance *196–99*
Manchester Rafters performance *242–43*
metabolic function *25, 136, 141*
myth creation *33–34, 38*
name *47–48*
Northampton Guild Hall performance *199–200*
nuclear war *see* eschatology
Oundle School performance *211*
performance space *18, 28–29, 104–07, 114–15*
'Persuasion' *17, 162*
pornography *85, 147–50, 173*
punk (relationship to) *74–76*
sampling *60, 161–62, 172, 175, 219*

Second Annual Report *98–99*
self-documentation *26, 40n10, 65–67*
serial killers *see* abjectness
Sheffield University first performance *188–90*
Sheffield University second performance *215–21*
'Slug Bait' *13, 123, 139, 151n25*
'Something Came Over Me' *238*
Southampton Nuffield Theatre performance *135*
'Still Talking/Walking' *201, 209, 211, 226n12, 235, 243*
structure versus anti-structure *137, 159, 211, 246–47, 261*
'Subhuman' *238*
termination *231, 244, 248–50*
Tesco *108, 123, 134–35, 137, 230*
'Trade Deficit' *15*
'United' *124–25, 127, 238*
United States performances *247–49*
'Very Friendly' *12, 242, 260*
Wakefield Industrial College performance *119, 126–41*
'Weapon Training' *162, 172, 201*
'What a Day' *157, 159, 162, 174–75*
Winchester Art School performance *136*
Winchester Hat Fair performance *55*
'Zyklon B Zombie' *84*
Top of the Pops *90, 124, 131, 150n4, 168, 170–71*
Toxic Graffitti/Grafity *260*
Tubeway Army *see* Numan, Gary
Tutti, Cosey Fanni *43, 147–49*

V
Vice Versa *195, 214, 222–23*

W
Wakefield *129–33*
war *172–73, 215, 236–38*
Westwood, Chris *126–28, 140, 157, 191, 195, 207, 235*
Whitehouse *143, 145, 256*
Who, The *12, 86, 90, 94*
Williams, Raymond *129*
Winter of Discontent *22–23, 153, 158, 160, 174–75, 177, 189*
Wire *202*
Worley, Matthew *23, 144, 149, 176, 258, 260, 263*

Y
Yorkshire Ripper *see* Sutcliffe, Peter

Z
ZigZag *126, 191*
1978 Throbbing Gristle feature *123*